INFRASTRUCTURE INVESTMENT IN INDONESIA

Infrastructure Investment in Indonesia

A Focus on Ports

Colin Duffield, Felix Kin Peng Hui and Sally Wilson

OpenBook Publishers

https://www.openbookpublishers.com

ISBN Paperback: 978-1-78374-821-1
ISBN Hardback: 978-1-78374-822-8
ISBN Digital (PDF): 978-1-78374-823-5
ISBN Digital ebook (epub): 978-1-78374-824-2
ISBN Digital ebook (mobi): 978-1-78374-825-9
ISBN XML: 978-1-78374-826-6
DOI: 10.11647/OBP.0189

Cover image: Unnamed Road, Juanga, Morotai Sel., Kabupaten Pulau Morotai, Maluku Utara, Indonesia, Morotai Selatan. Photo by Rizky Arief at Unsplash, https://unsplash.com/photos/msAY2oBDXHI
Cover design: Anna Gatti.

Contents

4.2.2 West Semarang Drinking Water Supply 92
4.2.3 National Capital Integrated Coastal Development 94
4.2.4 Bontang Refinery 96
4.2.5 Umbulan Springs Drinking Water Supply Project 98
4.3 Delivery of Infrastructure Projects: Australia 99
4.3.1 Channel Deepening Project, Victoria 100
4.3.2 M.7 Motorway, New South Wales 101
4.4 Benchmark Practices 103
4.4.1 Comparative Analysis 106
4.4.2 Findings 109
References 109

5. Port and Hinterlands **113**
J. Black and V. Roso

5.0 Introduction 113
5.1 Methodology 116
5.2 Literature Review Intermodal Terminals — Concept of Dry Ports 117
5.3 Sydney's Container Ports — History 119
5.4 Port Botany Container Terminals 122
5.5 Multi-modal Transport Access to Port Botany 128
5.6 Hinterland Intermodal Logistics Centres 133
5.6.1 Port Botany's Inland Terminals Pre-2010 133
5.6.2 Chullora Intermodal Terminal 136
5.6.3 Macarthur Intermodal Shipping Terminal (MIST) 136
5.6.4 Cooks River Intermodal Terminal (St Peters) 137
5.6.5 Yennora Intermodal Terminal 137
5.6.6 Villawood Terminal (Leightonfield) 138
5.6.7 Enfield Intermodal Logistics Centre 138
5.7 Moorebank Intermodal Terminal — Detailed Case Study of Dry Port 139
5.8 Funding and Financing Port, Terminals and Transport Access 144
5.9 Conclusions 146
References 149

Acknowledgements

This book is based on the collaborative international research conducted between The University of Melbourne, Universitas Indonesia and Universitas Gadjah Mada, on project initiation in ports and infrastructure projects in Indonesia and Australia. The editors would firstly like to acknowledge the generous funding and support from the Australia-Indonesia Centre (AIC) which made this possible. This funding came in the form of the Small Grant, Rapid Start Grant and a Strategic Research Grant. Special thanks must be given for the support received from the AIC's Research director Dr Richard Price and Research Manager Megan Power, and the Administrative team: Katrina Reid, Rebecca Hateley, Dr Maria Platt and Samantha Croy.

In Indonesia, the small grant received from the AIC and the travel support and case study materials provided by the Indonesian Infrastructure Initiative (IndII) group of Australia Aid is gratefully acknowledged. Special thanks for the support provided by Lynton Ulrich and Nur Hayati of IndII during the study. Aspects of this monograph have also been informed by direct communication with the Indonesian Co-ordinating Ministry for Economic Affairs. Also, special thanks for the inputs from Dr Luky Eko Wuryanto (who at the time was Deputi Bidang Koordinasi Infrastruktur dan Pengembangan, Kemenko Perekonomian), Dedy Supriadi Priatno (who at the time was Deputi Bidang Prasarana dan Sarana, Kementerian PPN/BAPPENAS — the key planning ministry) and Dr Hermanto Dardak (Wakil Menteri, Kementerian Pekerjaan Umum), as well as the staff at IndII who convened the meetings held with these senior Indonesian Officials.

A special mention goes to then Minister Robb (Australian Government) and then Premier Napthine (Victorian Government) for including the research team on trade delegations to Indonesia, and to Steve Richards of Aurecon for involving the research team in executive meetings with senior Indonesian Officials.

We thank Emeritus Professor John Black from the University of New South Wales, Professor Graeme Hodge from Monash University and Professor Danang Parikesit from Universitas Gadjah Mada for their valuable input at the academic workshop conducted in Melbourne in the early stage of the research. Professor John Black also contributed an entire chapter (Chapter 5) on port hinterland to this research monograph.

The editors would like to acknowledge the leadership of Associate Professor Sari Wahyuni, the co-lead for the Strategic Research Project in organising many of the tedious research activities such as the numerous stakeholder meetings and discussions in Jakarta, Indonesia. As the project co-lead, Associate Professor Sari also contributed two chapters (Chapters 7 and 8) to the research monograph. We also acknowledge the time, support and advice of our team member, Professor Danang Parikesit. As a senior academic and a policy expert, Professor Danang was instrumental in providing direction for research in Indonesia as well as valuable inputs in discussions. Professor Danang contributed a solid chapter on the critical importance of land transport in Indonesia (Chapter 11).

The editors would also like to acknowledge the input of all postgraduate research student contributions, Vijayshree Behal for her contribution to Chapter 4, Andrew Chin and Hanlong Huang for their co-contributions to Chapter 6, Haya Al-Daghlas for her contribution to Chapter 9, Waskitha Galih for his co-contribution to Chapter 10 and Said Basalim for his co-contribution to Chapter 11. We also wish to acknowledge research assistant Regina Duffield for her contribution to Chapters 1 to 3. In addition, we thank Vijayshree, Haya, Waskitha and Said for their assistance with the focus group discussions (FGDs).

We would also like to thank our colleagues at Institute Technologi Sepuluh Nopember (ITS), Dr Hera Widyastuti and Dr Saut Gurning and their colleagues for their support in arranging meetings with stakeholders during the Surabaya phase of the Strategic Research Project. Special mention to Bernardus Djonoputro of Deloitte Indonesia for his generous advice on the conduct of research in Indonesia.

We would also like to thank Dr Dewanti and Wiratno Wahyu Wibowo from the Centre for Transportation and Logistics Studies, Universitas Gadjah Mada for their assistance with the project.

We are extremely grateful to the participants of the focus group discussions held in Jakarta, Indonesia and Melbourne, Australia, survey participants, conference participants, interview participants in both Surabaya and Jakarta, in particular to management and staff of Pelindo II and Pelindo III, Teluk Lamong Port, Port of Tanjung Priok and the Terminal Pertikimas Surabaya. Special thanks must also go to the contribution from Sri Bagus from Bappenas, the Indonesian National Planning Agency and Dr Salusra Widya from LKPP, the Indonesian National Procurement Agency for their inputs and support, and Dr Nofrisel, Director of Operation and Development, PT Bhanda Ghara Reksa (Persero) BGR Integrated Logistics Solution. This has contributed to the rich pool of research data collected for the project.

In Australia, we acknowledge the contribution of the management and staff of the following port organisations who have given up so much of their time to support and participate in our research: Port of Melbourne (Don Fosdyke), DP World Melbourne (Vlad Jotic) and VICT, Ports Australia (Michael Gallagher), and The Chartered Institute of Logistics and Transport in Australia (CILTA) and the Supply Chain and Logistics Association of Australia (SCLAA) for their support in advertising the online survey. Their involvement has contributed to the research. In addition to the participants mentioned previously, special thanks also to the following for their presentations at the Port Competitiveness and Financing Workshop and Conference held in Melbourne on the 4–6 April 2018 including Mark Switkowski, Stan Roche (Austrade), Michael Tuckfield, Venkat Naidu (AECOM) and Leith Doody (former Australian Trade commissioner).

We also want to acknowledge University staff and postgraduate students both in Australia and Indonesia who have helped in various phases of the research that were organised as part of the bigger research project: from Melbourne — Dr David Wilson and Dr Kim Hassall; postgraduate students who took on various roles as Research Assistants — from Australia — Hanif Arief Wisesa, Putri Fatkhiyatul Ulya, Praditya Hadi Prabowo, Lydwina Adhisty, Steffen Utama, Garinata Sabatini Trema, Shabrina Austin Ghaisani, Bisma Anugerah

Subarno, Renold Partogi Lumbantoruan (Togi), and Elisa Mackowiak (intern from France), and Andrew Grisinger as a student during his post graduate study — and from Indonesia: Aditya Ridwan Nasution and Prisca Lidya Patty.

Finally, we acknowledge the support of our department leaders, Professor Abbas Rajabifard and Enterprise Professor Greg Foliente at The University of Melbourne for their continued support in promoting Engineering Management research.

Preface

Leith Doody[1] and Bernardus Djonoputro[2]

For Indonesia to join the top ten major global economies club by 2025, the average GDP per capita per annum would need to rise from USD 3,000 today to USD 15,000 and GDP per se to a heady USD 4.5 trillion (nearly five times the current GDP). It would need to do so in the space of less than ten years.

To achieve this a two-pronged approach will be required: acceleration, and expansion. Underpinning such development is the need for strengthened connectivity not only throughout the archipelago, but also the Association of Southeast Asian Nations (ASEAN). Additionally, such development requires the strengthening of human resources capability, as well as the smart use of science and technology.

Growth Centres, connectivity and infrastructure are considered the main building blocks of Indonesia's economic corridors. This connectivity needs to be developed through ICT and ebusiness, improved logistics through transport and refined business policies — practices and processes such that international trade and investment grows commensurate with expectations. Currently logistics costs in Indonesia are a crippling 25% of GDP. Critical infrastructure needs and areas for improvement include: roads, seaports (ferries and container and bulk trade), airports, public transport via a modern metro system and connected rail freight routes. Underpinning these productivity improvements is the need for

---

1   Ex Australian Trade and Investment Commissioner and Minister to Indonesia.
2   Director Asia, Deloitte.

   https://doi.org/10.11647/OBP. 0189.13

clean water, reliable energy and electricity and better access to social infrastructure such as hospitals and schools.

In a call to action, Pak Suryo Sulisto, former Chairman of Kadin and indeed a major driver for improved infrastructure in Indonesia, at an AusAid event held at the Indonesian Centre for Infrastructure Workshop on 10 July 2014, bluntly stated:

> Indonesia today has the highest logistics costs in Asia, which costs the country billions of dollars in losses… Unless we can build world class infrastructure, we will not be competitive and will lose out not only to the likes of China but also the Philippines…

The impediments and constraints are real: a lack of financing and funding, a propensity for major natural disasters such as earthquakes, volcanic eruptions and tsunamis, along with major congestion on transport routes and dated/poorly maintained vehicles using these networks.

Indonesia is not alone in facing infrastructure difficulties. In Australia, the need for additional funding to underpin the pipeline of identified nationally significant infrastructure projects remains a challenge. Infrastructure Australia's CEO, Mr Phil Davies, recently reflected on the infrastructure project list updated in March 2018 (this included $55bn worth of projects, with $25bn worth of ongoing projects moved off the list) with his observation that "governments and oppositions need to be more disciplined around proper planning, evaluating all available options, and seeking the solutions with positive cost-benefit ratios prior to a funding announcement".[3]

The impediments to achieving adequate infrastructure in Australia have numerous similarities to those mentioned previously: a lack of funding, the need for policy reform such that Australia's productivity can improve, and a tyranny of distance that imposes growing pressures on major cities but leaves rural and remote communities with inequitable access to infrastructure services. There are also numerous natural disasters in the form of floods, bushfires and cyclones.

The articles presented in this book provide a valuable resource for policy makers in Indonesia and Australia as they insightfully explore

---

3   Bagshaw, E 2018. 'Infrastructure chief says government and business have failed to deliver for Australians', 24 June, *Sydney Morning Herald*, https://www.smh.com.au/politics/federal/infrastructure-chief-says-government-and-business-have-failed-to-deliver-for-australians-20180622-p4zn7a.html.

economic, transport, policy and finance aspects of infrastructure investment.

We commend this book to those who are passionate advocates of finding practical solutions to creating sustainable infrastructure and successful business relationships between Indonesia and Australia. The creation of such infrastructure and business relationships would contribute to a more sustainable growth between our two great nations, who are significant and complementary economies and the closest of neighbours.

Foreword

This monograph charts the research undertaken by the policy and finance team within the infrastructure cluster of the Australia-Indonesia Centre (AIC). The research conducted was an international collaboration between The University of Melbourne, Universitas Indonesia and Universitas Gadjah Mada into project initiation in ports and infrastructure projects in Indonesia and Australia, with funding and support from the AIC. An outline of the research approach and collaboration is provided in the paper titled 'Collaborative international industry-university research training in infrastructure projects: an Australian-Indonesian case study' by Hui et al. 2018.[1]

The material presented in this monograph relates to research into efficient facilitation of major infrastructure projects, with an emphasis on infrastructure investment and a focus on port planning and development. Prominence was initially given to examining infrastructure investment in Indonesia and then relating this to the infrastructure environment in Australia. This approach has contributed to a better understand of how Indonesia and Australia can improve infrastructure investment and more particularly investment that enhances how ports function.

The lessons learnt in port infrastructure projects can also be broadly applied to large infrastructure projects. Efficient initiation and facilitation processes in rail infrastructure, road infrastructure, water infrastructure or energy infrastructure are also needed especially when these projects compete for the same pot of government funds.

The outline of the monograph is as follows:

 https://doi.org/10.11647/OBP.0189.14

Chapter 1: Infrastructure Investment in Indonesia — The Economic Context.

Authors: Professor Colin F. Duffield, Regina Duffield, Dr Sally Wilson

The first chapter sets the scene for infrastructure investment in Indonesia from an economic perspective. It takes into consideration the country's geography, its government, its growing population, its economy, and its investment and infrastructure needs.

Chapter 2: Infrastructure Planning, Challenges and Risks.

Authors: Professor Colin F. Duffield, Regina Duffield, Dr Sally Wilson

The second chapter briefly outlines relevant national and international plans and initiatives to assist with infrastructure investment and development in Indonesia. It then presents and discusses the challenges, barriers, risks and issues associated with delivering the required infrastructure necessary to underpin the economic growth and reform strategies for Indonesia. The chapter then presents some results from a survey of port executives, government officials, financiers and consultants undertaken in both Indonesia and Australia into efficient facilitation of major infrastructure projects with a focus on port planning and development.

Chapter 3: Funding and Financing Infrastructure: Indonesia and Australia.

Authors: Professor Colin F. Duffield, Regina Duffield, Dr Sally Wilson

The third chapter explores the financing mechanisms available and funding required to support infrastructure investment in Indonesia. The Australian situation is also considered. A range of alternate investment approaches are explored as well as priority areas for investment in Indonesia and Australia. The relative effectiveness of various financing methods are explored from the perspective of Indonesian and Australian respondents to the port planning and development survey.

Chapter 4: Efficient Facilitation of Major Infrastructure Projects

Authors: Professor Colin F. Duffield, Dr Felix Kin Peng Hui, Vijayshree Behal

The fourth chapter considers the processes involved in implementation of major infrastructure projects. It identifies the theoretical processes to instigate projects and compares them to the real-world practices that are being implemented in Indonesia and Australia with a focus on case study examples. A comparison with the Gateway review process undertaken for implementation of major infrastructure projects in Australia is presented.

Chapter 5: Port and Hinterlands: The Combined Infrastructure Costs of Seaports, Intermodal Terminals and Transport Access, Port Botany, Sydney.

Authors: Emeritus Professor John Black, Associate Professor Violeta Roso

The fifth chapter commences with a review of the literature on intermodal terminals (dry ports). It then examines the symbiotic relationships between port and hinterland, including investment costs (in current Australian dollars using an inflation calculator), with an historical case study that focuses on Port Botany in Sydney, Australia's second largest container port. The historical backdrop is important for researchers to understand the social, economic and environmental effects of port locational decisions on its hinterland. Specifically, the development of Port Botany has been associated with environmental and social conflicts due to landside constraints and community action. The problem of increasing container volumes handled in seaports requires adequate land to be available nearby or in the immediate hinterland for port-associated functions with efficient inland multi-modal transport access. The relevance to Indonesian ports is discussed.

Chapter 6: Comparative Efficiency Analysis of Australian and Indonesian Ports.

Authors: Dr Felix Kin Peng Hui, Professor Colin F. Duffield, Andrew Chin, Hanlong Huang

A comparative analysis of Australian and Indonesian port efficiency is presented in the sixth chapter. The analysis utilises the Data Envelope Analysis model to quantify and measure the efficiency of ports, focusing on port and container cargoes. Ports included in the benchmarking included major Australian, Indonesian and Chinese international ports. International benchmarking of port facilities provides an opportunity to identify areas for improvement.

Chapter 7: Innovation in Port Development: The Quad Helix Model.

Author: Associate Professor Sari Wahyuni

The seventh chapter presents a comprehensive case study from Japan on how an Academic-Business-Community-Government plus bank partnership can be nurtured to create innovation through various strategies, including engagement with key stakeholders for local industrial vitalization, analysis for new industries, support for creating an industrial vitalization plan, and support for collaboration with other regions.

Chapter 8: Revealing Indonesian Port Competitiveness: Challenge and Performance.

Authors: Associate Professor Sari Wahyuni, Alif Azadi Taufik, Dr Felix Kin Peng Hui

The eighth chapter considers Indonesian port competitiveness. It notes that the Indonesian government is in the midst of planning broad policies and strategies concerning maritime and port development and has recently provided a reform package to improve logistics in the country to improve the supply chain. Results from focus group meetings, a detailed questionnaire and in-depth interviews with key port industry stakeholders and financial bodies in Indonesia are presented. Problematic factors contributing to port problems were identified from the perspective of research participants. The chapter identifies important aspects of port competitiveness: government support, business support and operational performance. Despite general support towards the government policies in facilitating port investment, there seems to be a substantial gap between policy expectation and policy realisation.

Chapter 9: Initial Investigation into the Effectiveness of Australian Ports' Governance and Management Structures.

Authors: Haya Al-Daghlas, Dr Felix Kin Peng Hui, Professor Colin F. Duffield

The ninth chapter considers effectiveness of port governance and management structures in Australia. It briefly reviews Australian port reform, before considering private, local and international investment in Australia; the make-up of investors in major city ports in Australia; and the need to carefully assess foreign investment in critical infrastructure. Asset recycling in Australia is discussed. Factors identified from focus group discussions (in Australia) with key port stakeholders that help improve or act as obstacles to governance/policy, and that help improve or hinder management structures in ports, are also presented.

Chapter 10: Alternative Ways to Finance Major Port Projects: Seaports in Indonesia.

Authors: Waskitha W. Galih, Associate Professor Ruslan Prijadi

Various alternatives of port infrastructure project financing are explored in the tenth chapter. The insights and perspectives of various Indonesian seaport industry stakeholders on financing of infrastructure projects are presented from findings from an online survey, focus group discussions and in-depth interviews conducted in Indonesia. A detailed case study of the New Priok Container Terminal One (NPCT-1) is used to illustrate how different scenarios of financing schemes would affect the project risks allocation, and the project value itself. The first scenario examines the project's current financing structure — the contractual relationships between the project company, its sponsors, lenders and the government. The second scenario is built under a what-if assumption where the project is assumed to be financed under a Public Private Partnership (PPP) scheme with an annuity availability payments feature.

Chapter 11: The Critical Importance of Land Transport when Considering Port Development: the Case of Three Indonesian Ports.

Authors: Professor Danang Parikesit, Said Basalim, Wiratno Wahyu Wibowo

The eleventh chapter discusses the intricate relationship between ports and their hinterland and the critical importance of land transport when considering port development. The chapter considers the integration between a port and an industrial area. Multimodal operations of ports are discussed through a comprehensive review of the international literature which considers the following issues: regionalisation and spatial control, structural and organisation challenges of multi-mode port operation, and the disruption of land access to ports. Three Indonesian port case studies are then presented: Belawan Port in Medan, North Sumatera; Tanjung Priok Port in Jakarta; and Tanjung Perak/Teluk Lamong Port Terminal in Surabaya. The case studies touch on a variety of issues: traffic congestion in and around ports; control of inbound and outbound traffic at ports; empty trips; land-use management and local-through access traffic separation; dedicated toll access; the use of inland waterways as an alternative transport mode; dedicated rail service from an industrial area/special economic zone; expansion of rail services; use of intermodal systems; IT solutions; the green port concept; inter terminal freight transport; infrastructure that can guarantee efficient freight movement. The chapter concludes with several policy recommendations.

Chapter 12: Potential Infrastructure Enhancements for Ports and Cities: Conclusions, Future Research and Policy Concepts.

Authors: Professor Colin F Duffield, Associate Professor Sari Wahyuni, Professor Danang Parikesit, Dr Felix Kin Peng Hui, Dr Sally Wilson

The final chapter of this research monograph draws together key points from each of the chapters. It summarises key findings from the research and poses questions that would benefit from future/ further research.

The compilation of this research monograph highlights the importance of collaborative international research as a model for capacity building and knowledge transfer. This research monograph has been a true collaborative venture between the research partners from The University of Melbourne in Australia, and Universitas Indonesia and Universitas Gadjah Mada in Indonesia. It has built goodwill between the research participants and has resulted in strengthened professional relationships and increased engagement between the university research partners. The collaborative approach also enabled greater engagement with key port stakeholders within both countries and enhanced the understanding of the common problems faced by both countries.

Author Biographies

Editors

Colin Duffield is Professor in Engineering Project Management and Deputy Head of the Department of Infrastructure Engineering at The University of Melbourne. He is also a fellow of the Law School and formerly a Director of Infrastructure Australia. Colin has extensive experience in the governance of long-term contracts and the interaction between policy, technical matters, risk management, financing and contractual arrangements as they apply to infrastructure. Colin has been involved in infrastructure delivery for public and private clients; an advisor to projects on risk and project structuring; and an independent reviewer and researcher of major engineering contracts.

Dr Felix Kin Peng Hui is a Senior Lecturer and Academic Specialist in the Department of Infrastructure Engineering at The University of Melbourne, and he teaches engineering management and marketing management to engineers at postgraduate level. He has a diverse industry background having spent more than 25 years at senior levels in manufacturing of machine tools, precision engineering, semiconductors, and infrastructure. He has also consulted widely to organisations seeking continuous improvements to optimise their operational efficiency. His research interests are in the areas of operational process optimisation, operational efficiency, lean systems, organisational development, and change management for sustainability. Dr Hui is a registered professional engineer and is also Fellow of the Institute of Managers and Leaders, ANZ.

Dr Sally Wilson is a Research Fellow in the Department of Infrastructure Engineering at The University of Melbourne working with Professor Colin Duffield and Dr Felix Hui on the study into infrastructure policy and finance as part of the Infrastructure Cluster Agenda of the Australia-Indonesia Centre. She is a consultant pharmacist with wide experience as a clinical pharmacist in the hospital and community sectors. She has worked as a Research Fellow in the Department of Epidemiology and Preventive Medicine at Monash University and on numerous interdisciplinary programs and projects in primary care. She has broad experience in healthcare service-based research and has recently been Project Manager on a National Health and Medical Research Council study. She has previously assisted on a major infrastructure study in the Department of Infrastructure Engineering at The University of Melbourne related to the Victorian Regional Rail Project.

Chapter Authors

John Black was appointed as the Foundation Professor of Transport Engineering at the University of New South Wales (UNSW), Sydney in 1984 and is now an Emeritus Professor. Since 1968 his research has included all modes of transport and their economic, social and environmental impacts. He has an extensive record of the supervision of Indonesian higher degree students from 1974 to the present. Since 1978 he has worked as a researcher and consultant in Indonesia that includes: leading capacity building for Bina Marga on the 10-year Indonesian steel bridge replacement program funded by the Australian Government: co-director (with Professor Danang Parikesit) of reform in the transport sector and Public Private Partnerships funded by the Australian-Indonesian Governance Research Partnership; advisor to PT SMI on the Jakarta-airport rail link.

Violeta Roso is an Associate Professor at Department of Technology Management and Economics, Chalmers University of Technology,

Gothenburg, Sweden, where she is also Director of Doctoral studies. She has been researching dry ports since 2003 and today is the leading researcher within the subject with numerous highly cited publications. Violeta has acted as a visiting academic at the University of New South Wales (UNSW) in Sydney, Australia; and at the University of North Florida (UNF), Florida, USA. She supervises PhD and Master's students, and teaches Master's and postgraduate courses.

Danang Parikesit is a Professor of Transportation Engineering in the Department of Civil and Environmental Engineering at Universitas Gadjah Mada. Former policy advisor to the Minister of Public Works (2010–2014), Professor Parikesit is currently appointed by the Government of Indonesia as the Head of the Indonesia Toll Road Authority. He is also a commissioner of the PT Pelni, an Indonesia state owned shipping company.

Associate Professor Sari Wahyuni, Faculty of Economics and Business, University of Indonesia is the founder of the South East Asian Journal of Management and currently serves as the President of the Indonesian Strategic Management Society. She was the Director of the University of Indonesia's Institute of Management and Associate Professor of International Business at Nottingham University, Malaysia Campus. Sari is also a consultant for many multinational companies and government bodies in Indonesia. Her research interests are in strategic management, especially on regional economic development, national competitiveness, international business strategy, strategic alliances, human resources, international negotiations.

Ruslan Prijadi is Associate Professor of corporate finance in the Department of Management, Faculty of Economics and Business, Universitas Indonesia.

Haya Al-Daghlas is a PhD candidate in the Department of Infrastructure Engineering at The University of Melbourne. Haya obtained her BSc. In Civil Engineering from the University of Jordan in 2009. In 2016 Haya completed her Master's degree in Engineering Project Management at The University of Melbourne/School of Engineering, with first-class honours. Haya has worked in the field of engineering project management for several years and she was recently appointed as a member of the Board of Directors at Melbourne Maritime Heritage Network.

Regina Duffield is a biomedicine graduate from The University of Melbourne and was a research assistant in the Department of Infrastructure Engineering at The University of Melbourne.

Vijayshree Behal is a Master of Engineering (Civil with Business) graduate from the Department of Infrastructure Engineering, The University of Melbourne, and was a student at the time of the project.

Andrew Chin, and Hanlong Huang are Master of Engineering (Civil) graduates from the Department of Infrastructure Engineering, The University of Melbourne, and were students at the time of the project.

Said Basalim is a PhD Candidate in the Civil Engineering Department, Transport Engineering at Universitas Gadjah Mada. Said is also a lecturer in the Faculty of Engineering at the University of Tanjungpura in West Kalimantan.

Waskitha Weninging Galih is a Master of Management student at Universitas Indonesia in the Faculty of Law.

Wiratno Wahyu Wibowo is a researcher in the Centre for Transportation and Logistics Studies (Pustral) at Universitas Gadjah Mada. Wiratno is an associate researcher of Professor Danang.

Alif Azadi Taufik was a student in the Department of Management, Faculty of Economics and Business, Universitas Indonesia.

1. Infrastructure Investment in Indonesia — The Economic Context

C. F. Duffield,[1] R. Duffield,[2] and S. Wilson[3]

1.0 Introduction to Indonesia

Located in South-East Asia between the Indian and Pacific Oceans, Indonesia represents the world's largest archipelagic country. Its 17,000 equatorial islands, of which only 6,000 are inhabited, experience a tropical climate characterised by high rainfall, humidity and temperatures. The country is rich in natural resources including coal, minerals, gold, copper, nickel, oil, gas and fertile land (giving rise to agricultural products). It is also prone to natural disasters and home to the most volcanoes of any country in the world, with more than 75% of the population living within 100 km of a Holocene volcano (active within the last 11,700 years) (Smithsonian Institution 2015). For example, in early August 2018 a series of earthquakes and aftershocks hit the island of Lombok displacing an estimated 20,000 people.

1   Professor of Engineering Project Management, Deputy Head of Department (Academic), Dept. of Infrastructure Engineering, The University of Melbourne
2   Research Assistant, Dept. of Infrastructure Engineering, The University of Melbourne.
3   Research Fellow, Dept. of Infrastructure Engineering, The University of Melbourne.

https://doi.org/10.11647/OBP.0189.01

Indonesia shares land borders with Malaysia, East Timor and Papua New Guinea and is closely neighboured by Australia, Singapore and the Philippines. Also of note is its proximity to China and India, the two largest and fastest growing economies in the world, and its position along major sea lanes which link the Indian Ocean to the South China Sea and the Pacific Ocean. This central location, in combination with other factors such as its rich resources and demographic composition, make Indonesia an attractive location for foreign trade, investment and political and business affairs.

1.1 Government

1.1.1 National

President Suharto's long-standing dictatorship fell in 1998 and Indonesia has since operated as an independent democratic republic. The political system consists of three branches: the legislative; the executive; and the judicial branch.

The People's Consultative Assembly (MPR) forms the legislative branch and comprises the House of Representatives (DPR) and the Council of Regional Representatives (DPD). The MPR is responsible for drawing up and passing laws, providing policy guidance and overseeing the performance of the President and government agencies.

The executive branch consists of the President and Vice-President, as elected by the Indonesian electorate, as well as the cabinet, as appointed by the President. The President is the Chief Executive, the Head of State and Commander-in-Chief of the Armed Forces. The most recent elections in 2014 saw the appointment of a new Government, headed by President Joko Widodo (Jokowi).

The Judiciary is based on the Supreme Court, with most legal cases being dealt with by the public, military, religious and administrative courts.

1.1.2 Regional

Indonesia is divided administratively into thirty-four provinces and hundreds of districts and municipalities. These are headed by Governors and Regents, with elected provincial and council assemblies. In 1999, most government control and tax-raising powers were decentralised to these regional governments through the 'Regional Autonomy Law' (Law no. 22/1999). Many policies, laws and regulations now differ significantly between regions.

1.2 Population

At the most recent census in 2010 (BPS 2015a), the population of Indonesia was 238 million people. Currently, the estimated population is approximately 260 million (Indonesia Investments, 2017; World Bank 2017). This makes it the fourth most populous nation in the world (making up 3.5% of the world's total population) and the most populous nation in South-East Asia making up 40.6% of the South-East Asian population (United Nations 2015a; World Economic Forum 2015a). Almost 45% of this population is <25 years of age (United Nations 2015a), meaning there will be a large number of people ready to enter the workforce and who will drive economic growth in the coming decades.

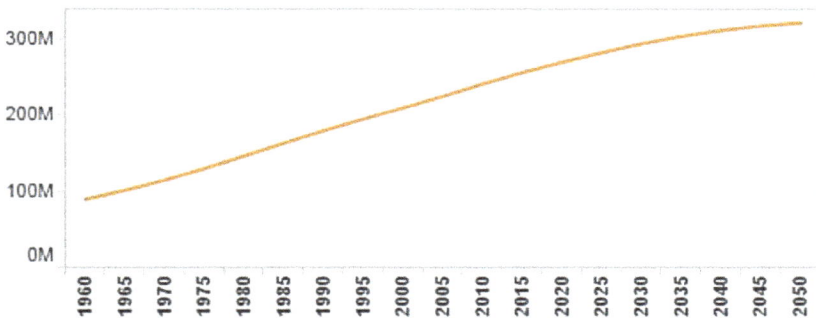

Fig. 1.1 Historical and projected populations of Indonesia, 1960–2050. Source: World Bank 2015a.

Population growth has been rapid and is forecast to continue to reach approximately 305 million people by 2035 (National Development Planning Agency 2013) and 322 million by 2050 (BPS 2015a; United Nations 2015a; World Bank 2017) (Fig. 1). The middle class and urban populations are increasing significantly. From 2003–2010 the middle class grew by 61.73%, with over seven million people being newly elevated into this category each year (World Bank 2011). An additional eight or nine million people are currently entering the middle class segment each year and numbers are expected to reach 140–150 million by 2020, approximately double the middle class population of 2012 (Rastogi et al. 2013). Urbanisation is also occurring at one of the fastest rates in the world, increasing by about 4% per year (World Bank 2014a). Currently 54.5% of the population (World Bank 2016a) is residing in the urban areas of Indonesia and this is predicted to rise to over 65% by 2035 (National Development Planning Agency 2013) and about 71% by 2050 (BPS 2015a; United Nations 2015b).

However, a large proportion of the country still lives in poverty. As at September 2014, over twenty-seven million people (11% of the population) were living on less than USD1 per day (BPS 2015b) and approximately one hundred million people (40% of the population) on less than USD2 per day — the standard international definition of 'poor' (Asian Development Bank 2015a). A further sixty-eight million people are classified as 'vulnerable', living on just above USD2 per day (Asian Development Bank 2015a). The country's human development index (an indicator of per capita income, life expectancy and education levels) of 0.684 in 2014 saw it ranked 108th in the world, alongside Egypt, Botswana and Palestine (United Nations Development Programme 2014). While the situation has been improving, the rate of progress is declining and the large gap between rich and poor is growing (Asian Development Bank 2015a). BPS, In September 2017, reported that the percentage of poor in Indonesia was 10.1% of the population (BPS 2017).

1.3 Economy

Except for several short-term dips, since the 1970s, the Indonesian economy has been steadily growing. Drastic political and financial reforms allowed the country to experience incredibly rapid growth from 1998 onwards, remaining reasonably unaffected during the 2008 GFC. Indonesia now ranks as the largest economy in South-east Asia and the 16th largest economy in the world with an expected nominal GDP of USD 873 billion (International Monetary Fund 2015). The economic growth has been largely attributed to high domestic consumption as a result of a rising middle class with increasing levels of disposable income.

However, decreased demand from key export markets for Indonesia's main commodity products, and a slowing down of domestic consumption, have resulted in a decline in the rate of growth since 2011, with real GDP growth dropping from 5.6% in 2013 to 5% in 2014 and

4.9% in 2015 (World Bank 2015b). Recent projections indicate a growth of 5.1% in 2017 (World Bank 2018). The country's global competitive ranking, which improved significantly from 50th in 2013 to 38th in 2014 and 34th in 2015, saw a setback in the 2015–2016 Global Competitiveness Report with a ranking of 37. For comparison, Singapore was ranked 2nd, Malaysia 18th, Thailand 32nd, the Philippines 47th and Vietnam 56th (World Economic Forum 2015a). In the 2017–2018 report, Indonesia now ranks 36th with Singapore ranked 3rd, Malaysia 23rd, Thailand 32nd, the Philippines 56th and Vietnam 55th.

Following improved household consumption and external demand (Asian Development Bank 2015b), real GDP growth was expected to rise again in 2016 to 5.1% (International Monetary Fund 2015, October) and estimated to be 5.5% in 2017 before rising to around 6% in 2020 (International Monetary Fund 2015, October; World Bank 2015b). The World Bank (2018) Global Economic Prospects reports real GDP growth for 2016 and estimates growth of 5.1% for 2017, 5.2% for 2018 and forecasts 2020 growth of 5.3%. The long term outlook is also positive, with predictions that Indonesia will be the 7th largest economy in the world by 2030 (Oberman et al. 2012) and the 4th largest by 2050 (Hawksworth and Chan 2015). Factors that are expected to facilitate this growth include Indonesia's young population, rising urban and middle class populations, low national debt, abundant natural resources, regulatory reforms, increased macroeconomic stability and growth in infrastructure development (Austrade and DFAT 2015; Smith et al. 2015). However, reaching full economic potential will rely upon continued reforms in order to take advantage of the promising environment (World Bank 2014a).

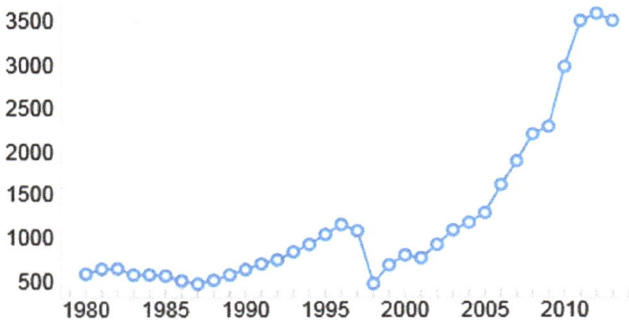

Fig. 1.2 Indonesian GDP per capita in USD, 1980–2013.
Source: World Economic Forum 2015b.

Under the master plan for the acceleration and expansion of Indonesia's economic development — MP3EI — the Indonesian Government has set an adventurous target to become a member of the top ten global economies by 2025. This would mean that average GDP per capita would rise from USD 3,000 today to USD 15,000 and GDP per se — a heady USD 4.5 trillion (some five times the current GDP). It is intended to achieve this through a two-pronged process of acceleration and expansion. The process involves strengthening connectivity, not only throughout the archipelago but also the Association of Southeast Asian Nations (ASEAN) region.

1.3.1 Investment

Domestic consumption can no longer be relied upon as the core driver to reach Indonesia's economic targets. The key to achieving the forecast growth will be an increase in foreign direct investment (FDI). With an expanding population, high consumption and enormous growth potential, Indonesia is well-placed as a favourable destination for many foreign investors. Indeed, foreign investment increased from USD 16.1 billion in 2010 to 24.5 billion in 2012 and 28.5 billion in 2014 (BKPM 2015) to 28.9 billion USD in 2016 (BKPM 2017a). Indonesia's credit rating by global rating agency Fitch Ratings was also upgraded in 2012 and confirmed in 2014 to Investment Grade 'BBB-/stable outlook', in recognition of the country's macroeconomic stability (KPMG Indonesia 2015; Fitch Ratings, 2014; Ho and Sapahutar 2017). However, the pace of FDI growth has slowed, with foreign investment realisation in January–September period up by a modest 14.6% in 2014, 16.8% in 2015 and a 12% increase in 2016, compared to increases of 26.1% and 22.4% in 2012 and 2013 respectively (BKPM 2015; Global business guide Indonesia 2015; BKPM 2017b). Despite the attractiveness of the region, there remain many disincentives to potential investors in Indonesia. These will be explored in the next chapter addressing challenges, risks and issues.

1.4 Infrastructure

For nearly two decades following the Asian economic crisis of 1997, both public and private spending on infrastructure in Indonesia was

FDI

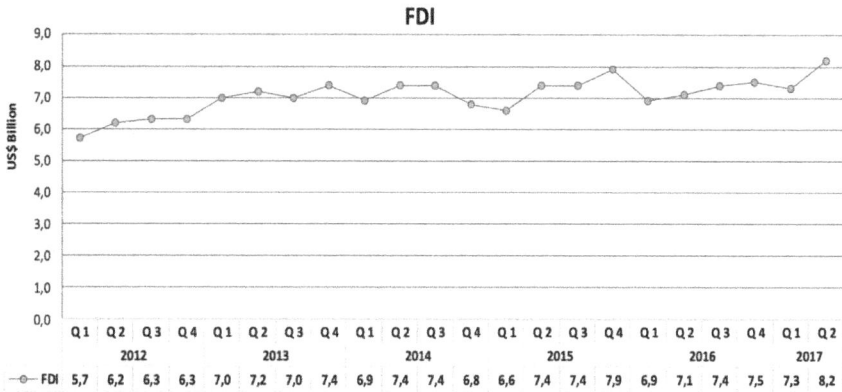

	Q1	Q2	Q3	Q4	Q1	Q2	Q3	Q4	Q1	Q2	Q3	Q4	Q1	Q2	Q3	Q4	Q1	Q2	Q3	Q4	Q1	Q2
	2012				2013				2014				2015				2016				2017	
FDI	5,7	6,2	6,3	6,3	7,0	7,2	7,0	7,4	6,9	7,4	7,4	6,8	6,6	7,4	7,4	7,9	6,9	7,1	7,4	7,5	7,3	8,2

Fig. 1.3 Investment realisation of FDI 2012–June 2017 in USD per quarter.
Source: BKPM 2017b.

Notes:

- 2010, 2011 and 2012, exchange rate USD 1 = Rp 9,000

- 2013 (Q I and Q II), exchange rate USD 1 = Rp 9,300 (based on State Budget 2013)

- 2013 (Q III and Q IV), exchange rate USD 1 = Rp 9,600 (based on Revised State Budget 2013)

- 2014 (Q I, Q II and Q III) exchange rate USD 1 = Rp 10,500 (based on State Budget 2014)

- 2014 (Q IV) exchange rate s USD 1 = Rp 11,600 (based on Revised State Budget 2014)

- 2015 (Q I, Q II, Q III and Q IV) exchange rate USD 1 = Rp 12,500 (based on Revised State Budget 2015)

- 2016 (Q I and Q II) exchange rate USD 1 = Rp 13,900 (based on State Budget 2016) — 2016 (Q III and Q IV) exchange rate USD 1 = Rp 13,500 (based on Revised State Budget 2016)

- 2017 (Q I and Q II), exchange rate USD = Rp 13,300 (based on State Budget 2017) (BKPM 2017b)

neglected. Underinvestment has left the country with both insufficient quality and quantity of roads, airports, railways and ports, with the current infrastructure being overcrowded, in poor condition and extremely inefficient. The resulting high costs of transportation and logistics contributed to Indonesia's low ranking of 53rd out of 160 countries in the 2014 Logistics Performance Index (World Bank 2014b) and 63rd of 160 in 2016 (World Bank 2016b). The Indonesian Chamber of Commerce and Industry (KADIN Indonesia) stated that logistics costs accounted for around 15% of Indonesia's GDP, compared to 8–9% in surrounding ASEAN countries (KADIN Indonesia MP 2015). In addition, many Indonesian's have only limited access to piped water, electricity, health care and education.

The Government of Indonesia has begun to address these issues, with increased spending over a number of years allowing the *infrastructure score* to improve from 3.7 (ranked 78th out of 144 nations) in 2012–2013 (World Economic Forum 2012) to 4.2 (ranked 61st out of 148 nations) in 2013–2014 (World Economic Forum 2013). However, this was still below the average score of the ASEAN nations (approximately 4.3) and did not improve in 2014 or 2015, with the country ranking 62nd out of 140 nations (World Economic Forum 2015a). However, in 2017 the infrastructure score increased slightly (4.5) with the current ranking of 52nd out of 137 countries on infrastructure (World Economic Forum 2017).

It has been emphasised by many observers that ongoing investment in infrastructure will be crucial for the maintenance of economic growth in Indonesia. With a growing population and increasing urbanisation, as well as global changes in climate, the demand for infrastructure development is ever increasing. Inefficiencies and high costs arising from poor connectivity present a major limitation both to the development of many industries and to attracting foreign investment. Upgrades to infrastructure, and in particular ports, will be necessary to take advantage of increased trade opportunities, especially with the formation of the ASEAN economic community (AEC) in 2015. Improvements will also help to raise quality of life, decrease the divide between rural and urban centres and reduce overall poverty

One of the most significant and pressing issues for Indonesia is how the country is going to fund, finance and deliver the infrastructure necessary to underpin the economic growth and reform strategies for the country. Reform is required to overcome the major gap between the demand for, and the provision of, infrastructure. There are persistent difficulties in the areas of gaining approvals, finance, governance and project delivery that have resulted in poor project selection and poor project preparation (OECD 2012; Parikesit et al. 2012; Wibisono, Delmon, and Hahm 2011; Center for Infrastructure Development, 2012).

The World Bank and the OECD also identified the need for a unified voice to identify and support priority projects and to provide guidance on best practice for the delivery of projects and the Indonesian government has responded through the establishment of the Public Private Partnership (PPP) centralised unit within the Ministry of Finance that works closely with the Directorate for PPP Development in the Indonesian National Development Planning Agency (BAPPENAS), the National Committee for the Acceleration of Infrastructure Provision (KKPPI) for policy formulation and the State Infrastructure Guarantee Company for PPP projects.

Growth centres and infrastructure development are considered the main building blocks of the proposed Indonesian economic corridors. ICT and transport infrastructure improvements in roads, seaports, airports, water, energy, power and social needs are critical, all of which require significant funds. The Indonesian government has estimated that it will only be able to provide approximately 35% of the funds required and that local and international finance is being sought to participate in infrastructure investments via the use of PPPs as alternative sources of development financing. Specific barriers to this plan remain as the current legal and regulatory regimes do not readily accommodate the PPP funding mechanism.

A recent news report related to attracting private funding for infrastructure in Indonesia noted that Indonesia is now sending delegations to China to attract private funds for infrastructure projects, according to the World Bank's Private Participation in Infrastructure report. The report highlighted that Indonesia attracted USD 15 billion to 11 projects. In 2015 President Jokowi announced that more than USD 400 billion will be spent to accomplish 247 national strategic projects by 2019 (Roughneen 2017). Since President Jokowi took office in 2014, 30 of the projects — worth Rp 94.8 trillion (USD 6.7 billion) — have been completed (Himwan and Hapsari 2018; Ganesha 2018).

Research is required to develop and refine Indonesian infrastructure project procurement systems and to appropriately integrate these systems into processes and practice. This involves the development of an internationally attractive market; reform of internal project delivery processes; reform of legal and regulatory systems, reform such that an integrated and streamlined mechanism for infrastructure provision is developed that is appropriate not only for highly populated and developed regions such as West Java (Jakarta) but also for the balance of provinces across the archipelago.

Although there has already been major reform in how infrastructure is planned in Indonesia, the gap between demand and provision of infrastructure remains. Ongoing research into how infrastructure investment decisions should be made is required to inform the changes, advancements and reforms to infrastructure provision and management that are necessary. The next chapter focuses on Indonesian infrastructure planning, challenges and risks.

References

Asian Development Bank 2015a. *Summary of Indonesia's poverty analysis,* www. adb.org/sites/default/files/publication/177017/ino-paper-04-2015.pdf

Asian Development Bank, 2015b. *Indonesia: Economy — Excerpt from Asian development outlook 2015 update,* www.adb.org/countries/indonesia/economy

Austrade and DFAT 2015. *Why ASEAN and why now?,* Canberra: Department of Foreign Affairs and Trade, dfat.gov.au/about-us/publications/documents/why-asean-and-why-now.pdf

BKPM 2015, *Domestic and Foreign Direct Investment Realization in Quarter III and January-September 2015,* 22 October 2015.

BKPM 2017a. *Domestic and foreign direct investment realization in quarter,* www. bkpm.go.id/images/uploads/investasi_indonesia/file/Bahan_Paparan_-_Eng_-_TW_IV_2016-250117_FINAL.pdf

BKPM 2017b. *Domestic and foreign direct investment realization in quarter II and January-June 2017,* www.bkpm.go.id/images/uploads/investasi_indonesia/file/2%29_Paparan_Bahasa_Inggris_Press_Release_TW_II_dan_Jan_Juni_2017.pdf

Badan Pusat Statistik (BPS) 2015a. *Population statistics,* sp2010.bps.go.id/index. php/site/topik?kid=1andkategori=Jumlah-dan-Distribusi-Penduduk

Badan Pusat Statistik (BPS) 2015b. *Poverty statistics,* https://www.bps.go.id/publication/2016/11/03/0131ac39a63150db11dfab04/data-dan-informasi-kemiskinan-kabupaten-kota-tahun-2015.html

Badan Pusat Statistik (BPS) 2017. *Poverty statistics,* www.bps.go.id/statictable/2014/01/30/1494/jumlah-penduduk-miskin-persentase-penduduk-miskin-dan-garis-kemiskinan-1970-2017.html

Center for Infrastructure Development 2012. 'Solving problems of inertia in implementaton of Public Private Partnership for infrastructure provision', in *Business Dialog Report,* p. 20, Jakarta, Indonesia: Prasetiya Mulya Business School.

Fitch Ratings 2014. *Fitch affirms Indonesia at 'BBB-'; Outlook stable*, www.fitchratings.com/site/pr/922055

Ganesha, A 2018. 'Indonesia improves in getting private money for infrastructure', *Jakarta Globe*, jakartaglobe.id/business/indonesia-among-top-5-countries-utilizing-the-most-private-money-for-infrastructure-last-year/

Global Business Guide Indonesia 2015. *Indonesia in 2015: Economic and political renewal shifts investment focus*, www.gbgindonesia.com/en/main/why_indonesia/indonesia_in_2015_economic_and_political_renewal_shifts_investment_focus.php

Hawksworth, J and Chan, D 2015. *The World in 2050: Will the shift in global economic power continue?*, PwC, www.pwc.com/gx/en/issues/the-economy/assets/world-in-2050-february-2015.pdf

Himawan, A and Hapsari, DK 2018. 'Here is a list of 30 infrastructure projects that have been completed by Jokowi', *Suara*, www.suara.com/bisnis/2018/04/19/150203/ini-daftar-30-proyek-infrastruktur-yang-telah-diselesaikan-jokowi

Ho, Y and Sipahutar, T 2017. 'Indonesia wins Fitch Rating upgrade months after S and P move', *Bloomberg News*, www.bloomberg.com/news/articles/2017-12-21/indonesia-wins-fitch-credit-rating-upgrade-months-after-s-p-move

International Monetary Fund 2015. *World economic outlook database*, www.imf.org/external/pubs/ft/weo/2015/02/weodata/weoselgr.aspx

Indonesia Investments 2017. 'Population of Indonesia', *Indonesia Investments*, www.indonesia-investments.com/culture/population/item67

KADIN Indonesia MP 2015. 'Government needs a breakthrough to suppress logistics cost', *BSD Bulletin — Indonesia Trade & Investment News October 2015*.

KPMG Indonesia 2015. *Investing in Indonesia*, https://assets.kpmg/content/dam/kpmg/pdf/2016/07/id-ksa-investing-in-indonesia-2015.pdf

National Development Planning Agency 2013. *Projected population Indonesia 2010–2035*, indonesia.unfpa.org/sites/default/files/pub-pdf/Policy_brief_on_The_2010_%E2%80%93_2035_Indonesian_Population_Projection.pdf

National Development Planning Agency 2013. *Proyeksi penduduk Indonesia 2010–2035*, Central Bureau of Statistics (Badan Perencanaan Pembangunan Nasional), www.bappenas.go.id/files/5413/9148/4109/Proyeksi_Penduduk_Indonesia_2010-2035.pdf

Oberman, R, Dobbs, R, Budiman, A, Thompson, F and Rosse, M 2012. *The archipelago economy: Unleashing Indonesia's potential*, McKinsey Global Institute, www.mckinsey.com/~/media/mckinsey/featured%20insights/asia%20pacific/the%20archipelago%20economy/mgi_unleashing_indonesia_potential_executive_summary.ashx

OECD 2012. *Reviews of regulatory reform*: *Indonesia — Strengthening co-ordination and connecting markets,* read.oecd-ilibrary.org/governance/oecd-reviews-of-regulatory-reform-indonesia-2012_9789264173637-en#page1

Parikesit, D, Black, J and Strang, J 2012. *Towards a refocused Indonesian national delivery process for infrastructure*: *A concept for a centre of evidence-based policy analysis of infrastructure and PPP, GREAT initiative,* unpublished report for AUSTRADE, Department of Foreign Affairs and Trade.

Rastogi, V, Tamboto, E, Tong, D and Sinburimsit, T 2013. *Indonesia's rising middle-class and affluent consumers*: *Demographic and regional shifts,* BCG Henderson Institute, www.bcgperspectives.com/content/articles/center_consumer_customer_insight_consumer_products_indonesias_rising_middle_class_affluent_consumers/?chapter=3#chapter3

Roughneen, S 2017. 'Southeast Asian ports thirst for more seaborne trade', *Nikkei Asian Review,* asia.nikkei.com/Economy/Southeast-Asian-ports-thirst-for-more-seaborne-trade

Smith, J, Satar, R, Boothman, T and Harrison, G 2015. *Building Indonesia's future*: *Unblocking the pipeline of infrastructure projects,* PwC, www.pwc.com/id/en/capital-projects-infrastructure/Building%20Indonesia's%20future.pdf

Smithsonian Institution 2015. *Global volcanism program — the Indonesia region,* volcano.si.edu

United Nations 2015a. *World population prospects, the 2015 revision,* esa.un.org/unpd/wpp/

United Nations 2015b. *World urbanisation prospects, the 2015 revision,* esa.un.org/unpd/wup/

United Nations Development Programme (UNDP) 2014. *Human development reports — Human Development Index (HDI),* hdr.undp.org/en/content/human-development-index-hdi-table

Wibisono, A, Delmon, J and Hahm, H 2011. *Unlocking the public-private partnerships deadlock in Indonesia,* World Bank, documents.worldbank.org/curated/en/603611468043468438/pdf/750940WP0P11580eadlock0in0indonesia.pdf

World Bank 2011. *Indonesia economic quarterly*: *2008 again?* World Bank, www-wds.worldbank.org/external/default/WDSContentServer/WDSP/IB/2011/03/18/000333037_20110318015637/Rendered/PDF/601520revised010IEQ1Mar20111english.pdf

World Bank 2014a. *Indonesia*: *Avoiding the trap — Indonesia development policy review 2014,* World Bank, www.worldbank.org/content/dam/Worldbank/document/EAP/Indonesia/Indonesia-development-policy-review-2014-english.pdf

World Bank 2014b. *Logistics performance index — global rankings 2014,* lpi.worldbank.org/international/global

World Bank 2015a. *Population estimates and projections — Indonesia,* datatopics. worldbank.org/hnp/popestimates

World Bank 2015b. *Global economic prospects: having fiscal space and using it,* World Bank, www.worldbank.org/content/dam/Worldbank/GEP/GEP2015a/pdfs/ GEP15a_web_full.pdf

World Bank 2016a. *World development indicators: Indonesia,* data.worldbank.org/ country/indonesia

World Bank 2016b. *Logistics performance index — global rankings 2016,* lpi. worldbank.org/international/global/2016

World Bank 2017. *Health, nutrition and population,* datatopics.worldbank.org/ health/population

World Bank 2018. *Global economic prospects, January 2018: Broad-based upturn, but for how long?* World Bank, openknowledge.worldbank.org/bitstream/ handle/10986/28932/9781464811630.pdf

World Economic Forum 2012. *The global competitiveness report 2012–13,* www3. weforum.org/docs/WEF_GlobalCompetitivenessReport_2012-13.pdf

World Economic Forum 2013. *The global competitiveness report 2013–14,* www3. weforum.org/docs/WEF_GlobalCompetitivenessReport_2013-14.pdf

World Economic Forum 2015a. *The global competitiveness report 2015–16,* www3.weforum.org/docs/gcr/2015-2016/Global_Competitiveness_ Report_2015-2016.pdf

World Economic Forum 2015b. *The global competitiveness report 2015–16: country profiles — Indonesia,* reports.weforum.org/global-competitiveness-report-2015-2016/economies/#economy=IDN

World Economic Forum 2017. *The global competitiveness report 2017–2018,* www3. weforum.org/docs/GCR2017-2018/05FullReport/TheGlobalCompetitiveness Report2017%E2%80%932018.pdf

2. Infrastructure Planning, Challenges and Risks

C. F. Duffield,[1] R. Duffield,[2] and S. Wilson[3]

2.0 Introduction

As already mentioned in the previous chapter, there is an evident need for improved infrastructure in Indonesia. The Government of Indonesia (GoI) has recognised this, incorporating targets and strategies into a number of national plans which aim to address the issues. The development of infrastructure in Indonesia is also likely to be affected by other large-scale plans, initiatives or doctrines in the region. This chapter briefly outlines relevant national and international plans and initiatives to assist with infrastructure investment and development in Indonesia, and then presents and discusses the challenges, risks and issues associated with delivering the required infrastructure necessary to underpin the economic growth and reform strategies for Indonesia. It details the context for focusing on the development of waterways and ports.

2.1 Infrastructure Plans
2.1.1 National Plans, Agencies and Institutions

Several government agencies, organisations and institutions have been established in Indonesia to help facilitate, drive, coordinate or

---

1   Professor of Engineering Project Management, Deputy Head of Department (Academic), Dept. of Infrastructure Engineering, The University of Melbourne.

2   Research Assistant, Dept. of Infrastructure Engineering, The University of Melbourne.

3   Research Fellow, Dept. of Infrastructure Engineering, The University of Melbourne.

 https://doi.org/10.11647/OBP.0189.02

assist with project preparation. These agencies and institutions further provide guidance on infrastructure development and project planning and delivery within the country.

The National plans set an agenda for national development, economic growth and infrastructure development.

2.1.1.1 *Bappenas and Bappenda*

Bappenas, the National Development Planning Agency, is a central government organisation responsible for national development planning and budgeting (annual, five-year and long-term) and works with Ministries and local government and agencies so that development planning is more structured, strategic and comprehensive. Bappenas now sits as a Ministry under the President Joko Widodo (KementerianPPN/ Bappenas 2017). It is also in charge of planning, evaluation and implementation of Public Private Partnerships (PPPs) and coordinates the PPP program. Bappenas releases a PPP Book annually aimed at presenting "reliable information to prospective investors on national PPP projects in the pipeline" (Bappenas 2015a; ERIA 2014). The projects fall under two categories based on readiness: ready to offer projects and projects under preparation. Projects that have been tendered are also listed (Bappenas 2017).

Bappenas coordinates the planning process of projects funded by external loans. It compiles several external loan planning documents including the *List of Medium-Term Planned External Loans* or *Daftar Rencana Pinjaman Luar Negeri Jangka Menengah (DRPLN-JM)/Blue Book* and the *List of Planned Priority External Loans* or *Daftar Rencana Prioritas Pinjaman Luar Negeri (DRPPLN)/Green Book*.

The Blue Book contains the planned programs and projects which are appropriate to be funded by external loans for the medium-term period, while the Green Book lists planned projects that have a funding indication and are ready to be negotiated within the yearly effective period (Bappenas 2015b; Kementerian PPN/Bappenas 2016a, 2016b). The projects detailed in these books are based primarily on identified needs but do not fully consider the resource implications required to implement the projects described. This has led to few of the projects being deemed "bankable".

Bappenda is the regional co-ordinator for developments. It has responsibility for implementing projects in the region through the application of Bappenas's policies. Bappenda seeks to ensure projects are undertaken sustainably and that the financial governance is appropriate. It also manages local approvals, property and local tax revenue (http://bappenda.ntbprov.go.id/).

2.1.1.2 Master Plan for the Acceleration and Expansion of Indonesian Economic Development 2011–2025 (MP3EI)

In May 2011, the Government of Indonesia released its master plan aimed at transforming Indonesia into a developed nation with an even distribution of wealth and living standards across its regions and an economy within the global top ten by 2025. This ambitious target will involve boosting GDP per capita from approximately USD 3,500 (International Monetary Fund 2015) to USD 14,250–15,500 and nominal GDP from approximately USD 880 billion (International Monetary Fund 2015) to USD 4–4.5 trillion (KP3EI 2012a; Bappenas 2011b; Bappenas 2011a).

MP3EI outlines three main strategies in order to achieve this rapid economic growth: the establishment of six geographically defined economic corridors (Sumatra Economic Corridor, Java Economic Corridor, Kalimantan Economic Corridor, Sulawesi Economic Corridor, Bali-Nusa Tenggara Economic Corridor, and Papua-Kepulauan Maluku Economic Corridor (Fig. 2.1));[4] the improvement of national and international connectivity; and the strengthening of human resource capacity, science and technology (Bappenas 2011b; Bappenas 2011a; KP3EI 2012b).

Realisation of these plans will rely heavily upon improved infrastructure and hence this is a major focus of the MP3EI. Of the total IDR 4012 trillion of investment needed across the six corridors, approximately IDR (Indonesian Rupiah) 1725 trillion (or 43%) is

---

4   The development themes for the six economic corridors identified are: Sumatra EC-centre for production and processing of natural resources as nation's energy reserves; Java-driver for national industry and service provision; Kalimantan-centre for production and processing of national mining and energy reserves; Sulawesi-centre for production and processing of national agricultural, plantation, fishery, oil and gas and mining; Bali-Nusa Tenggara gateway for tourism and national food support; Papua-Kepulauan Maluku centre for development of food, fisheries, energy, and national mining.

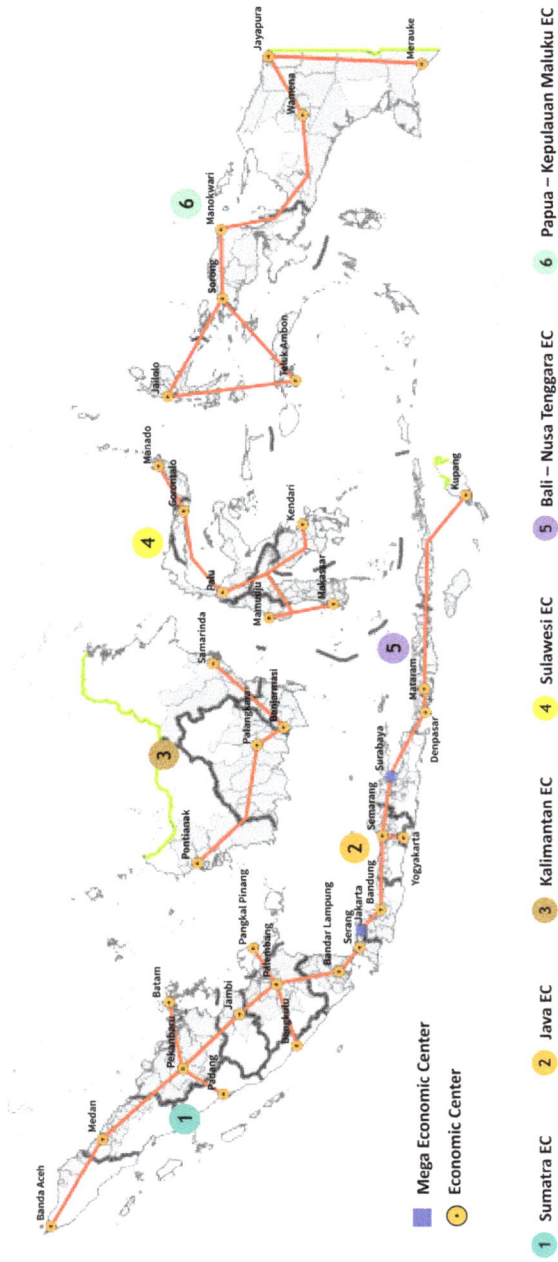

Fig. 2.1 Indonesian Six Economic Corridors identified for the MP3EI. Source: Ministry of National Development Planning/National Development Planning Agency, 2011 (Bappenas 2011a), *Masterplan Acceleration and Expansion of Indonesia Economic Development 2011–25*. Coordinating Ministry for Economic Affairs.

expected to go towards infrastructure development (Strategic Asia 2012), with approximately 24% earmarked for power and energy, 23% for roads and toll roads, 13% for railways, 10% for ICT, 8% for ports, 2% for airports and 2% for water and utilities (Oxford Business Group 2014). The majority of this funding will need to be sourced from State Owned Enterprises (SOEs) and private companies, largely through PPP arrangements.

The government claims to have made decent progress within the first three years of the plan, with 197 projects being launched by the end of June 2014. This is around 20% of the total 1048 infrastructure projects committed to between 2011 and 2025 and the head of the National Development Planning Agency (BAPPENAS) is optimistic that the planned projects will go ahead (Sipahutar 2014). However, others have criticised the plan for moving at a slow pace (Sambhi 2015) and so far the majority of funding has come from SOEs and government funding (Sipahutar 2014). Private participation has been disappointing and very few projects have been successfully implemented through the PPP scheme. It is hoped that further advancements will be made in the coming years as regulatory and institutional reforms help to stimulate the interest of private and foreign investors (Gustely 2015).

2.1.1.3 National Long-term Development Plan 2015–2025 (Rencana Pembangunan Jangka Panjang Nasional abbreviated to RPJPN)

The National Long-term Development Plan (RPJPN) 2005–2025 for Indonesia includes a broad range of targets regarding social, environmental and macroeconomic development, with an overarching objective to improve quality of life, equality and progression in an environmentally sustainable fashion (Government of the Republic of Indonesia and United Nations in Indonesia 2015).

Specific goals of the RPJPN are to:

- Achieve per capita income for residents' equivalent to middle income countries
- Reduce unemployment to less than 5%
- Reduce the number of poor people to less than 5%

- Increase both the human development index (HDI) and the Gender Development Index (GDI) scores

The RPJPN is divided into four stages. The first two stages of reform have largely been achieved with the country now progressing to stage three of the plan, refer below.

RPJPN 1 — 2005–2009 Reform the Republic of Indonesia such that the country is secure, peaceful, just and democratic, with enhanced prosperity.

RPJPN 2 — 2010–2014 Increase the quality and capacity of human resources in science, technology and strengthen economic competitiveness.

RPJPN 3 — 2015–2019 Enhance economic competitive advantage based on available natural resources, quality human resources and capability in science and technology.

RPJPN 4 — 2020–2025 Realize self-sufficiency through accelerated development in all fields with an economic structure that is based on competitive advantage.

In line with the general focus of the Jokowi government appointed in October 2014, the 2015–2019 medium term plan places a strong emphasis on infrastructure development. The government has set ambitious targets to improve basic infrastructure and connectivity involving a predicted total of IDR 5,519 trillion in investments (Smith et al. 2015a). Approximately 20% of these funds are to be directed towards road and toll road projects; a further 20% will go towards connectivity programs involving railways, urban transportation, sea transportation and aviation; and the final 60% is planned for basic services such as electricity, energy, gas, clean water, waste management, housing and information technology (Priatna 2014).

The state budget was originally expected to fund about 22% of the planned infrastructure projects, with an additional 6% to come from State Owned Enterprises (SOEs) and a 50% financing gap to be filled by the private sector (Priatna 2014). However, in January 2015 the Widodo Government abolished generous fuel subsidies, which were set to consume more than 10% of the state budget. This contributed significantly to their ability to increase the infrastructure spending target by 63% in 2015 (IDR 290 trillion) and a further 12% in 2016 (IDR 312 trillion) compared to 2014 (IDR 178 trillion). National and regional government funding is now estimated to account for 50% (IDR 2,761 trillion) of total infrastructure investment from 2015–2019. SOEs are expected to finance 19%, leaving 31% to be covered by private companies (Smith et al. 2015a; Hutapea 2015).

However, PricewaterhouseCoopers (PwC) Indonesia predicts a shortfall of approximately 19% in government infrastructure spending between 2015 and 2019 due largely to systemic issues which are likely to continue causing project bottlenecks (Smith et al. 2015a). The Asian Development Bank (ADB) has also suggested that annual infrastructure spending will need to reach 6.2% of GDP by 2020 in order to meet Indonesia's needs (Sipahutar 2015). The 2015–2019 capital infrastructure budget allocation represents only around 2.9% of GDP per year, which is below the approximate average of 5.5% of GDP for developing countries (Sukaesih 2014). That said, PwC Indonesia believes sufficient domestic and international funding is available, so long as Indonesia can provide a conducive environment to attract the required amount of private investment (Smith et al. 2015a).

2.1.1.4 *Committee for Acceleration of Priority Infrastructure Delivery*

By way of the Presidential Regulation no. 75 of 2014, the Committee for Acceleration of Priority Infrastructure Delivery (KPPIP) was established to co-ordinate and facilitate the development of National Strategic Projects and Priority Projects. Whilst the committee reports directly to the President and the Coordinating Ministry of Economic Affairs, it included representation from the Ministries of Finance and National Development along with representatives from Bappenas and the Minister of Agrarian Affairs. The Committee (KPPIP) was established to become a coordinating unit in the decision-making process to address issues related to lack of coordination between stakeholders, to facilitate 'debottlenecking' (removal of bottlenecks) efforts, to provide support for priority projects and to provide incentives and disincentives schemes to accelerate project realisation (KPPIP 2016).

In February 2016, the KPPIP released thirty priority projects for the country based on consideration of top down priorities as proposed by the President/Vice President, and on bottom up projects as proposed by the Ministries, Institutions and Regional governments.

There was little overlap between the thirty KPPIP priority projects with the blue book recommended projects from Bappenas, the MP3EI projects or specific projects as nominated by Institutions and Agencies, referred to in Fig. 2.2.

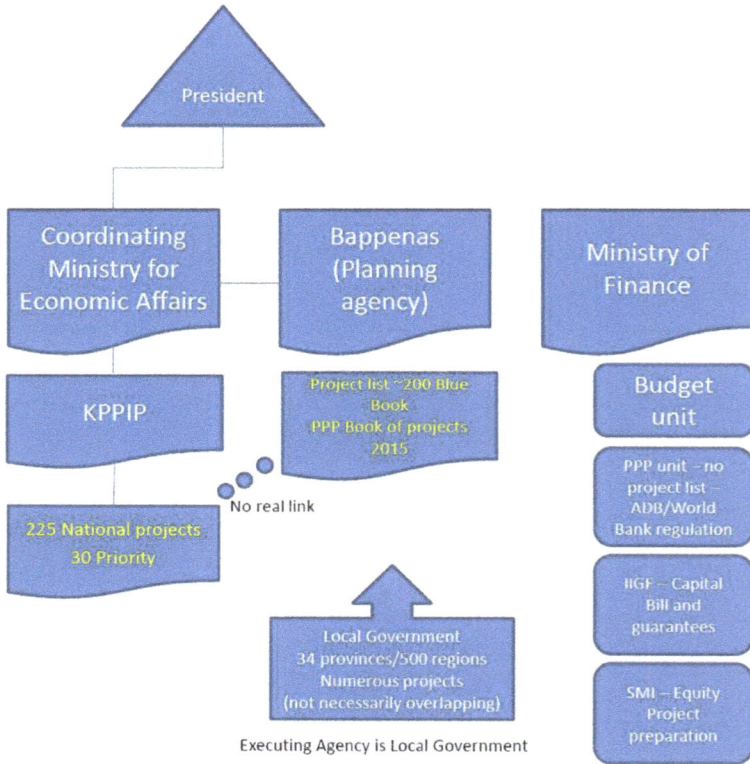

Fig. 2.2 Relationships between various Indonesian project planning agencies and authorities (figure by the authors)

Specific projects have historically been put forward by Bappenas and Local Governments yet as Indonesia has sought to address the pressures of rapid development, projects may emerge from KPPIP, Bappenas, Local Government or via the numerous mechanism available to attract international finance and/or funds. The Public Private Partnership unit may prioritise projects likely to attract international finance, the World Bank (and or the Asian Development Bank) may provide funds for priority initiatives, the Indonesia Infrastructure Guarantee Fund (IIGF) seeks to identify projects worthy of underwriting, while PT Sarana

Multi Infrastruktur (SMI) — a governmental infrastructure financing company — seeks to raise finance for projects. Once financed, projects gather pace as priorities.

Since its inception in 2014, KPPIP has set about to achieve co-ordination and project prioritisation as detailed in Fig. 2.3 KPPIP process for coordinating project outcomes (Source: KPPIP, 2016).

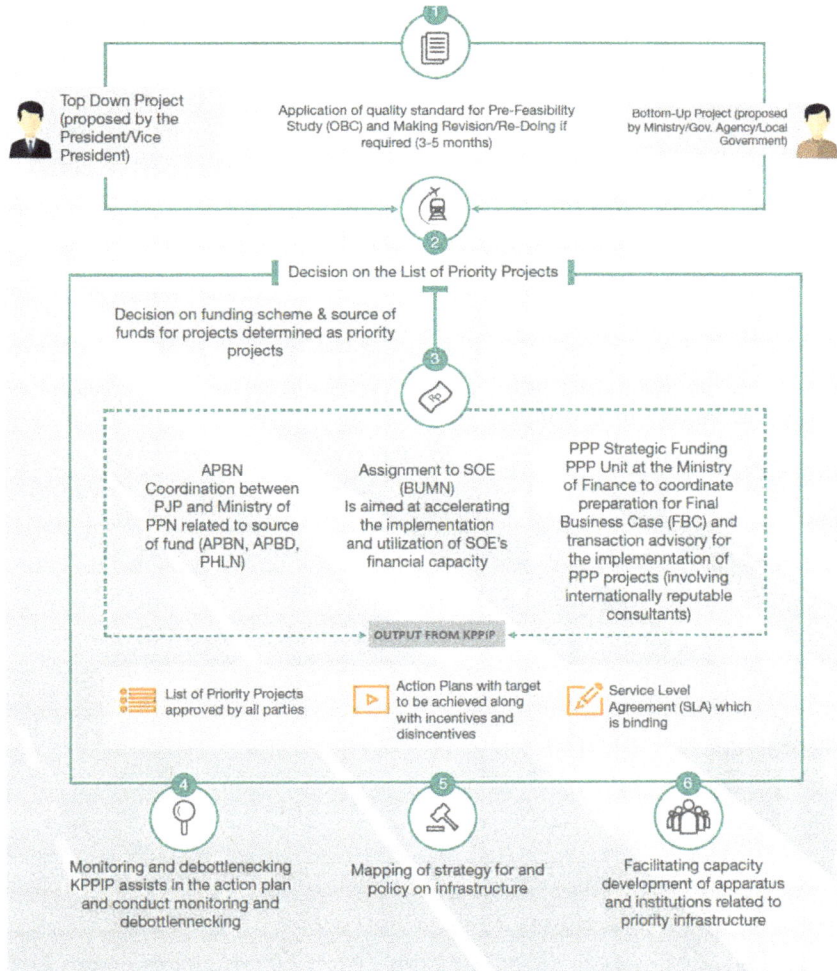

Fig. 2.3 KPPIP process for coordinating project outcomes. Source: KPPIP, 2016.

In addition to setting priority projects in 2016, KPPIP also assisted in improved project preparation for the following projects:

- Panimbang-Serang Toll Road
- Jakarta-Bandung High Speed Railway
- Bontang Oil Refinery
- Synchronization between the PPP unit in the Ministry of Finance and the Ministry of National Development Planning/ Bappenas

They also clarified project funding schemes for a range of projects and assisted to improve regulations and overcome bottlenecks.

Even though synergies exist between Central Government Agencies, the provinces and Local Government still have a level of autonomy with respect to the prioritisation of projects.

2.1.1.5 *Indonesian Maritime Doctrine 2014*

President Joko Widodo ('Jokowi') has highlighted maritime development as a key focus of his five-year term. The country currently suffers from a severe lack of inter-connectivity and inefficient port facilities hinder both national and international maritime commerce. The average dwell time of Indonesia's main port in Jakarta is 6.4 days, much higher than the dwell times of 1.5 and 3 days in nearby Singapore and Malaysia, respectively (Piesse 2015). In his maritime doctrine, Jokowi outlined plans to upgrade or construct twenty-four seaports and deep seaports over five years as a part of the 'sea toll road' program. The resulting increase in domestic connectivity and reduced transportation costs are expected to boost economic development through enhanced trade and competitiveness.

Furthermore, it is hoped that the improved infrastructure and bigger ports will provide a platform for increased international shipping traffic. By expanding diplomatic attention beyond the Pacific and the Association of Southeast Asian Nations (ASEAN) regions and into the Indian Ocean, Jokowi intends to establish Indonesia as a 'global maritime axis', acting as a powerful international hub for sea trade. The policy also outlines plans to improve national security and expand the fishing and shipbuilding industries (Shekhar and Liow 2014; Piesse 2015).

As a part of the National Medium Term Development Plan 2015–2019, the majority of funding for Jokowi's maritime vision is being sought from private and foreign direct investment. In December 2014 the government stated that approximately USD 7 billion was needed from foreign investors for the planned sea toll road project, "a coordinated network of ports designed to better handle international traffic and streamline more local trade" (Dodd 2015). Investment interest is strong and there are already a number of companies, development banks and foreign governments taking part, with upgrades to some of the ports now underway (Sambhi 2015; Dodd 2015). In November 2015 the government also launched a subsidised freight service program along its 'sea toll road', linking major ports between Java, Papua, Maluku and Riau Islands (*The Jakarta Post* 11 November 2015, editorial). While the government certainly faces challenges ahead, the maritime doctrine has largely been received with support and positivity.

2.1.2 International Plans

There are several plans from bodies, other than the Indonesian government, with relevance to the development of infrastructure in Indonesia.

2.1.2.1 ASEAN (Association of Southeast Asian Nations) Connectivity Agenda

The 2011–2015 Master Plan on ASEAN connectivity included strategies for the development of roads, railways, ports, aviation facilities, ICT and electricity (ASEAN 2010). Discussions on a post-2015 ASEAN Connectivity agenda were held at the 6th ASEAN Connectivity Symposium in October 2015 (ASEAN 2015).

2.1.2.2 APEC (Asia-Pacific Economic Cooperation) Connectivity Blueprint 2015–2025

Initiated in 2013 by Indonesia, the APEC connectivity blueprint outlines targets and strategies for the strengthening of physical, institutional and people-to-people connectivity within the Asia-Pacific region. Included in this blueprint are plans to improve both regional and domestic infrastructure in the sectors of maritime, air, roads, railways, ICT and energy. A key focus will be to improve the investment climate and encourage private sector participation through PPP arrangements. To this end, an APEC PPP Experts Advisory Panel was created, which will support a pilot PPP centre established within Indonesia's Ministry of Finance (APEC 2014, Andres 2015). The role of this PPP centre will be to provide technical expertise, assist in the development and reviewing of project structures, remove bottlenecks and identify problems with the aim of increasing coordination and overall delivery of infrastructure projects (APEC 2013). The APEC connectivity blueprint also contains methods for increasing infrastructure quality through improved project assessment and evaluation practices (APEC 2014).

2.1.2.3 Master Plan of ASEAN Connectivity (MPAC) 2025

The MPAC 2025 was ratified in 2016 with a focus on five strategic areas: sustainable infrastructure, digital innovation, seamless logistics, regulatory excellence and people mobility. The strategic objective of sustainable infrastructure is to increase public and private infrastructure investment in each ASEAN Member State, as required; and to significantly enhance evaluation and sharing of best practices on infrastructure productivity in ASEAN. This would include project preparation, improving infrastructure productivity and capability building. Another objective of sustainable infrastructure would be to increase deployment of smart urbanisation models across ASEAN. A strategic objective related to seamless logistics is to lower supply chain costs and improve speed and reliability of supply chains in each ASEAN member state (ASEAN 2016).

The MPAC noted a projected undersupply of skilled and semi-skilled workers in Indonesia by 2030.

2.1.2.4 21st Century Maritime Silk Road Initiative

In 2013, the President of China announced his vision to build a trade network or 'Maritime Silk Road' running from China through Indonesia, into the Indian Ocean and beyond. Upgrades to Indonesian maritime infrastructure will have clear benefits for Chinese trade and indeed the Chinese foreign minister has expressed that the Chinese government is willing to contribute to Indonesian infrastructure projects (Piesse 2015). Both President Widodo and the Indonesian presidential advisor for foreign policy, Rizal Sukma, have indicated that Indonesia's Maritime Doctrine and China's Maritime Silk Road Initiative are highly complementary and contain overlapping aims (Piesse 2015). According to the Chinese Ambassador to ASEAN, Xu Bu, ASEAN is a key starting point for the 21st Century Maritime Silk Road Initiative and China intends to increase China-ASEAN maritime cooperation (Bu 2015). The Maritime Silk Road complements the Silk Road Economic Belt (which is focused on infrastructure development across Central Asia) and together these make up the One Belt One Road initiative (Szechenyi 2018).

2.1.2.5 Indonesia-Malaysia-Thailand Growth Triangle Implementation Blueprint 2012–2016

The Indonesia-Malaysia-Thailand Growth Triangle (IMT-GT) is a subregional economic cooperation program that was established in 1993. Following the 2007–2011 Roadmap for Development, which delivered modest results, the cooperation has established more solid frameworks and strategies for delivering projects in the 2012–2016 implementation blueprint. One of the aims of the program is to strengthen infrastructure linkages, connectivity and transport in the region, with a focus on five specific land and maritime connectivity corridors. Included in the Blueprint are six priority infrastructure projects within Indonesia, amounting to a total estimated cost of USD 4545 million to be covered by the Indonesian government, Asian Development Bank and the private sector (Asian Development Bank 2012). The mid-term review found that project implementation in transport and infrastructure was encouraging (Asian Development Bank 2015). However, the review also noted that "most major (transport) projects in the priority corridors (in the IMT-GT) were still in the feasibility, design or pre-construction stage". The IMT-GT implementation blueprint for 2017–2021 has now been adopted.

2.2 Challenges, Risks and Issues Affecting Infrastructure Processes and Development in Indonesia

The Indonesian Government has set ambitious targets for improvements to infrastructure, but many challenges and issues stand in the way of meeting these targets. The main challenge is funding.

The Indonesian Government needs funding from the private sector and while there is great potential for investing in the Indonesian economy, investment remains below the targets set by the Indonesian Investment Co-ordinating Board (BKPM). The Indonesian Government has estimated that it will only be able to provide approximately 35% of funds required and that local and international finance is being sought to participate in infrastructure investments via the use of PPPs as alternative sources of development financing (Duffield 2014).

There are several in-country issues and risk factors that are responsible for reducing the interest of foreign investors. Many of these factors, such as problems with regulations and processes, are a common cause of project bottlenecks. Such delays not only deter investors but are a direct hindrance to the progression of infrastructure development.

The next section explores these issues and risk factors. It discusses the challenges that must be addressed by researchers to address some of these infrastructure system barriers and examines what has been done to date.

2.2.1 Issues and Risks

As already mentioned, lack of infrastructure in Indonesia, in particular in transportation, logistics and water treatment, is impeding economic, business and social development in Indonesia (OECD 2016). This discourages competitiveness and foreign investment as well as international trade (OECD 2016).

The World Economic Forum Global Competitiveness Report presents information and data related to competitiveness on 137 countries around the world. Competitiveness is defined as "the set of institutions, policies and factors that determine the level of productivity of an economy, which in turn sets the level of prosperity that the economy can achieve" (World Economic Forum 2017).

In 2017/18 in the Global Competitiveness Index, Indonesia ranked 36 out of 137 countries (score 4.68) an improvement from 2016/17 when it was ranked 41 (score 4.52) (Fig. 2.4).

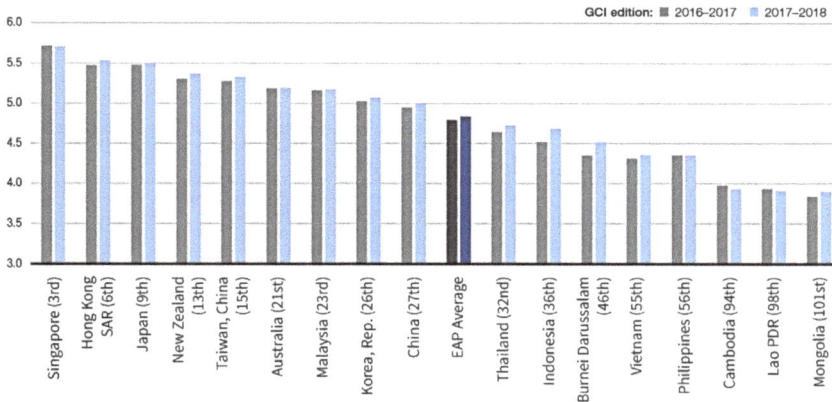

Fig. 2.4 Global Competitiveness Index* scores for East Asia and Pacific countries. Source: World Economic Forum 2017, The Global Competitiveness Report 2017–2018.

*The GCI measures all indicators on a 1–7 scale and aggregates the scores to find a final overall GCI score. The higher the score the better the measure being assessed.

The 2017/18 Global Competitiveness Report notes that Indonesia (amongst major emerging markets) is becoming a centre for innovation. However, there is a need for the country to increase the readiness of its people and firms to adopt new technology. In terms of technological readiness, Indonesia is ranked 80th despite progress in the last decade (World Economic Forum 2017).

Labour market efficiency is reported as 96th, with the ranking attributed to "excessive redundancy costs, limited flexibility of wage determination, and a limited representation of women in the labour force".

In terms of Infrastructure, Indonesia ranked 52 out of 137 countries with quality of port infrastructure ranked 72 (World Economic Forum 2017).

Numerous issues have been identified as problematic to doing business in Indonesia (World Economic Forum 2016). The most problematic factors for doing business in Indonesia, as identified by business executives in a survey from the World Economic Forum's Executive Opinion Survey 2016 and again in 2017, are shown in Fig. 2.5 and 2.6 respectively. A comparison between the two figures highlights the shift in problematic factors over this period. *Corruption, inefficient government bureaucracy* remained number 1 and 2 as most problematic in 2017, but *access to financing* rose in rank replacing *inadequate supply of infrastructure* as number 3. *Policy instability* also rose to 5th position as most problematic to doing business in Indonesia.

Most problematic factors for doing business   Source: World Economic Forum, Executive Opinion Survey 2016

Corruption	11.8
Inefficient government bureaucracy	9.3
Inadequate supply of infrastructure	9.0
Access to financing	8.6
Inflation	7.6
Policy instability	6.5
Poor work ethic in national labor force	6.3
Tax rates	6.1
Inadequately educated workforce	5.6
Tax regulations	4.8
Foreign currency regulations	4.6
Government instability	4.1
Poor public health	4.0
Crime and theft	4.0
Insufficient capacity to innovate	3.7
Restrictive labor regulations	3.7

Fig. 2.5 The most problematic factors for doing business in Indonesia 2016. Source: World Economic Forum 2016, Global Competitiveness Report 2016–2017.*

*This chart summarizes those factors seen by business executives as the most problematic for doing business in their economy. The information is drawn from the World Economic Forum's Executive Opinion Survey (the Survey). Note: From the list of **sixteen factors**, respondents to the World Economic Forum's Executive Opinion Survey were asked to select the five most problematic factors for doing business in their country and to rank them between 1 (most problematic) and 5. The score corresponds to the responses weighted according to their rankings.

Separate to the World Economic Forum (WEF) survey which examines factors problematic for doing business in the country, the World Bank also conducts research into the "ease of doing business" to provide an economy profile for 190 economies in the world (World Bank 2018). These items provide an objective measure of business regulations and their enforcement across 190 economies and selected cities.

In 2017, Doing Business (DB) Rankings were conducted on ten topics (Figs. 2.7 and 2.8):

- *Starting a business*: Procedures, time, cost and paid-in minimum capital to start a limited liability company

- *Dealing with construction permits*: Procedures, time and cost to complete all formalities to build a warehouse and the quality control and safety mechanisms in the construction permitting system

Most problematic factors for doing business   Source: World Economic Forum, Executive Opinion Survey 2017

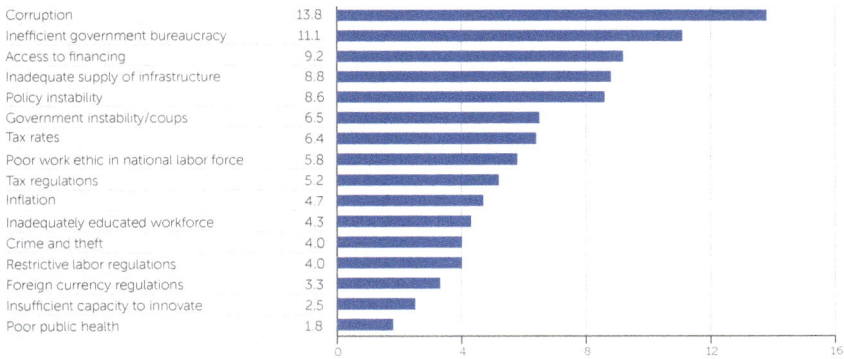

Corruption	13.8
Inefficient government bureaucracy	11.1
Access to financing	9.2
Inadequate supply of infrastructure	8.8
Policy instability	8.6
Government instability/coups	6.5
Tax rates	6.4
Poor work ethic in national labor force	5.8
Tax regulations	5.2
Inflation	4.7
Inadequately educated workforce	4.3
Crime and theft	4.0
Restrictive labor regulations	4.0
Foreign currency regulations	3.3
Insufficient capacity to innovate	2.5
Poor public health	1.8

Fig. 2.6 The most problematic factors for doing business in Indonesia 2017. Source: World Economic Forum 2017, The Global Competitiveness Report 2017–2018.

- *Getting electricity*: Procedures, time and cost to get connected to the electrical grid, the reliability of the electricity supply and the transparency of tariffs

- *Registering property*: Procedures, time and cost to transfer a property and the quality of the land administration system

- *Getting credit*: Movable collateral laws and credit information systems

- *Protecting minority investors*: Minority shareholders' rights in related-party transactions and in corporate governance

- *Paying taxes*: Payments, time and total tax rate for a firm to comply with all tax regulations as well as post-filing processes

- *Trading across borders*: Time and cost to export the product of comparative advantage and import auto parts

- *Enforcing contracts*: Time and cost to resolve a commercial dispute and the quality of judicial processes

- *Resolving insolvency*: Time, cost, outcome and recovery rate for commercial insolvency and the strength of the legal framework for insolvency

In 2018, *Labour market regulation* — flexibility in employment regulation and aspects of job quality — was added as an indicator.

Rankings on Doing Business topics - Indonesia

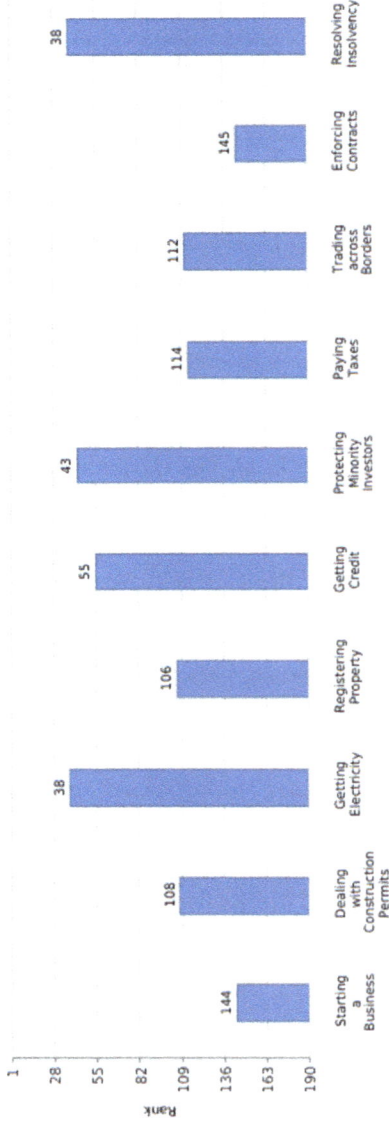

Topic	Rank
Starting a Business	144
Dealing with Construction Permits	108
Getting Electricity	38
Registering Property	106
Getting Credit	55
Protecting Minority Investors	43
Paying Taxes	114
Trading across Borders	112
Enforcing Contracts	145
Resolving Insolvency	38

Fig. 2.7 World Bank Rankings on Doing Business topics — Indonesia. Source: World Bank 2018. Doing Business 2018 — Indonesia. World Bank Group.

Distance to Frontier (DTF) on Doing Business topics - Indonesia

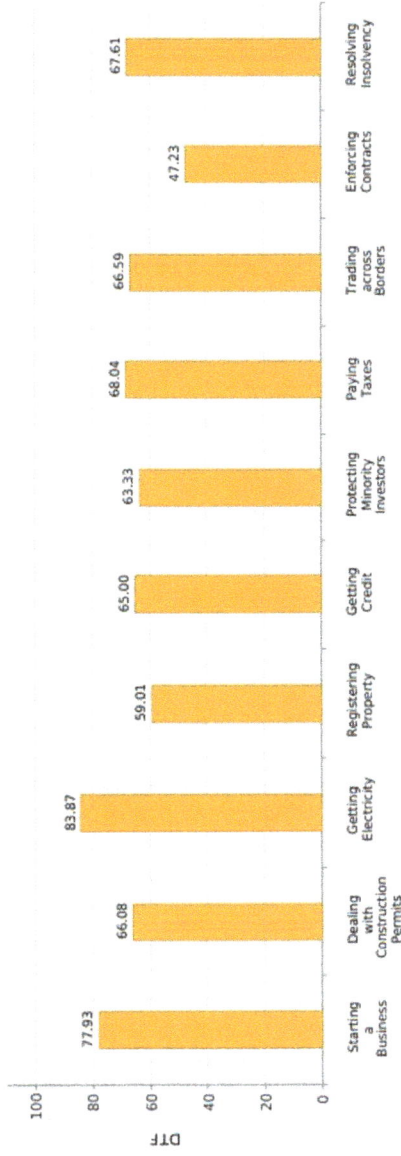

Fig. 2.8 Distance to Frontier (DFT) on Doing Business topics — Indonesia.
Source: World Bank 2018. Doing Business 2018 — Indonesia.

The ease of doing business rank for Indonesia is 72 (out of 190) and the Doing Business 2018 distance to frontier (DTF) is 66.47 (out of 100).[5]

2.2.1.1 Corruption

Corruption throughout the political, judicial and corporate domains has been an ongoing problem within Indonesia. Corruption continues to feature as the most problematic factor for doing business in Indonesia as seen in The World Economic Forum's executive opinion survey (Figs. 2.5 and 2.6).

In the Corruption Perceptions Index in 2014, Indonesia was ranked 107th out of 175 countries, tracking alongside Albania, Ecuador and Ethiopia (Transparency International, 2014). In 2017 Indonesia was ranked 96 out of 180 countries with a score of 37 out of 100 (where 0= highly corrupt and 100=very clean) (Salas 2018) (https://www.transparency.org/country/IDN).

A lack of trust in the system can be a major deterrent for investors and corrupt practices may curb the development of a sound infrastructure investment framework. However, approaches taken to tackle corruption (outlined below) appear to be improving the situation.

What Is Being Done?

In March 2012, the Indonesian Government issued the National Strategy of Corruption Prevention and Eradication which has medium and long-term plans to achieve the vision of an anti-corruption nation.

The corruption eradication commission — Komisi Pemberantasan Korupsi (KPK) — was established in 2002/3 (Indonesian investments 2017). This is the main public anti-corruption institution. The Commission is a government agency envisaged to free Indonesia from corruption by investigating and prosecuting cases of corruption as well as monitoring the governance of the state. The KPK is required to:

---

5   The distance to frontier (DTF) measure shows the distance of each economy to the "frontier," which represents the best performance observed on each of the indicators across all economies in the *Doing Business* sample since 2005. An economy's distance to frontier is reflected on a scale from 0 to 100, where 0 represents the lowest performance and 100 represents the frontier. The ease of doing business ranking ranges from 1 to 190.

- "Coordinate with, and supervise, other institutions authorised to fight corruption.

- Conduct preliminary investigations, investigations and prosecutions of corruption.

- Seek to prevent corrupt activity.

- Monitor state governance" (Centre for Public Impact 2016).

Opinions are divided regarding the success of this agency, but there are indications that corruption is improving — for instance, the 2015 global competitiveness report indicated that 'Indonesia improve[ed] on almost all measures related to bribery and ethics' (World Economic Forum 2015). Transparency International notes that the slight improvement in the corruption index for Indonesia may be from the work of Indonesia's leading anticorruption agency acting against corrupt individuals (Salas 2018).

President Jokowi is committed to combatting corruption (Indonesian Investments 2016, 2017). Media reports indicate that the President is encouraging the Police, the Corruption Eradication Commission (KPK) and the prosecution office to strengthen their commitment and cooperation in fighting corruption (Antaranews.com 2015).

2.2.1.2 Environmental Risks

Indonesia is situated on the Pacific Ring of Fire and hence is at an extremely high risk of experiencing floods, tsunamis, earthquakes and volcanic eruptions. The resulting damage to infrastructure comes at a high cost and given the choice, investors may be inclined to support less risky projects.

Poor quality of build is also a concern in areas prone to natural disasters or extreme weather phenomena.

2.2.1.3 Land Acquisition

The process of acquiring land for the implementation of infrastructure projects has been a common cause of project delays and cancellations. Lack of clear regulations regarding land rights, such as land acquisition for public use and the provision of compensation to land owners, has often led to lengthy and complicated disputes.

Issues, such as informal land ownership in Indonesia, have resulted in increased 'rights to land' claims during land acquisition processes, with some land owners holding onto their land as long as possible as a project progresses, so as to benefit from land appreciation during that time (KPMG Indonesia 2015).

According to the Indonesia Infrastructure Initiative, it takes a minimum of 4–5 years to identify and acquire land for a major project in Indonesia (Lee 2015). The government has taken a number of steps to try and establish a clear administrative process and legal framework to deal with this issue.

A 2015 report from PwC (Smith et al. 2015a) lists land acquisition as one of several economy wide factors for success, stating that: "Land acquisition has historically delayed many projects. The new law is welcome, but it is too soon to tell whether this will solve the problem. The lack of clear, nationwide land tenure recognised by the national and subnational government agencies as well as the courts will remain an ongoing challenge."

What Is Being Done?

In 2012, a new law on Land Procurement for Public Interest (UU no. 2/2012) was introduced to try and speed up the process of land acquisition. It addressed the revocation of land rights to serve public interest, introduced procedural time limits and ensured safeguards for land-right holders (KPMG 2015; Indonesian investments 2016).

Since then, the new Government has released Presidential Regulation no. 30 of 2015 on Land Acquisition for Public Projects. This regulation facilitates private investment during the land acquisition process which can be "refunded from the state budget based on the calculated projected return on investment" (GBG Indonesia 2015).

National Land Agency (BPN)

In addition, Presidential Regulation no. 63 of 2013 on National Land Agency (BPN) is expected to facilitate land acquisition through organisational changes to BPN, such as the establishment of regional BPN offices and a deputy office for land procurement.

A 2015, a PwC report with research by Oxford Economics (and a subsequent 2016 report) notes that "Land acquisition bill: Law no. 2/2012 and Presidential Regulation no. 71/2012 regarding Land Acquisition for Public Interest, effective as of 2015, limit the land acquisition procedure to 583 days and allows for revocation of land rights in the public interest. This is crucial as many projects have been held up by extended land acquisition disputes" (Smith et al. 2015a, 2016).

2.2.1.4 Transaction Law

In 2015, a new Rupiah Transactions Regulation (Bank Indonesia Regulation no. 17/3/PBI/2015) was introduced, which mandates the use of Indonesian currency for all transactions on some projects. This is likely to make such projects less attractive to foreign investors (Smith et al. 2015a). New regulations continue to be released.

2.2.1.5 Public Private Partnership (PPP) Process

Sourcing private funding for infrastructure projects is expected to be predominantly achieved through PPP arrangements. However, there are problems with the current PPP framework in Indonesia: the current framework discourages private investors from entering into such agreements, while a lack of project success stories weakens confidence in the system.

Unclear regulations; unclear or complicated/inefficient processes; problems of excessive bureaucracy within government institutions; lack of coordination among central, provincial and regional governments all result in bottlenecks in PPP procurement. All projects currently listed as 'ready for tender' in the 2013 PPP book are stalled (Smith et al. 2015a). This remains the case in 2016 (Smith et al. 2016).

Many projects are not designed, documented and structured in line with international best practices (Smith et al. 2015a). There is a need for new risk management tools to avoid infrastructure project development, delivery and financial risks falling to the private sector, when they were traditionally the responsibility of the Government.

According to a 2014 McKinsey report (Lin 2014), "Most PPP projects are stuck in the preparation and transaction stages."

What Is Being Done?

Improvements to regulatory framework

Presidential Regulation no. 38 of 2015 on Cooperation between Government and Business Entity in Infrastructure, as a replacement of Presidential Regulation 67/2005 and its amendments, established clearer and more detailed stipulations about unsolicited proposals, cooperation agreements and Government's support and guarantees to projects, among other points (Bappenas, 2015). This allows for performance-based annuity schemes which are a more appropriate risk model for many of the proposed PPP projects in Indonesia.

Improvements to institutional framework

As mentioned earlier in this chapter, the Committee for Acceleration of Priority Infrastructure Delivery (KPPIP) was established to co-ordinate and facilitate the development of National Strategic Projects and Priority Projects. Since its inception in 2014, KPPIP has set about to achieve co-ordination and project prioritisation. The establishment of KPPIP should help with coordination among governments.

Currently the organisation is chaired by the Minister of the Coordinating Ministry for Economic Affairs (CMEA) and the head of BAPPENAS. It was formed at the initiative of BAPPENAS, the Ministry of Finance and the Coordinating Ministry of Economic Affairs, in recognition of the need to create an effective coordination framework with strong political leadership to reinforce its infrastructure program in general, and that of PPPs in particular.

KPPIP has a "crucial role in priority projects development and implementation, starting from project selection up to ground-breaking — positioned as the Project Management Office (PMO) for priority projects. It also has a central role in coordinating related stakeholders in priority projects implementation through the action plan development facilitation, monitoring and debottlenecking as well as providing incentives and disincentives schemes to accelerate the project realization" (KPPIP 2016).

The Indonesia Infrastructure Guarantee Fund (IIGF) (see Chapter 3) provides guarantees against infrastructure risks for projects under the PPP scheme and reduces risk for private investors (Indonesian investments 2016).

A 2015 PwC report noted that "Presidential Regulation no. 67/2005 has just been superseded by Presidential Regulation no. 38/2015 to stimulate investment in Public Private Partnership projects by expanding eligible sectors and offering a more favourable legal framework" (Smith et al. 2015a; Smith et al. 2018).

Several public finance institutions such as the Indonesia Infrastructure Guarantee Fund (IIGF), Indonesia Infrastructure Finance Company (PT SMI) and PT Indonesia Infrastructure Finance (IIF) have been set up to support measures/reforms introduced by the Indonesian Government to aid private sector participation (Smith et al. 2015a; Smith et al. 2018). These are briefly outlined in Chapter 3.

2.2.1.6 Political Instability

There is always a certain level of political risk involved when investing in a project — for example, a change in government or regulation may lead to project delays or cessations. Given the election of a new and popular government in 2014, this risk is currently quite low. However, there is a lack of united Parliamentary support for President Jokowi. Disagreements within his own party and a disruptive opposition may hinder reforms relevant to the implementation of the infrastructure program.

2.2.1.7 Regulatory and Legal Uncertainty

Unclear, conflicting laws and regulations contribute to uncertainty — for example, uncertainty on the right of the private sector to participate in a specific project. A lack of coordination exists between the central, provincial, and regional governments (Smith et al. 2015a). Infrastructure sector specific laws are inconsistent and there is wide variation between sectors. A strong, centralised strategy for infrastructure and PPPs, with clearly defined roles for different levels of government would help address this (Smith et al. 2015a).

Coordination is essential for infrastructure development to be effective. Regional autonomy contributes to regional regulations conflicting with central government law. Lack of clarity and alignment increases risk for the private sector. This may lead to double taxation.

Government policy must be streamlined to allow for a bigger participation from the private sector. Regulations must be clear and without any possibility for misinterpretation in order to encourage trust and maximize participation from investors to build much-needed industries and infrastructure. In order to achieve the above objectives, all existing regulatory frameworks must be evaluated, and strategic steps must be taken to revise and change regulations

2.2.1.8 Lack of Projects

Despite an infrastructure deficit, there is a lack of projects in the pipeline. According to Gustely, this is due to a general lack of institutional capacity and capability. Contracting government agencies fail to efficiently develop, prepare and execute projects (Gustely 2015).

However, total projects in the 2015 PPP Book increased to 38, compared to 27 projects in the 2014 book due to new proposals submitted by ministries and local government.

2.2.1.9 Insufficient Human Capital

Rapid economic growth and deficiencies in education have led to a demand for skilled professionals and technicians greater than available supply. This is despite there being a large potential workforce in Indonesia.

There is a problem with workers falling short of employer expectations, and skills not being "up to scratch" — the minimum wage may not match low productivity. Lack of skills leads to bottlenecks and project delays. Indonesian labour laws are intended to safeguard employees. Minimum wages can vary across regions and industries (KPMG 2015).

The employers' ability to terminate underperforming workers is heavily restricted under labour laws, and high severance and termination benefits are payable. This is particularly relevant once a project reaches the phase of construction as it may result in decreased efficiency and increased times to complete projects, leading to increased costs — a risk factor that may deter investors.

Shortages of skilled labour are not helped by tightening immigration regulations.

The quality of human resources is a big challenge for Indonesia. Currently only about 50% of workers in Indonesia have enjoyed primary school education, and only 8% have a formal diploma. Quality of human resources is affected by access to quality education and health facilities, as well as access to basic infrastructure.

2.2.1.10 Bureaucracy

Inefficient government bureaucracy features second on the list of most problematic factors for doing business in Indonesia from the World Economic Forum, Executive opinion survey (World Economic Forum 2016; World Economic Forum 2017; Figs. 5 and 6). A 2015 KPMG report mentions that "excessive bureaucracy and a lack of coordination at the ministerial level was considered to be undermining the country's business environment" (KPMG 2015).

What Is Being Done?

Investment coordinating Board BKPM

A 2015 PwC report noted that "the Investment Coordinating Board, BKPM One Stop Service now provides a centralised licensing point for certain sectors, which should increase the efficiency of the investment approval process" (Smith et al. 2015a). It acts as the primary interface between business and government and is authorized to "boost domestic and foreign direct investment through creating a conducive investment climate" (BKPM 2015). The BKPM serves as a 'front office' for investor relations through packaging information on show-case projects or the marketing of projects.

As mentioned earlier, the World Bank and the Organisation for Economic Co-operation and Development (OECD) identified the need for a unified voice to identify and support priority projects, and to provide guidance on best practice for the delivery of projects. The Indonesian government has responded through the establishment of the Public Private Partnership (PPP) centralised unit within the Ministry of Finance that works closely with BAPPENAS, the KKPPI for policy formulation and the State Infrastructure Guarantee Company for PPP projects.

Public Private Partnership Central unit (P3CU)

The Public Private Partnership Central Unit (P3CU) is seen as an independent, centralized organization dedicated to a wide range of PPP related functions, such as policy formulation, provision of guidance and dissemination of information. It will have access to fiscal budget allocation decisions. "This dedicated unit will be placed under a high-level political leadership and decision-making institution that has the authority to:

- coordinate across planning and fiscal agencies;

- decide on cross-ministerial conflict resolution;

- drive legislative improvements." (Parikesit and Laksmi 2015).

The P3CU will be responsible for ensuring policy consistency, quality control and transparency, establishing standards and principles that all transactions must follow, and monitoring the execution for compliance. The unit was formed due to the devolution of planning, preparation and transaction to ministries and contracting agencies — P3CU will assist line ministries and local governments in identifying, preparing, and implementing PPP projects. The unit will prioritize PPP projects according to their development impact and their readiness toward implementation.

The roles for P3CU include: reviewing project evaluation carried out by the PPP nodes, assessing requests for Government support to PPP projects and coordinating such support with the Ministry of Finance, publishing status reports on PPP projects and disseminating relevant information, preparing guidelines and manuals for PPP projects, and building capacity in the PPP nodes (Bappenas 2015).

2.2.1.11 Economic Outlook

While the long-term economic outlook for Indonesia is positive, there is a risk that projected growth targets will not be reached. Success relies upon a enough investment to boost growth and provide employment for the rapidly growing population. If the estimated growth of 8–9% that is required to support the fifteen million people entering the workforce by 2020 (World Bank 2014a) is not achieved, an increasing number of unemployed will place a strain on society and stunt economic performance. Some may also fear the impact of unequal wealth distribution and a growing number of people living below the poverty line.

2.2.1.12 Foreign Currency

Currency exchange rates present a risk to investment in any foreign economy. Since early 2014 the Indonesian Rupiah has been experiencing significant depreciation, putting potential investors at risk of exchange losses.

2.2.1.13 Dispute Resolution

The Judicial system in Indonesia needs significant reform — Indonesian courts are not the preferred method for investors enforcing contractual rights. "There are frequent reports that Indonesia's judiciary institutions are not free from corruption and are not fully independent from the other political branches. Litigation can be unpredictable in terms of outcomes, protracted and time consuming." (Indonesia Investments, 'General Political Outline of Indonesia').

2.2.2 Research into Barriers to Doing Business in Indonesia and Australia

A research project into the **Efficient Facilitation of Major Infrastructure Projects** was undertaken between 2016–2018 to enhance our understanding of which investment strategies and options facilitate project initiation that attracts international engagement for major infrastructure development in Indonesia and Australia, with a focus on ports.

This research project is a collaboration between The University of Melbourne and The Universitas Indonesia, Universitas Gadjah Mada and Institut Teknologi Sepuluh Nopember as part of the work from the Australian-Indonesia Centre Infrastructure Cluster Research Group research project.

As part of the study, an online questionnaire was developed for key stakeholders associated with ports in both Indonesia and Australia. The focus of the survey was *Port Planning and Development* and sought to investigate:

- Which investment strategies and options facilitate project initiation that attracts international engagement?

- How to effectively plan and develop existing ports and new ports to increase regional and national productivity?

- What related infrastructure development is necessary to support the port and port development?

The full research methodology is outlined in Appendix 1.

A question related to *Investment decisions — Barriers to doing business* was incorporated into both the Australian and Indonesian surveys. **Twenty-nine** factors were listed.

The factors listed in the 'barriers' question incorporated:

- The **sixteen factors** that the ***World Economic Forum (WEF)*** uses in their Executive Opinion Survey;

- The **ten indicators** used by the ***World Bank (WB)***; and

- **Three additional factors** included in the questionnaires: *affordable energy availability, land acquisition* and *regulatory uncertainty* which were identified as issues in Indonesia and already highlighted above (KPMG 2015, Smith et al. 2015a) and which were therefore added as potential barriers to doing business. These factors are also of concern and interest in Australia.

Survey participants were asked to indicate on a scale of 1–5 which of the twenty-nine factors listed were most problematic for doing business in their respective countries, when 1 is most problematic and 5 least problematic. Their mean scores are shown in Fig. 2.9. Even though this scoring method was not consistent with how the World Bank determine their "ease of Doing Business" rankings[6] and no weighting was applied to the mean scores (as is the case for the WEF Executive Opinion Survey),

---

6   The World Bank Ease of Doing Business Index covers 11 areas of business regulation across 190 economies although only 11 areas are reported in rankings and DTF score. Results are based on standardised case scenarios and usually located in the largest business city of each economy.

the responses received to this question gave a valuable perspective from key stakeholders associated with ports in both countries. The results also aligned with concerns reported in the literature and findings from the WEF survey.

Based only on the factors used in the WEF survey, results from the online port planning and development survey show that corruption, inefficient government bureaucracy, policy instability, inadequate supply of infrastructure and government instability were the 5 most problematic for doing business in Indonesia (Fig. 2.9).

In Australia, based on the WEF factors, inadequate supply of infrastructure, policy instability, restrictive labour regulations, poor work ethic in the national labour workforce and tax regulations were the top five most problematic factors for doing business. This is further illustrated in Figs. 2.9 and 2.10.

If we examine all *twenty-nine factors* ranked, according to how problematic they are, by key port stakeholders in Indonesia and Australia, the most problematic issues identified in this survey for Indonesia were *corruption, inefficient government bureaucracy, policy instability, inadequate supply of infrastructure, regulatory uncertainty* and *land acquisition.* In Australia, based on the full twenty-nine factors, *inadequate supply of infrastructure, policy instability, affordable energy availability, restrictive labour regulations,* and *land acquisition* were identified as key barriers from the perspective of the port stakeholders surveyed.

Fig. 2.10 schematically shows the spread of factors, and the degree to which these factors are problematic in Indonesia and Australia. The figure clearly shows that many of the challenges and risks raised earlier in this chapter are relevant to key port stakeholders in Indonesia. *Corruption* is a much bigger issue from the perspective of respondents from Indonesia than from the perspective of Australian port stakeholders. *Policy instability* and *inadequate supply of infrastructure* are considered problematic for both countries.

The next chapter in this research monograph will focus on funding and mechanisms to finance infrastructure investment in Indonesia.

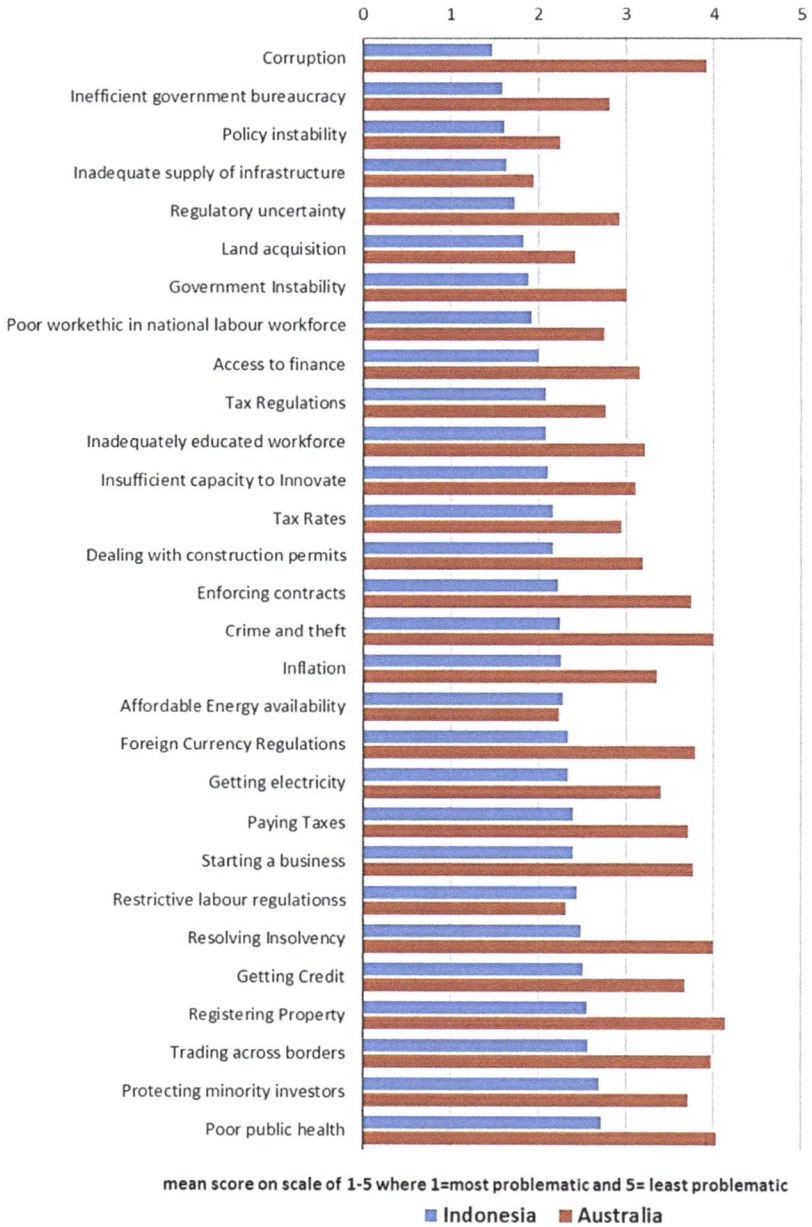

Fig. 2.9 Barriers to doing business in Indonesia and Australia (sorted by mean score — most problematic to least for Indonesia) (Figure by the authors)

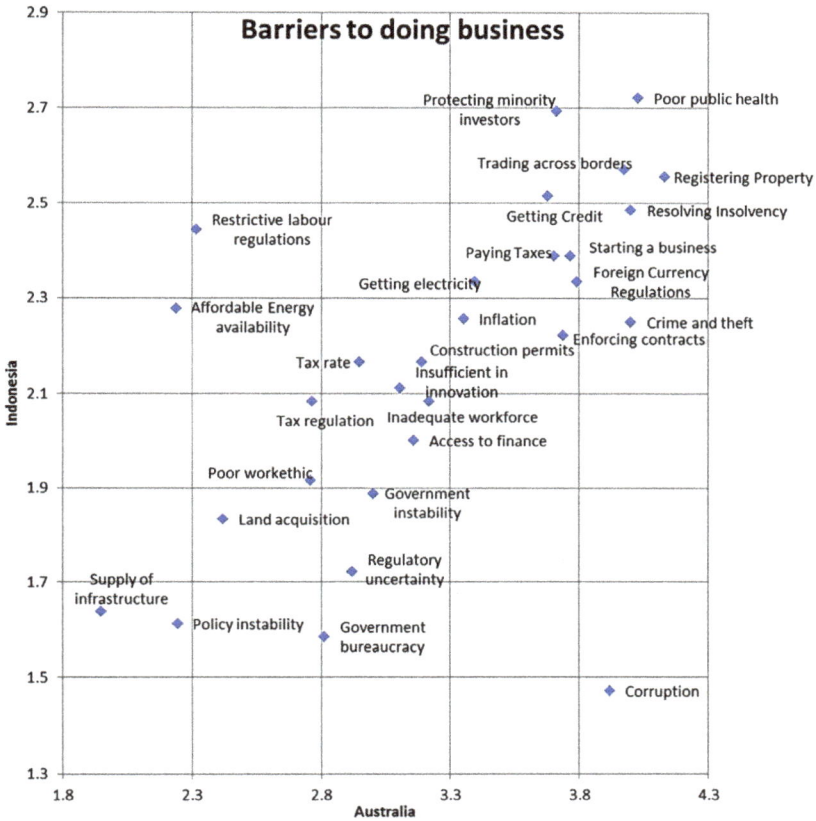

Fig. 2.10 Barriers to doing business — a comparison of Indonesia and Australia*
(Figure by the authors)

*Lower values correspond to the factor shown being more problematic (1=most problematic, 5=least problematic)

References

APEC 2013. *Annex A — An APEC PPP experts advisory panel and pilot PPP centre,* paper presented at the APEC Finance Ministerial Meeting, www.apec. org/Meeting-Papers/Sectoral-Ministerial-Meetings/Finance/2013_finance/ annexa

APEC 2014. *Annex D — APEC connectivity blueprint for 2015–2025, Leaders' Declaration,* www.apec.org/Meeting-Papers/Leaders-Declarations/2014/2014_ aelm/2014_aelm_annexd.aspx

ASEAN 2010. 'Master plan on ASEAN connectivity', *ASEAN Secretariat*, www. asean.org/storage/images/ASEAN_RTK_2014/4_Master_Plan_on_ASEAN_ Connectivity.pdf

ASEAN 2015. 'ASEAN convenes the sixth connectivity symposium', *ASEAN Secretariat*, www.asean.org/asean-convenes-the-sixth-connectivity-symposium

ASEAN 2016. 'Master plan on ASEAN connectivity 2025', *ASEAN Secretariat*, www.asean.org/storage/2016/09/Master-Plan-on-ASEAN-Connectivity-20251.pdf

Asian Development Bank 2012. *IMT-GT implementation blueprint 2012–2016*, www.adb.org/sites/default/files/page/34235/imt-gt-implementation-blueprint-2012-2016-july-2012.pdf

Asian Development Bank 2015. *IMT-GT implementation blueprint 2012–2016 Mid-term Review*, www.jpp.moi.go.th/media/files/02_02_59_DOC_8_-_MTR__ FINAL_web_4Apr2015_1.pdf

Bappenas (Ministry of National Development Planning/National Development Planning Agency) 2011b. *Masterplan for acceleration and expansion of Indonesia economic development 2011–2025*, Coordinating Ministry for Economic Affairs, ASEAN_Indonesia_Master Plan Acceleration and Expansion of Indonesia Economic Development 2011-2025 (3).pdf

Bappenas (Ministry of National Development Planning/National Development Planning Agency) 2011a. *Masterplan for acceleration and expansion of Indonesia economic development 2011–2025*, Coordinating Ministry for Economic Affairs, in ASEAN Briefing Dezan Shira and Associates, ASEAN_Indonesia_Master Plan Acceleration and Expansion of Indonesia Economic Development 2011-2025 (9).pdf

Bappenas (Ministry of National Development Planning/National Development Planning Agency) 2015a. *Public Private Partnerships (PPP) 2015. Infrastructure projects plan in Indonesia*, www.bappenas.go.id/files/1514/4041/0522/ppp_ book_2015.pdf

Bappenas (Ministry of National Development Planning/National Development Planning Agency) 2015b. *List of planned priority external loans* www.bappenas. go.id/files/2814/4524/3464/drppln-2015.pdf

Bappenas (Ministry of National Development Planning/National Development Planning Agency) 2017. *Public Private Partnerships. Infrastructure projects plan in Indonesia*, www.bappenas.go.id/files/9314/8767/3599/PPP_BOOK_2017. pdf

BKPM (Indonesian Investment Coordinating Board) 2015. *About BKPM — Profile of institution*, www.bkpm.go.id/en/about-bkpm/profile-of-institution

Bu, X 2015. 'Maritime Silk Road can bridge China-ASEAN cooperation', *The Jakarta Post*, www.thejakartapost.com/news/2015/08/05/maritime-silk-road-can-bridge-china-asean-cooperation.html

Centre for Public Impact 2016. *Indonesia's anti-corruption commission: the KPK, Centre for Public Impact,* www.centreforpublicimpact.org/case-study/indonesias-anti-corruption-commission-the-kpk/

Dodd, C 2015. 'Indonesia launches massive port expansion', *FinanceAsia,* www.financeasia.com/News/394905,indonesia-launches-massive-port-expansion.aspx

Duffield, CF 2014. *Discussion paper for the Australia-Indonesian research centre research summit: infrastructure,* Working Paper, The University of Melbourne.

ERIA 2014. *PPP country profile. Indonesia,* EAIC Advisory-Economic Research Institute for ASEAN and East Asia (ERIA), PPP_in_Indonesia_ERIAsummary_March_2014.pdf

Global Business Guide (GBG) Indonesia 2015. *Indonesia's land acquisition laws: On paper only?,* www.gbgindonesia.com/en/property/article/2016/indonesia_s_land_acquisition_laws_on_paper_only_11365.php>

Government of the Republic of Indonesia and United Nations in Indonesia 2015. *Government-United Nations Partnership for Development Framework (UNPDF) 2016–2020: Fostering sustainable and inclusive development,* Republic of Indonesia and The United Nations System in Indonesia, pp. 1–60, www.unicef.org/about/execboard/files/Indonesia-UNPDF_2016_-_2020_final.pdf

Gustely, E 2015. 'How do foreign investors perceive opportunities in Indonesian infrastructure?', *Journal of the Indonesia Infrastructure Initiative Prakarsa,* 22, October, pp. 4–6.

Hutapea, TP 2015. *Overview of Indonesia's infrastructure landscape,* presentation at Investment Coordinating Board (BKPM), www.iesingapore.gov.sg/~/media/IE%20Singapore/Files/ASIR/Workshop1_Tamba_Hutapea.pdf

Indonesian Investments. 'General political outline of Indonesia', *Indonesia Investments,* https://www.indonesia-investments.com/culture/politics/general-political-outline/item385

Indonesian Investments 2016. 'Infrastructure development in Indonesia', *Indonesia Investments,* www.indonesia-investments.com/business/risks/infrastructure/item381

Indonesian Investments 2017. 'Corruption in Indonesia', *Indonesia Investments,* www.indonesia-investments.com/business/risks/corruption/item235>

International Monetary Fund (IMF), 2015. *World economic outlook database,* www.imf.org/external/pubs/ft/weo/2015/02/weodata/weoselgr.aspx

Kementerian PPN/Bappenas 2016a. *Revised list of planned priority external loans (DRPPLN) 2016 Green Book,* www.bappenas.go.id/id/data-dan-informasi-utama/publikasi/drpln-jm-dan-drpphln/

Kementerian PPN/Bappenas 2016b. *Blue Book (DRPLN-JM) 2015–2019. List of medium-term planned external loans 2015–2019 Book 1 and 2,* 2016 Revision., www.bappenas.go.id/id/data-dan-informasi-utama/publikasi/drpln-jm-dan-drpphln/

Kementerian PPN/Bappenas 2017. *Kementerian Perencanaan Pembangunan Nasional/Badan Perencanaan Pembangunan Nasional,* www.bappenas.go.id/en/profil-bappenas/sejarah/

KPPIP 2016. *About KPPIP,* Komite Percepatan Penyediaan Infrastruktur Prioritas (Committee for Accelleration of Priority Infrastructure Delivery), www.kppip.go.id/en/about-kppip/

KP3EI 2012a. *MP3EI — Background,* www.kp3ei.go.id/en/main/content2/69/68

KP3EI 2012b. *MP3EI — Main Strategy,*www.kp3ei.go.id/en/main/content2/69/83

KPMG Indonesia 2015. *Investing in Indonesia — 2015,* www.assets.kpmg.com/content/dam/kpmg/pdf/2016/07/id-ksa-investing-in-indonesia-2015.pdf

Lee, J 2015. 'Indonesia's road infrastructure: Accelerating the private sector contribution', *Journal of the Indonesia Infrastructure Initiative: Prakarsa,* 22, pp. 22–7.

Lin DY, 2014. *Can public private partnerships solve Indonesia's infrastructure needs?,* McKinsey and Company, www.mckinsey.com/indonesia/our-insights/can-ppps-solve-indonesias-infrastructure-needs

OECD 2016. *OECD Economic surveys: Indonesia,* OECD Publishing, www.oecd.org/eco/surveys/indonesia-2016-OECD-economic-survey-overview-english.pdf

Oxford Business Group 2014. *The report: Indonesia 2014,* www.oxfordbusinessgroup.com/indonesia-2014

Parikesit, D and Laksmi, IN 2015. *Research report. Critical review of Indonesia PPP regulations and frameworks. Challenges and ways forward,* 1st ed, PT Penjaminan Infrastruktur Indonesia (Persero), www.iigf.co.id/institute/media/kcfinder/docs/iigf-ppp-regulatory-frameworks.pdf

Piesse, M 2015. *Strategic analysis paper: The Indonesian maritime doctrine: Realising the potential of the ocean,* Future Directions International, www.futuredirections.org.au/wp-content/uploads/2015/01/FDI_Strategic_Analysis_Paper_-_The_Indonesian_Maritime_Doctrine.pdf

Priatna, I D S 2014. *Workshop on the establishment of an Indonesia institute for infrastructure development effectiveness,* presentation at BAPPENAS.

Priyambodo, RH 2015. 'President Jokowi wants synergy in fight corruption', *Antara News,* www.antaranews.com/en/news/99005/president-jokowi-wants-synergy-in-fight-corruption

Salas, A 2018. 'Slow, imperfect progress across Asia Pacific', *Transparency,* www.transparency.org/news/feature/slow_imperfect_progress_across_asia_pacific

Sambhi, N 2015. 'Jokowi's 'Global maritime axis': Smooth sailing or rocky seas ahead?', *Security Challenges*, 11:2, pp. 39–55.

San Andres, EA 2015. *APEC connectivity blueprint: Objectives, targets, and strategies. National Seminar on Integrated Intermodal Transport Connectivity, Yogyakarta, Indonesia*, www.unescap.org/sites/default/files/Session%204%20 APEC%20Connectivity%20Blueprint.pdf

Schwab, K 2016. *The global competitiveness report 2016–2017*, World Economic Forum, www3.weforum.org/docs/GCR2016-2017/05FullReport/TheGlobal CompetitivenessReport2016-2017_FINAL.pdf

Schwab, K 2017. *The global competitiveness report 2017–2018*, World Economic Forum, www.cdn.indonesia-investments.com/documents/Global-Competitiveness-Report-2017-2018-Indonesia-Investments.pdf

Shekhar, V and Liow, JC 2014. 'Indonesia as a maritime power: Jokowi's vision, strategies, and obstacles ahead', *The Brookings Institution*, www.brookings. edu/articles/indonesia-as-a-maritime-power-jokowis-vision-strategies-and-obstacles-ahead/

Sipahutar, T 2014. 'Govt claims MP3EI progress, financing remains a key issue', *The Jakarta Post*, www.thejakartapost.com/news/2014/09/05/govt-claims-mp3ei-progress-financing-remains-a-key-issue.html

Sipahutar, T 2015. 'Fiscal reform continues with capex boost', *The Jakarta Post*, www.thejakartapost.com/news/2015/12/11/fiscal-reform-continues-with-capex-boost.html

Smith, J, Satar, R, Boothman, T and Harrison, G 2015a. *Building Indonesia's future: Unblocking the pipeline of infrastructure projects*, PwC, www.pwc.com/ id/en/capital-projects-infrastructure/Building%20Indonesia's%20future.pdf

Smith, J, et al. 2016. *Indonesian infrastructure: Stable foundations for growth*, PwC, www.pwc.com.au/publications/asia-practice-indonesian-infrastructure-stable-foundations-for-growth.html

Smith, J, Wiryawan, A, Irawan, M, and Ray, D, 2018. *Public Private Partnerships*, PwC, www.pwc.com/id/en/industry-sectors/cpi/public-private-partnerships. html

Strategic Asia 2012. 'Implementing Indonesia's economic master plan (MP3EI): Challenges, limitations and corridor specific differences', presentation available at www.scribd.com/document/129770011/Implementing-the-MP3EI-Paper-pdf

Szechenyi N (ed.) 2018. *China's Maritime Silk Road. Strategic and economic implications for the Indo-Pacific region*, Centre for Strategic and International Studies, Washington, www.csis-prod.s3.amazonaws.com/s3fs-public/ publication/180404_Szechenyi_ChinaMaritimeSilkRoad.pdf?yZSpudmFyA RwcHuJnNx3metxXnEksVX3

Sukaesih, M 2014. 'Analysis: Alternative sources of funding for infrastructure development', The *Jakarta Post*, p. 14, www.thejakartapost.com/news/2014/ 09/24/analysis-alternative-sources-funding-infrastructure-development. html

Transparency International 2014. *Corruption Perceptions Index 2014*: *Results*, www.transparency.org/cpi2014/results

World Bank 2018. *Doing business 2018*: *Indonesia*, World Bank Group, www. doingbusiness.org/content/dam/doingBusiness/country/i/indonesia/IDN. pdf

World Economic Forum 2015. *The global competitiveness report 2015–2016 Country profiles — Indonesia*, http://reports.weforum.org/global-competitiveness-report-2015-2016/economies/#economy=IDN

3. Funding and Financing Infrastructure: Indonesia and Australia

C. F. Duffield,[1] R. Duffield,[2] and S. Wilson[3]

3.0 Introduction

Funding and financing remain a major hurdle for delivering planned infrastructure projects in Indonesia. While the Government of Indonesia has increased their spending, significant amounts of foreign investment will be required to fill the financing gap. Countries like Australia also face continuing challenges to fund their infrastructure ambitions. However, for the right project, they appear to be able to attract international finance.

As mentioned earlier in Chapter 1, growth centres and infrastructure development are considered the main building blocks of the proposed Indonesian economic corridors. As such, ICT and transport infrastructure improvements in roads, seaports, airports, water, energy, power and social needs are critical. The Indonesian Government has estimated that it will only be able to provide approximately 35% of funds required

---

1   Professor of Engineering Project Management, Deputy Head of Department, Dept. of Infrastructure Engineering, The University of Melbourne.
2   Research Assistant, Dept. of Infrastructure Engineering, The University of Melbourne.
3   Research Fellow, Dept. of Infrastructure Engineering, The University of Melbourne.

    https://doi.org/10.11647/OBP.0189.03

and that local and international finance is being sought to participate in infrastructure investments via the use of Public Private Partnerships (PPPs) as alternative sources of development financing.

This chapter seeks to establish the current mechanisms adopted for infrastructure finance in Indonesia and Australia, and to establish the likely success of the more commonly available financing mechanisms for any given situation. More specifically, the research seeks to identify *which investment strategies and options facilitate project initiation that attracts international engagement.* It draws on recent international literature, the outcomes from a major survey, focus group meetings, interviews of key professionals in Indonesia and Australia, and specific case study examples from both countries. The qualitative investigation concentrates on the needs and reflections for port developments in both countries and uses the Port sector to draw examples to amplify the financing mechanisms under discussion.

The chapter is structured as follows: first, it critiques a range of scenarios for private investment; second, it identifies the actual investment mechanisms being used in both countries; and, finally, it explores the strengths and weaknesses of the alternatives for specific projects.

3.1 Potential Sources of Infrastructure Financing

Emerging nations appear to have more options for funding and financing projects than exist for developed nations. This is due to potential investment from foreign aid, as well as the desire of economically strong countries to expand their influence into emerging economies and thus gain a strategic commercial footing for future growth. The range of financing scenarios considered are:

1. Direct financing out of government budget. *Direct financing comes from the investors' corporate internal budget if internal procedures permit. It may include debt financing, but such loans are secured at an organisational level rather than at project level.*

2. Direct company facilitation — potentially with expanded business model that incorporates supply chain integration, e.g. industrial zone adjoining port facilities.

3. Foreign Direct Investment, inter-country grants or loans e.g. World Bank, Asian Development Bank (ADB), Japan International Cooperation Agency (JICA).

4. Public Private Partnerships (PPPs) in a variety of broad categories: (a) user charge like toll roads; (b) availability PPP payments (these PPP are generally facilitated through transactional processes, but they are also sometimes developed by a direct approach from the private sector).

5. Special Economic Zones or preferential concessional loans.

6. Asset recycling — leasing. *Asset recycling is a technique where capital tied up in long-term assets can be freed up for new investment by releasing the contract of an asset, for a period of time, for payment. In so doing the revenue generated from the asset is foregone for the term in lieu of an upfront payment.*

7. Privatisations are mentioned but due to their unpopularity in both countries they are not considered in detail in this chapter.

Each financing option carries a greater or lesser opportunity for private sector involvement. Direct government investment — whether by internal investment, the use of special economic zones or via engagement with other countries — places control within government, which also brings the responsibility to facilitate solutions. If government ownership is relaxed, a range of options emerge that may attract international finance (refer to Fig. 3.1), although these options bring differing levels of control, costs and risk profiles. It is worth noting that over the last thirty years in Australia, the balance of publicly controlled infrastructure construction compared with private investment has swung considerably to the private sector. This is due to mining expansions, asset sales and the use of Public Private Partnerships (Fig. 3.2).

Specific sources of finance differ depending on the facilitation mechanism adopted. Preferred mechanisms for raising finance in Indonesia and Australia are discussed later in this chapter. Firstly, however, some specific consideration of the financing scenarios focused on are considered.

Greater options for financing but generally at a cost

Private/sale

Asset recycling/Lease

PPP

Franchise

Outsource

Government

**Higher risk
Less government control**

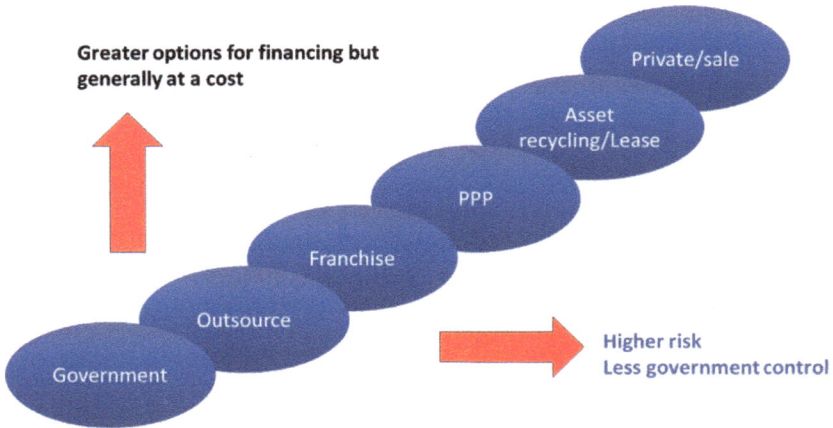

Fig. 3.1 Increased opportunity for private sector finance (Figure by the authors)

3.2 Discussion of the Specific Financing Scenarios

3.2.1 Direct Governmental Financing

As mentioned previously, all countries have infrastructure plans that exceed their budgetary capacity. This has necessitated a range of alternative approaches and it is in the broader approaches that divergence between individual countries becomes evident.

As a Federation of States, Australian governments attract revenue from a variety of sources. At a federal level, taxation from individuals and entities is the primary source of revenue, whereas specific states generate revenue as duties, fees and royalties and receive distributions from the Federal government, and, from time to time, specific grants and/or co-funding for major infrastructure projects. States and Territories in the main have primary responsibility for the direct provision of infrastructure with the Federal government retaining responsibility for matters of national importance. The Australian Government and State and Territory Governments commit to infrastructure investments via their budgetary processes and much attention has been placed on developing detailed business cases to assist in prioritising projects for investment. Long-term strategic infrastructure planning is undertaken both within government departments and agencies, and by so called 'I' bodies like Infrastructure Australia and Infrastructure New South Wales.

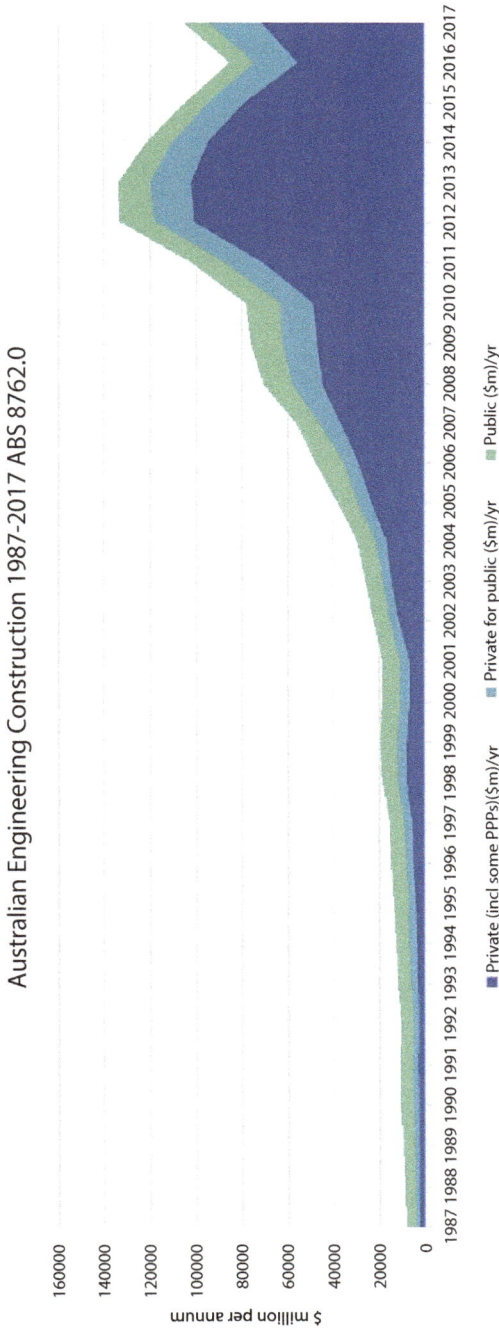

Fig. 3.2 Private versus public engineering construction in Australia (Figure by the authors)

The choice of ownership model and arranging specific project finance is in the control of the delivering government. The financial markets in Australia are mature, with regulation regarding foreign investment, consumer protection and banking regulations being managed at the federal level. While it is hard to specifically quote the need for infrastructure, based on Infrastructure Australia's 2018 priority list of projects, there is an immediate need for development of ninety-six projects at an estimated cost of some AUD 55 billion. This call for funds far outstrips the approximate AUD 13 billion available capital for projects per annum.

Like Australia, Indonesia has three levels of government, all with specific responsibility for the provision of infrastructure. However, control of procurement of infrastructure and investment decisions tend to be driven top down from the Indonesian Government. This system has the advantage of consistency but often faces the burden of a long and protracted democratic process to gain support for major investment decisions. Being an emerging economy, the revenue base in Indonesia is smaller than for Australia. Nonetheless, long-term planning of infrastructure is managed by its planning agency Bappenas and complemented from time to time by direct intervention from the President via agencies such as KPPIP who assist in developing and accelerating a plan of priority infrastructure projects.

Bappenas details its infrastructure forecasts in the 'Blue book'. In the 2017 Blue Book there was a forecast requirement of some USD 35 billion over the four-year projection, this is again well in excess of the available budget of approximately USD 9 billion over the same period.

Several funds and financial entities have been established by the Indonesian government and their Ministry of Finance (MoF) to facilitate financial support for infrastructure projects. These are outlined below.

3.2.1.1 Indonesia Infrastructure Guarantee Fund (IIGF)

The IIGF, also known as PT PII, was established by the Government of Indonesia as a State-Owned Enterprise (SOE) under the Ministry of Finance (MoF) in December 2009.

The IIGF provides guarantees for the financial obligations of the Government Contracting Agency (GCA) under a Contracting

Agency, Ministry, Regional government, State Owned Enterprises or Public Private Partnership (PPP) contract to mitigate contractual risks stemming from the government's actions and inactions. These include breach of contract by the GCA, delays in obtaining permits/licenses, changes in the law, and so forth.

The entity provides government guarantees or credit enhancements only to PPP projects that are financially feasible. Providing guarantees will leverage private investments in infrastructure projects. As the fund's capital is still limited, the guarantees are backed up by co-guarantors, including the World Bank (WB) (supporting since September 2012), as well as by the MoF when necessary. An objective of the IIGF is to improve transparency and governance on guarantee provisions (Indonesia infrastructure guarantee fund 2017).

3.2.1.2 *PT Sarana Multi Infrastruktur (Persero) (PT SMI)*

PT SMI was originally set up as a non-bank financial institution (infrastructure financing institution) established by the Government of Indonesia in February 2009 and wholly owned by the Ministry of Finance (MoF). The institution provides alternative sources of project financing by working with stakeholders to obtain appropriate financing solutions for infrastructure projects.

PT SMI promotes PPPs in financing infrastructure projects in Indonesia. It acts as facilitator and catalyst for infrastructure development in Indonesia, including the promotion of the Public Private Partnership scheme and funding activities in various infrastructure-related sectors in the form of debt, equity and mezzanine financing.

For PPP projects, PT SMI has mainly acted in an advisory role at the project preparation stage (PT Sarana Multi Infrastruktur (Persero) 2017).

3.2.1.3 *Indonesia Infrastructure Finance (PT IIF)*

PT IIF was established by the MoF through PT SMI in 2010. It is an infrastructure financing company, majority privately owned. It is funded through equity participation by PT SMI, the Asian Development Bank (ADB), the International Finance Corporation (IFC), the Deutsche

Investitions-und Entwicklungsgesellschaft mbH (DEG) and Sumitomo Mitsui Banking Corporation (SMBC), and subordinated loans from World Bank and the Asian Development Bank (PT Indonesia Infrastructure Finance 2019; KPMG Indonesia 2015).

PT IIF focuses on commercially viable infrastructure projects and offers fund-based products (e.g. long-term financing in IDR), non-fund-based products (e.g. guarantees), and fee based services (e.g. syndication) (PT Indonesia Infrastructure Finance 2019).

3.2.1.4 Viability Gap Fund (VGF)

The VGF was recently established on the basis of *MoF Regulation no. 223 of 2012* and contributes a part of the construction cost of well-prepared PPP projects in the form of cash to enhance the project's financial viability (ERIA 2014 March; Ministry of Finance Republic of Indonesia 2016).

3.2.1.5 Land Funds

The Government of Indonesia has several forms of land funds for land acquisition or clearance. For instance:

- Land capping fund — provides compensation for toll road investors against a significant increase in land prices.

- Land Revolving Fund — temporarily covers land acquisition costs for toll road projects, to be reimbursed by the project's investors

- Centre for Government Investment (PIP) — under the Ministry of Finance — prepares Pre-financing for land acquisition.

It is concluded that, regardless of the sound initiatives implemented by either Australia or Indonesia, there remains a gap between the available funds for infrastructure investment and the critical needs identified.

3.2.2 Direct Company Facilitation

Direct investment by companies is an excellent solution where control and regulation of the investment decision is dictated by the market and a company's view on the risk — return trade off. Exhibit 3.1 provides an example of direct company facilitation in Indonesia. Attraction of company facilitation of infrastructure development becomes a Business to Business transaction and such arrangements are best arranged using standard international commercial principles. These principles and business practices provide companies with a mechanism where they can balance their strategy with forecast current and future returns on their investments. Confidence in such transactions transcends specific in-country requirements, provided that companies have confidence that sovereign risks will not emerge, that a specific country has a stable and peaceful economy and that business is conducted using sound governance practices.

The strong private investment in infrastructure experienced in Australia, refer to Fig. 3.2, has been underpinned by substantial private sector business investment.

Exhibit 3.1 Example of Direct Company Facilitation for Port Development in Indonesia

PT Terminal Teluk Lamong, a subsidiary of PT Pelabuhan Indonesia III (Persero), was built as a development from Tanjung Perak Port. Equipped with ecofriendly and semi-automatic equipment, PT Terminal Teluk Lamong serves as the best solution to reduce density and accelerate the process of distributing goods flows especially from and to the Eastern Indonesia region.

PT Terminal Teluk Lamong serves loading and unloading container and dry bulk services. Through the availability of modern equipment, Terminal Teluk Lamong is able to drive and boost the economy in Indonesia.

3.2.3 Foreign Direct Investment (FDI)

Emerging nations generally enjoy support from wealthier countries by way of foreign aid, grants and preferential loan schemes that are granted on humanitarian grounds, foreign trade support and from time to time to seek alignment of a country for specific purposes such as resolutions within the United Nations. The schemes of arrangement vary from donations, "trade for aid" arrangements, and aid for commercial support of the donating country, to long-term loans that are provided with an expectation that the loans will be repaid in the future. Current commitments to Indonesia under such schemes add to some USD 12 billion which is inclusive of funds provided by the World Bank, ADB,[4] JICA,[5] IFAD,[6] Exim Bank and aid from countries such as: Korea, Germany, Hungary, Spain, Australia, and the UK. This foreign support, whilst welcomed, nonetheless does not bridge the funding gap for infrastructure. In the context of specific Indonesian investment, in ports, the following exhibits 3.2 and 3.3 provide a range of typical styles of support provided.

Exhibit 3.2 Examples of Foreign Direct Investments Available for Port Development in Indonesia

World Bank

In May 2015, the President of the World Bank, Jim Yong Kim, announced that the institution would support Indonesia's maritime development plans by providing both advice and funding. The World Bank plans to work with public and private stakeholders while contributing up to USD 12 billion over the next three to four years towards projects which will improve maritime logistics and connectivity, such as upgrades to seaports and access roads (The World Bank 2015).

ASEAN Infrastructure Fund (AIF) and Asian Development Bank (ADB)

In order to address the infrastructure investment needs of the ASEAN region, member countries of ASEAN together with the Asian Development Bank (ADB) established the ASEAN Infrastructure Fund (AIF) in 2011. Supported by 10 shareholder nations and the ADB (Asian Development Bank 2016a), the AIF is expected to provide up to USD 300 million in loans per year for regional projects involving the development of roads, railways, power, clean water supply and other critical fund power upgrades in Indonesia (Asian Development Bank 2013, December) and since then at least three other projects in Indonesia have been approved to receive joint funding from the AIF and ADB (Asian Development Bank 2016b).

---

4   Asian Development Bank.
5   Japan International Cooperation Agency.
6   The International Fund for Agricultural Development.

Asian Infrastructure Investment Bank (AIIB)

Established by China in October 2014, the Asian Infrastructure Investment Bank (AIIB) is an alternative to the World Bank and Asian Development Bank aimed at improving regional cooperation and connectivity through infrastructure development. In June 2015, Indonesia joined the twenty other nations who are part of the USD 50 billion bank, providing opportunity for investment in its infrastructure (Meharg et al. 2015).

Silk Road Infrastructure Fund

In November 2014, the President of China, Xi Jinping, announced that China would contribute USD 40 billion to establish the Silk Road Fund as a part of its Silk Road Economic Belt and 21st Century Maritime Silk Road Initiatives. This funding source was refined to the 'Belts and Road' initiative announced in 2016. The fund is supported by investors such as the China Development Bank, the Export-import Bank of China and China Investment Corporation (Silk Road Fund 2016) and has already invested in its first project (Jia 2015). Implications of the Maritime Silk Road for Indonesia are discussed above and Xi Jinping has pledged to sponsor Indonesian maritime projects through both the Silk Road Fund and the AIIB (Tiezzi 2015).

Exhibit 3.3 Examples of Specific Country Support for Port Development in Indonesia

Japan

Due to rising labour costs in China and tension over territorial disputes, Japan is increasingly shifting its investment to the ASEAN region (Piesse 2015). In 2014, President Widodo called upon Japan to invest in infrastructure in Indonesia, and Kishida, the then Minister for Foreign Affairs of Japan, agreed to provide support for Indonesia's maritime development plans (Purnamasari 2014). A report into Indonesia's development and Japan's cooperation noted that "eight out of a total of 28 gateway ports in Indonesia, 12 non-commercial ports in eastern Indonesia, and 10 ferry ports across the country were developed" (JICA 2018).

China

With their complementary development plans, Indonesia and China have agreed to develop a "maritime partnership". China has promised to encourage Chinese firms to invest in Indonesian infrastructure and the government also intends to provide funding to Indonesian projects through the AIIB and Silk Road Fund (Tiezzi 2015).

Australia

Commercial, trade and political ties are strengthening between Australia and Indonesia. As a part of Indonesia Australia Business Week in December 2015, the then Australian Minister for Trade and Investment, Andrew Robb, led a program involving 360 Australian business people aimed at encouraging increased investment, trade and business links with Indonesia (Robb 2015). The Indonesia-Australia Comprehensive Economic Partnership Agreement currently under negotiation is also likely to deepen the Australian Indonesian relationship and enhance bilateral trade and investment). As stated by Andrew Robb, "when you deepen trade and commercial ties, new investment inevitably follows", and Australia has expertise to offer Indonesia in the field of infrastructure (Robb 2015).

3.2.4 Public Private Partnerships

In the broadest definition Public Private Partnerships (PPPs) are arrangements that involve the private sector in the delivery of service outcomes expected of public infrastructure. Such arrangements generally involve the construction of major infrastructure. The capital required for this investment is at least partially provided by private finance through the facilitation of debt and equity arrangements.

In Australia, PPPs have enabled the acceleration of both economic and social infrastructure projects over the last twenty-five years. Considering the most populated states of New South Wales (NSW) and Victoria, in excess of seventy-five large projects have been undertaken as PPPs to a value in excess of AUD 85 billion. These projects have always been arranged as hard money, high risk transfer commercial contracts with long-term concessions deeds ranging from seven years to over thirty years in duration. These PPPs account for approximately one third of the major project investments undertaken over the period, and the services provided have helped establish best practice in the industries where the model is used. Typically, economic infrastructure such as road and water treatment facilities have been structured on a user charge mechanism, whilst social infrastructure projects such as hospitals and schools have used a term payment mechanism provided by the government, known as an availability payment.

Attempts to use similar commercial contract-based PPPs have been less successful in Indonesia. Some excellent outcomes have been achieved by the Independent Power providers in the provision of power stations and there were early examples of toll roads. The toll roads have been criticised for their commercial structuring, and it has been difficult to arrange long-term private finance for other transactions brought to the market. Schemes such as the West Semarang Drinking Water supply project have relied heavily on viability gap funding and infrastructure guarantees to facilitate a bankable transaction. The Umbulan Springs Water Supply project is another PPP project in Indonesia that has recently been contracted after considerable support from government and foreign assistance to overcome funding gaps and concerns regarding the proposed risk transfer and governance arrangements.

In the context of Ports, Indonesia has successfully used the Landlord PPP model (Fig. 3.3) described by the World Bank[7] at Tanjung Priok in Jakarta. This landlord PPP model has facilitated the joint venturing of Hutchinson Ports and Pelindo II (a government agency) to reform the operations and efficiency of the Jakarta International Container Terminal at Tanjung Priok. The ownership control remains with government while gaining operational excellence from a private operator.

3.2.5 Special Economic Zones or Preferential Concessional Loans

The concept of governments attracting foreign investment through the provision of zones with special, investor-friendly regulatory and tax concessions is not new, yet such approaches do not always achieve

---

7   World Bank, World Bank Port Reform Tool Kit, Module 3: Alternative Port Management Structures and Ownership Models, https://ppiaf.org/sites/ppiaf.org/files/documents/toolkits/Portoolkit/Toolkit/module3/index.html

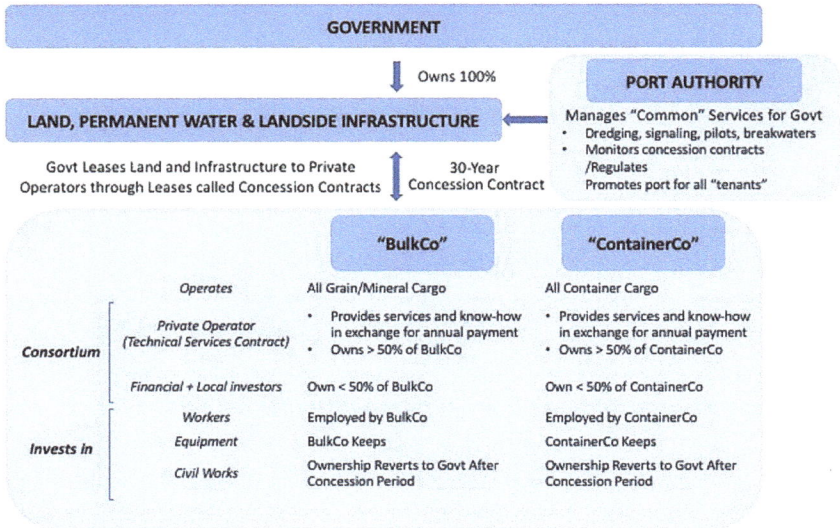

Fig. 3.3 Landlord Port Model (Figure by the authors based on the World Bank resource, https://ppp.worldbank.org/public-private-partnership/library/landlord-port-structure-graph-pdf)

their strategic objective. In 2017, Indonesia announced a major strategy to attract foreign investment using special economic zones (SEZs) with specific industrial foci. Their locations are detailed in Fig. 3.4. Of these SEZs, the first three proposed zones are Mandalika, Maloy Batuta Trans Kalimantan, and Palu.

Fig. 3.4 Proposed new Indonesian Special Economic Zones. Source: Indonesia Investments   2017,   https://www.indonesia-investments.com/business/business-columns/indonesia-seeks-to-develop-more-special-economic-zones/item7962?

One of the first SEZs developed in Indonesia was Batam. The strategy adopted for this investment was based primarily on its proximity to Singapore rather than its inherent strategic advantage. The new SEZ locations are far more strategically located, although the findings from a 2013 comparison of SEZs in Indonesia, Malaysia, Thailand and China by Wahyuni (2013) concluded that there is no universal 'cookie-cutter' approach to tackle development problems, since experiences, situations and practices differ dependent on the local context.

This message equally holds true for Australia's Northern Australian Infrastructure Facility established in 2016.[8] The objective of this facility was to attract business to the north of Australia through the provision of concessional loans. Mandatory criteria for the proposed project to be eligible for financial assistance are as follows:[9] the project must involve the construction or enhancement of Northern Australia economic infrastructure; it must be of public benefit; it must be located in, or have a significant benefit for, Northern Australia; the loan provided must be repaid or refinanced; and there must be an Indigenous engagement strategy. Unfortunately, the uptake of the concessional loan arrangement was very slow, necessitating a revamp of arrangements in 2018. On discussing the viability of these concessional arrangements with industry it became evident that, first and foremost, companies make their investment decisions based on the risk return equation over the long-term. Concessional arrangements were secondary considerations.

3.2.6 Asset Recycling

In the 2014–2015 Australian budget a policy to stimulate asset recycling was launched. Asset recycling is a mechanism to forward sell the revenue stream of an asset, generally under the terms of a long-term lease, thus releasing the long-term capital locked in the value of an asset to working capital that can be used to invest in new initiatives. The asset recycling transaction resembles a sale whereby the government values its asset and the time discounted value of the revenue stream and commits to enter a long-term lease of the facility should the private sector offer a

---

8 NAIF Northern Australian Infrastructure Facility, http://www.naif.gov.au/about-us/naif-governance/

9 Northern Australia Infrastructure Facility Investment Mandate Direction 2018, dated 24 April, https://www.legislation.gov.au/Details/F2018L00567

price and terms deemed to enhance the government's position should it retain the asset. The Australian policy sought to stimulate more asset recycling initiatives by states and territories by incentivising successful asset recycling arrangements with a 15% bonus of the price received to further stimulate investment in infrastructure. The scheme closed in 2016.

Major facilities for which the management and stewardship of the assets changed as a result of the asset recycling program are detailed in Table 3.1.

Table 3.1 Major Australian asset recycling transactions (Table compiled by authors from various publicly available websties and data sources relating to the facilities)

Facility	Term of the agreement	Consideration (AUD)
Port of Melbourne (Vic)	50 years (transaction 1 Nov 2016)	9.7 billion
Poles and wires — electrical network (NSW)	99 years	34.1 billion
Port Botany and Port Kembla	99 year (31 May 2013)	5.0 billion[10]
City Renewal Precinct sites (ACT)	Sale	60 million
Darwin Port (NT)	99 year (Nov 2016)[11]	506 million[12]
Port of Newcastle	98 year	1.71 billion[13]
Port of Brisbane	99 year	2.3 billion[14]

The release of the assets detailed in Exhibit 3.3 raised community discussions regarding the sale of strategic public facilities. The direct investment of the proceeds of these sales has underpinned major economic stimulation in the participating jurisdictions, particularly

10 NSW Auditor-General's Report: Financial Audit, Vol. 8: Focusing on Transport and Ports, 2013, https://www.audit.nsw.gov.au/sites/default/files/pdf-downloads/2013_Dec_Report_Volume_Eight_2013_focusing_on_Transport_and_Ports.pdf
11 Port of Darwin, *Darwin Port Handbook*, June 2017, https://www.darwinport.com.au/sites/default/files/uploads/2017/Darwin%20Port%20Handbook%20June%202017_0.pdf
12 Ian Kirkwood, 'Questions over ownership of Port of Newcastle shareholder Hastings Fund Management', *Newcastle Herald*, 23 March 2016, https://www.newcastleherald.com.au/story/3809984/port-move/
13 Ibid.
14 Chris O'Brien and Melinda Howells, 'Government leases Port of Brisbane for $2.3b', ABC News, 11 November 2010, https://www.abc.net.au/news/2010-11-10/government-leases-port-of-brisbane-for-23b/2331972

NSW and Victoria. There is strong emerging evidence[15] that Customer Focused private sector involvement in public infrastructure enhances outcomes rather than detracting from the services received. Further, it also appears that the involvement of large investment houses has focused port investments on the wider supply chain rather than simply port management.

Asset recycling has not been adopted in Indonesia.

3.2.7 Discussion

When the six investment strategies (presented above) are considered, it is evident that no one solution is appropriate in every situation.

Direct government sponsorship is ideal, but there are insufficient resources for those projects deemed urgent.

Direct company facilitation is effective, although risk aversion by many companies (and their bankers) often means that sound projects cannot raise the necessary finance in a timely manner.

Direct Foreign Investment frequently provides a lifeline in emerging economies yet long-term reliance on arrangements from other countries is not sustainable.

Public Private Partnerships appear to be most successful when executed effectively, but there are many examples where the projects do not attract the required finance, or are questioned for the value they bring.

Special Economic Zones and preferential concessional loans bring much optimism that the arrangements will create a quantum market shift, yet the examples of failure or under performance appear far too common.

Asset recycling provides a mechanism to unlock capital from existing assets, but the approach raises many questions regarding the long-term stewardship of assets and the need for intergenerational equity.

A detailed survey and a series of workshops with industry leaders was undertaken in order to understand how both countries may overcome the lack of finance for infrastructure projects, and how best to prioritise the investment of scarce resources in the port sector. The next section details the collective wisdom regarding financing port infrastructure projects.

---

15   Infrastructure Australia, *Improving Public Transport: Customer Focused Franchising,* May 2017, https://www.infrastructureaustralia.gov.au/sites/default/files/2019-06/customer-focused-franchising.pdf

3.3 The Market's View of How Best to Finance Port Infrastructure Projects: Indonesia and Australia

3.3.1 Introduction

To gain an understanding of the actual financing approaches being successfully implemented in Australian and Indonesian ports, a comprehensive sequence of surveys, interviews and workshops were conducted during 2017/18. The detailed method adopted for collection of this data is provided in Appendix 1. Of specific relevance to the funding and financing issues were questions broadly relating to:

- Is there sufficient finance to meet the development demand in a timely manner?

- What are the priority areas requiring investment?

- What are the barriers to doing business in Indonesia or Australia?

- What financing mechanisms have proven popular and successful?

The analysis adopted in this section relies on statistical analysis of the results where Means, standard deviation, ANOVA analyses and F tests for significance have been considered. The results are presented primarily for those findings deemed to be statistically significant.

3.3.2 Do the Current Government Policies Support and Facilitate Investment?

Survey participants in Indonesia and Australia were asked whether the current government policies in their respective countries are supporting and facilitating investment. Interestingly, in Indonesia 82% of respondents (n=45) indicated 'yes' — that the government policies in their country support and facilitate investment — whilst 11% indicated they do not and 7% did not know. In Australia only 47% of respondents (n=43) indicated that the government policies in their country support and facilitate investment while 40% said they do not and a further 14% did not know.

3.3.3 Is There Sufficient Finance to Meet the Development Demand in a Timely Manner?

Two fundamental starting questions were: (a) Is there sufficient finance? And (b) Is your port attracting sufficient finance? The results are summarised in Figures 3.5 and 3.6. Unsurprisingly, as seen in Fig. 3.5, nobody thinks there is too much finance available for infrastructure investment, while few people think that too much is being spent on their port (Fig. 3.6). More interesting is the confirmation that Indonesia generally considers there to be a lack of finance, while, in Australia, respondents consider finance is available and adequate (combined ('neither too much or too little' and 'about right') 68% of respondents Fig. 3.5).

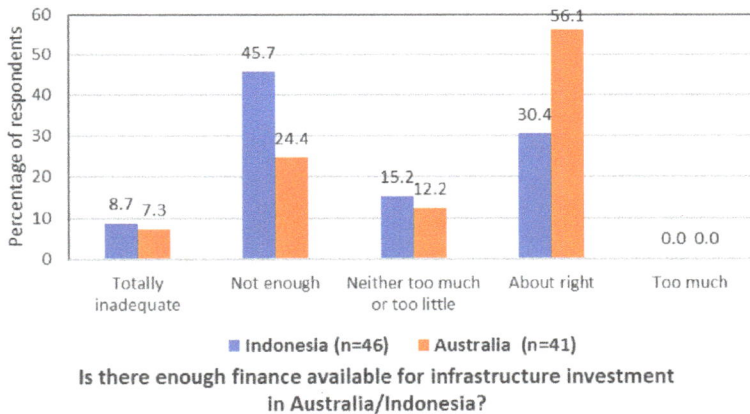

Fig. 3.5 Availability of finance (Figure by the authors)

Indonesian respondents tended to consider that their ports were attracting enough finance for infrastructure development (63%) whereas a smaller proportion of Australian respondents shared this view for their ports (50%, Fig. 3.6).

A higher proportion of respondents from Australia felt that the level of administration/control associated with the decision making process for infrastructure projects in their country was 'too much' (22.5%, n=40) compared with respondents from Indonesia (4.7%, n=43) whereas more Indonesian respondents felt it was 'about right' in their country.

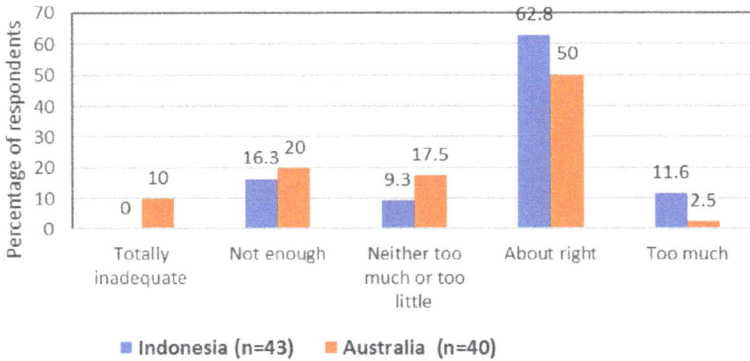

Fig. 3.6 Port is attracting enough finance (Figure by the authors)

In summary it is concluded that:

- Current government policies are perceived to be supporting and facilitating direct government investment in Indonesia, more so than in Australia where investment is dominated by the private sector.

- Australia seems to have access to finance whereas Indonesia would like more.

- Ports appear to get more attention in Indonesia than in Australia. This is not surprising as the Indonesian President has made port enhancements a priority for the country.

- Some think Australia has excessive administration/control mechanisms.

3.3.4 Priority Areas Requiring Investment

Survey participants were asked to indicate how important it is to make investment decisions in water infrastructure, transport, energy and materials handling to improve ports and the level of importance of developing these areas (Figs. 3.7–3.10). All respondents to the online surveys in Indonesia and Australia agreed that transport improvements are required (Fig. 3.7). Water and energy appear to require specific attention in Indonesia (Figs. 3.8 and 3.9 respectively).

The online port surveys also took into consideration *ports in general* and the importance of developing various areas listed where investment

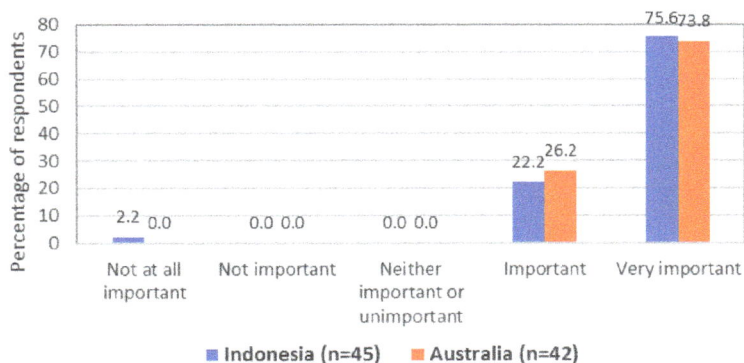

Fig. 3.7 The importance of making investment decisions in transport to improve ports (Figure by the authors)

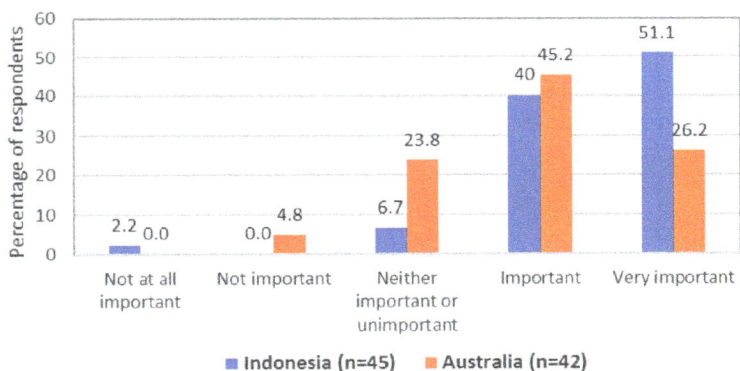

Fig. 3.8 The importance of making investment decisions in water infrastructure to improve ports (Figure by the authors)

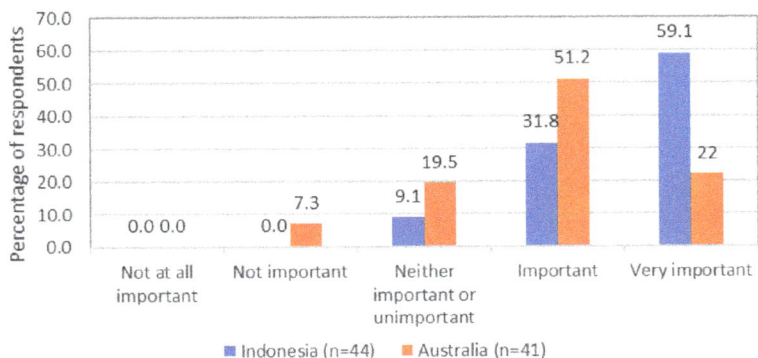

Fig. 3.9 The importance of making investment decisions in energy to improve ports (Figure by the authors)

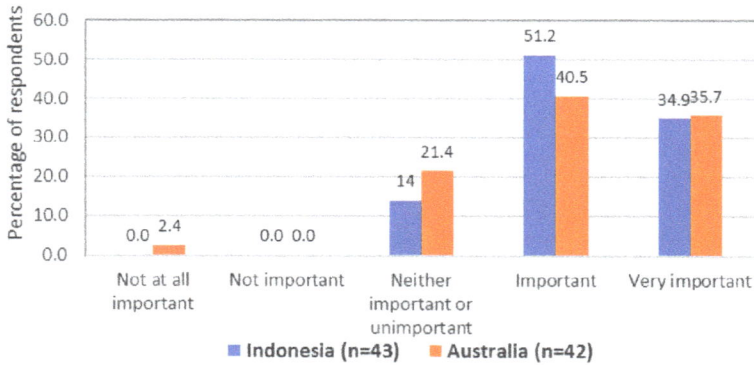

Fig. 3.10 The importance of making investment decisions in materials handling to improve ports (Figure by the authors)

should be directed to improve port operations for Indonesia (Fig. 3.11) and for Australia (Fig. 3.12). Road connectivity features highly for both countries.

The Indonesian port survey responses showed that road connectivity was most important ('very important') followed by seaside facilities, and then channel depth (Fig. 3.11).

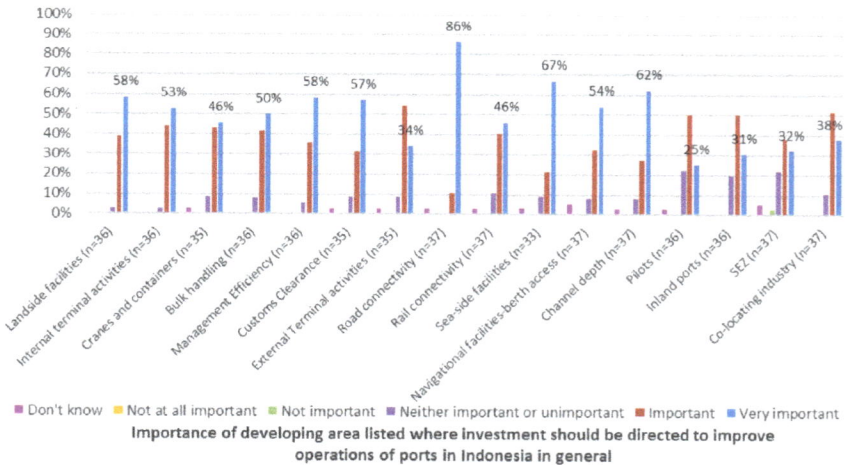

Importance of developing area listed where investment should be directed to improve operations of ports in Indonesia in general

Fig. 3.11 Level of importance of developing areas listed where investment should be directed to improve operations of PORTS in general in Indonesia. (Figure by the authors)

In the Australian port survey, responses to this question showed that road and rail connectivity were the most important ('very important') areas to be developed to improve port operations in general (Fig. 3.12).

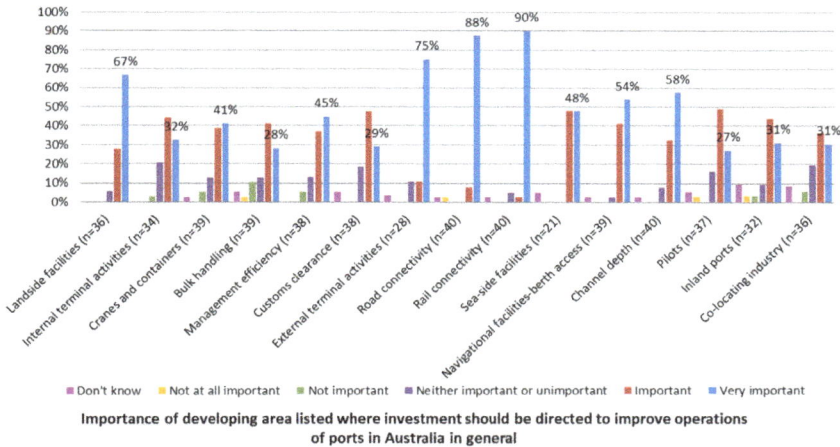

Importance of developing area listed where investment should be directed to improve operations
of ports in Australia in general

Fig. 3.12 Level of importance of developing areas listed where investment should be directed to improve operations of PORTS in general in Australia. (Figure by the authors)

3.3.5 Research Relevance to Funding and Finance

The relative effectiveness of twenty-nine financing mechanisms was explored for Indonesia and Australia in the online surveys (Tables 3.2 and 3.3). The tables combine the responses to 'not at all effective' and 'ineffective' and combine those for 'effective' and 'highly effective'. The tables do not include the responses from respondents who indicated they 'don't know'.

There are some differences in financing mechanisms that are available in the two countries. For Indonesia these are: Indonesian bank finance, World Bank, Asian Development Bank, Asset Sale, Incentive SEZ.

For Australia the unique financing mechanisms are: Australian bank finance, International financing, Outright asset sale, Arrangement of special tax zone, and Arrangement of incentives to attract investment e.g. special taxation arrangements.

Table 3.2 Relative effectiveness of various funding mechanisms —
Indonesia (Table by the authors)

INDONESIA	Not at all effective / ineffective	Neither effective or ineffective	Effective / highly effective	n
Direct government finance (from budget/bonds)	6.3%	40.6%	53.1%	32
Government agency finance	9.4%	34.4%	56.3%	32
Indonesian bank finance	3.1%	21.9%	75%	32
International bank finance	10%	43.3%	46.6%	30
Foreign government / International government finance	17.2%	34.5%	48.3%	29
Direct inter-country grants or loans	17.2%	27.6%	55.1%	29
World bank	6.5%	32.3%	61.3%	31
Asian Development bank	6.5%	38.7%	54.9%	31
Private port operator finance	0%	38.7%	61.3%	31
Third party logistics operator finance	6.5%	38.7%	54.8%	31
Direct company facilitation	6.3%	31.3%	62.5%	32
Asset recycling: leasing or sale	13.8%	48.3%	37.9%	29
Asset sale	29.1%	45.2%	25.8%	31
Franchise	27.5%	34.5%	37.9%	29
Lease	29.1%	29%	42%	31
Public private partnerships (PPP)	3.3%	26.7%	70%	30
PPP Government guaranteed	0%	26.7%	73.3%	30
Viability gap funding (funding provided to meet shortfall/deficiency of funds for infrastructure project funding)	3.3%	36.7%	60%	30

INDONESIA	Not at all effective / ineffective	Neither effective or ineffective	Effective / highly effective	n
Availability funding	6.3%	25%	68.7%	32
PPP with 'in kind' — construction support	3.2%	29%	67.8%	31
Fully demand risk transfer (full risk of traffic volume is transferred to the private sector)	25%	35.7%	39.3%	28
PPP Capital contribution	0%	55.2%	44.8%	29
PPP Availability payments	0%	46.4%	53.6%	28
PPP Availability payments with capital contribution	0%	42.9%	57.1%	28
Asset roll over (sell and then reinvest)	12.5%	46.9%	40.7%	32
Market led proposals	10%	30%	60%	30
Arrangement of incentives to attract investment e.g. SEZ	3.3%	26.7%	70%	30
Direct foreign investment	18.8%	28.1%	53.2%	32
A combination of the above, please list below and indicate relative effectiveness here*	8.7%	34.8%	56.5%	23

n=number of respondents (NB: does not include 'don't know' responses)

*Options listed by respondents include:

- 'Funding assistance from any party with a grant nature to soft loan over a selective program'.
- 'Government Budget and International financial institutions'.
- 'This question is based on opinion alone or according to existing conditions? The existing ones right now are almost all not effective, only funding with Government Budget is running, even then is not effective. While the PPP scheme should be the solution of funding, the private companies are given the restrictions in the share, causing also not effective, because it is not possible to become a major fund provider but may only have a share that is not major. It should be the question in this

case, How Important is your opinion, if the question is effective or not, nothing is effective'.

- 'Reduce Pelindo dominance'.
- 'The Port 'owner' must have a very heavy level of control. All of the above must lead to non-government and city interference'.
- 'Domestic bank loan mixed with international loan'.

Table 3.3 Relative effectiveness of various funding mechanisms —
Australia (Table by the authors)

AUSTRALIA	Not at all effective / ineffective	Neither effective or ineffective	Effective / highly effective	n
Direct government finance (from budget/bonds)	9.7%	19.4%	70.9%	31
Government agency finance	12.6%	25%	62.5%	32
Australian bank finance	6.1%	9.1%	84.8%	33
International bank finance	0%	16.7%	83.3%	30
Foreign government / International government finance	24.1%	41.4%	34.5%	19
Direct inter-country grants or loans	34.6%	38.5%	26.9%	26
International financing	13.3%	20%	66.7%	30
Private port operator finance	11.8%	8.8%	79.4%	34
Third party logistics operator finance	6.5%	32.3%	61.3%	31
Direct company facilitation	3.4%	34.5%	62.1%	29
Asset recycling: leasing or sale	13.3%	20%	66.6%	15
Outright asset sale	21.3%	24.2%	54.5%	33
Franchise	22.2%	37%	40.7%	27
Lease	15.1	15.2%	69.7%	33
Public private partnerships (PPP)	14.3%	28.6%	57.1%	14

AUSTRALIA	Not at all effective / ineffective	Neither effective or ineffective	Effective / highly effective	n
PPP Government guaranteed	17.2%	17.2%	65.5%	29
Viability gap funding (funding provided to meet shortfall/deficiency of funds for infrastructure project funding)	22.2%	22.2%	55.5%	27
Availability funding	27.3%	27.3%	45.4%	22
PPP with 'in kind' — construction support	26.9%	19.2%	53.8%	26
Fully demand risk transfer (full risk of traffic volume is transferred to the private sector)	19.2%	34.6%	46.2%	26
PPP Capital contribution	16.7%	12.5%	70.8%	24
PPP Availability payments	19%	28.6%	52.4%	21
PPP Availability payments with capital contribution	23.8%	23.8%	52.4%	21
Asset roll over (sell and then reinvest)	32.1%	17.9%	50%	28
Market led proposals	7.4%	14.8%	77.7%	27
Arrangement of special tax zone	28.6%	19%	52.4%	21
Arrangement of incentives to attract investment e.g. special taxation arrangements	25.9%	11.1%	62.9%	27
Direct foreign investment	25.8%	12.9%	61.3%	31
A combination of the above, please list below and indicate relative effectiveness here*	23.1%	38.5%	38.5%	13

n=number of respondents (NB: does not include 'don't know' responses)

*Only two respondents indicated the relative effectiveness of a combination of the finance vehicles listed and one listed that vehicle and its relative effectiveness:

- 'Government guaranteed funding of port infrastructure and private funding of terminal operations and logistics'.

- 'Port context + government policy would more than likely dictate the allowable funding strategies; in SW WA ports privately funded infrastructure is the most acceptable method for in-port works (marine) whereas the government seems prepared to fund lanside (landside) works (rail loop; road over rail bridge)'; (*relative effectiveness: highly effective*).

NB. For some forms of financing the response numbers were low.

Indonesian bank finance followed by government guaranteed PPP were perceived to be most effective by Indonesian survey respondents.

Australian bank finance and international bank finance were perceived to be most effective by Australian survey respondents.

3.4 Concluding Remarks

In this chapter the international research team conducted both qualitative and quantitative research employing online surveys, focus group discussions and in-depth interviews to identify projects and initiatives that are critical to the funding and financing of infrastructure projects associated with ports in Australia and Indonesia.

There are various findings in our research:

- There are never sufficient funds to meet the expectations associated with the large capital expenditure required for infrastructure development. Developed countries like Australia can readily raise the finance for such investments provided the investment is underwritten by a AAA credit rated government. Nonetheless, balancing the level of debt with the ongoing cost of finance remains a challenge.

- For an emerging nation such as Indonesia there are additional challenges in raising finance due to sovereign risk, perceptions of governance and the depth of their in-country financial market. The options available to decision makers are important. Among the various options, some, particularly PPPs, look very viable.

- The asset recycling model as a financing mechanism for infrastructure projects has been successful in Australia.

- Enabling and directing investments toward landside connectivity constitute the critical issues pertaining to Indonesian and Australian port infrastructure decisions.

- Infrastructure projects are usually nationally significant investments that provide much needed social and economic benefits. Decision makers are often faced with challenging tasks of prioritising and allocating scarce financial resources. In the case of significant infrastructure investments such as port projects, specific guidance on the critical issues will help with decision making to ensure that value is delivered.

- Through our study in the Australian ports, it was observed that the asset sale model is an effective financing mechanism for port infrastructure development, with the asset lease being the most agreeable among other asset sale options.

- Our research in Australia also found that the enabling effects of directing investment to landside transport as a means of improving port operations is crucial. Investment funds should be directed towards transportation facilities as a priority area. Reduction of traffic bottlenecks in road and rail infrastructure near the ports are also areas identified that need to be addressed. Investment in rail and road connectivity is a significant means of improving port operations. However, it is recognized that it is a challenge to implement rail networks as the main mode of freight transportation to and from ports as currently rail networks prioritise passenger trains as opposed to freight trains, which may lead to increased dwell times and increased costs due to resulting disruption to the whole supply chain. A possible solution to these challenges is the development of inland hubs co-located with industrial and warehouse areas.

- The Indonesian study shows support for government policies for investment facilitation. Future research can develop more comprehensive solutions to increase port competitiveness in Indonesia through the problems identified in our study.

- Financing options that are available for infrastructure projects in Indonesia would differ from those in Australia. The study gained insights from the Indonesian seaport stakeholders into the issues, barriers, and improvement of port infrastructure financing and the most effective financing vehicle for port infrastructure projects. The survey finds that Indonesian domestic banks syndication and Public Private Partnership (PPP) schemes with government fiscal support are two most awaited financing vehicles. In reality, however, the domestic banks have limited capacity and the PPP schemes are still ineffective as shown by our researchers.

References

Asian Development Bank 2013. 'Indonesia power project marks first loan of ASEAN Infrastructure Fund', *News Release*, www.adb.org/news/indonesia-power-project-marks-first-loan-asean-infrastructure-fund

Asian Development Bank 2015. *The ASEAN Infrastructure Fund (Infographic)*, www.adb.org/news/infographics/asean-infrastructure-fund

Asian Development Bank 2016a. *ASEAN Infrastructure Fund Overview*, www.adb.org/site/aif/overview

Asian Development Bank 2016b. *ASEAN Infrastructure Fund projects*, www.adb.org/site/aif/projects

ERIA 2014. *PPP country profile. Indonesia*, http://www.eria.org/projects/PPP_in_Indonesia_ERIAsummary_March_2014.pdf

Indonesia Infrastructure Guarantee Fund 2017. *Business-guarantee overview*, PT Penjaminan Infrastruktur Indonesia (Persero), www.iigf.co.id/en/business/overview

Infrastructure Australia 2017. *Improving Public Transport: Customer Focused Franchising*, https://www.infrastructureaustralia.gov.au/sites/default/files/2019-06/customer-focused-franchising.pdf

Jia, C 2015. 'Silk Road Fund makes first investment', *China Daily USA*, www.chinadaily.com.cn/cndy/2015-04/22/content_20502525.htm

Japan International Cooperation Agency (JICA) 2018. *Indonesia's development and Japan's cooperation: Building the future based on trust*, www.jica.go.jp/publication/pamph/region/ku57pq00002izqzn-att/indonesia_development_en.pdf

Kirkwood, I 2016. 'Questions over ownership of Port of Newcastle shareholder Hastings Fund Man-agement', *Newcastle Herald*, 23 March, https://www.newcastleherald.com.au/story/3809984/port-move/

KPMG Indonesia 2015. *Investing in Indonesia,* assets.kpmg/content/dam/kpmg/pdf/2016/07/id-ksa-investing-in-indonesia-2015.pdf

Meharg, S, Kirono, DGC, Butler, JRA, McEachern, S and Hajkowicz, S 2015. *Australia-Indonesia Centre megatrends: Infrastructure,* report prepared for the Australia-Indonesia Centre, Monash University, publications.csiro.au/rpr/download?pid=csiro:EP158505&dsid=DS2

Ministry of Finance Republic of Indonesia 2016. *Public Private Partnership. Government support and facilities for PPP project in Indonesia.*

NAIF Northern Australian Infrastructure Facility, http://www.naif.gov.au/about-us/naif-governance/

Northern Australia Infrastructure Facility Investment Mandate Direction 2018, https://www.legislation.gov.au/Details/F2018L00567

NSW Auditor-General 2013. Report: Financial Audit, Vol. 8: Focusing on Transport and Ports, https://www.audit.nsw.gov.au/sites/default/files/pdf-downloads/2013_Dec_Report_Volume_Eight_2013_focusing_on_Transport_and_Ports.pdf

O'Brien, C and Howells, M 2010. 'Government leases Port of Brisbane for $2.3b', ABC News, 11 November, https://www.abc.net.au/news/2010-11-10/government-leases-port-of-brisbane-for-23b/2331972

Piesse, M 2015. Strategic Analysis Paper: The Indonesian maritime doctrine: Realising the potential of the ocean, *Future Directions International,* futuredirections.org.au/wp-content/uploads/2015/01/FDI_Strategic_Analysis_Paper_-_The_Indonesian_Maritime_Doctrine.pdf

PT Indonesia Infrastructure Finance (PT IIF) 2019. *Overview.*

Port of Darwin 2017. Darwin Port Handbook, https://www.darwinport.com.au/sites/default/files/uploads/2017/Darwin%20Port%20Handbook%20June%202017_0.pdf

Purnamasari D, 2014. 'Jokowi asks for Japan's help on infrastructure projects', *The Jakarta Globe,* 12 August.

Robb, A 2015. 'After the IABW 2015: Growing Australia's business with Indonesia's middle class', *Australian Financial Review.*

Silk Road Fund 2016. *Silk Road Fund home page,* www.silkroadfund.com.cn/enwap/27363/index.html

The World Bank 2015. 'The tale of two ports in Indonesia', *The World Bank*: *News,* www.worldbank.org/en/news/feature/2015/05/26/the-tale-of-two-ports-in-indonesia

Tiezzi, S 2015. 'Indonesia, China seal "maritime partnership"', *The Diplomat,* thediplomat.com/2015/03/indonesia-china-seal-maritime-partnership/

Wahyuni, S 2013. *Competitiveness of special economic zone: Comparison between Indonesia, Malaysia, Thailand and China, Hak Cipta, Jakarta,* Jakarta: Salemba Empat.

4. Efficient Facilitation of Major Infrastructure Projects

C. F. Duffield,[1] F. K. P. Hui,[2] and V. Behal[3]

4.0 Background and Context

Indonesia is currently experiencing a "major infrastructure deficit" brought on by decades of neglect and poor asset management (Ray and Ing 2016; Barker, 2017). Although the Government of Indonesia (GoI) is working towards a reform by diverting the focus of the state budget to this area, a substantial amount of private investment is necessary to fill the gap in funding that is required to meet the targets of efficiency in infrastructure (Ray and Ing 2016). It seems that the GoI has devised a plan to overcome this issue through privatisation of existing State Owned Enterprises (SOEs) and delivering funds from the state budget to them to realise their goals of infrastructure development (Abednego and Ogunlana 2006). In addition to this, Atmo, Duffield and Wilson (2015) suggest that whilst local investment from private entities may substantially contribute to some of the smaller projects, the larger infrastructure projects that are vital for national social

---

1   Professor of Engineering Project Management, Deputy Head of Department (Academic), Dept. of Infrastructure Engineering, The University of Melbourne.
2   Senior Lecturer and Academic Specialist, Dept. of Infrastructure Engineering, The University of Melbourne.
3   Research Assistant, Dept. of Infrastructure Engineering, The University of Melbourne.

and economic growth require a considerable amount of investment that may only be provided by foreign parties. Moreover, the current system for risk allocation and lack of transparency in the system have managed to deter foreign investors from Public Private Partnership (PPP) schemes in Indonesia (Atmo et al. 2015; Ray and Ing 2016; Olken 2007; Abednego and Ogunlana 2006). Risks of extensive delays in the project's implementation timelines and the government's tendency to be "stronger on announcements than implementation" have led to the cautious response from foreign markets despite the various reforms in regulation that have been brought upon by the Jokowi government (Ray and Ing 2016, p. 2; Manning 2015).

Whilst several writers have attributed a lack of quality infrastructure as the primary contributor towards a decrease in economic and social development (Negara 2016; Barker 2017); Sandee (2016) highlights the importance of soft issues such as regulations and policy coordination in addition to the hard issues like infrastructure for the economic and social development of a nation, and Basri (2016) validates this point. Furthermore, Flyvbjer (2005) discusses the need for reform in policy regulations and planning for large infrastructure projects. This specifically focuses on the issues of misrepresentation of data to win stakeholder support, as well as the issues with cost estimations and planning that lead to the overall cost of project exceeding the projected costs by a large sum, contributing to a lack of trust between the parties, and hence a lower likelihood of future investment (Flyvbjerg 2005).

The Jokowi government has recently been working to overcome these issues in their release of ten new economic policy packages, released between the period of September 2015 to February 2016, in an attempt to support investment in key areas of focus, infrastructure being one of them (Manning 2015; Ray and Ing 2016). Nevertheless, the President's attempt to attract and welcome foreign investors to Indonesia has been met with scepticism on whether the new policy packages will deliver (Ray and Ing 2016). Several occurrences in the past, where the projects have been bottlenecked due to systematic errors, not only serve as a deterring factor for future foreign investors, the unclear boundaries on risk allocation, opaqueness within the system and the lack of state support to carry out the implementation seem to have established a reputation for Indonesia (Pangeran et al. 2012).

Foreign investment in Indonesian infrastructure is imperative to improve its attractiveness, stability and functionality for other trades, making Public Private Partnerships (PPP) a viable option for procurement of infrastructure projects (Pangeran et al. 2012). Taking into account, the current failures in the system, the Jokowi government has established a web of supporting government organisations to support the investors and planners in implementation of PPP infrastructure projects through the various stages in the process for procurement (Haryanto 2015), (Ray and Ing 2016); this has been summarised in Fig. 4.1 Project support system. This Figure also highlights the several changes in the Presidential Regulations that have been made to support the implementation process through each stage, addressing the various factors that have acted to deter foreign investors in this area (Haryanto 2015). Furthermore, Committee for Acceleration of Priority Infrastructure Delivery (KPPIP) has been created as a government organisation to review the progress of priority infrastructure projects in Indonesia and accelerate their delivery (KPPIP 2016; Haryanto 2015).

Other notable regulatory reforms include the establishment of the Indonesian Infrastructure Guarantee Fund (IIGF), supported by the World Bank, that provides a government guarantee for political and legal risks pertaining to the project (Ministry of Finance 2012) and (Atmo et al. 2015). Not only does this increase the investor's confidence in the system by increasing the government's accountability towards the project; the establishment of the IIGF also encourages transparency in the system, hence increasing the chances of the project's successful implementation (Atmo et al. 2015). In addition to this, PPP institutions have also been set up and clear guidelines on the PPP implementation process have been established to maximise the benefits for potential future PPP partnerships (Indra 2011).

This chapter looks at the processes involved in implementation of major infrastructure projects. It identifies the theoretical processes to instigate projects and compares them to the real-world practices that are being implemented in Indonesia and Australia by looking at case study examples. This chapter primarily focuses on PPP procurement of projects, although projects using other procurement strategies may be used as case examples.

Preparation | **Bidding Process** | **Construction**

Project Development Facility (PDF)

- Assist GCA on PPP project preparation

Managing entity:
- PT SMI and PT IIF
- Ministry of Finance under its new PPP unit

Institutional Reform

- Establishment of KPPIP
- Empowerment of existing institutions (PT SMI, IIGF) to fill in the gap in enhancing project bankability

Managing entity:
- CMEA
- Ministry of Finance

Viability Gap Funding (VGF)

- Contributes to construction cost to increase project's financial viability

Managing entity:
Ministry of Finance based on GCA proposal

Government's commitment:
49% max per project

Guarantee Funds

- Guaranteeing government's contractual obligations under infrastructure concession agreements

Managing Entity:
Indonesia Infrastructure Guarantee Fund (IIGF) – wholly owned by MoF

Government's commitment:
US $450 Million

Tax Facilities

- MoF Regulation no. 159/PMK.010.2015
- Tax holiday for pioneer sectors (listed below) will be further expanded
  - Base metal
  - Oil refinery
  - Basic petrochemical
  - Machinery
  - Renewable energy
  - Telco equipment

Managing entity:
Ministry of Finance

Availability Payment

- Concessionaire receive sum of money periodically from government after the completion of an asset

Managing entity:
Ministry of Finance

Progress:
Ministry of Finance regulation on Availability Payment has been ratified

Land Revolving Fund

- Support land acquisition for toll road projects
- Government of Indonesia provides bridging finance for the private sector

Managing entity:
Ministry of Public Work and Public Housing

Government's commitment:
US $489 Million

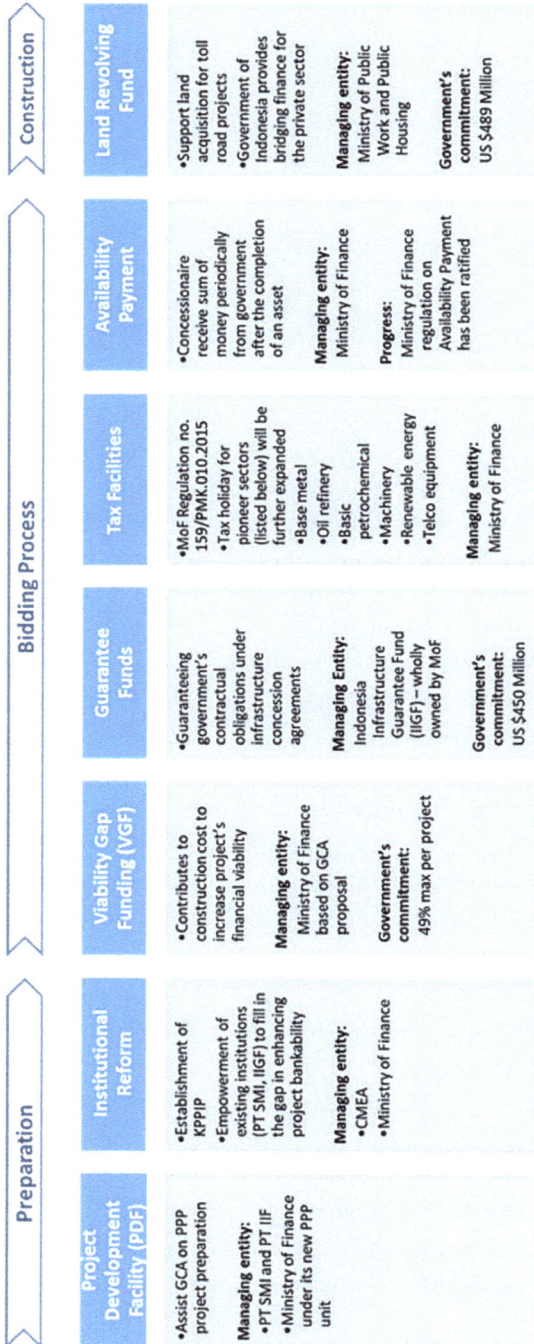

Fig. 4.1 Project support system (Figure by the authors based on data. Source: Haryanto 2015)

4.1 Risk Allocation and Management

Private investment is necessary to overcome the financial obstacles in procurement of infrastructure projects in Indonesia (Duffield et al. unpublished). Whilst PPP arrangements are a viable option for attracting private investment in infrastructure projects (Pangeran et al. 2012; Atmo et al. 2015), there are several risks associated with such schemes, especially when international parties are involved (Pangeran et al. 2012). The large capital investment requirements and the lack of flexibility in contractual agreements increase the level of risk involved with the project, making effective risk management and a clear system of risk allocation critical factors for the overall project success (Dixon, Pottinger and Jordan 2005; Hardcastle, Edwards, Akintoye and Li 2005; Pangeran et al. 2012; Abednego and Ogunlana 2006). However, as Abednego and Ogunlana (2006) clearly highlight, different perspectives may exist on proper risk allocation between parties in PPP schemes, often creating conflict that must be managed through effective project management to ensure successful project implementation.

In addition to this, Pangeran et al. (2012) emphasises the importance of correct risk identification and management as there is a danger in underestimation of risks and their allocation to parties that do not have the necessary expertise or resources to manage them to the level of adequacy required. Furthermore, the quality of the decision-making process throughout the development of the project is also reliant on an effective risk management system (Dixon et al. 2005; Li et al. 2005); providing an overall benefit to the project in the following ways, as highlighted in the Public Private Partnerships report by the Department of Finance and Administration, Australian Government (2006):

1. Improving the project's performance by early risk identification.

2. Improving the planning process by taking the risks into account.

3. Supporting robust decision making.

Furthermore, inadequate risk assessment and management has the potential to result in increased project costs, substantial delays in project delivery and an inability to achieve the full potential of benefits received from the project's implementation (Ng and Loosemore 2006; Dixon et al. 2005). Additionally, it must be acknowledged that risk management must continue from the project planning, through to the execution and construction stages, as stated by Pangeran et al. (2012). The exposure to risk for the private entity throughout the project's lifetime has been addressed by the Presidential Regulation 67/2005 that was later amended by Presidential Regulation 13/2010, Presidential Regulation 78/2010 (Indra 2011; Atmo et al. 2015; Ministry of Finance 2012). These address the provision of government support and guarantees to the private entity engaged in a PPP agreement to effectively reduce the risks that the investors may be exposed to throughout the planning and implementation stages of the project (Ministry of Finance 2012).

4.2 Delivery of Infrastructure Projects: Indonesia

Several case studies have been analysed to identify the factors which cause delays in major project implementation. The projected schedule dates for major processes for these projects have been researched and summarised using Gantt charts shown in this section. The scheduled dates and expected timelines have been sourced from media releases and the government department report published for priority infrastructure projects (KPPIP 2016). The legend used for these charts is shown in Fig. 4.2 Legend used for project schedule charts below.

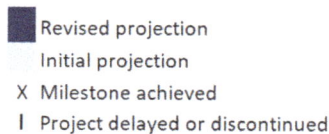

■ Revised projection
  Initial projection
X Milestone achieved
I Project delayed or discontinued

Fig. 4.2 Legend used for project schedule charts (Figure by the authors)

The following cases have been studied for this study:

1. Jakarta Sewerage System.
2. West Semarang Drinking Water Supply System.
3. National Capital Integrated Coastal Development Phase A.
4. Bontang Oil Refinery.
5. Umbulan Springs Water Supply Project.

The location of these case studies has been overlaid on the map shown below.

Fig. 4.3 Case study locations (map source: Amin (2015))

4.2.1 Jakarta Sewerage System (JSS)

The project to improve Jakarta's Sewerage System has been ongoing since it was first initiated in the early 1970s (Independent Evaluation Group (IEG) 2012). However, due to funding constraints and a lack of knowledge and expertise in this area, only a pilot phase of this project was delivered in 1991 (The World Bank 2017). Further phases have been initiated several times but failed to deliver due to a lack of funding availability (Smith, Wiryawan and Ray 2017). Table 4.1 Jakarta Sewerage System summarises the key aspects of this project and Fig. 4.4 shows the project implementation timeline for the various processes in this project.

Table 4.1 Jakarta Sewerage System

Project owner	Provincial Government of DKI Jakarta
Location	DKI Jakarta
Investment value (Zone 1)	IDR 8 trillion
Funding scheme	Potential for state budget with foreign loan (Japan) for Zone 1, funding scheme for other zones is yet to be determined, potential for Public Private Partnership (PPP)
Construction commencement (Zone 1)	2018
Commercial Operation (Zone 1)	2021

Source: KPPIP (2016).

DKI Jakarta is now ranked as the second lowest capital city in South East Asia for sanitation, with the current coverage ratio only being 4% of the total area (Basu 2016; KPPIP 2016). The city is the Indonesian capital for government, business and industry; however, the quality of water and sanitation has worsened over the years despite the recent development of the city (KPPIP 2016).

This project is especially necessary for effective implementation of the National Capital Integrated Coastal Development project, listing the Jakarta Sewerage System project as a priority project for implementation (KPPIP 2016).

Fig. 4.4 highlights the major delays in completion of the processes involved with this project. The expected date projections for the processes seem to not have been met and the project is currently experiencing extensive delays due to issues associated with land acquisition.

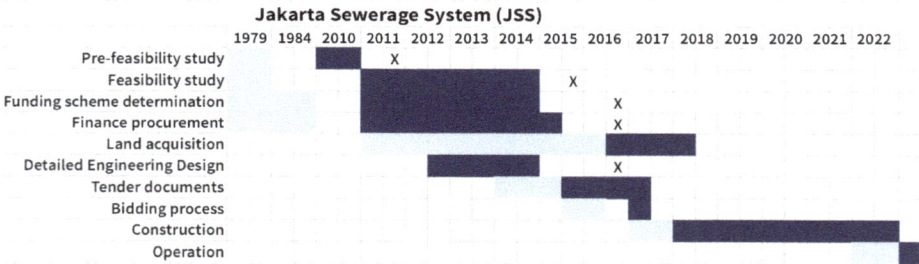

Fig. 4.4 Jakarta Sewerage System project implementation schedule
(Figure by the authors)

4.2.2 West Semarang Drinking Water Supply

The West Semarang Drinking Water Supply (SPAM) project is expected to resolve the current shortage of raw drinking water supply in Semarang (KPPIP 2016). There are currently over 60,000 families in thirty-one subdistricts that have no access to drinking water (Puspa 2016). Table 4.2 West Semarang Drinking Water Supply summarises the key information for this project; Fig. 4.5 shows the coverage area and location of the SPAM for this project. This project is expected to supply these families with water and aid in reduction of ground water usage, which is currently being extracted to extreme levels (Puspa 2016; KPPIP 2016).

Table 4.2 West Semarang Drinking Water Supply

Project owner	Municipal Government of Semarang
Location	Semarang, Central Java
Investment value	IDR 1,170 billion
Funding	State Budget (APBN), Local government budget (APBD) and Tirta Moedal PDAM of Semarang City
Construction commencement (planned)	2018
Commercial Operation	2022

Source: KPPIP (2016).

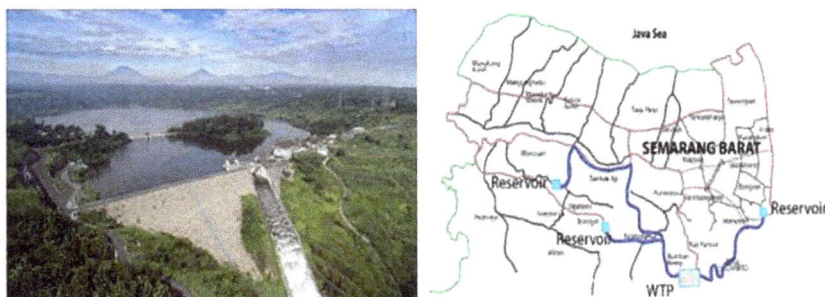

Fig. 4.5 West Semarang SPAM (left), supply map (right)
(image source: Amin (2015)).

Viability Gap Funding (VGF) has been approved for this project in 2015, assisting prospective private investors to meet funding requirements (Investor Daily 2015). A Public Private Partnership (PPP) scheme was initially proposed for this; however, it was revised when a change in direction was recommended by the Vice President (Sulistyoningrum 2016). This was to revise the funding option from a PPP to a State Owned Enterprise (SOE) to accelerate the implementation of this project.

Recent developments include division of the project funding to three sources: State Budget (APBN), Local Government Budget (APBD) and Tirta Moedal PDAM of Semarang City (Puspa 2016). The project was initially expected to commence construction in July 2015; however, funding availability and land acquisition have been a source of delay to its implementation (Investor Daily 2015). Although the funding has now been finalised, the land issue has been deemed to be 'complicated' and the project is awaiting land acquisition. If land is finalised within 2017, the construction may commence in 2018 (Puspa 2016). However, this seems unlikely at this stage, judging by the current progress. Fig. 4.6 West Semarang Drinking Water Supply project implementation schedule shows the timeline for its implementation.

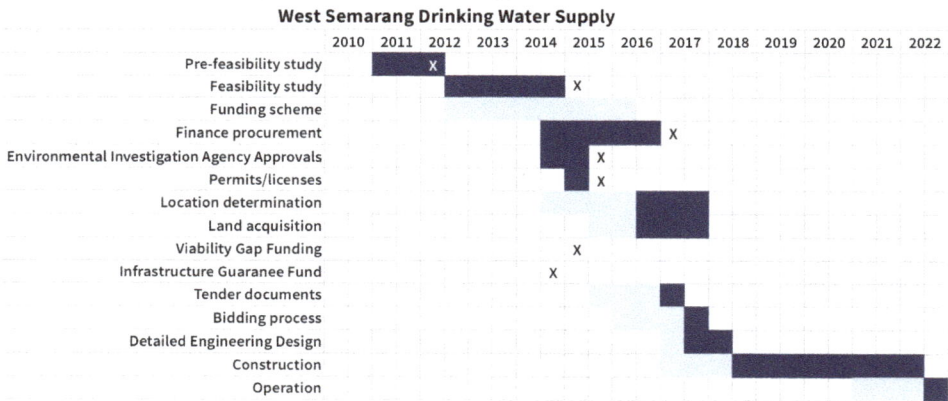

Fig. 4.6 West Semarang Drinking Water Supply project implementation schedule (Figure by the authors)

4.2.3 National Capital Integrated Coastal Development

More than 50% of Jakarta's population currently lives in the coastal area, with a significant proportion of the city's economic activities taking place here (KPPIP 2016). Jakarta is home to thirteen rivers and 40% of the city's coastal low land area is lower than the tidal surface (KPPIP 2016). Furthermore, excessive ground water extraction due to drinking water supply shortage has led to land subsidence, exacerbating the impact of floods (Sherwell 2016). This makes National Capital Integrated Coastal Development (NCICD) project necessary for long-term sustainability of the area. Table 4.3 highlights some of the key information for this project.

Table 4.3 National Capital Integrated Coastal Development

Project owner	Provincial Government of DKI Jakarta, Ministry of Public Works and Public Housing (MOPWandPH)
Location	DKI Jakarta
Investment value	IDR 26 trillion (Phase A), IDR 600 trillion (all phases)
Funding scheme	State and Regional budget (Phase A), potential for PPP for other phases
Construction commencement (planned)	2016 (initial plan)
Commercial Operation	2018 (initial plan)

Source: KPPIP (2016).

There are three phases to the completion of this project (KPPIP 2016):

1. Improving the existing coastal protection

2. Further development of the west outer giant seawall to be constructed 2018–2022

3. Construction of the east outer giant seawall (planned for after 2023)

The NCICD is supported by the Royal Dutch Embassy with the total investment amounting up to USD 40 billion (Sherwell 2016). However, the project was halted in December 2016 due to stakeholder concerns of the immediate negative impact of this project on the livelihood and welfare of the Jakarta Bay residents (Transnational Institute 2016). Interference from local groups had initially led to halting of the project to conduct further environmental impact studies and discussions with the local groups to come to a sustainable solution to solve the water problems for the residents of Jakarta Bay (Transnational Institute 2016). Some key information regarding the project has been highlighted in Table 4.3 National Capital Integrated Coastal Development, while Fig. 4.7 National Capital Integrated Coastal Development project implementation schedule gives timeline projections of the implementation process.

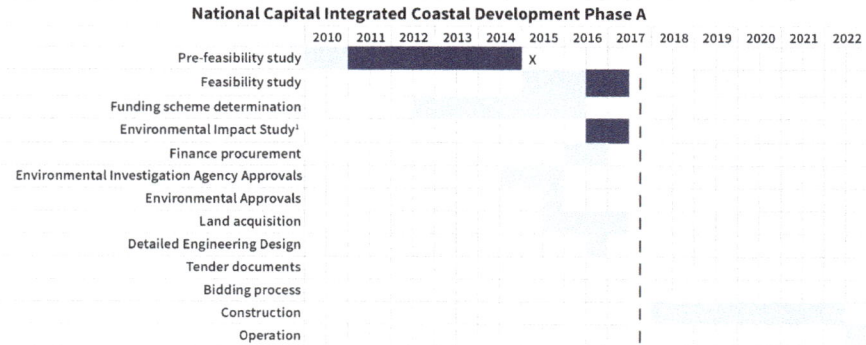

Fig. 4.7 National Capital Integrated Coastal Development project implementation schedule (Figure by the authors)

■ Revised projection
Initial projection
X Milestone achieved
I Project delayed or discontinued

In July 2017, it was announced that this project will be terminated and the Indonesian capital will be relocated, as reported in the Jakarta Post (2017).

4.2.4 Bontang Refinery

The Bontang Refinery construction project, located in East Kalimantan, aims to produce 235,000 barrels of oil per day to satisfy the domestic demand for fuel. Some of the key information for this project, as sourced from the report for priority infrastructure projects, has been summarised in Table 4.4 Bontang Oil Refinery. Indonesia's increasing need for fuel and vision to achieve energy security require a significant growth in the domestic refinery industry, as will be facilitated by several refinery projects that are currently in the pipeline for implementation (KPPIP 2016).

Table 4.4 Bontang Oil Refinery

Project owner	PT Pertamina (awaiting determination)
Location	Bontang, East Kalimantan
Investment value	IDR 75–140 trillion
Funding scheme	Potential for PPP scheme (awaiting determination)
Construction commencement (planned)	2018
Commercial Operation	2022

Source: KPPIP (2016).

The Bontang Refinery project has attracted the interest of several foreign investors and global refinery companies were invited to participate in the tender process in February 2017, with the business partners expected to be named by April 2017 (Tempo.co 2017). However, no alliances have yet been announced, as of October 2017.

Although the KPPIP report (2016) did not expect any significant issues with its timeline due to land already being allocated and the presence of supporting infrastructure (road access, jetty, etc), the project

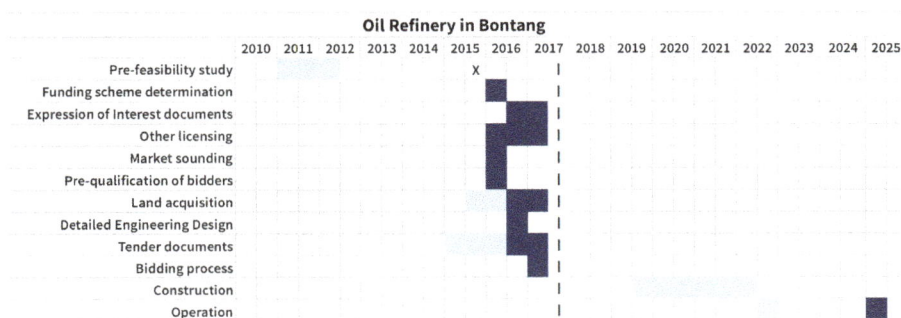

Fig. 4.8 Bontang Oil Refinery project implementation schedule
(Figure by the authors)

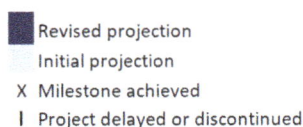

Revised projection
Initial projection
X Milestone achieved
I Project delayed or discontinued

has recently been met with major delays due to issues with the financial capacity of the project's major shareholder, PT Pertamina (Singgih 2017). Whilst the ground-breaking for this project was previously projected to begin in 2017 (Indonesia Investments 2016); it was later revised to 2019 due to low interest from foreign investors (Asmarini and Tan 2017). The projected operational date for the project has recently been revised to 2025 due to Pertamina's financial obligations (Singgih 2017). Fig. 4.8 Bontang Oil Refinery project implementation schedule aims to illustrate some of these date projections and the project's process timeline.

4.2.5 Umbulan Springs Drinking Water Supply Project

The Umbulan Springs Drinking Water Supply (SPAM) project has been in the planning stage since 1973 (Syarizka 2016), making it well over forty years before the construction was able to recently begin in July 2017 (PwC 2017). Table 4.5 Umbulan Springs Drinking Water Supply Project summarises the key information for this project and Fig. 4.9 shows an approximate timeline of the processes involved in the implementation of this project.

Table 4.5 Umbulan Springs Drinking Water Supply Project

Project owner	PT Medco Energi Internasional, Tbk. and PT Bangun Cipta Kontraktor
Location	East Java Province
Investment value	IDR 2050 Billion
Funding scheme	Public Private Partnership (PPP)
Construction commencement (planned)	2017
Commercial Operation	2019

Source: Syarizka (2016).

This is the first regional water supply project that will be implemented under a Public Private Partnership (PPP), managed by the central and regional governments (Susanty 2016). After experiencing extensive delays for over forty years, the Infrastructure Guarantee Funding (IGF) was allocated in 2006 as a risk sharing mechanism for this project (Susanty 2016). This, along with the government subsidy Viability Gap

Umbulan Springs Drinking Water Supply Project

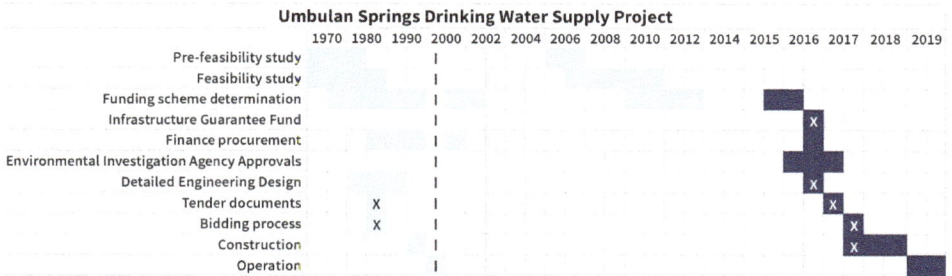

Fig. 4.9 Umbulan Springs project implementation schedule
(Figure by the authors)

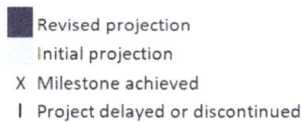

■ Revised projection

 Initial projection

X Milestone achieved

I Project delayed or discontinued

Funding (VGF), has led to an increase in its bankability for private investors, attracting them to invest in the Umbulan Springs Drinking Water Supply project (Syarizka 2016).

The bidder for this project was chosen in 1989; however, negotiations between the GoI and the selected bidder failed when it was determined that no guarantee funding would be allocated to the project, leading to a termination of the contract (Chemonics International, Resource Management International, Sheladia Associates 1994). Recently, the government support of the project with the Infrastructure Guarantee Fund has worked as a risk sharing mechanism, attracting the private investors to carry out this project.

4.3 Delivery of Infrastructure Projects: Australia

This chapter looks at two case studies from Australia: the Channel Deepening Project for the Port of Melbourne in Victoria; and the M7 Motorway in Sydney, New South Wales. The Australian cases have been analysed similarly to the Indonesian case study analysis earlier in this chapter. Official reports, news and media releases were closely followed to be able to draw a Gantt chart of the Australian case studies to show their projected timelines and the processes implemented for a successful project commencement.

4.3.1 Channel Deepening Project, Victoria

The Channel Deepening Project for the Port of Melbourne in Victoria involved dredging into the Port Phillip Bay, removing approximately twenty-two million cubic metres of sand and silt, to enable passage of the larger shipping vessels into the port (Department of Infrastructure and Transport 2010). Moreover, dredging is necessary to avoid Melbourne from becoming a backwater and limiting further access to the shipping vessels (Millar 2008). The Table below summarises the key features of this project.

Table 4.6 Channel Deepening Project, Victoria

Project owner	Port of Melbourne
Location	Port Phillip Bay
Investment value	AUD 969 million
Procurement scheme	Alliance
Construction commencement (planned)	2008
Commercial Operation	2010

Source: Department of Infrastructure and Transport (2010).

The Channel Deepening Project was announced in 2000. Thereafter, the project development and planning took more than six years (Department of Infrastructure and Transport 2010). The economic viability and the environmental safety were thoroughly investigated to ensure limited impact on the surrounding economy and ecology. The overall project was completed on time and within budget of AUD 969 million under an Alliance contract.

The project has involved some of the most stringent environmental requirements to date, including 150 environmental control measures and 60 project delivery standards (Department of Infrastructure and Transport 2010). These were continuously monitored during the timeline of the project's implementation and after beginning the commercial operation by independent experts (Cooke 2007). These are a result of extensive environmental impact studies and community protests against the dredging activities due to possible social and environmental impacts (unknown author 2008; Lucas 2007). Furthermore, as a risk contingency program, an environmental protection bond has been paid to the government by the Port of Melbourne (Lucas and Murphy 2007). Some delays were experienced in the final stages of the project due to stakeholder action in the form of public protests.

Fig. 4.10 Channel Deepening Project implementation schedule outlines the timeline for the implementation processes of this project. This figure shows the projected durations for each of the processes in the shadings, with the lighter colour signifying the earliest projections and the darker shading highlights any changes that may have been made to these projections as a result of circumstances surrounding the project. The dates when the processes were finally completed have been marked by the 'X'. Overall, the Port of Melbourne's projected dates seem to have been met successfully with the project reaching operation stage within time and budget constraints.

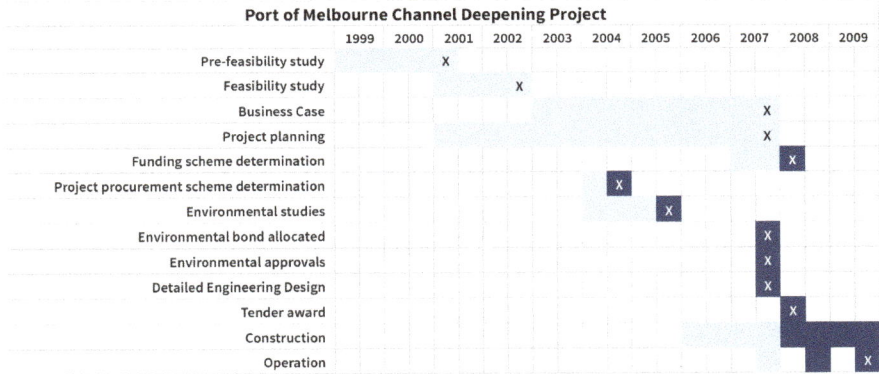

Port of Melbourne Channel Deepening Project

	1999	2000	2001	2002	2003	2004	2005	2006	2007	2008	2009
Pre-feasibility study			X								
Feasibility study				X							
Business Case									X		
Project planning									X		
Funding scheme determination										X	
Project procurement scheme determination						X					
Environmental studies							X				
Environmental bond allocated									X		
Environmental approvals									X		
Detailed Engineering Design									X		
Tender award										X	
Construction											
Operation											X

Fig. 4.10 Channel Deepening Project implementation schedule
(Figure by the authors)

■ Revised projection
  Initial projection
X Milestone achieved
| Project delayed or discontinued

4.3.2 M7 Motorway, New South Wales

The M7 Motorway is a substantial part of the New South Wales (NSW) government's orbital strategy to dramatically reduce travel time across western Sydney (Roads and Maritime Services 2015). The motorway spans 40 km and consists of four lanes. It has reduced approximately 60,000 vehicles per day from the existing western Sydney road network, reducing the congestion and delays in this area.

Table 4.7 below summarises the key attributes of the project.

Table 4.7 M7 Motorway, New South Wales

Project owner	NSW Roads and Traffic Authority (RTA)
Location	Sydney, New South Wales
Investment value	AUD 1.65 billion
Procurement scheme	PPP
Construction commencement (planned)	February 2003
Commercial Operation	December 2005

Source: CIMIC, n.d.

The initial concept for this project was introduced in the 1960s by the NSW Department of Main Roads (Department of Infrastructure and Transport 2010). The Sydney Area Transportation Study in 1974 suggested the need for the highway and a possible corridor for this route to address the future residential and industrial growth areas. A Build Own Operate Transfer (BOOT) Public Private Partnership was selected as the procurement model to accelerate the delivery of this project. Benchmark practices, as outlined by the Gateway Review Process were followed in the implementation of this project.

This motorway project had invited the largest private funding of AUD 2.23 billion into public infrastructure with only AUD 360 million being provided by the federal government to support the replacement of the Cumberland Highway in the National Highway Network (Department of Infrastructure and Transport 2010). Furthermore, the preliminary design and the features of the motorway invited community consultation to ensure their cooperation and satisfaction with the new motorway. In fact, some changes to the route were made as a result of this to minimise the environmental impact of the new motorway. In addition to this, all levels of the government (local, state and federal) were engaged throughout the duration of the project to ensure their cooperation and a high level of stakeholder management. This has proven to be beneficial for the project in the long term, ensuring that it meets the needs and expectations of stakeholders.

Fig. 4.11 M7 Motorway project implementation schedule outlines the timeline for the implementation processes of this project. This figure shows the projected durations for each of the processes in the shadings. The dates when the processes were finally completed have been marked by the 'X'. Overall, the projected dates seem to have been met successfully with the project completing construction well before the required date set in 2007. This may be attributed to the PPP procurement model that incentivises early completion (Department of Infrastructure and Transport 2010).

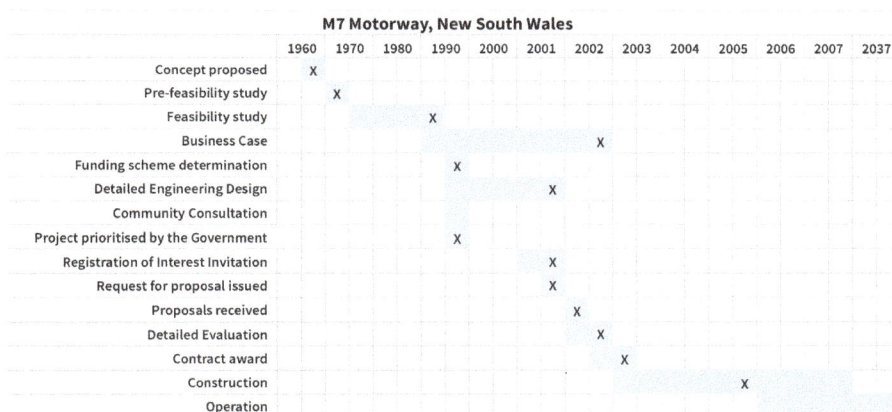

M7 Motorway, New South Wales

	1960	1970	1980	1990	2000	2001	2002	2003	2004	2005	2006	2007	2037
Concept proposed	X												
Pre-feasibility study		X											
Feasibility study				X									
Business Case								X					
Funding scheme determination					X								
Detailed Engineering Design							X						
Community Consultation													
Project prioritised by the Government					X								
Registration of Interest Invitation							X						
Request for proposal issued							X						
Proposals received							X						
Detailed Evaluation								X					
Contract award									X				
Construction											X		
Operation													

Fig. 4.11 M7 Motorway project implementation schedule (Figure by the authors based on Department of Treasury and Finance n.d.)

■ Revised projection
  Initial projection
X Milestone achieved
I Project delayed or discontinued

4.4 Benchmark Practices

Fig. 4.12 Gateway Review Process (left) in comparison to Indonesian case studies (right) shows the benchmark process for implementation of major infrastructure projects in Australia, the Gateway Review System.

Australian Gateway Review Process

Case Studies

Define program and early development stage

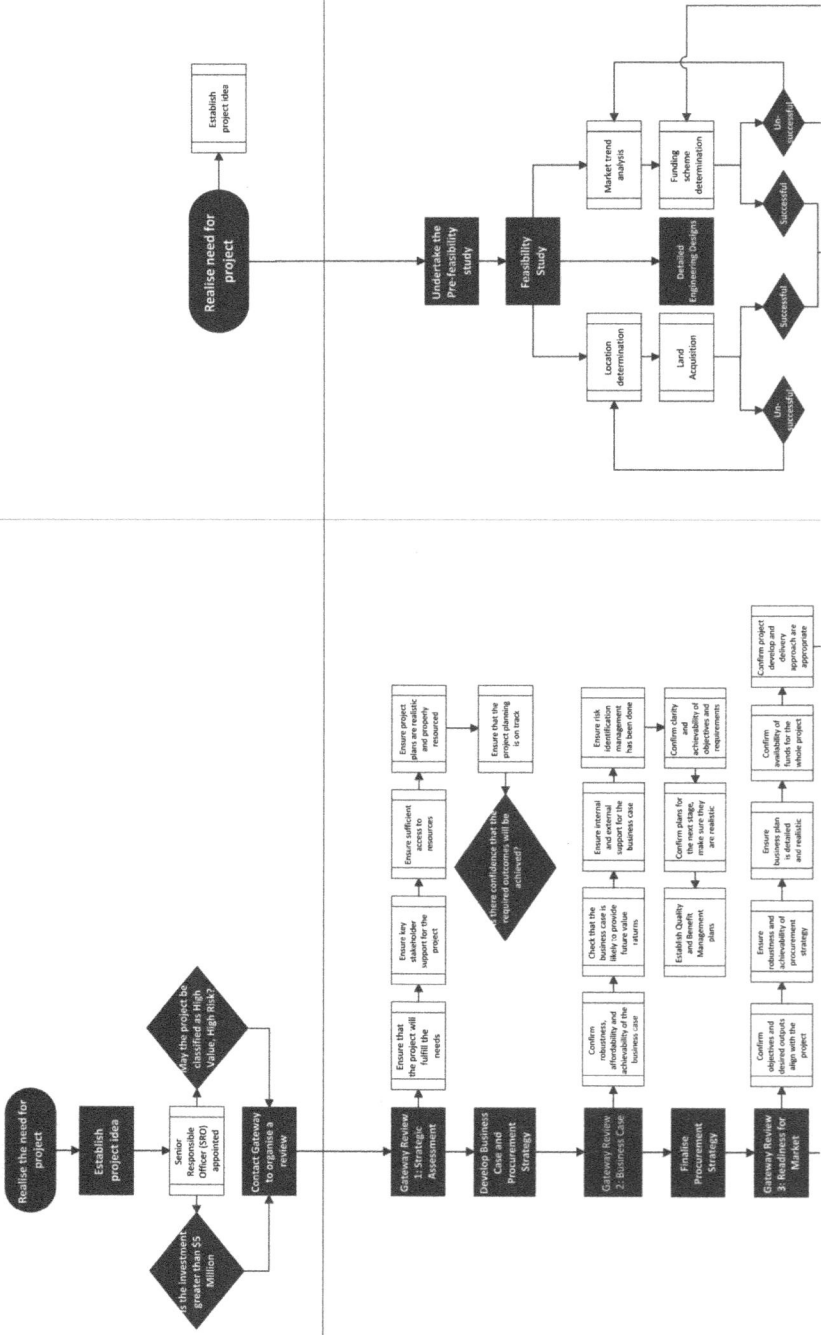

Program execution stage

Realise the need for project

Establish project idea

Senior Responsible Officer (SRO) appointed

May the project be classified as High Value, High Risk?

Is the investment greater than $5 Million

Contact Gateway to organise a review

Gateway Review 1: Strategic Assessment
- Ensure that the project will fulfill the needs
- Ensure key stakeholder support for the project
- Ensure sufficient access to resources
- Ensure project plans are realistic and properly resourced
- Ensure that the project planning is on track
- Is there confidence that the required outcomes will be achieved?

Develop Business Case and Procurement Strategy

Gateway Review 2: Business Case
- Confirm robustness, affordability and achievability of the business case
- Check that the business case is likely to provide future value returns
- Ensure internal and external support for the business case
- Ensure risk identification and management has been done
- Confirm plans for the next stage, make sure they are realistic
- Confirm clarity and achievability of objectives and requirements

Finalise Procurement Strategy
- Establish Quality and benefits Management plans

Gateway Review 3: Readiness for Market
- Confirm objectives and desired outputs align with the project
- Ensure robustness and achievability of procurement strategy
- Ensure business plan is detailed and realistic
- Confirm availability of funds for the whole project
- Confirm project develop and delivery approach are appropriate

Realise need for project

Establish project idea

Undertake the Pre-feasibility study

Feasibility Study

Location determination

Market trend analysis

Land Acquisition

Funding scheme determination

Detailed Engineering Designs

Un-successful

Successful

Successful

Un-successful

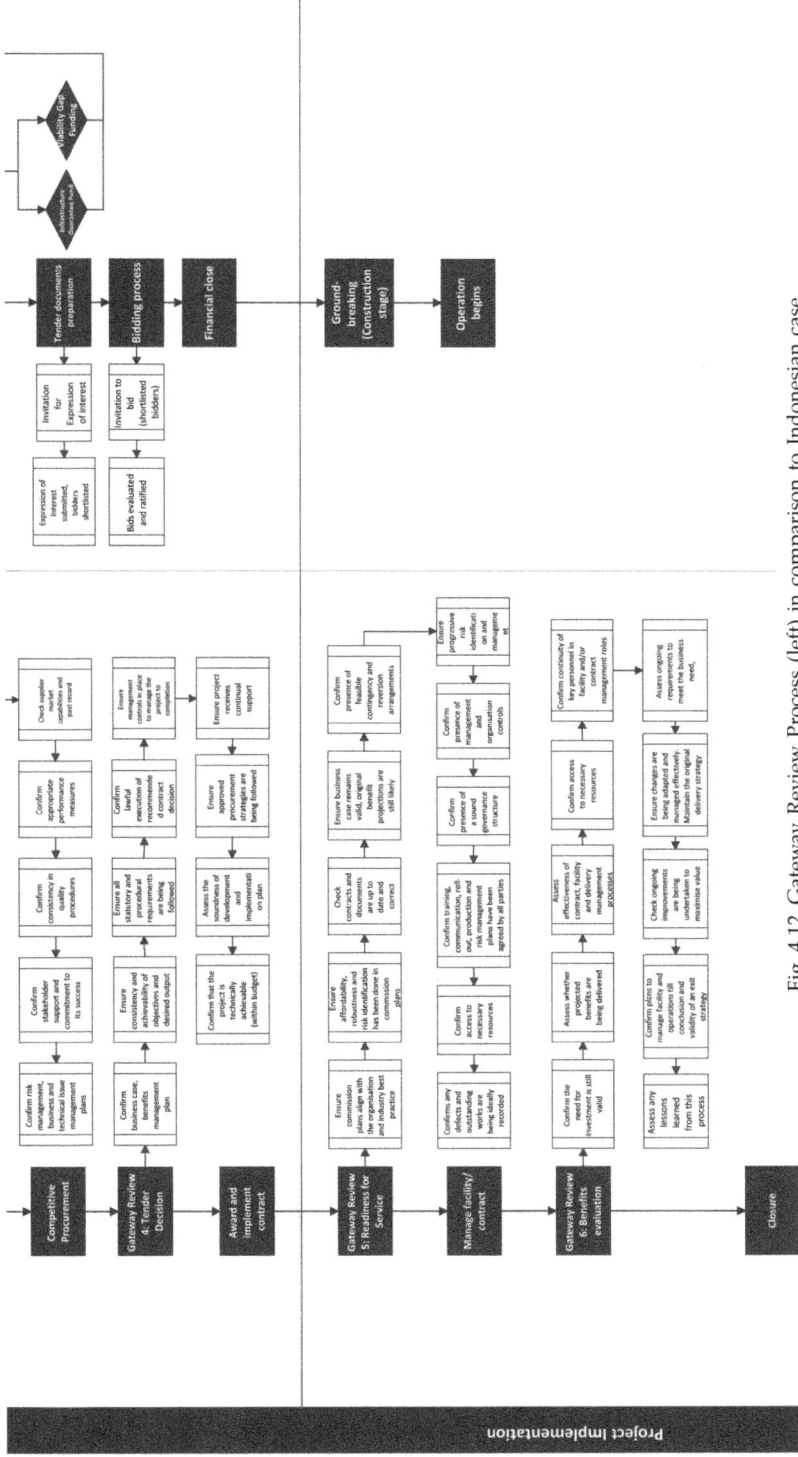

Fig. 4.12 Gateway Review Process (left) in comparison to Indonesian case studies (right) (Figure by the authors based on Department of Treasury and Finance, n.d.)

This system requires a thorough review to be conducted at each of the major milestones in the implementation of projects that are classified as high value, high risk (HVHR) projects (Department of Treasury and Finance n.d.). Projects may be assigned to be a high value, high risk project if they have a value greater than AUD 5 million or may be vulnerable to a significant risk.

Fig. 4.12 Gateway Review Process (left) in comparison to Indonesian case studies (right) highlights the points at which the review is undertaken and the processes that may need to be completed in the lead up to the review of a typical project. The review is conducted by a panel of field experts that are independent to the project owner, service provider and the government.

This system aims to identify any errors with the business case or in other stages of the project as they occur to mitigate their effect on the project's value and the timeline of the project's implementation. Strengthening the business case through an external review system in its early stages may potentially be value-adding over the entire lifecycle of the project.

4.4.1 Comparative Analysis

The case studies discussed in this chapter show a comparison of high value, high risk infrastructure project implementation in Australia and Indonesia. A common trend gathered from these is that a delay or an interruption during a project's initial stages often leads to extensive delays or interruptions to its overall completion. Inadequate pre-feasibility studies, poor stakeholder management, policy or regulation bottlenecks and financial constraints are the key underlying factors that lead to these delays.

Over the time that it takes for a project to be implemented, the needs of the public magnify and modify. This is especially true for the Umbulan Springs, where it was initially announced in the 1960s and was in its planning stage since 1973; it is now projected to be delivered by 2019. By the time it is delivered, the needs of the residents would have multiplied due to population growth and climate change. Therefore, even after the project will be delivered, the capacity of the system will still not be adequate to meet its needs. Furthermore, the overall quality of the infrastructure, which has been attributed as an important factor for social and economic growth, would not have improved to the level expected as a result of this project. Jakarta Sewage System is a similar project that was expected to have been completed based on its initial pre-feasibility studies in 1979; however, these feasibility studies were again undertaken in 2010 and the project was expected to be delivered by 2021.

For infrastructure development to result in a nation's social and economic growth, it must meet the pre-defined needs. However, needs change over time and projects must be delivered as early as possible (within time constraints) to ensure the needs are still relevant.

Furthermore, since a project does not begin to deliver on its value until it is implemented, and since the financial costs of a project increase for each unit of time it is delayed or stagnant, any delay in the project can cause a significant financial dent to its overall budget. As so many projects in Indonesia and Australia are already competing for financial support and funding allocation, it is imperative that each project is delivered on time and within budget. This can lead to more projects being supported for implementation, over time leading to an overall increase in the quality of infrastructure and therefore, social and economic growth.

One of the key differences between Australia and Indonesia in terms of large infrastructure project implementation is forecasting and incorporating future needs in the initial stages of the project. The M7 Motorway in New South Wales is a prime example where the pre-feasibility studies began in 1966, and finally delivered decades later, much like the Umbulan Springs Project in Indonesia. A key point of difference between these is that the M7 Motorway project was developed based on predictions of population growth along that corridor, recognising the need for a high capacity motorway. Furthermore, while the studies for the project began in 1966, it was ensured that the design and funding remained up to date as they were only completed leading up to the project's implementation. Having done this, it may be asserted that the project and the current needs of the city were considered and served by the project.

Another key difference is that the date projections for different major milestone phases include a risk contingency period in Australia. This was highlighted by the Port of Melbourne Case Study, Channel Deepening Project in Victoria. As interruption or factors causing delay are mostly external to the project, it can be difficult to predict when they may arise. Allowing a contingency period to accommodate such factors can be highly useful in stakeholder management; which, if not managed adequately, may lead to further delays. In addition to this, the dates for smaller milestone achievement are not widely published to public sources in the Australian case studies, as opposed to the case studies in Indonesia. Taking this into account, and the additional risk contingency period, delays caused by stakeholders are reduced, allowing the project to meet the date of final completion within time (as publicised). The Channel Deepening Project is a great case study for this, as it was subjected to significant stakeholder caused interruption and yet was able to make the deadline for final completion, end of 2009.

Here, it must be highlighted that this section does not compare between projects in Australia and Indonesia due to their geographical differences, rather between projects that followed the benchmark processes as opposed to not. The M7 Motorway in Sydney and the Channel Deepening project for the Port of Melbourne both followed the Gateway Review Process as a benchmark process guideline for their implementation. The Gateway Review process supports the importance of a linear, logical process, milestones to be met and a major review by an external party taking place after each major milestone. This aims to identify any problem areas through external consultation and ensure all pre-requisites are met as progress is made towards the next milestone. This allows for any discrepancies to be picked up and magnified through progress into the project. Furthermore, the project plan is reviewed and developed accordingly and maintained regularly to ensure it is up to date.

Through study of the Indonesian case studies mentioned in this chapter, it was identified that the project progress is done in a non-linear model where several tasks towards key goals are in the pipeline at any one time, as also highlighted in Fig. 4.12. While this is an attempt to fast track the project due to regulatory and legislative bottlenecks, it often tends to lead to other delays where slight discrepancies may be overlooked and cause major consequences at a later stage. Furthermore, this has contributed to a lack of transparency and a loss of confidence for financial investors.

4.4.2 Findings

A key point of difference between the two systems, and a factor causing delay for projects in Indonesia, is the absence of an external expert review mechanism for major projects. As highlighted by the literature, one of the major contributory factors for project delays is improper planning mechanisms (Department of Treasury and Finance, n.d.). Therefore, a robust business case is key for the successful implementation of a project, and an expert review panel for the project and each of its processes may be able to identify any factors lacking from the initial study that may be a later cause of concern and result in the ultimate delay or termination of the project.

Furthermore, a third-party review mechanism increases the confidence for a prospective investor, increasing the bankability of the project and hence attracting private investors.

References

Abednego, MP and Ogunlana, SO 2006. 'Good project governance for proper risk allocation in public-private partnerships in Indonesia', *International Journal of Project Management*, 24:7, pp. 622–34.

Amin, TM 2015. *PPP opportunities of water supply projects in Indonesia*, Ministry of Public Works and Housing, Republic of Indonesia, National Supporting Agency for Water Supply System Development.

Asmarini, W, Tan, F and Heavens, L 2017. Pertamina looks for partner to take majority stake in Bontang refinery project, *Hydrocarbon Processing*, www.hydrocarbonprocessing.com/news/2017/02/pertamina-looks-for-partner-to-take-majority-stake-in-bontang-refinery-project

Atmo, G, Duffield, C and Wilson, D 2015. 'Attaining value from private investment in power generation projects in Indonesia: An empirical study', *CSID Journal of Sustainable Infrastructure Development*, 1:1, pp. 65–79.

Australian Government, Department of Finance and Administration 2006. *Public Private Partnerships*: *Risk management*, www.finance.gov.au/sites/default/files/FMG_Business_Case_Development.pdf

Barker, J 2017. 'STS, governmentality, and the politics of infrastructure in Indonesia', *East Asian Science, Technology and Society*: *An International Journal*, 11:1, pp. 91–9, www.doi.org/10.1215/18752160-3783565

Basri, MC 2016. 'Comment on "Improving connectivity in Indonesia: the challenges of better infrastructure, better regulations, and better coordination"', *Asian Economic Policy Review*, 11, pp. 239–40, www.doi. org/10.1111/aepr.12139

Basu, M 2016. '96% of Jakarta has no sewage system', *Government Insider*, www. govinsider.asia/inclusive-gov/96-of-jakarta-has-no-sewage-system/

Chemonics International, Resource Management International, Sheladia Associates 1994. *Description of existing private sector participation projects and Public Private Partnership projects in Indonesia — and an analysis of lessons learned*, United States Agency for International Development, www.pdf. usaid.gov/pdf_docs/PNACB657.pdf

CIMIC n.d. *WESTLINK M7*, CIMIC, https://www.cimic.com.au/our-business/ projects/completed-projects/westlink-m7

Cooke, D 2007. 'Bay dredge to go ahead', *The Age*, 1 November, www.theage. com.au/news/national/bay-dredge-to-go-ahead/2007/10/31/1193618943809. html

Department of Infrastructure and Transport 2010. *Infrastructure planning and delivery: Best practice case studies*, Commonwealth of Australia, www. infrastructure.gov.au/infrastructure/publications/files/Best_Practice_Guide. pdf

Department of Treasury and Finance n.d. *Gateway — overview*, www.dtf.vic. gov.au/Publications/Investment-planning-and-evaluation-publications/ Gateway/Gateway-review-process-Guidance-materials

Flyvbjerg, B 2005. *Policy and planning for large infrastructure projects: Problems, causes, cures*, World Bank Policy Research Working Paper, www.doi. org/10.1596/1813-9450-3781

Jakarta Post 2017. 'Government to prepare capital's relocation', *The Jakarta Post*, 4 July, www.thejakartapost.com/news/2017/07/04/government-to-prepare-capitals-relocation.html

Haryanto, R 2015. *Getting into infrastructure game: Regulatory framework in the procurement process for funding schemes*, KPPIP, www.austrade.gov. au/.../1418/IABW_Infra_Rainier-Haryanto.pdf.aspx

Independent Evaluation Group (IEG) 2012. *Sewerage and sanitation: Jakarta and Manila*, The World Bank Group, www.lnweb90.worldbank.org/oed/ oeddoclib.nsf/DocUNIDViewForJavaSearch/4BE7A12A7DD3B01A852567F 5005D897C

Indonesia Investments 2016. *Indonesian Government seeks investors for Bontang Oil Refinery*, www.indonesia-investments.com/news/todays-headlines/ Indonesian-government-seeks-investors-for-bontang-oil-refinery/item6485?

Indra, BP 2011. *PPP policy and regulation in Indonesia*, Ministry of National Development Planning/National Development Planning Agency (BAPPENAS), http://www.oecd.org/gov/regulatory-policy/47377646.pdf

Investor Daily 2015. 'Government reviews West Semarang SPAM', *Investor Daily*, www.indii.co.id/index.php/en/news-publication/weekly-infrastructure-news/government-reviews-west-semarang-spam

KPPIP 2016. *KPPIP's Report for August-December 2015*, KPPIP, www.kppip.go.id/en/publication/kppip-semester-reports/

Lucas, C 2007. 'Dredge may raise water level in bay', *The Age*, www.theage.com.au/news/national/dredge-may-raise-water-level-in-bay/2007/10/31/1193618976026.html

Lucas, C and Murphy, M 2007. 'Ready, set - start dredging', *The Age*, www.theage.com.au/news/national/ready-set--start-dredging/2007/10/31/1193618975646.html

Manning, C 2015. 'Jokowi takes his first shot at economic reform', *East Asia Forum*, www.eastasiaforum.org/2015/09/13/jokowi-takes-his-first-shot-at-economic-reform/

Millar, R 2008. 'Options abound but easy choices are few', *The Age*, www.theage.com.au/news/national/options-abound-but-easy-choices-are-few/2008/02/01/1201801037863.html

Ministry of Finance 2012. *Government fiscal and financial support on infrastructure project*, Republic of Indonesia, Fiscal Policy Office, World Export Development Forum.

Negara, SD 2016. 'Indonesia's infrastructure development under the Jokowi administration', *Southeast Asian Affairs*, pp. 145–65.

Olken, BA 2007. 'Monitoring corruption: Evidence from a field experiment in Indonesia', *Journal of Political Economy*, vol. 115, no. 2, pp. 200–49.

Pangeran, M, Pribadi, K, Wirahadikusumah, R and Notodarmojo, S 2012. 'Assessing risk management capability of public sector organizations related to PPP scheme development for water supply in Indonesia', *Civil Engineering Dimension*, 14:1, pp. 26–35, www.doi.org/10.9744/ced.14.1.26-35

Puspa, A W 2016. 'Drinking water supply: Land for West SEMARANG SPAM prepared', *Bisnis Indonesia*.

PwC 2017. *Vice President inaugurates construction of Umbulan SPAM*, PwC.

Ray, D and Ing, LY 2016. 'Addressing Indonesia's infrastructure deficit', *Bulletin of Indonesian Economic Studies*, 52:1, pp. 1–25, www.doi.org/10.1080/00074918.2016.1162266

Roads and Maritime Services 2015. '*M7*', Roads and Maritime Services, NSW Transport, www.rms.nsw.gov.au/projects/key-build-program/building-sydney-motorways/m7.html

Sandee, H 2016. 'Improving connectivity in Indonesia: The challenges of better infrastructure, better egulations, and better coordination', *Asian Economic Policy Review*, 11, pp. 222–38, www.doi.org/10.1111/aepr.12138.

Sherwell, P 2016. '$40bn to save Jakarta: the story of the great Garuda', *The Guardian*, www.theguardian.com/cities/2016/nov/22/jakarta-great-garuda-seawall-sinking

Singgih, VP 2017. 'Finances halt Pertamina projects', *The Jakarta Post*, www.pressreader.com/indonesia/the-jakarta-post/20170608/281539405928906

Smith, J, Wiryawan, A and Ray, D 2017. *Kemen PUPR collaborates with Japan to provide IPALs up to face detection device*, PwC, www.pwc.com/id/en/media-centre/infrastructure-news/june-2017/kemenpupr-collaborates-with-japan-to-provide-ipals-up-to-face-de.html

Sulistyoningrum, Y 2016. Infrastructure projects tender for West Semarang SPAM postponed, *Bisnis Indonesia*, http://indii.co.id/index.php/en/news-publication/weekly-infrastructure-news/infrastructure-projects-tender-for-west-semarang-spam-postponed

Susanty, F 2016. Drinking water project contract signed after 43-year delay, *The Jakarta Post*, www.pressreader.com/indonesia/the-jakarta-post/20160722/282029031582155

Syarizka, D 2016. Drinking water supply: Certainty for Umbulan Project, *Bisnis Indonesia*, www.indii.co.id/index.php/en/news-publication/weekly-infrastructure-news/drinking-water-supply-certainty-for-umbulan-project

Tempo.co. 2017. 'Pertamina to name partner on Bontang Refinery Project in April', *Tempo.co.*, www.en.tempo.co/read/news/2017/02/14/056846281/Pertamina-to-Name-Partner-on-Bontang-Refinery-Project-in-April

The World Bank 2017. *Jakarta sewerage and sanitation project (JSSP)*, The World Bank, www.worldbank.org/P003827/jakarta-sewerage-sanitation-project-jssp?lang=en

Transnational Institute 2016. *National Capital Integrated Coastal Development (NCICD) project in Jakarta Bay*, TNI, www.tni.org/es/node/23337

The Age 2008. 'Protest buzz as Queen steams in', *The Age*, www.theage.com.au/news/national/protest-buzz-as-queen-steams-in/2008/01/29/1201369136015.html

5. Port and Hinterlands

The Combined Infrastructure Costs of Seaports, Intermodal Terminals and Transport Access, Port Botany, Sydney

J. Black[1] and V. Roso[2]

5.0 Introduction

From time immemorial, goods and commodities have been transferred from water to land. As specialised trade developed, such as tribute trade from Japan to China (Black and Lee 2016) primitive wharfs and harbours were created. This would also be the case with early Indonesian ports catering for the spice trade (Maguin 2017). As domestic and international trade increased in volume and ship technology improved, so did the need for more efficient intermodal transfers and space landside for port functions. Suitable deep-water seaports were located on the coast, within natural harbours or up-river but with limited thought given to landside space requirements. In the modern economy, pressures of globalisation, in particular, the widespread introduction of container ship technology from the late 1960s onwards (and associated storage, stuffing and un-stuffing containers and port access by road and rail)

1   Emeritus Professor of Transport Engineering, University of New South Wales, Sydney.
2   Associate Professor, Chalmers University of Technology, Gothenburg, Sweden.

    https://doi.org/10.11647/OBP.0189.05

have forced governments to re-evaluate these constrained ports and seek alternative solutions (Rimmer and Black 1982) such as dry ports, or intermodal logistics terminals.

Bird (1971) has developed conceptual models of the historical evolution of port locations and developments, but the broad strategic policy options are threefold. The first is an obvious one, and that is to find an entirely new location for the port, but political pressures to capitalise on sunk investments and avoid trade going to another city often render this option infeasible. The second policy option is to reclaim land from the ocean or the bay as has been done, for example, for the Japanese Hanshin ports or Tokyo Bay (Pernice, n.d.). This option is also being followed in the expansion of Tanjung Priok, Jakarta. The third option is to transfer some of the port-associated functions into the hinterland by locating, constructing and operating intermodal terminals or dry ports (Heaver et al. 2001; Roso 2008; Roso and Rosa 2012; Panova and Hilmola 2015), as in the case of Port Botany, Sydney. Physically constrained ports with their terminal operators have become involved in developing dry ports (Roso 2009, 2008; Ng and Gujar 2009; Wilmsmeier et al. 2011; Bask et al. 2014), where the functions may be classified by distance from the port: close; midrange; and distant (Roso et al. 2009).

Whilst chosen for its distinctiveness with operational intermodal terminals, it is a fact that today there are still few ports in the world that have as many functioning close inland intermodal terminals as in metropolitan Sydney serving Port Botany (Roso 2013). This symbiotic relationship between port and hinterland, including investment costs, is examined with an historical case study. Case studies usually contain unique characteristics where some of the experience and lessons learnt are not necessarily transferable to other cities, including ports in Indonesia located in large cities.

However, the case study methodology is justified for this book chapter because Port Botany in Sydney has several close intermodal terminals already operational, and has two more that are at the advanced planning stage. What makes this case study of Sydney unique is that a major research study (Butlin 1976) anticipated the need for such intermodal facilities at the very time that containers and coal loaders were being taken out of Port Jackson (Sydney Harbour) with plans to relocate them to a new port on Botany Bay in 1969 (Black and Styhre

2015; Black and Styhre 2016). The development of Port Botany has been a continuous story of environmental (and other) conflicts from the days that container shipping was removed from Mort Bay in Sydney Harbour because of landside constraints and community action that stopped the container trucks from using narrow residential streets in Balmain (Rimmer and Tsiporous 1977). It is this historical study of conflicts (and the corresponding capital investments to eliminate such conflicts), including conflicts as recent as mid-2018 that will resonate with policy makers and researchers with the Indonesian ports of Tanjung Priok and Surabaya.

The essence of a universal problem is that increasing container volumes handled in seaports require adequate land to be available nearby for port-associated functions and they must have efficient inland multi-modal transport access. Port Botany is Australia's second largest container port handling over 2 million TEU, approximately one third of the nation's maritime containers. Container volumes are expected to increase annually over the next decade and projected to reach seven million TEU by 2031 (Transport for New South Wales 2013). Export and import of containers are rather balanced in amount of TEU, with East Asia being the leading region for full container imports. Given this growth, stakeholders have expressed concerns about the landside operations at Port Botany: they claim there are inefficiencies in the flow of containers into and out of the stevedores' premises at the port, which are resulting in congestion, particularly for road haulers. This is a general issue that resonates in other ports of the world. Issues surrounding suburban freight terminals, or dry ports, are a sub-set of the wider social and environmental problems of the interactions of seaports with their hinterlands.

In the case of seaports in metropolitan Sydney over the past five decades, we describe when the location for a new container port was selected by the New South Wales (NSW) Government to relieve the fragmented and site-constrained port facilities in Port Jackson. We also explain why this sub-optimal location on Botany Bay had insufficient land available for its longer-term expansion. The historical backdrop is important for researchers to understand port locational decisions. The location in the 1970s was predicated on road haulage serving the new port but subsequent governments have changed policy to encourage a mode share of 40% on rail so the whole issue of hinterland transport access is examined in some detail. Part of recent government policy has been to boost intermodal logistics terminals in metropolitan Sydney. However, the case study of Moorebank (maximum capacity of two million TEU), which started in 2003 with operations to commence soon, demonstrates that has not been without controversy. Moorebank Intermodal Terminal is one example of a Public Private Partnership infrastructure project in its development and financing and so the traditional role of governments managing and funding ports is examined through both the privatisation of Port Botany and through the national government's encouragement of asset recycling. The conclusions contain broad port and hinterland issues that require careful consideration in the Indonesian context.

5.1 Methodology

The methodology adopted in the study of implementation and financing of new container ports and dry ports is as follows. To set the context for the case study of metropolitan Sydney, we compare recommendations associated with resolving the Port Botany's environmental and social problems in the 1970s against how successive governments have formulated (palliative) policies based on comprehensive research by Butlin (1976), Rimmer and Black (1982), Black and Styhre (2016), and other government and private-sector inquiries (for example, NSW Parliamentary Librarian 1976; NSW Government 1980a,b, 2011; Infrastructure Partnership Australia 2007). Infrastructure costs are derived from various sources including project websites and New South Wales Department of Treasury annual budget appropriations.

An extensive review of the literature on dry ports was undertaken to include in this chapter. This archival research is supported by studies based on in-depth interviews with key stakeholders on ports and dry ports (Roso 2008; Roso 2013; Roso et al. 2015). Interviews in these studies have been undertaken with different actors of the transport system, such as seaport managers, inland terminal managers, rail and road operators, as well as policy makers. In addition, secondary data sources, such as internal company reports and internet-based documents, were combined with site visits in order to ensure validity through triangulation (Golicic and Davis 2012).

5.2 Literature Review Intermodal Terminals — Concept of Dry Ports

Intermodal transport refers to the freight supply chain using at least two different modes of transport for the movement of intermodal units (containers, semi-trailers or swap bodies) between origin and destination with one bill of lading, i.e. without handling freight itself during transhipment (Rutten 1998; van Klink and van de Berg 1998; Nierat 1996). Reduced energy consumption, optimisation of the usage of the main strengths of each mode (European Commission 2000a), reduction of congestion on road networks, and low environmental impacts (Woxenius et al. 2004; Kreutzerberger et al. 2003) are considered to be the advantages of intermodal (road-rail) transport.

There is a substantial body of research available on how to find the optimal location for these terminals (Rutten 1998; Macharis and Verbeke 1999; Arnold et al. 2004; Flämig and Hesse 2011; Wang et al. 2017) and how to improve the efficiency of the road-rail terminals (Kozan 2000; Ballis and Golias 2002; Awad-Núñez et al. 2014). Höltgen (1995) deals with the basic problem of differentiation between "conventional" transhipment terminals and the various types of large-scale, intermodal logistics centres. The definitional issue is that the concept for intermodal logistics centres varies from country to country. A substantial amount of research has been completed, in general, about the concept (Roso 2008; Roso et al. 2009; Ng and Gujar, 2009; Notteboom and Rodrigue 2010; Rodrigue et al. 2010; Veenstra et al. 2012; Roso 2013). Inland intermodal terminals should: contribute to intermodal transport; promote regional economic activity; and improve land use and local goods distribution. These features may also be applied to a dry port — an inland intermodal terminal that has direct rail connection to a seaport, and where customers can leave and/or collect their goods in intermodal loading units, as if the transaction was directly with the seaport (Roso et al. 2009). As well as transhipment, which a conventional inland intermodal terminal provides, services such as storage, consolidation, depot, track and trace, maintenance of containers, and customs clearance are available at dry ports.

The quality of access to a dry port, and the quality of the road-rail interface, determines the dry port's performance (Bask et al. 2014).

However, the quality of inland access depends on the behaviour of a large variety of actors, such as government planning agencies, regulatory authorities, terminal operators, freight forwarders, transport operators, and port authorities and this requires coordination between all actors involved (de Langen and Chouly 2004; Van Der Horst and de Langen 2008). Scheduled and reliable high-capacity transport by road and rail to and from the seaport is a prerequisite. Bergqvist et al. (2010) identified factors affecting the development process and the time needed to establish intermodal road-rail terminals: profitability; financiers; political entrepreneurs; location; large local shippers; and the road traffic authorities. The authors conclude that profitability, combined with an enthusiastic and committed political entrepreneur, are the most vital factors for the success and pace of the development process (ibid). Haralambides and Gujar (2011) argue that Public Private Partnership investments should be supported by governmental pricing policies and guidelines to secure successful dry port implementation. Implementation of a close dry port in a seaport's immediate hinterland increases the terminal capacity of the seaport and with it comes the potential to increase productivity because larger container ships will be able to call at the seaport (Roso et al. 2009; Black et al. 2018), provided that the seaway is not constrained by the necessary draft depth.

With a dry port implementation, the seaport's congestion from numerous trucks at the landside interface is avoided because one train can substitute some thirty-five trucks (in the European context as noted by Roso et al. 2009). The benefits from dry ports derive from the modal shift from road to rail, resulting in reduced congestion at the seaport gates, and their surroundings, as well as reduced external environmental effects along the route (Roso 2007; Roso et al. 2009; Lättilä et al. 2013). A reduced number of trucks on the roads generates less congestion, fewer accidents, lower road maintenance costs and less vehicle emissions; as much as 25% (Roso 2007) and 32–45% (Lättilä et al. 2013) less emissions. A study conducted in Finland concludes that implementation of dry ports would cause "reduction in both, emissions and total transportation costs" (Henttu and Hilmola, 2011). Although road carriers would lose market share, in countries such as Australia, where long trailers are restricted to pass through city roads, a dry port is a good solution from their perspective as well. In addition to the general benefits to the environment, and the quality of life for residents by shifting container flows from road to rail, the dry port concept mainly offers seaports a possibility to increase their throughput without physical expansion at the site of the port. It therefore constitutes a "movement" of the seaport's "interface" inland (Roso et al. 2009) and, effectively, extends the reach of the seaport inland (Wilmsmeier et al. 2011).

The concept of a dry port should facilitate more efficient port access. The movement of the seaport's interface inland shifts container flows from road to rail. This results in a reduction of road transport to and from the seaport, along with the broad social and environmental benefits associated with such a reduction (Henttu and Hilmola 2011; Hanaoka and Regmi 2011; Roso 2013, Black et al. 2018). Various types of inland intermodal terminals that fit into the concept of dry ports have been developed and studied around the world, for example in China (Beresford et al. 2012), Japan (Yoshizawa 2012), India (Ng and Gujar 2009), the United States (Rodrigue et al. 2010; Roso et al. 2015), Asia (Hanaoka and Regmi 2011), Russia (Korovyakovsky and Panova 2011), Australia and New Zealand (Roso 2008 and 2013; Black et al. 2018) and Europe (Flämig and Hesse 2011; Henttu and Hilmola 2011; Monios 2011; Bask et al. 2014).

As noted above, success in the development of seaports, and of inland terminals, depends on the behaviour of a large variety of actors. However, the devil is in the detail when it comes to co-operative behaviour and co-ordination with real-world examples. In practice, locating dry ports within an already developed metropolitan space, such as Sydney or Jakarta, is a tricky balance between evidence-based land-use and transport analysis and the politics at the local, metropolitan, state and national scales. In order to understand suburban terminal location issues in metropolitan Sydney we must first explain the historical context.

5.3 Sydney's Container Ports — History

Sydney was a port at Sydney Cove before it became a city. When the First Fleet of nine ships entered Port Jackson on 26 January 1788 to establish a penal colony for British convicts that became the first European settlement on the continent, British Government policy was to establish friendly relations with indigenous Australians, but it was not long before conflict erupted (Australian Museum 2015; FitzSimons 2019). Subsequent urban evolution reflects the multiple ripple effects caused by dis-equilibrating external influences, induced in the 19th and 20th centuries largely by the changing nature of world capitalism. Domestic responses to the container ship revolution have only partially resolved re-occurring conflicts (Rimmer and Black 1982, p. 230). From the late 1960s to the present day, these responses have taken the form of infrastructure developments — essentially shifting problems from one place to another — where "the community has a limited capacity for absorbing spatial dissonance" (Rimmer and Tsipouras 1977, p. 12).

The port systems of Sydney have developed rapidly since the 19th century in response to a continuing sequence of external stimuli and Australia's changing role in the world economy. The Australian Federal Government held a Conference on Containerisation in 1966 to seek assistance from the State port authorities (Under the Australian Constitution, maritime commercial ports are the statutory responsibility of state and territory governments) in providing facilities for containerised cargo, mitigating the effects of the reduction in water-side employment and minimising inter-union disputes. In Port Jackson it turned out to be a problem of lack of land availability for container operations. As a consequence, the Maritime Services Board (MSB — the Sydney port authority at the time), "became committed to the redevelopment of port facilities to cater to the new order" (Brotherson 1975, p. 34).

Initially, Port Jackson was partially redeveloped with the first container terminal (leased to a British consortium (Seatainer Terminals Pty. Ltd)) opened in 1969 at White Bay on 10.9 hectares of reclaimed land. A 10.1-hectare MSB facility on Glebe Island was opened in 1973. Although the Commonwealth Government suggested these facilities would be adequate for "the foreseeable future", it was later conceded that these two terminals were half the area required. This necessitated decentralised depots at Villawood and Chullora for container handling. In turn, this aggravated strife between the Waterside Workers Federation of Australia and the Federated Storemen and Packers Union over who should handle containers in off-wharf depots — the court decision going in favour of the latter union. The third container port in Port Jackson at

Mort Bay had a depth of water of 9.5 m that proved insufficient for the second generation of container ships that were introduced in 1975. The fourth container terminal was at Darling Harbour.

Mort Bay faces northeast onto Sydney Harbour on the Balmain peninsula where the predominantly residential and industrial streets have 10m-wide road pavements feeding onto the only main road into and out of the peninsula — Darling Street. Not surprisingly, the container movements by trucks met with great hostility from residents of Balmain and Rozelle, who complained vocally that the Maritime Services Board had approached the planning for containers from a narrow, "silo" maritime perspective. This situation led to the preparation of a report by residents arguing for the earliest elimination of cargo trucking through Balmain. The report cited evidence of pedestrian accidents, noise intrusion, pollution, structural damage to pavements, fear of damage to parked cars, and a 5 to 10% drop in property values along truck routes. Australian National Line figures indicated that approximately 1000 trucks moved in and out of Mort Bay during a sixty-six-hour working week. In November 1974, Mort Street residents counted up to seventy-nine trucks per hour during peak periods (Rimmer and Black 1982, p. 237).

The environmental backlash was so severe that Australian National Line (ANL) quit the congested site at Mort Bay in April 1980 for Port Botany which offered improved "operational and environmental conditions" (Rimmer and Black 1982, p. 237). (The importing of cars by ship that previously occurred at Glebe Island was relocated to Port Kembla in November 2008.) Forewarned by the confrontation between residents of Balmain and ANL, the residential community of Botany, located around the new port on Botany Bay, feared similar environmental issues when that port became operational.

In 1978/9, 69% of all general cargo was containerised with 349,337 TEU containers annually passing through these four terminals in Port Jackson (Rimmer and Black 1982, Table 12.2, p. 231). A survey in June 1978 showed that on a typical day, 650 containers were moved by road and 450 containers were moved by rail (Edgerton et al. 1979). The truck traffic generated by the containers in Port Jackson and Port Botany inevitably led to conflicts with surrounding residents and with other road users, especially during the morning peak-hour. As a New South

Wales Government Inquiry noted, the "container vehicle, even in a sea of cars, stands out as an elephant amidst a flock of pigeons" (NSW 1980a, vol. I, p. 89).

5.4 Port Botany Container Terminals

It was the unanticipated growth of container traffic through Port Jackson, and the environmental backlash from resident action groups on the Balmain peninsula, that forced the government to review its plans for Port Botany and to incorporate container terminals there. Brotherson (1975) explains the relevant history behind the need to relocate some port functions from Sydney Harbour to an entirely new port on reclaimed land in Botany Bay. Port functions to handle containers in Port Jackson were becoming increasingly constrained in the post-Second World War era because of the lack of suitable land to store full and empty containers. The NSW State Government wanted to maintain Sydney as Australia's premier port, so a decision was made in 1969 to construct container facilities in Botany Bay. Table 5.1 gives a time line of key events.

Table 5.1 Port Botany — Key Events 1969–2018 (Table by the authors)

Date	Key Events
1969	NSW State Government decision to construct container facilities in Botany Bay
1971	The NSW Government establishes the State Pollution Control Commission (SPCC) but with no regulatory powers
June 1971	Construction of Port Botany commences on 600ha of reclaimed land in Botany Bay
November 1974	SPCC takes over regulatory functions of water and air and regulation of municipal garbage disposal from the NSW Health Commission
1976	Publication by Professor Noel Butlin of book on the impact of Port Botany Bay
1979	NSW Environmental Planning and Assessment Act became law whereby development proposals, such as ports and intermodal terminals are scrutinised in the public arena through environmental impact assessments
December 1979	Port Botany opens

Date	Key Events
30 June 1995	Maritime Services Board was abolished under the *Ports and Maritime Administration Act 1995*, and Sydney Ports Corporation was established
September 2011	NSW Government announced its intention to refinance state owned assets including Port Botany
12 April 2013	99-year lease of State-owned port assets Port Botany and Port Kembla awarded to the NSW Ports consortium.
September 2018	Cruise Ship Terminal mooted for Port Botany after Federal Government rules out Garden Island as a suitable terminal location

Construction of Port Botany started in June 1971, the years before environmental impact assessment and subsequent public inquiry became NSW Government policy. The new port involved the physical transformation of Botany Bay through dredging, construction of a high breakwater to counter storm surges in the bay and reclamation of a large area at a cost of about AUD 621 million (in 2016 prices). A V-shaped entrance channel 19.2 m deep was dredged in the mouth of Botany Bay to accommodate 200,000 DWT tankers ostensibly designed for petroleum imports and bulk cargoes. In 2018, the maximum draught remains at 12.7 m. Hence, the northern foreshore of the bay involved reclamation of about 225 hectares of land and a re-entrant basin dredged to 15.3 m of depth with nearly 2 km of wharfage to accommodate two container terminals, each with three berths (Fig. 5.1).

From the outset, The Botany Bay Project established by the Australian Academies (Science, Social Science and Humanities) criticised the government's decision to relocate container facilities to this location because it disregarded:

> the land-use impact on the hinterland, the effects on city design, the social disturbances to city residents, the efficiency and economic rationality of the investment project and the social implications for the land environment (Butlin 1976, p. 94).

The Botany Bay project drew attention to several issues that have haunted Port Botany operators from the 1970s to the present day: the area's poor landward connections to the emerging industrial lands in

Fig. 5.1 Port Botany Container Terminals. Source: https://www.nswports.com.au/
assets/Uploads/PDFs-General/MAP-PB-New-for-website.pdf

the outer western suburbs of Sydney; the area's limited rail access to the
port; and constraints imposed not only by its location (immediately to
the port's north-west is Sydney International and Domestic Airport), but
also, significantly, by community intolerance. The present-day pattern
of container truck movements is illustrated in Fig. 5.2, where projections
show a similar spatial pattern of intensified traffic in 2036.

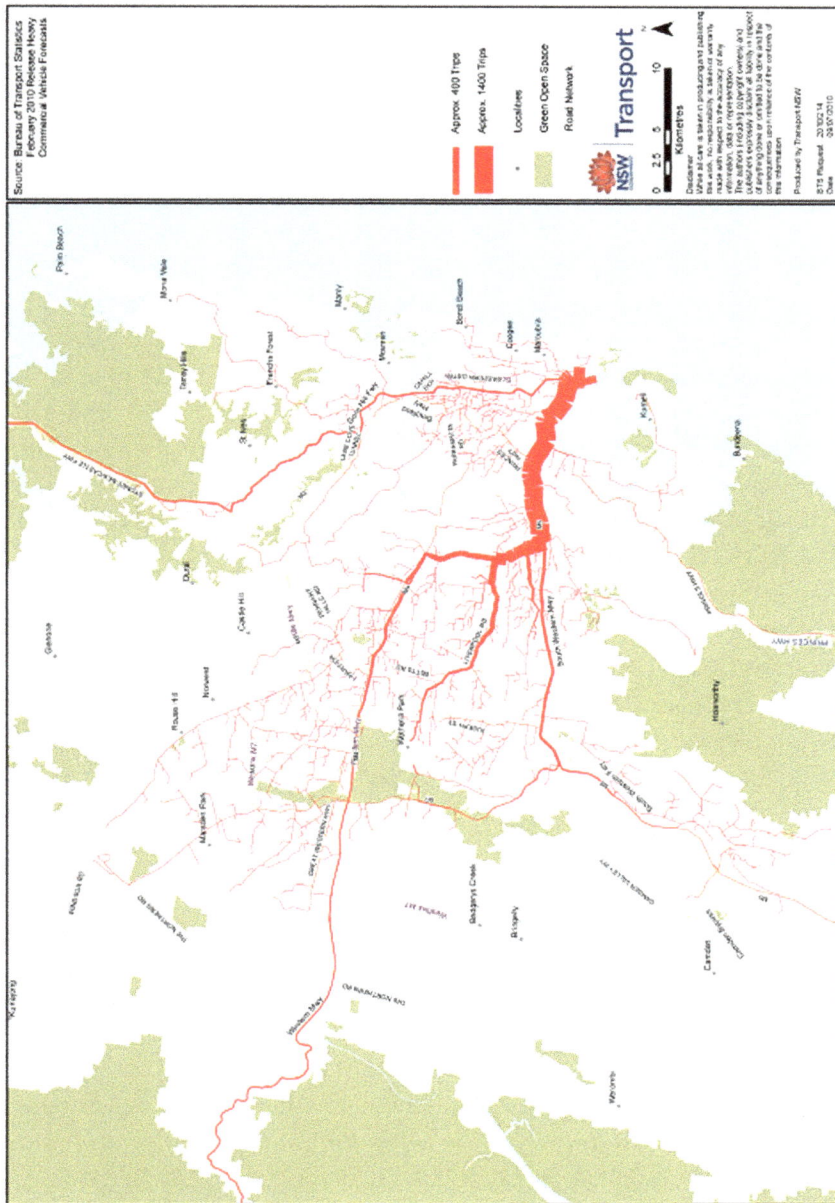

Fig. 5.2   Heavy Commercial Vehicles Trips from Port Botany, Average Weekday, 2006. Source: Bureau of Transport Statistics 2010.

The growth in container traffic has forced local councils around the port to react with specific zoning policies, while the co-location with Sydney Airport has imposed additional pressures on land. The County of Cumberland Planning Scheme (1951) recognised the growing importance of Sydney Airport and Port Botany combined as a centre of economic activity and generator of traffic activities in the future, at a time when international shipping was the dominant mode for passengers and cargo. The document then suggested the need for allocating some extra space within, and in close proximity to the port and airport in order to accommodate these activities. The scheme zoned a total area of 308.44 hectares to be used as port and airport-oriented land-uses.

The local government Interim Development Order no. 19, which was enacted on 16 September 1977, allocated another 80 hectares of land in the surrounding areas of Sydney airport for airport-related land-use (Jatmika 2001). At this time, other parcels of land still followed the land-use zonings stipulated in the County of Cumberland Planning Scheme. In 1987, the Botany Local Council issued Local Environmental Plan (LEP) no. 32 as the main instrument for the land-use development planning and control. The major aims of the LEP were: to encourage local economic development; to provide efficient public services and amenities; to promote better environmentally-based development; and to encourage port and airport-related economic activities. The specific objectives were: to promote airport-oriented business as the major activity, whilst accommodating some seaport-associated activity developments; to foster a mixed-use of land for those industrial activities that are compatible with airport-related industries; to improve the landscape and streetscape of the zone; and to discourage traffic-generating land-use development within the zone.

The spatial pattern of change caused by the gateway port-dependent industries (such as cargo services, customs broker, transport and forwarding agents, warehouse, courier, airline and sea liner agents, importers, export agents, transport service and shipping companies) in the adjacent municipality to Sydney port and airport — Botany Municipality — has provided the basis for research policy analysis. In the designated study area, where fieldwork and interviews were undertaken in 1971 (Black et al. 2012), general industry dominated: only two carrier firms (out of twenty-eight firms) were related to gateway port activities. These two companies accounted for 8% of all firms. It was only after the establishment of the LEP in 1987 that the number of port and airport-related firms increased significantly. The number of port and airport-related sites accounted for only 8% in 1971, increased to 29% in 1991 and 43% in 2001. By 2011, the port and airport-related sites accounted for sixteen sites (46% of the total sites). In 2009, Botany Bay Council issued the Botany Bay Planning Strategy 2031 stating unequivocally that both Sydney Airport and Port Botany have a national economic significance and will continue to become one of the Australia's gateway ports in the future (SGS Economics and Planning 2009).

In maintaining the port as a global gateway, an uneasy tension in the aspirations of the Botany Bay Planning Strategy arises between, on the one hand, ensuring employment areas near the port are protected and are able to accommodate port-related activity and businesses, and, on the other hand, ensuring port activities do not further compromise residential amenity. The growth of gateway port activities will require extra space to cater for the increasing demand for off-site employment sites. This expansion compromises the amount of land available for residential development and undermines the state government's policy on increasing residential densities throughout inner Sydney. Only around 108 hectares of the local government area (LGA) is comprised of unconstrained residential land (SGS Economics and Planning 2009, p. 6). This unconstrained residential-zoned land comprises only one third of the total residential-zoned land in the whole of the Botany Local Government Area. Without careful planning, increased port activity and related truck and rail freight traffic will impinge on future residential amenity. The strategy suggests that additional residential development should be directed to areas away from the rail freight corridor and truck routes. It further suggests that areas already affected should be considered for alternative, non-residential zoning over time (SGS Economics and Planning 2009, p. 78).

The New South Wales Government has aspirations to make Port Botany the largest container port in Australia. Recently, Port Botany underwent a major expansion of its container port facilities to cope with the growing volumes of trade. The expansion — one of the largest port projects ever to be undertaken in Australia in the last 30 years — entailed the design, construction, procurement and the eventual awarding to

Hutchison Port Holdings (HPH) of the 3rd Stevedore contract (NSW Ports 2015). The NSW Government then called for long-term leases for the operation of two of Australia's largest ports. Port Kembla is Australia's largest vehicle import hub and the largest grain-handling terminal in New South Wales and Port Botany is the country's second largest container port.

The New South Wales Government retains regulatory oversight of port matters, and the Australian Competition and Consumer Commission (ACCC) has established a price-monitoring regime to ensure transparency as Port Botany is now operated by the private sector. The successful private sector partner was NSW Ports, who obtained the concession for ninety-nine years. The winning consortium — IFM Investors, AustralianSuper, QSuper and Abu Dhabi Investment Authority — made an upfront payment of AUD 5.07 billion: AUD 4.31 billion for Port Botany and AUD 760 million for Port Kembla (Infrastructure Australia 2014, p. 22). In addition, the consortium pays an annual fee of AUD 5 million to the State Government under the lease agreement. The proceeds are allocated to the State Government's investment fund, Restart NSW, to help pay for large infrastructure projects (including the 33 km-long WestConnex roads project) under the policy of asset recycling. In September 2018, the Sydney Transport Partners consortium, led by Transurban (who operate seven of Sydney's existing toll roads) paid AUD 9.3 billion to the New South Wales Government for a 51% share of the motorway that is expected to open for traffic in 2023 (Saulwick et al. 2018).

5.5 Multi-Modal Transport Access to Port Botany

The relocation of port activities from Port Jackson to Port Botany altered the modal split of containers to and from Sydney Ports, because the terminals at Port Botany were designed for trucks. When fully operational, 53% of the containers previously carried by rail to and from Port Jackson were transferred to truck to and from Port Botany. Furthermore, there was a shift in the orientation of trip patterns with container trucks moving westwards through Rockdale where the alternative routes were unsuitable for heavy vehicles. The arguments made by import/export companies at the time were that either container traffic does not cause any environmental problems, or if they do, "operational, practical and financial considerations would make alternatives less desirable, if not impractical" (Rimmer and Black 1982, pp. 239–40).

Naturally, local government councils in the Botany Bay sub-region strongly opposed the projected flows of containers through their municipalities and pressure mounted on the NSW State government for the greater use of rail instead of new road construction. The State Rail Authority proposed two options: that 70% of containers could be carried by rail by establishing depots inland from the port at Cooks River, Rozelle, Chullora and Villawood; or that containers with origins and destinations in a defined zone in the outer western suburbs be trucked to Chullora and Villawood then with a rail connection to Botany Bay. The Commission of Inquiry into the Kyeemagh-Chullora Road (NSW 1980a), which examined the major road deficiencies linking the new port with industrial areas, eventually recommended the latter, rail-based scheme be adopted. This recommendation was never implemented.

The current Sydney Freight Network with access to Port Botany via the Botany Goods Line is shown in Fig. 5.3. The Australian Rail Track Corporation (ARTC) and the NSW Rail Corporation (now Sydney Trains) signed a Deed of Agreement for the Metropolitan Freight Network (MFN) Lease and License. In December 2008, ARTC commenced the first phase of the MFN lease, with the lease of the Port Botany Rail Yard. Subsequent leases for Enfield West to Sefton and Port Botany to Sefton Park Junction were executed in July 2011 and August 2013, respectively. The timing of the MFN leases generally coincided with major capital projects (ARTC 2015, p. 3).

For example, ARTC developed, as a potential candidate for funding from the Nation Building Program 2009–2014, a staged upgrading program for the Metropolitan Freight Network and Port Botany line to meet projected growth in demand for container transport by rail. This proposal was successful (Infrastructure Australia 2018). The Port Botany Rail Link (PBRL) project is in two phases. A third phase has now been funded under the current Infrastructure Investment Program. A Federally funded AUD 75 million project — Stage 3 upgrade of the 18 km South Sydney Freight Line — involving track reconditioning, concrete re-sleepering, new rails, new drainage and new retaining structures is due for completion in 2019. The 2018–2019 Federal Budget, announced on 4 May 2018, allocated AUD 400 million including new rail bridges, civil works and duplicated rail tracks across the 2.9 km length of the freight line between Mascot and Botany, along with the construction of a 1.4 km passing loop between Cabramatta and Warwick Farm. When completed by the Australian Rail Track Corporation Ltd, the project will support freight logistics and supply chain activities of existing intermodal terminals such as at Enfield and Chullora and Moorebank (under construction) (http://roadsonline.com.au/port-botany-rail-line-to-undergo-400m-upgrade/).

In addition, the Port Botany Expansion Project entailed the design, construction, procurement and eventual awarding to Hutchison Port Holdings of the 3rd Stevedore contract. This part of the Project has now been completed and Hutchinson commenced operations from the 3rd Terminal in 2014. NSW Ports has begun investigating future requirements at the Port Botany Rail Terminal to receive a greater number of train movements. Investigations include the future construction of multiple rail mounted gantries (ARTC 2015, p. 6).

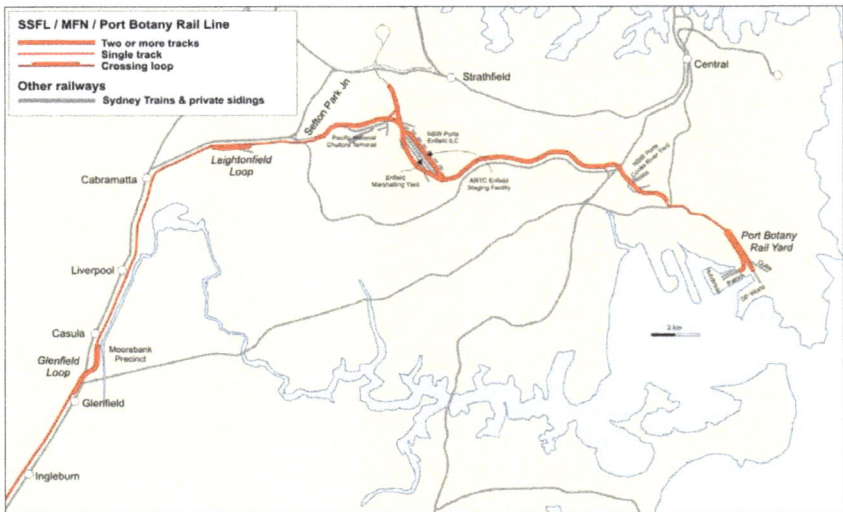

Fig. 5.3 Southern Sydney Freight Network and Port Botany Rail Line.
Source: ARTC 2015, Fig. 1.2, p. 6

However, the transport industry has stridently opposed the imposition of any regulations on the choice of transport mode for containers. For thirty-five years, inadequate truck routes accessing Port Botany continue as an unresolved problem. In 2011, around 20% of containers were carried into and out of Port Botany by rail — well below the state government's target of 40% set in 2005 for 2011. The Botany Bay Planning Strategy 2031 suggests that the port will be at its most competitive and efficient where support infrastructure such as heavy truck routes and arterial roads, and rail infrastructure, provide ease of movement to and from the facility. It further suggests that infrastructure investment will deliver that promise within the next decade.

The Independent Pricing and Regulatory Tribunal of New South Wales (2008) reviewed the interface between the stevedores and the haulage companies, recommending options for improving efficiency. These options included the use of road instead of rail, where rail is constrained by track configurations within the port terminals; and the finding of suitable train paths through the metropolitan rail network. Improvements to the vehicle booking system (VBS) operated by the stevedores and the introduction of the Port Botany Landside Improvement Program, introduced through regulation in February 2011, largely eliminated the truck queues that had previously extended around the port precinct where waiting from two to four hours was common (NSW Freight 2013).

The Federal Government has intervened in this long-standing wrangle between State and local governments. For many decades, the State and Territory Governments have been the key players in the port planning process, wherein both Federal and Local Governments have a relatively low level of involvement. Uncoordinated port planning and development, as identified above, has caused trade barriers and relatively high transaction costs as well as inefficient funding allocations. The main objectives of the national ports strategy are: to promote sustainable port development by enhancing port-related freight movements; to minimise the negative externalities of the freight movements; and to influence the policy making process associated with freight movements. There are four crucial issues that need to be dealt with for all Australian ports:

- Effective legal and governance frameworks.

- Land-use planning enhancement and the preservation of a transport corridor.

- The future requirements of port facilities, involving road and railway lines.

- Future planning and development of port and freight facilities which is coordinated nationally.

The road strategy is illustrated in Fig. 5.4. The recent sale of the WestConnex Motorway to Transurban will provide the NSW Government with money to build the Airport road link under its Assets Recycling Policy.

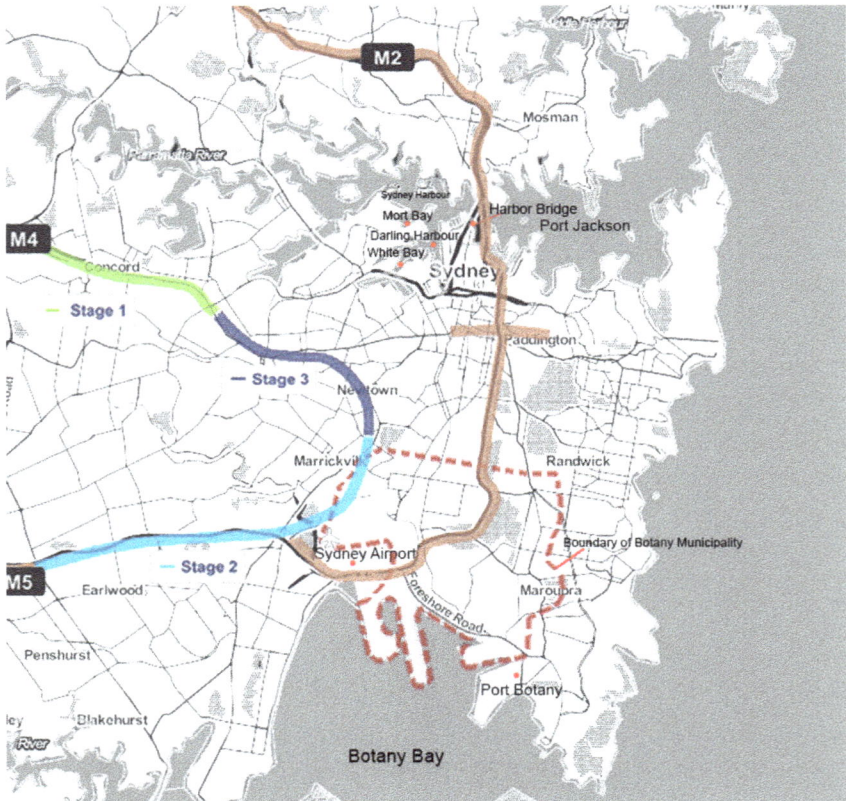

Fig. 5.4 Motorway Connections Proposed Between Sydney Airport and Port Botany (Figure by the authors)

5.6 Hinterland Intermodal Logistics Centres

In order to implement the above policies and strategies for developing Port Botany, the NSW Government allocated AUD 483 million to develop a network of Intermodal Terminals, such as the enhancements of Botany and Enfield Rail Yards (NSW Transport and Infrastructure 2010). The main target of the development is to increase the share of container consignment by rail to 40%. The growth of trade activities and container flows will also increase the demand for land to cater for the economic development. The NSW Government, through its Freight Strategy, endorsed a plan for a new network of intermodal terminals to support the movement of containers by rail. The new terminals will supplement the existing capacity, and reduce delivery times and costs. The areas identified as intermodal sites include Enfield, Moorebank and another site in western Sydney that is yet to be identified.

5.6.1 Port Botany's Inland Terminals Pre-2010

Several intermodal terminals that were located within the Sydney metropolitan area nearly a decade ago are listed in Table 5.2. These are primarily located in close proximity to areas of concentrated industrial distribution. The total planned capacity is limited in some cases by the availability of freight train paths through the Sydney metropolitan network. The total estimated capacity of these terminals is about 695,000 TEU. These intermodal terminals service the port or function as a transfer point for interstate cargoes. Sydney Ports Corporation (2008) recognised the need to expand the intermodal network within Sydney as a prerequisite for the greater use of rail in alignment with an NSW Government transport policy objective — in fact, the expected capacity for TEU containers has increased by over 5.5 times. The NSW Government Metropolitan Strategy outlined a proposed network of additional intermodal terminals in the central-west, south-west and west of metropolitan Sydney to meet predicted demand (Sydney Ports Corporation 2008).

The NSW Government proposed new facilities at Enfield, Moorebank and Eastern Creek. Sydney Ports Corporation developed a proposal for an Intermodal Logistics Centre at Enfield that provides an intermodal facility to cater for demand generated in central-west Sydney (Table 5.3).

Table 5.2 Metropolitan Sydney intermodal terminals, 2008

Location	Operators	Siding Length (Metres)	Estimated Capacity (TEU)
Camellia	Patrick PortLink	300	80 000
Chullora	Pacific National (inter-state)	680	300 000
Cooks River	Maritime Container Services	500	150 000
Villawood	Mannway	350	20 000
Minto	Macarthur Intermodal Shipping Terminal	390	45 000
Yannora	Patrick PortLink/QR National	500	50 000

Source: Sydney Ports Corporation (2008).

The private sector proposed an expansion of the Macarthur Intermodal Shipping Terminal at Minto and a joint venture arrangement between Kaplan Investment Funds, QR National and Stocklands for a new intermodal facility at Moorebank. The inclusion of warehousing and freight support services within each site is a mitigation strategy to reduce the number of large truck movements within the local community surrounding the terminal facilities.

Descriptive details of each terminal follow, while a broad overview of their TEU capacity is supplied in Table 5.3.

Table 5.3 Sydney suburban intermodal terminals — TEU capacity

Location	Operator	Capacity* TEU	Comments
Chullora	Pacific National	600,000	Announced in 2015 increasing from 300,000 to 600,000.
MIST	Qube	200,000	Capacity as stated on Qube website.
Cooks River	MCS	500,000	NSW Ports advice.
Yennora	Qube	200,000	Qube advice.
Villawood (Leightonfield)	Toll/DPW	180,000	Toll / DP World announcement.

Location	Operator	Capacity* TEU	Comments
Enfield	NSWPorts	500,000	Planning approval for 300,000.
Moorebank	Qube	1,550,000	Planned to commence operations in 2017. IMEX and interstate.
Total		3,730,000	

Source: ARTC (2015), Table 2.1, p. 13

The existing and proposed terminals are shown in Fig. 5.5.

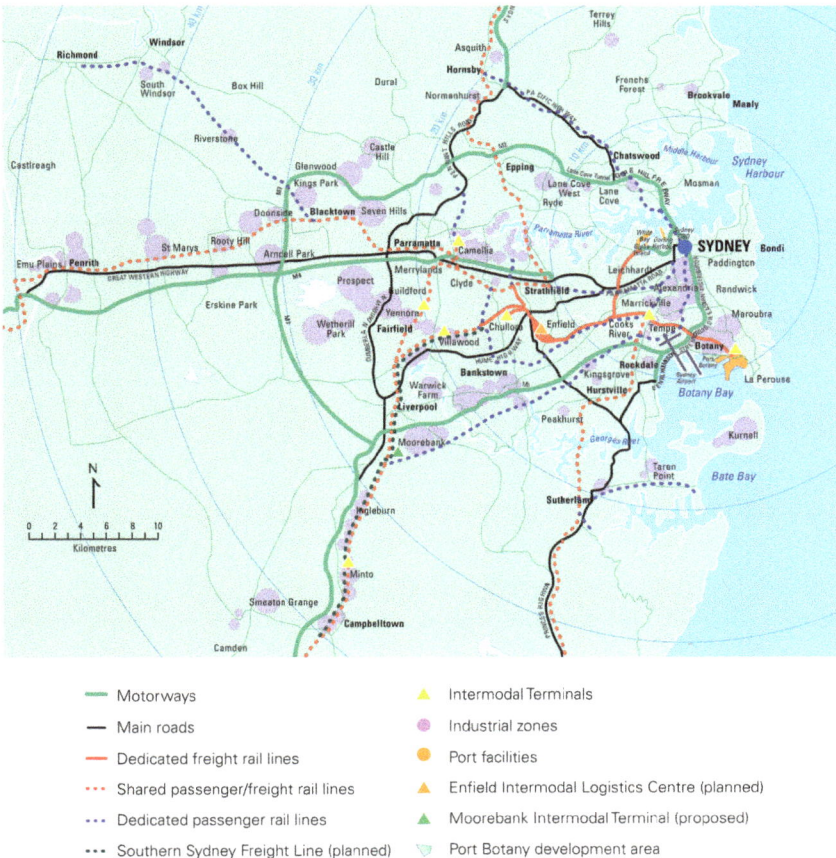

Fig. 5.5 Location of existing and proposed freight terminals for Port Botany
Source: Sydney Ports Corporation 2008

5.6.2 Chullora Intermodal Terminal

Chullora, Pacific National's facility, is the main interstate terminal geographically close to the centre of the city, located immediately to the south of the Sydney Operations Yard. However, the drift of freight intensive activity to the west and south means that it is effectively to the east of the major industrial concentrations. The terminal is situated about 25 km from Port Botany and has four 680 m-long rail sidings that accommodate about forty trains a week, resulting in a total throughput of 300,000 TEU/year (Sydney Ports Corporation 2008; Roso 2013). In 2015 that capacity was doubled. The facility is equipped with two gantry cranes; however, it does not offer customs clearance since it is used only for domestic freight movements (Roso 2013). Two new rail mounted gantries were commissioned earlier in 2015, increasing the capacity of the terminal from 300,000 to 600,000 TEU/year where the plan is to use the terminal for import/export containers (ARTC 2015). This facility can receive 1500 m trains for break-up and shunting into the terminal itself. Expansion of the terminal is complicated due to the presence of endangered species around the site and interaction with the RailCorp facilities to the east.

5.6.3 Macarthur Intermodal Shipping Terminal (MIST)

The Macarthur Intermodal Shipping Terminal (MIST) site located at Minto is a 16-hectare intermodal facility that has an annual throughput capacity of up to 200,000 TEU. In 2012, Qube acquired MIST from the Independent Transport Group (ITG). As part of the transaction Qube acquired the freehold property at Minto with warehousing and its rail terminal, locomotives and wagons from ITG (ARTC 2015). The terminal is entirely privately owned and run by MIST who saw the potential in using rail for the transport of containers to the seaport, and, in agreement with the seaport, but with its own investments, started a rail shuttle to/from the seaport. Services offered at the terminal are container haulage and transshipment between rail and road, storage, warehousing, maintenance of containers, customs clearance, quarantine, reefer storage, and packing/unpacking (Roso 2013). The 45 km-long shuttle services (approximately 4 per day) currently operate on the Sydney rail network between Minto and the connection to the metropolitan freight network at Sefton Park Junction. The terminal's throughput is about 65,000 TEU a year (in 2010), of which one third is for exports. Besides the rail connection to the seaport, the terminal has rail connections to other inland terminals where empty containers (from the seaport) are dispatched to be filled with grains for export (Roso 2013). On its 600 m-long rail sidings the terminal is able to accommodate long trains that will result in increased rail volumes. There is about 25,000 m² of covered storage in use and an additional 10,000 m² of warehouse.

5.6.4 Cooks River Intermodal Terminal (St Peters)

The Cooks River Intermodal Terminal is adjacent to the dedicated rail freight line 10 km from the port and is owned by NSW Ports and operated by Maritime Container Services Pty Limited (MCS). The 17.3-hectare intermodal terminal and empty container site with 14,500 TEU capacity was purchased by Sydney Ports in October 2005 and is currently utilised by container operators. The Cooks River Rail Depot and Empty Container Park (ECP) at St Peters receives empty containers from importers to be cleaned, stored and repaired before being sent for export loading or empty export. With 150,000 TEU throughput, the facility contributes to the port's strategy to manage the growth of containers by rail (Roso 2013). During 2012 work was undertaken to upgrade and expand the Cooks River facility. This has included the extension of existing rail sidings to allow for trains of 600 m in length.

5.6.5 Yennora Intermodal Terminal

Yennora Intermodal Terminal, operated by Qube, is located about 30 km from Port Botany in the Western suburbs between Granville and Liverpool on the main southern railway line. There are two 530 m-long rail sidings, and the total storage capacity for the facility is 5,000 full and 9,000 empty containers (ARTC 2015). The facility is mainly oriented towards the port market, though Aurizon (Australia's largest rail freight operator) also uses Yennora as its Sydney inter-state terminal. Rail services to the port are restricted to outside of the morning and afternoon peak passenger periods. This terminal was originally developed as the central wool warehouse facility for NSW, but has been gradually redeveloped as an integrated multi-user intermodal terminal/ warehouse facility and is owned by Stockland.

5.6.6 Villawood Terminal (Leightonfield)

Villawood (for the purposes of rail operations commonly known as Leightonfield) — operational since 2004 and situated about 26 km from Port Botany — is owned by Toll and is used for steel distribution. It also operated as an intermodal terminal for export containers for a number of years up to 2012/13. In addition to a transshipment function the terminal offers services of storage (open and covered), maintenance of containers, packing/unpacking of containers and freight forwarding. The terminal connects to the Southern Sydney Freight Line (SSFL) and has two main rail sidings, currently 300 m in length (ARTC 2015). Toll and DP World announced a 50/50 joint venture to redevelop Villawood and operate it is an import/export terminal for up to 185,000 TEU commencing in 2017 (ARTC 2015). As of June 2018, investigations into determining a suitable corridor are taking place to extend the Southern Sydney Freight Line from Leightonfield to the planned Outer Sydney Orbital freight rail corridor near Luddenham (www.transport.nsw.gov.au).

5.6.7 Enfield Intermodal Logistics Centre

Sydney Ports Corporation has developed an Intermodal Logistics Center at its 60-hectare marshalling site at Enfield with the purpose to relieve the congested roads by moving more containers by rail to/from Port Botany. Plans for Enfield started with planning approval in 1997 (Roso 2008; Sydney Ports Corporation 2008) and the completion of a statutory environmental assessment (Sinclair Knight Merz 2005). In September 2007, the NSW Minister of Planning issued approval under Part 3A of the Environmental Planning and Assessment Act 1979 for the construction, operations and associated works pertaining to the Enfield Intermodal Logistics Centre (ILC) — located on the site of the former Enfield Railway Marshalling Yards. Following community outrage, Strathfield Council pursued legal advice to challenge the State Government's approval of the development. At the Council meeting on 5 February 2008, after receiving advice from two barristers that it was unlikely to succeed with the legal action, the Council decided to not proceed.

The terminal was planned for 500,000 TEU per year but an independent review recommended that it was too large for the site and suggested a total of 300,000 TEU per annum. The site delivers an integrated logistics centre with an intermodal facility at the core. The development consists of: an intermodal terminal in a 13 hectare-area, where a total of 300,000 TEU can be moved into and out of the site; five warehouses close to 52,500 m² where around one third of the import containers would be unpacked for delivery and one sixth of the containers packed for export; two road access points linking to Roberts Road and the Hume Highway through industrial areas; empty container storage areas; and on-site traffic management and queueing. The terminal has a warehouse for the packing and unpacking of containers and short-term storage for unpacked cargo, as well as an empty container storage facility depot for later packing or transfer by rail. In December 2015, rail-based transport company Aurizon entered into a Heads of Agreement with NSW Ports to take on the role as the Intermodal Terminal Operator for the Enfield ILC.

The existing freight line between Port Botany and Enfield/Chullora is a dedicated freight rail line. It operates as a single line in its own corridor from Botany Yard to Cooks River, east of the Princes Highway. From Cooks River to Marrickville the line is duplicated. From Marrickville to west of Campsie Station, the freight rail line is duplicated and runs in a shared corridor (separate lines) with passenger trains (Bankstown Line), passing through Dulwich Hill, Hurlstone Park, Canterbury and Campsie. It departs from the shared corridor west of the Loch Street Bridge and proceeds to Enfield and Chullora.

5.7 Moorebank Intermodal Terminal — Detailed Case Study of Dry Port

The Australian and NSW Governments identified the Moorebank precinct as a key strategic location to increase intermodal capacity by an additional two million TEU (NSW Government 2013, p. 122). The Moorebank terminal was first proposed in 2003 while the South Sydney Freight Line, completed in 2013, was first conceived in 1985.

The implication is that land-use and transport planning, which have long time horizons, requires Governments to be made aware of the long-term consequences for freight of their land-use planning decisions (ARTC 2015). The precinct is owned by the Australian Government (158 hectares) and by the Sydney Intermodal Terminal Alliance (SIMTA) who own 83 hectares.

The Moorebank Intermodal Terminal (MIT) is a 241-hectare intermodal freight precinct in the south-western Sydney suburb of Moorebank consisting of an import-export (IMEX) rail terminal, inter-state terminal and up to 190 hectares of onsite warehousing. The Australian Government first announced its plan to relocate the School of Military Engineering to enable the construction of the terminal on its freehold land in September 2004. A private-sector joint venture — SIMTA — was formed in 2007 to develop an IMEX-only terminal and onsite warehousing at Moorebank. SIMTA had planned to build this on its freehold land that was purchased from the Australian Government in 2003. The SIMTA site is situated directly across Moorebank Avenue from the School of Military Engineering land. The original sale was on a leaseback arrangement, where the Australian Department of Defence signed a ten-year lease (with two five-year extensions at Defence's sole discretion) for the Defence National Storage and Distribution Centre's (DNSDC) operations to remain on the site.

Following the Australian Government's consideration of various studies that it had commissioned, the project's implementation commenced in April 2012. The Moorebank Intermodal Company (MIC) is a Government Business Enterprise (GBE). It was established in December 2012 and assumed full responsibility from the Department of Finance and Deregulation for the delivery of the project. Development consent was required under both Commonwealth and State legislation: The Commonwealth Environment Protection and Biodiversity Conservation Act 1999; and the NSW Environmental Planning and Assessment Act 1979. Parsons Brinkerhoff (2014) prepared the Moorebank Intermodal Terminal Environmental Impact Statement under NSW State Government regulations that went on public exhibition.

On 3 June 2016, the NSW Planning Assessment Commission approved MIC's Stage 1 "State significant development" Concept Approval for an intermodal terminal on the MIC owned land at Moorebank. To give an idea of the scale of this project, if superimposed over Sydney's CBD it would stretch from Circular Quay (in the north) to Chinatown (in the south), and from Darling Harbour (in the west) to William Street (in the east). During operations, MIC's main role will be to monitor SIMTA's compliance with its open access obligations requiring IMEX and inter-state terminals to be operated on a non-discriminatory basis. Any transport operator providing freight transport services may gain access to the terminal.

Given the Commonwealth of Australia's agenda of improving the nation's economic efficiency of national ports, KPMG were commissioned by the Australian Department of Finance and Deregulation to prepare a Detailed Business Case that contains advice, analysis and recommendations for consideration by the Commonwealth of Australia in its deliberations on a proposed intermodal terminal at Moorebank (KPMG, Deloitte and Parsons Brinkerhoff 2012). A governance framework was selected to enable the Moorebank Intermodal Terminal to be delivered by an entity with 'an appropriate commercial focus while maintaining effective Government oversight'.

A large component of MIC's first year was comprised of setting up its operations: engaging a range of key advisory firms to support a competitive procurement process to find a private sector delivery partner; and undertaking market interactions. Following an expression of interest (EoI) process in early 2014, SIMTA was selected by MIC as the preferred private-sector partner (from a total of five respondents) to be responsible for the delivery of the precinct. The two entities entered into a formal direct negotiation process in May 2014, achieving financial close on 24 January 2017. The project is now in its delivery phase.

During 2017, the National Audit Office of Australia assessed whether the contractual arrangements that were put in place for the delivery of the Moorebank Intermodal Terminal would provide value for money and achieve the Australian Government's policy objectives for the project (ANAO 2017). The report found that value for money progressively eroded during the negotiation of the contractual arrangements that took place over thirty-two months. Negotiating directly with one respondent, rather than the original plan of maintaining competitive tension, gave rise to a number of risks. These risks were identified, and mitigation strategies were formulated but never implemented.

Importantly for logistics operations, the contracts provided no assurance that non-discriminatory open access is likely to be available within all aspects of the intermodal precinct. The contractual framework does not apply to all elements of terminal operations. It only partially applies to the rail shuttle service between Port Botany and MIT and internal transfers within the terminal precinct but does not apply to warehouse operations. Key detailed documents that are required for implementation of effective open access arrangements are under development.

The deal is complicated. The Commonwealth funds about AUD 370 million of the development, and, importantly, the rail connection between the terminal and the Southern Sydney Freight Line (Fullerton 2015). Sydney Intermodal Terminal Alliance (SIMTA) — a consortium of Australia's import/export logistics company Qube Holdings and Australia's largest rail freight operator Aurizon Holdings — delivers most of the capital (approximately AUD 1.5 billion over the first ten years), including the terminal infrastructure and warehousing, and contributes eighty-three hectares of land to the development. Qube's investment is around AUD 250 million over the first five years. Also, Qube will be working with other partners for the development of the warehousing precinct — about an AUD 800 development probably over a five-year horizon from now.

Initially, the 241-hectare site will handle 250,000 import-export (IMEX) containers a year from about 2018/9, and ultimately up to 1.05 million IMEX containers a year, and up to 500,000 inter-state containers a year. There will be up to 850,000 m² of warehouses where containers can be unpacked before delivery to their final destination. Also, there is the possible future relocation of Moorebank Avenue external to the precinct (subject to future planning approval) that will remain open for public use. Substantial biodiversity offsets protected from development, including vegetation on the eastern bank of the Georges River, will be enhanced and preserved to comply with Commonwealth and State environmental planning legislation.

According to ARTC (2015), the following assumptions have been made concerning future IMEX volumes: Port Botany IMEX shuttle services to and from Moorebank are expected initially to have a 250,000 TEU capacity, and ultimately to have a capacity of 1.05 million containers (twenty foot equivalents or TEU's) per year in IMEX freight by 2028. Moorebank Intermodal, servicing the inter-state market, is predicted to start-up in 2020 with steadily increasing volumes and an ultimate capacity of 500,000 inter-state containers per year by 2028.

The project proponents claim ambitious goals: taking 3,000 trucks off the road; removing 40,000 tonnes of carbon a year from the air; and reducing the cost of importing and exporting by 20 to 25% (Fullerton 2015). The New South Wales Government fully recognises the impacts such a terminal will have on the local road network and obtained money from the Federal Government under its Nation Building 2 program to undertake transport modelling and economic analyses to determine the optimal road upgrade package to meet the needs of the Moorebank facility. The impact on road investment, plus other issues, has been the essence of community objections to this proposal, including a gross underestimation of traffic generation (van den Bos n.d.). The implications of this underestimation of traffic are that the externalities associated with the terminals are also underestimated: road traffic accidents; vehicle emissions; and noise pollution. Furthermore, the report argues that the intermodal terminals will attract the co-location of low-density industries and the Liverpool Local Government will find it difficult to meet its employment targets under the State Metropolitan Planning Strategy.

The Moorebank Intermodal Terminal — Traffic and Transport Impact Assessment (prepared by Parsons Brinkerhoff) analysed New South Wales Roads and Maritime Services' crash data for the years 2008–2013 for the section of Moorebank Avenue between the East Hills Railway Line and south of the intersection with the M5, and for the section of the M5 between the Hume Highway and Heathcote Road intersections (Moorebank Intermodal Company 2015, pp. 22–23). The project proponents noted both roads were accident "black spots". The project proponents proposed treatments and their potential individual impact on the type of accidents that occur (Moorebank Intermodal Company 2015, Table 9.39). Further investigations by the NSW Roads and Maritime Services have led to a recommended package of works of about AUD 500 million.

The Liverpool Community Independent Team argued that there are more appropriate, more efficient and more economical solutions for the location of new intermodal terminals. One solution is to move the problem elsewhere — to Eastern Creek. The second solution is to move the problem out of metropolitan Sydney entirely — south to Port Kembla — exploiting a rail corridor between Maldon and Dombarton. While the project has long been on the planning books, it is seen by all governments as uneconomical. The Moorebank Intermodal Terminal is another example of port-generated conflicts — specifically, the lack of the local community's tolerance of governments delivering large infrastructure projects "in their backyards".

5.8 Funding and Financing Port, Terminals and Transport Access

Government-owned ports typically obtain capital and operating costs from government annual budget appropriations. In the case of ports in Sydney (Port Jackson and Port Botany) the New South Wales Government Maritime Services Board was a statutory authority responsible directly to the minister — effectively operating as a "silo" within the governance arrangements of the state. In such arrangements there was little incentive for financial discipline, and, in the absence of economic, social and environmental assessments, it is impossible to estimate the costs of constructing Port Botany that includes its external costs. Nowadays, completely different processes are in place, with the New South Wales Government formulating State strategic and economic plans. Individual infrastructure projects must undergo detailed scrutiny through submission of their strategic and final business cases to Cabinet for whole of government approval (or rejection), before making their way into the capital works program of the respective government line agencies. Sydney Ports Corporation was formed to introduce more commercial practices.

The New South Wales Government aspires to make Port Botany the largest container port in Australia. Recently, Port Botany underwent a major expansion of its container port facilities to cope with the growing volumes of trade — one of the largest port projects ever to be undertaken in Australia in the last thirty years. It entailed the design, construction, procurement, and the eventual awarding to Hutchison Port Holdings (HPH) of the 3rd Stevedore contract (NSW Ports 2015). The Government called for the operation of long-term leases (ninety-nine years) for two of Australia's largest ports. Port Kembla is Australia's largest vehicle import hub and the largest grain-handling terminal in New South Wales and Port Botany is the country's second largest container port. The winning consortium — IFM Investors, AustralianSuper, QSuper and Abu Dhabi Investment Authority — made an upfront payment of AUD 5.07 billion–AUD 4.31 billion for Port Botany and AUD 760 million for Port Kembla (Infrastructure Australia 2014, p. 22). In addition, the consortium pays an annual AUD 5 million to the State Government under the lease agreement.

The construction costs associated with this asset amount to approximately AUD 1.6 billion in 2016 prices as adjusted by the Reserve Bank of Australia inflation calculator. The Foreshore Road in Botany was purpose built for truck access to and from the ports, but its construction costs would require searching records of the former New South Wales Department of Main Roads. The cost of recent upgrades to roads in the vicinity of the port and airport are about AUD 700 million. Of course, it is incorrect to allocate the hinterland road costs exclusively to the port and its movement of freight because of the close location of a major domestic and international airport as well of other road users. The Botany Goods line served the former coal-fired power station at Bunnerong but recent rail upgrades can be costed at AUD 75 million. The biggest unknown in these estimates of capital costs is the intermodal terminals in metropolitan Sydney. This sum must be substantial. The latest terminal under construction at Moorebank is a Public Private Partnership involving some AUD 1.9 billion of Government and private capital.

Table 5.4 presents a partial analysis of the capital costs of Port Botany, some of the distributed dry port capital costs and hinterland transport construction costs only where data are readily available. Further research is needed to account for all of port associated infrastructure in the hinterland and to allocate the proportion attributable to port vehicles on the road. However, the table gives an impression of the relative breakdown of the very long-term capital costs of port development and enabling infrastructure in the hinterland. Clearly, the capital costs in the logistics chain extend well beyond the costs of building a container port, as do the externality costs of the emissions of ships in port (Styhre et al. 2017), container truck emissions, noise and loss of residential amenity.

Table 5.4 Approximate construction costs of Port Botany and enabling
infrastructure (Australian Dollars in 2016 prices)

Infrastructure	Construction Cost (AUD millions)
Port Botany	621
Terminal 3 Container Terminal Dredging	800
Terminal 3 landside Wharf	200*
Enfield Intermodal Terminal and Port Botany yards	483
Cooks River — development application for grain silo	10
Moorebank Inter-Modal Terminal**	1870
Botany Goods Rail Line Phase 3	75
Airport/Port Road Upgrades	700

* Private sector confidential — estimate only

** Private Sector plus Commonwealth Government

(Table by the authors, data from various government websites)

5.9 Conclusions

Issues surrounding suburban intermodal terminals, or dry ports, are a sub-set of the wider economic, social and environmental problems of the interactions of seaports with their hinterland. This is clearly demonstrated through historical analysis of port development in Sydney, as noted by Butlin (1976, p. 8, italics in the original):

> *most of the problems that have arisen with respect to Port Botany derive from the statutory obstacles to the integration of the Port with its hinterland and with the whole of metropolitan land-use planning.*

Historically, ports have been developed with little thought given to their impacts on the hinterland. Stevedores have seen their prime task of the contractual arrangements with shipping companies to load and unload containers in the port terminal (IPART 2008). The problems of not taking a holistic approach to planning ports as part of an urban system are many.

The first issue of relevance to Indonesian ports considering expansion is therefore the role of regulators and the statutory planning processes in place and whether reform is desirable. Port expansion *in situ* can only occur if port activities encroach into surrounding residential, commercial and industrial areas, or if land is reclaimed from the sea. Both options bring into play the regulatory powers of national, state and local governments. At the forefront of any battle to develop port facilities will be the local government in which the port is located. In the case of Port Botany we have shown how local government has imposed land-use zoning policies to facilitate port (and airport) related activities.

The national governments sometimes may add fuel to the fire of such conflicts in port development. On what sounds like an echo from the past, the Australian government recently released a Smart Cities Plan and noted "urban development pressures around airports, seaports and intermodal facilities need to be carefully managed to prevent these important economic hubs and corridors from being constrained and to reduce their impacts on surrounding communities" (Commonwealth of Australia 2016, p. 16). Nevertheless, given the Federal Government's policy of making gateway ports (seaports and airports) the engines of economic productivity, it seems that port-hinterland research funding is essential to support the aspirations of this Smart Cities Plan.

A related issue is the role of governments at the national and state (provincial) levels in port planning, development and operations. When addressing the general logistics or supply-chain management problem, what is the appropriate role of governments and other stakeholders in the planning of seaports and dry ports in any urban system? This is essentially a question of political economy, and our case study of Sydney can only provide some guidance. The means of regulating urban system growth, mechanisms of resolving environmental conflicts and the relative power of political parties and different stakeholders and the community to influence planning and development decisions remain as research topics of relevance today when studying maritime ports. This clearly represents an important topic of investigation for Indonesian ports.

Another issue of relevance to Indonesia is the queueing of trucks on streets surrounding the ports and the general problem of road traffic congestion in the ports' hinterlands. The Sydney case study, with its stevedore vehicle booking system (VBS), indicates the importance of information technology in reducing congestion around ports. The key road access to and from Port Botany is the Foreshore Drive linking the Southern Cross Drive that tunnels under the airport's two parallel runways before joining the M5 toll road to the west of the port, but these are capacity constrained. Under construction as of 2018 is the WestConnex Motorway project linking the M5 and M4 tollroads that will also provide better road access between Port Botany and its metropolitan hinterland. From Marrickville to the wharves at Port Botany is the Botany Goods line that connects to the shared passenger and freight rail network of metropolitan Sydney, including the route to the Enfield inter-modal freight terminals. As of 2018, there is construction work to upgrade this railway. However, the evidence is that governments throughout the world struggle with effective policies to encourage transport companies to ship containers by rail instead of roads.

Finally, a well-functioning network of inland terminals is crucial to achieve the goal of shifting freight from road to rail. In the case of Port Botany, there has been clear cooperation between national and state governments on providing suitable land for the terminals. Port Botany, and its close inland intermodal terminals, is a very distinctive port globally because there are very few other ports with such a well-developed network of close, inland intermodal terminals in their metropolitan hinterlands. The most recent terminal project at Moorebank was delivered through a public-private sector partnership involving a New South Wales State Government Enterprise and SIMTA, but as noted this has not been without controversy. Moorebank intermodal logistics terminal was first conceived in early 2000, demonstrating the problematic aspect of long timeframes for development of significant infrastructure to support the transport of containers to and from ports. For Indonesian researchers, the literature on the success factors of locating dry ports cited in this chapter are worthy of careful study.

Finally, it is worth speculating on the value of research into ports and their hinterlands both for Australian and Indonesian researchers. There is little appetite to fund evidence-based policy analysis in the Australian transport sector. As one anonymous, senior government transport bureaucrat put it: "there are no votes in conducting such studies: Ministers love to cut the ribbon on an infrastructure project and not to worry about on-going maintenance nor potential problems." Nevertheless, given the Federal Government's policy of making gateway ports (seaports and airports) the "engines of economic productivity" it seems that port-hinterland research funding is needed to learn from the outcomes of past policies and to determine those transport policy options that will not burden economic, social and environment costs on future generations. Independent analyses are needed in the era of Public Private Partnerships for inter-modal terminals, as demonstrated by the controversy surrounding Moorebank Intermodal Terminal.

References

Andersson, D and Roso, V 2016. 'Developing dry ports through the use of value-added services', *Commercial Transport*, pp. 191–201, https://doi.org/10.1007/978-3-319-21266-1_12

ARTC, 2015. *2015–2024 Sydney metropolitan freight strategy*, www.artc.com.au/uploads/2015-Sydney-Metro-Strategy-Final.pdf

Awad-Núñez, S, González-Cancelas, N, Soler-Flores, F and Camarero-Orive, A 2015. 'How should the sustainability of the location of dry ports be measured? A proposed methodology using Bayesian networks and multi-criteria decision analysis', *Transport*, 30:3, pp 312–19, https://doi.org/10.3846/16484142.2015.1081618

Bacon, W and Dalley, E 2015. 'New coalition forms against carcinogenic WestConnex', *AltMedia*, www.altmedia.net.au/westconnex-is-filthy-business/104038

Bask, A, Roso, V, Hämäläinen, E and Andersson, D 2014. 'Development of seaport — dry port dyads: Two cases from Northern Europe', *Journal of Transport Geography*, 39, pp. 85–95, https://doi.org/10.1016/j.jtrangeo.2014.06.014

Beavis, P, Black, J, Macgill, I, Woxenius, J and Moore, S 2007. *Distributed function hinterland: Interface design for the coordination of container freight services*, presented at the *11th World Conference on Transport Research Society Conference*, Berkeley, California: University of California Berkeley.

Bergqvist, R, Falkemark, G and Woxenius, J 2010. 'Establishing intermodal terminals', *World Review of Intermodal Transportation Research*, 3:3, pp. 285–302, https://doi.org/10.1504/WRITR.2010.034667

Beresford, A, Pettit, S, Xu, Q and Williams, S 2012. 'A study of dry port development in China', *Maritime Economics and Logistics*, 14:1, pp. 73–98.

Bird, J 1971. *Seaports and Seaport Terminals*, London, UK: Hutchinson.

Black, DA and Black, JA 2009. 'A review of the urban development and transport impacts on public health with particular reference to Australia: Trans-disciplinary research teams and some research gaps', *International Journal of Environmental Research and Public Health*, 6:5, pp. 1557–96, https://doi.org/10.3390/ijerph6051557

Black, J and Lee, JM 2016. *Osaka ports from ancient times to the Meiji Restoration: Institutions and organisations,* paper presented at the 7th IMEHA International Congress 'Old worlds, new worlds? Emerging themes in maritime history', 27 June — 1 July, Murdoch University, Perth, Australia.

Black, J, Roso, V, Marušić, E and Brnjac, N 2018. 'Issues in dry port location and implementation in metropolitan areas: The case of Sydney, Australia', *Transactions on Maritime Science,* 7:1, pp. 41–50, https://doi.org/10.7225/toms. v07.n01.004

Black, J and Styhre, L 2015. *Environmental conflicts in port cities: A case study of Port Jackson and Port Botany in Metropolitan Sydney,* paper presented at the WCTRS Special Interest Group A2 'The port and maritime sector: Key developments and challenges', 11–12 May, Department of Transport and Regional Economics, University of Antwerp, Antwerp, Belgium.

Black, J and Styhre, L 2016. *The Sydney Botany Bay Project legacy: Identification and resolution of port-based conflicts,* paper presented at the 7th International Congress of Maritime History, 27 June to 1 July, Murdoch University, Perth, Australia.

Black, J, Kyu, T, Roso, V and Tara, K 2013. *Critical evaluation of Mandalay dry port,* paper presented at the Proceedings 5th International Conference on Logistics and Transport, Sustainable Supply Chain Management in Asia Pacific, Doshisha University, Kyoto, Japan, www.researchgate.net/ publication/278678017

Black, J, Tara, K, Bista, S, Jatmika, H, and Lea, J 2012. *Transport infrastructure investment and sustainable employment in special economic zones — Evidence based policy analysis for Smart Cities,* keynote at the ADG Smart City Conference, 19–21 October, Guangzhou, Hong Kong, China.

Brotherson, WH 1975. 'Port operations in Australia', *Australian Transport,* 17:9, pp. 33–35.

Butlin, NG (ed.) 1976. *The Impact of Port Botany,* Canberra, Australia: Australian National University Press.

Commonwealth of Australia 2016. *Smart Cities Plan,* Canberra, Australia: Australian Government, Department of Prime Minister and Cabinet.

Cullinane, K and Wilmsmeier, G 2011. 'The contribution of the dry port concept to the extension of port life cycles', in *Handbook of terminal planning, operations research computer science interfaces series,* JW Böse (ed.), 49, Heidelberg, Germany: Springer, pp. 359–80.

De Langen, PW and Chouly, A 2004. 'Hinterland access regimes in seaports', *European Journal of Transport and Infrastructure Research,* 4:4, pp. 361–80.

Edgerton, D, James, G and Jordan, F 1979. *Port container movements in Sydney,* paper presented at the 5th Australian Transport Research Forum, Sydney, Australia, pp. 63–84.

FitzSimons, P 2019. *James Cook: The Story Behind the Man who Mapped the World*, Australia, Hachette Press.

Flämig, H and Hesse, M 2011. 'Placing dry ports: Port regionalization as a planning challenge — The case of Hamburg, Germany, and the Süderelbe', *Research in Transportation Economics*, 33:1, pp. 42–50, https://doi.org/10.1016/j.retrec.2011.08.005

Fullerton, T 2015. 'Qube's Moorebank Intermodal Hub a major infrastructure boost', *ABC News*, www.abc.net.au/news/2015-06-12/qube-moorebank-intermodal-hub-infrastructure/6541514

Golicic, SL and Davis, DF 2012. 'Implementing mixed methods research in supply chain management', *International Journal of Physical Distribution and Logistics Management*, 42:8–9, pp. 726–41, https://doi.org/10.1108/09600031211269721

Hanaoka, S and Regmi, M B 2011. 'Promoting intermodal freight transport through the development of dry ports in Asia: An environmental perspective', *IATSS Research*, 35:1, pp. 16–23, https://doi.org/10.1016/j.iatssr.2011.06.001

Heaver, T, Meersman, H and Van De Voorde, E 2001. 'Co-operation and competition in international container transport: Strategies for ports', *Maritime Policy and Management*, 28:3, pp. 293–306, https://doi.org/10.1080/03088830110055693

Henttu, V and Hilmola, O-P 2011. 'Financial and environmental impacts of hypothetical Finnish dry port structure', *Research in Transportation Economics*, 33:1, pp. 35–41, https://doi.org/10.1016/j.retrec.2011.08.004

Independent Pricing and Regulatory Tribunal 2008. *Reforming Port Botany's links with inland transport: Review of the interface between the land transport industries and the Stevedores at Port Botany, other industries — Final report*, New South Wales, Sydney, www.ipart.nsw.gov.au/files/sharedassets/website/trimholdingbay/final_report_-_reforming_port_botanys_links_with_inland_transport_-_march_2008.pdf

Infrastructure Australia 2014. *Infrastructure Financing*, Canberra, Australia: Infrastructure Australia.

Infrastructure Australia 2018. *Infrastructure priority list: Australian infrastructure plan — project initiatives and summaries March 2018*, Canberra, Australia: Australian Government.

Infrastructure Partnerships Australia 2007. *Integrated infrastructure planning — A new way forward, report to infrastructure partnership Australia — A case study of Sydney airport and Port Botany precinct*, Sydney, Australia: Strategic International Advisory Limited (SIAL).

Jatminka, HE 2001. *Economic, social and spatial impacts of major commercial airports and their management: A case study of Sydney (Kingsford Smith) airport*, unpublished PhD Thesis, Sydney, Australia: School of Civil and Environmental Engineering, The University of New South Wales.

Korovyakovsky, E and Panova, Y 2011. 'Dynamics of Russian dry ports', *Research in Transportation Economics,* 33:1, pp. 25–34, https://doi.org/10.1016/j. retrec.2011.08.008

KPMG, Deloitte and Parsons Brinkerhoff 2012. Advisory: *Department of Finance and Deregulation — Moorebank intermodal terminal project, detailed business case,* Sydney, Australia: Deloitte and Parsons Brinkerhoff.

Liverpool City Council 2014. *Moorebank intermodal terminal project*: *Peer review of the environmental impact statement, project number*: *112083-03/Report 001, Ver. 4,* Sydney, Australia: Cardo for Liverpool City Council.

Lättilä, L, Henttu, V and Hilmola, O-P 2013. 'Hinterland operations of sea ports do matter: Dry port usage effects on transportation costs and CO2 emissions', *Transportation Research Part E: Logistics and Transportation Review,* 55, pp. 23–42.

Manguin, P-Y 2017. *Ships and shipping in Southeast Asia, Subject*: *Economic/Business, science and technology, Southeast Asia,* Oxford, UK: Oxford University Press, https://doi.org/10.1093/acrefore/9780190277727.013.30

Monios, J, 2011. 'The role of inland terminal development in the hinterland access strategies of Spanish Ports', *Research in Transportation Economics,* 33:1, pp. 59–66, https://doi.org/10.1016/j.retrec.2011.08.007

Moorebank Intermodal Company 2016. *Annual report 2016,* Moorebank Intermodal Company, Sydney, Australia, www.micl.com.au/aboutus-annualreports/

Ng, AKY and Gujar, GC 2009. 'Government policies, efficiency and competitiveness: The case of dry ports in India', *Transport Policy,* 16:5, pp. 232–39, https://doi.org/10.1016/j.tranpol.2009.08.001

Ng, AKY and Pallis, AA 2010. 'Port governance reforms in diversified institutional frameworks: Generic solutions, implementation asymmetries', *Environment and Planning A,* 42:9, pp. 2147–67, https://doi.org/10.1068/a42514

Notteboom, TE and Rodrigue, J-P 2010. 'Inland terminals within North American and European supply chains', *UNESCAP Transport and Communications Bulletin for Asia and the Pacific,* 78, pp. 1–57.

NSW Freight 2013. *Port Botany Landside Improvement Strategy*: *PBLIS — Three years on.*

NSW Government 1980a. *Commission of inquiry into the Kyeemagh-Chullora road (the Kirby Report) Volume I*: *Containers.*

NSW Government 1980b. *Report of the Royal Commission of enquiry into the New South Wales road freight industry (the McDonald Report).*

NSW Government 2011. *Port Botany and Sydney airport transport improvement program submission to infrastructure Australia.*

NSW Government 2013. *NSW freight and ports strategy,* https://www.transport. nsw.gov.au/sites/default/files/media/documents/2017/NSW_Freight_and_ Ports_Strategy-Full_Strategy-High_Resolution_0.pdf

NSW Parliamentary Librarian 1976. *Report of the Botany Bay Port and environment inquiry (the Simblist Report)*, NSW Parliamentary Papers 1976 (Second Session), no. 103, Sydney, Australia: Government Printer.

NSW Ports 2015. *Port Botany expansion*, www.nswportsbotany.com.au/projects-and-planning/port-botany-expansion/

Paixão, AC and Marlow, PB 2003. 'Fourth generation ports — A question of agility?' *International Journal of Physical Distribution and Logistics Management*, 3:4, pp. 355–76, https://doi.org/10.1108/09600030310478810

Panova, Y and Hilmola, O-P 2015. 'Justification and valuation of dry port investments in Russia', *Research in Transportation Economics*, 51:C, pp. 61–70, https://doi.org/10.1016/j.retrec.2015.07.008

Parola, F and Sciomachen, A 2005. 'Intermodal container flows in a port system network: Analysis of possible growths via simulation models', *International Journal of Production Economics*, 97:1, pp. 75–88, https://doi.org/10.1016/j.ijpe.2004.06.051

Parsons Brinkerhoff 2014. *Moorebank intermodal terminal project — Environmental impact statement Parsons Brinkerhoff for Sydney intermodal terminal alliance*.

Pernice, R, n.d. 'The issue of Tokyo Bay's reclaimed lands as the origin of urban utopias in modern Japanese architecture', *Journal of Architecture and Planning, Architectural Institute of Japan*, 613, pp. 259–66

Rimmer, PJ and Black, JA 1982. 'Land use — transport changes and global restructuring in Sydney since the 1970's: The container issue', in *Why Cities Change: Urban Development and Economic Change in Sydney*, RV Cardew, JV Langdale and D. Rich (eds.), Sydney, Australia: Allen and Unwin, pp. 223–45.

Rimmer, PJ and Tsipouras, A 1977. *Ports and urban systems: Framework and research needs in resolution of port-generated conflicts*, paper presented at the 3rd Australian Transport Research Forum, Melbourne, Australia, pp. 1–17.

Rodrigue, J-P, Debrie, J, Fremont, A and Gouvernal, E 2010. 'Functions and actors of inland ports: European and North American dynamics', *Journal of Transport Geography*, 18:4, pp. 519–29, https://doi.org/10.1016/j.jtrangeo.2010.03.008

Rodrigue, JP and Notteboom, T 2012. 'Dry ports in European and North American intermodal rail systems: Two of a kind?' *Research in Transportation Business and Management*, 5:4, pp. 4–15, https://doi.org/10.1016/j.rtbm.2012.10.003

Roso, V 2008. 'Factors influencing implementation of a dry port', *International Journal of Physical Distribution and Logistics Management*, 38:10, pp. 782–98, https://doi.org/10.1108/09600030810926493

Roso, V 2013. 'Sustainable intermodal transport via dry ports — Importance of directional development', *World Review of Intermodal Transportation Research*, 4:2–3, pp. 140–56, https://doi.org/10.1504/WRITR.2013.058976

Roso, V and Rosa, A 2012. 'The dry ports in concept and practice', in Song Dong-Wook and P. M. Panayides (eds.) *Maritime Logistics: A Complete Guide to Effective Shipping and Port Management*, London: Kogan Page, pp. 179–94.

Roso, V, Woxenius, J and Lumsden, K 2009. 'The dry port concept: Connecting container seaports with the hinterland', *Journal of Transport Geography*, 17:5, pp. 338–45, https://doi.org/10.1016/j.jtrangeo.2008.10.008

Roso, V, Russell, D, Ruamsook, K and Stefansson, G 2015. 'Inland port services for seaports' competitive advantage', *World Review of Intermodal Transportation Research*, 5:3, pp. 263–80, https://doi.org/10.1080/03088839.2018.1505054

Saulwick, J, Hatch, P and Visentin, L 2018. 'Transurban pays $9.3b for control of WestConnex', *The Sydney Morning Herald- News*.

SGS Economics and Planning 2009. *Randwick Economic Development Strategy*.

Sinclair Knight Merz 2005. *Intermodal Logistics Centre at Enfield Environmental Assessment*.

Styhre, L, Winnes, H, Black, J, Lee, JM and Le-Griffin, H 2017. 'Greenhouse gas emissions from ships in ports – Case studies in four continents', *Transportation Research D: Transport and Environment*, 54, pp. 212–24, https://doi.org/10.1016/j.trd.2017.04.033

Sydney Ports Corporation 2008. *Port Freight Logistics Plan: A Framework to improve road and rail performance at Port Botany*.

Transport for New South Wales 2016. *NSW ports record positive growth in freight on rail*.

Van Den Bos, N, n.d. *Moorebank intermodals: Key assumptions require deeper scrutiny*, Wetherill Park, NSW: Bright Print Group and Liverpool Community Independents Team.

Van Der Horst, MR and De Langen, PW 2008. 'Coordination in hinterland transport chains: A major challenge for the seaport community', *Maritime Economics and Logistics*, 10:1–2, pp. 108–29, https://doi.org/10.1057/palgrave.mel.9100194

Veenstra, A, Zuidwijk, R and Van Asperen, E 2012. 'The extended gate concept for container terminals: Expanding the notion of dry ports', *Maritime Economics and Logistics*, 14: 1, pp. 14–32, https://doi.org/10.1057/mel.2011.15

Wang, C, Chen, Q and Huang, R 2017. 'Locating dry ports on a network: A case study on Tianjin Port', *Maritime Policy and Management*, 45:1, pp. 1–18, https://doi.org/10.1080/03088839.2017.1330558

Wilmsmeier, G, Monios, J and Lambert, B 2011. 'The directional development of intermodal freight corridors in relation to inland terminals', *Journal of Transport Geography*, 19:6, pp. 1379–86, https://doi.org/10.1016/j.jtrangeo.2011.07.010

Yoshizawa, J 2012. *JR Freight Company's quest for intermodal freight transport*, ICHCA'S Cargo World 2011/2012.

6. Comparative Efficiency Analysis of Australian and Indonesian Ports

F. K. P. Hui,[1] C. F. Duffield,[2] A. Chin,[3] and H. Huang[4]

6.0 Introduction

Logistics is a critical element of a country's trading ability and is central to the economic growth of the country, since it enables effective connection of trade through both domestic and international logistics networks. Due to the close geographic proximity of Australia and Indonesia, trade plays an important role in each country's economy (DFAT 2019). In 2016, Australia came in 8th and 11th place as the principal import source and export destination for Indonesia respectively. Given the pivotal role of trading between the two countries, it is important to establish and analyse the efficiency of the major ports of the two countries. For this project, the Port of Melbourne was chosen as the focus for analysis as it is the largest container port in Australia. The Port of Surabaya was

---

1   Senior lecturer and Academic Specialist, Dept. of Infrastructure Engineering, The University of Melbourne.
2   Professor of Engineering Management, Deputy Head of Department (Academic), Dept. of Infrastructure Engineering, The University of Melbourne.
3   Master of Engineering graduate, Dept. of Infrastructure Engineering, The University of Melbourne.
4   Master of Engineering graduate, Dept. of Infrastructure Engineering, The University of Melbourne.

https://doi.org/10.11647/OBP.0189.06

chosen as the comparison study port in Indonesia. The major ports in Jakarta (Port of Tanjung Priok), Sydney (Botany Bay) and Perth were also used in the comparative analysis.

Port performance is extremely important for supporting the economy of the hinterland (Hung, Lu and Wang 2010; Lam and Yap 2016), which plays an important role in the logistics supply chain. The efficiency of the ports needs to be analysed and studied in order to improve the competitiveness of the port and terminal within the country and the region.

The Logistics Performance Index (LPI) captures the assessment of the entire logistic performance through a series of inputs and outcomes of the logistics supply chain and environment (Ojala and Celebi 2015). These indicators help regulators define the areas for policy regulations as well as inputs for operational assessment, such as customs, infrastructure, services quality and other service delivery performance that deals with cost, time and reliability outcomes.

Ports are an essential part of the logistic supply chain. In a similar manner, port efficiency can be measured through inputs and outputs, generally with a concept similar to the logistics performance index. Given the multiplicity of ports and types of cargoes handled, the choice of indicators for analyzing inputs and outputs, as well as their units of measurement, need to be carefully considered. The primary measures of the operational performance of ports are ship turnaround time; and crane handling rate in the port (Chung 1993). These measures are dependent on the port's infrastructure, available resources, types of cargoes (bulk, container TEU) and logistical interfaces. Asset and financial performance are important inputs and outputs to measure the port efficiency as they reflect the berth throughput, berth utilisation rate, and rate of return and turnover. Hence these variables were used in the efficiency analysis in this research. Due to the different ownership status of different ports and terminals, many past studies such as Chen, Pateman and Sakalayen (2017), Tongzon and Heng (2005) and Yuen, Zhang and Cheung (2013) have provided different views on how ownership structure can influence their efficiency and competitiveness. Therefore, part of this study also discusses how ownership structure might affect the efficiency of Australian and Indonesian container terminals.

The rest of this chapter provides a comparative analysis of the efficiency of Australian and Indonesian ports and terminals. The study also includes comparison with the Port of Shanghai, which is the largest container port in the world.

6.1 Literature Review

6.1.1 Logistics and Port Efficiency

Based on a World Bank (2016) report on port efficiency, Germany is ranked first on overall efficiency in the world and Singapore is ranked first in the Asian region, in terms of overall efficiency (LPI indicator) (see Fig. 6.1).

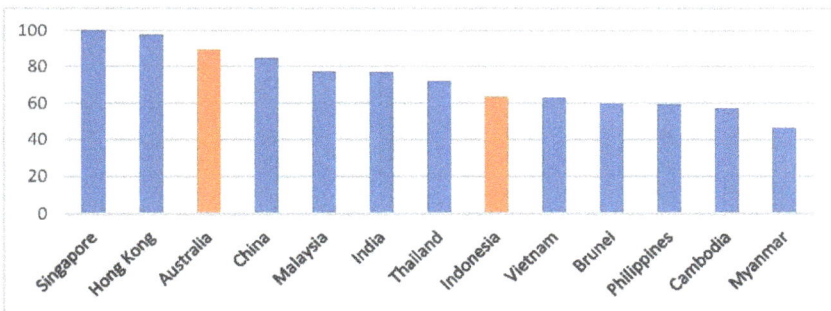

Fig. 6.1 Overall efficiency of ports *in Asian region* (*incl. Australia*) on country basis
(Figure by the authors based on World Bank 2016 data)

In the same report, the port infrastructure index showed that Australia and Indonesia are rated at 86% and 61% respectively, significantly behind Singapore the top ranked in the Asia region (see Fig. 6.2).

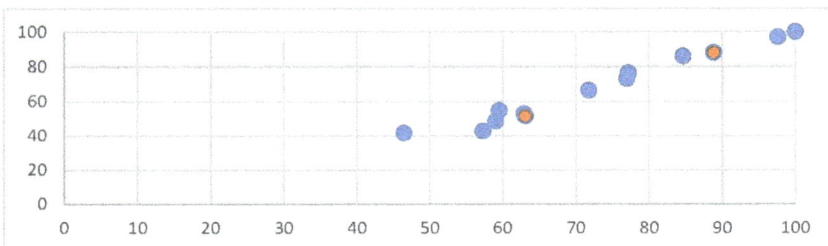

Fig. 6.2 Relationship between infrastructure and overall efficiency on country basis (Figure by the authors based on World Bank 2016 data)

It is interesting to note that Data envelopment analysis (DEA) was used to compare the overall port efficiencies over the provision of infrastructure. There appears to be a linear correlation between the provision of infrastructure and the port efficiency index (see Fig. 6.2). Cullinane et al. (2006) also observed that infrastructure investments and provisions have an influence in port operational efficiencies. It is clear that both Australia and Indonesia have room for improvement in relation to worldwide best practices.

6.1.2 Indonesia

The major international ports in Indonesia are located at Tanjung Priok, Jakarta and Tanjung Perak, Surabaya. These ports are close in distance to Australia and are central to Indonesia's logistics system, providing a strategic gateway for trade to the hinterland in Indonesia. They also provide gateways for domestic trade connections to neighbouring islands and provinces. This is an important role considering that these are critical infrastructure for a country with a large population of 255.5 million (DFAT 2014). Inter-island shipping alone accounts for more than 60% of the nation's sea cargo activities (World Bank Group 2013).

6.1.2.1 Port of Surabaya

The Port of Tanjung Perak is a major transportation hub in East Java and it serves as a gateway to the collection and distribution of goods around the country. Tanjung Perak contributes significantly to the economic development in the whole of Eastern Indonesia (Logistics Capacity Assessment 2017). It currently has an annual container throughput of 3.1 million TEU. Terminal Petikemas Surabaya (TPS) and Terminal Teluk Lamong (TTL) are two of the main terminals that handle containers and bulk in the port. TPS is 51% owned by the Government State Owned Enterprise Pelindo III and 49% by DP World, a large port operator based in the Middle-East.

Recent research by Seo et al. (2012), using DEA analysis, indicated that Surabaya has a relatively low efficiency rating when compared with other ASEAN ports. However, other studies that compared terminal level efficiency, found TPS to be a relatively efficient terminal in Indonesia, in terms of container throughput and utilisation (Andenoworih 2010; Syafaaruddin 2015). TPS is well equipped with modern facilities as well as being well-connected to industrial parks by rail and roads. Syafaaruddin (2015) used DEA analysis to show that TPS has a high ratio of capacity utilisation based on technical inputs.

Terminal Teluk Lamong (TTL) opened in 2015. It is owned by Pelindo III, a State Owned Enterprise and the first green port in Indonesia (Terminal Teluk Lamong 2015). It has world-leading infrastructure facilities and is also the first in Indonesia to implement "semi-automated equipment in yard services, automation gate-system and online transaction" (Terminal Teluk Lamong 2015). Recent studies by Rahmanto (2016) found that the Teluk Lamong Terminal is still a congested terminal with low port capacity issues. In recent years it has been considered to be one of the low performing ports of Surabaya due to its poor road infrastructure around the terminal. The principal difference between TPS and TTL is that TPS has private sector involvement (49% owned by DP World). It would be interesting to see whether private sector involvement plays a role in port efficiency (between TPS and TTL), and whether high tech, advanced, green automotive infrastructures can improve port efficiencies.

6.1.2.2 Port of Jakarta

The Port of Tanjung Priok (PTP) is the busiest port in Indonesia and is managed by PT Pelabuhan Indonesia Pelindo II, one of the four state-owned corporations that manage ports in Indonesia (IPC 2017). PTP is also home to the Jakarta International Container Terminal (JICT), a container terminal that is majority owned by Pelindo II under government control (Koperasi Pegawai Maritim) at 51%, with the remaining 49% under Hutchison Port Holdings.

Andenoworih (2010) and Syafaaruddin (2015) both used DEA analysis and reported consistent results showing that the Port of Tanjung Priok and JICT have relatively good efficiency scores, ranking highly against other smaller ports. It was noted that that Port of Tanjung Priok and JICT are situated within the high regional economic activity areas of Indonesia. However, both studies noted that there are still bottleneck issues with congestion and low port capacity issues. On the other hand, Afriansyah et al. (2017) explained that the Port of Tanjung Priok has both current internal and external issues associated with the port, one being that operational efficiency of the port is low and the other being that the bad integration of the information system causes long dwelling time. Tanjung Priok has a dwelling time of 4.58 days, which was attributed to the less than ideal information management system. Hill (2014) found that Tanjung Priok is the only port in ASEAN having not provided importers with a priority lane. Overall operational efficiency is low, with slow customs handling causing congestion issues, consistent with the findings of Afriansyah et al. (2017). This shows dwell time is an important input that has been used in past analysis and is a useful parameter in our study.

6.1.3 Australia

6.1.3.1 *Port of Melbourne*

The Port of Melbourne (POM) is the largest and busiest container and multi cargo port in Australia, with an annual container throughput of 2.64 million TEU (PR Newswire 2017). According to the Department of Foreign Affairs and Trade (2017), in the year 2014, Australia's top exports are iron ore, coal, gas, wheat (bulk), while top imports are crude petroleum, motor vehicles (roll on-roll off).

DP World and Patrick Terminals serve as stevedores for West and East Swanson Dock respectively. In 2016, it was announced that the Lonsdale Consortium had acquired the right to operate the Port of Melbourne for the next fifty years. The government believed that by doing this, they could simultaneously allow private sector involvement in the port and gain access to funds for the government budget, in the process receiving AUD 9.7 billion from leasing the commercial and management rights of the port.

Ghadehi, Cahoon and Nguyen (2016) highlighted that the Port of Melbourne lacks an intermodal rail that may have allowed loading and unloading to occur outside the dock. This view is shared by Lubulwa, Malarz and Wang (2011), who reported that container haulage mode from terminals are 95% trucks and 5% rail, well below the 30% target for rail in statistics obtained from 2010. The poor development of terminal rail infrastructure was reported to have caused inefficiency and congestion problems within the Port of Melbourne.

6.1.3.2 Port of Botany, Sydney

The Port of Botany in Sydney is managed by the New South Wales Ports Consortium. It holds a ninety-nine-year lease to the state-owned assets of the port. It is the second major container port in Australia, ranking after Melbourne, with an annual container throughput of 2.28 million TEU and 4.7 million tonnes of bulk handled at the port. The Botany Port has three private stevedores that co-manage container terminal berths: Patricks, DP World and Hutchinsons, Port of Botany, Sydney, was reported to be and deemed efficient using the variable return DEA model, but inefficient under the constant return to scale assumption (according to analysis from Tongzon (2001)). Similar to Fremantle Port (see below), it was suggested that the port undertake structural and technical reform to raise the efficiency level. To further add to the scope of the project, we included Port Botany and its container terminals for a comparative analysis against Indonesian ports using DEA techniques.

6.1.3.3 Port of Fremantle

Fremantle Port (Harbour) is the largest general cargo port of Western Australia and fourth largest container port of the country (Fremantle Ports 2017). It is strategically managed by Fremantle Ports, a Western Australia Government trading enterprise. Port of Fremantle is an important gateway from the western part of the country to the world, with annual container TEU's of 0.72 million handled (Maritime Report 2016). Compared to the other international ports in this efficiency analysis, it is slightly smaller in scale in terms of land area as well as annual container throughput handled.

Cheon, Dowall and Song (2010) highlight that Port of Fremantle is relatively inefficient when compared to other larger scale international ports. It was found that despite government restructuring of port ownership, efficiency was still not improved, given that ports of this size and scale should really focus on large scale port technical improvement rather than terminals structure that can improve their short-term scale efficiency. Another study by Tongzon (2001) stated that the port has a major slack in terminal area usage and labour input. The two studies strengthened the case that Fremantle Port may need strong and effective government reform to improve the technical areas of the port in order to achieve higher levels of trade volumes and efficiency.

6.1.4 China
2.1.4.1 Port of Shanghai

The Port of Shanghai is a major international port in China and has the highest container throughput in the world, with 36.5 million TEU annually (World Shipping Council 2017). Shanghai International Port (Group) Company Limited (SIPG) is the sole operator of the public terminals of the port. Wu and Goh (2010) and Yuen, Zhang and Cheung (2013) both stated that it is a relatively efficient port in terms of ownership structure, hinterland size and container terminal efficiency performance. Their studies used DEA (both CCR and BCC models) to reduce any scale differences in the efficiencies, and the results obtained were consistent. Wu and Goh (2010) used indicators of supply chain factors as inputs to the DEA analysis. These include: customs clearance, review procedures, and import and export lead time. Privatisation of the port was also found to be beneficial and had some positive influences on port efficiency (Yuen, Zhang and Cheung 2013). In this project, Shanghai port is used as a benchmark to provide an additional reference point to the comparisons of Indonesian and Australian ports.

6.1.5 Data Envelopment Analysis (DEA)

Data envelopment analysis (DEA) is a common tool used to measure efficiency based on the inputs and outputs variable of processes in port operations. DEA has recently been applied by several researchers to investigate the efficiency and productivity of port logistics operations. However, most of the inputs and outputs from past studies are directly related to the physical infrastructure of the port, such as cranes, number of berths, berth length, quay length, yard area etc. and with output of container throughput (TEU) (Almawsheki and Shah 2014). Kevin et al. (2004) analysed the application of DEA to container port production efficiency. Ada and Lee (2007), So et al. (2007), Salem et al. (2008) and Van Dyck (2015) have all conducted DEA efficiency analysis on Malaysia, Northeast Asia, Middle Eastern and West African seaports respectively. Since then, a significant number of port efficiency analyses have been completed using DEA. It is an appropriate tool for investigating the relative efficiency of selected ports in Australia and Indonesia. In this way, their efficiency as major trading partners can be compared and recommendations for improvement provided.

6.1.6 Private Sector Involvement

It is shown that port ownership structures have an influence on efficiency, and privatisation may not necessarily be beneficial to the port efficiency (Cullinane, Ji and Wang 2005; Chen, Pateman and Sakalayen 2017). Joint venture arrangements of port organisations and public/private partnership have been critiqued over the years. Tongzon and Heng (2005), Yuen, Zhang and Cheung (2013), Panayides et al. (2015) and Wanke and Barros (2015) did not fully reject the view that privatisation has no relationship to port efficiency. They concluded that it may bring some benefits to the management and operational activities of the ports. However, the government at the same time needs public participation in their reformed policies in order to fully maximise the potential of privatisation of ports.

6.1.7 Current Knowledge Gap

From the above literature review, it is apparent that previous studies focused largely on port level efficiency as a whole. Furthermore, most of this research was conducted more than five years ago. There is thus a gap in the understanding of efficiency at port terminal level. This study offers more insights for owners, port operators, stakeholders and future researchers on port operations and improvement opportunities. This study aims to do this by measuring and comparing efficiencies at port and terminal levels for the Ports of Melbourne, Fremantle, Botany, Surabaya, Jakarta, Shanghai and their container terminals. This chapter further investigates the effects of privatisation on efficiency of these ports and terminals. Due to the close proximity of Indonesia and Australia and the important trade relationship, this study provides valuable insights into performance of the major ports in Indonesia and Australia.

6.2 Methodology

6.2.1 Data Envelopment Analysis (DEA)

The Data Envelopment Analysis model was used to quantify and measure the efficiency of ports, focusing on port and container cargoes. DEA models allow for multiple inputs and multiple outputs without strong a-priori assumptions regarding production technology or error structure. There are two basic DEA models generally used in the applications. The first assumes constant returns to scale (CRS) and is named the DEA-CCR model after its authors Charnes, Cooper and Rhodes (1978). The second assumes variable returns to scale (VRS) and is called the DEA-BCC model, named after its authors Banker, Charnes and Cooper (1984). The efficacy of a Decision Making Unit (DMU) can be measure by weighted input variables.

6.2.2 Input and Output Variables

As outlined implicitly by Charnes et al. (1978), DEA models assume that factor inputs and factor outputs are discretionary. They are controllable and can be set up by the decision-maker. Based on earlier research, the input and output variables used in the port efficiency analysis are summarised in Table 6.1. The analysis presented in this chapter uses the latest available data sets from ports from 2015 annual reports and official government data.

6.2.2.1 Crane Rate

Crane rate is computed as the total number of containers handled divided by the total elapsed crane time. It is interpreted as a proxy measure for the productivity of capital at a container terminal.

6.2.2.2 Ship Rate

Ship rate is the average number of containers moved on or off a ship in an hour.

Table 6.1 Input and output variables used in the port DEA analysis.

Variable		Reference
Input	Land size	Kevin et al. (2004),
	Length of berths	Ada and Lee (2007)
	Number of berths	So et al. (2007)
	Number of cranes	Salem et al. (2008)
	Operating expense	
	Net assets	Cullinane and Wang (2010)
	Number of employees	Van Dyck (2015)
Output	Container throughput	
	Bulk throughput	
	Crane rate	
	Ship rate	

(Table by authors: based on data sourced from: Kevin et al. (2004), Ada and Lee, So et al. (2007), Salem et al. (2008), Cullinane and Wang (2010), Van Dyck (2015))

6.2.3 Mathematical Formulation of DEA

Let $y_k = \{y_{1k}, y_{2k}, ..., y_{sk}\}$ and $x_k = \{x_{1k}, x_{2k}, ..., x_{Mk}\}$ be the vectors of outputs and inputs for *DMU* k (k = 1, 2,.., n), where s and m are the number of outputs and inputs respectively. Outputs and inputs are converted into weighted virtual entities by the values of the production factors (u_r and v_i).

For DMU$_k$, the virtual output is calculated as in equation (1) and the virtual input is calculated as in equation (2). The efficiency is calculated as in equation (3).

$$X_k = u_1 x_{1,k} + u_2 x_{2,k} + ... + u_m x_{m,k} \tag{1}$$

$$Y_k = v_1 y_{1,k} + v_2 y_{2,k} + ... + v_s y_{s,k} \tag{2}$$

$$\text{Max } \theta_k = \frac{u_1 y_{1,k} + u_2 y_{2,k} + ... + u_m y_{m,k}}{u_1 x_{1,k} + u_2 x_{2,k} + ... + u_m x_{m,k}} = \frac{Y_k}{X_k} \tag{3}$$

Subject to

$$\text{DMU}_j = \frac{u_1 y_{1,j} + u_2 y_{2,j} + \dots + u_m y_{m,j}}{u_1 x_{1,j} + u_2 x_{2,j} + \dots + u_m x_{m,j}} = \frac{Y_j}{X_j} \leq 1 \tag{4}$$

$$u_1, u_2, \dots, u_m \geq 1 \tag{5}$$

$$v_1, v_2, \dots, v_m \geq 1 \tag{6}$$

Where, j is the number of DMU being evaluated in DEA. k is a generic DMU and θ_k its efficiency. Solving this fractional problem for each *DMU*, the efficiency scores $0 < \theta_k < 1$, ($k = 1, 2, \dots, n$). The DMUs with $\theta_k = 1$ are considered as efficient, and the ones with $\theta_k < 1$ are inefficient.

The efficiency score θ_k, obtained from the CCR model, represents the overall efficiency of DMU k. The most efficient selected ports can be set to the maximum efficiency DMU ($\theta_k = 1$)

$$\sum_{j=1}^{n} \lambda_j x_{ij} \leq \theta_k x_{i0}, \qquad\qquad i = 1, 2, \dots, m \tag{8}$$

$$\sum_{j=1}^{n} \lambda_j y_{rj} \leq \theta_k x_{i0}, \qquad\qquad r = 1, 2, \dots, s \tag{9}$$

$$\sum_{j=1}^{n} \lambda_j = 1, \qquad\qquad \lambda_j \geq 0 \tag{10}$$

6.2.4 Returns to Scale Structure

A DEA model can be either a Constant Returns to Scale structure (CRS) also known as DEA-CCR model, or a Variable Returns to Scale (VRS) known as DEA-BCC model, depicted in Fig. 6.3. In the case of a CRS, it is assumed that an increase in the inputs consumed would lead to a proportional increase in the outputs produced. In the VRS model, the outputs produced do not vary proportionately with the increase in inputs. They may increase; remain constant; or decrease with an increase in the inputs. The CRS version is more restrictive than the VRS, and usually yields a fewer number of efficient units. This also results in lower efficiency scores among all DMUs. The CRS is considered a special case of the VRS model.

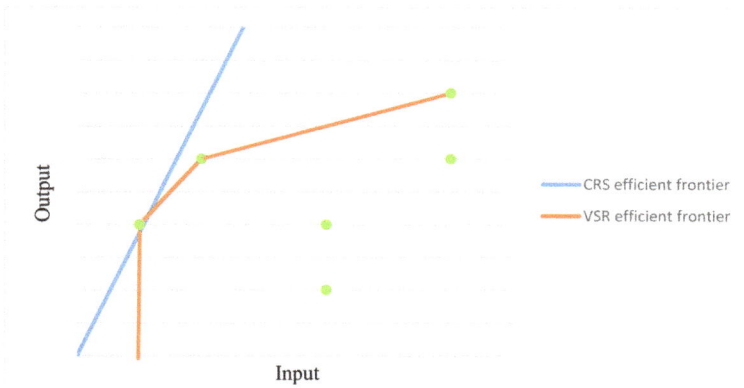

Fig. 6.3 Computing efficiency frontier in VRS and CRS model
(Figure by the authors)

6.2.5 Scale Efficiency

The scale efficiency of each DMU has been estimated using the efficiency scores obtained under the CCR and BCC models. In fact, the efficiency observed under the CRS model is the overall measure of technical and scale efficiency whilst the one deriving from the VRS model is pure technical efficiency. The scale efficiency can be used to indicate the efficiency of the DMU.

$$\text{Scale Efficiency} = \frac{\text{CCR efficiency score}}{\text{BCC efficiency score}} \qquad (11)$$

6.3 Results and Findings

6.3.1 Data Analysis

6.3.1.1 Port

To streamline the DEA analysis, the input data is divided into two groups: functional and operational. The functional inputs consist of land size, length of berths, number of berths and number of cranes — effectively describing the existing facilities and infrastructure of the port. These parameters indicate the physical hardware of the port and the ability of the port to handle the throughput objectively. In contrast, the operational inputs consist of operating expense, net assets and number of employees — in other words, the financial assets and human labour have been used as inputs in the ports. These parameters indicate the software of the ports and how much recourse has been used to operate the ports. The outputs used in DEA are the same for both functional and operational inputs: container throughput and bulk throughput.

The sample ports for DEA are shown in Table 6.2 while the characteristics of the variables used to estimate the relative efficiency of the sample ports are presented in Table 6.3. As shown in Table 6.3, the standard deviations of the port data variables are significantly large. This is due to the size and scale difference in the sample ports, especially for the Port of Shanghai, which is one of the biggest ports in the Asia Pacific area and consists of terminals and large throughput volume. Hence, this further strengthens our initial idea of analysing container terminals of the selected ports, where datasets gathered are more complete and more precisely reflect the operational side of the terminals.

Table 6.2　Sample ports for efficiency comparison (Table by the authors)

Country	Sample Ports
Australian	Port of Melbourne
Australian	Port of Fremantle, Fremantle
Australian	Port Botany, Sydney
Indonesia	Tanjung Priok Port, Jakarta
Indonesia	Tanjung Perak Port, Surabaya
China	Port of Shanghai

Table 6.3　Descriptive port statistics for input and output variables for DEA

	Variable	Max	Min	Mean	Medium	Std. Dev*
Input	Land size (hectares)	777.0	75.0	437.0	462.0	243.9
Input	Length of berths (km)	25.2	1.5	9.7	6.1	9.4
Input	Number of berths	76.0	12.0	36.8	28.5	26.3

	Variable	Max	Min	Mean	Medium	Std. Dev*
Input	Number of cranes	618.0	7.0	154.7	69.5	231.1
Input	Operating expense (million AUD)	4385.0	70.0	934.8	263.8	1696.8
Input	Net assets (million AUD)	12145.0	102.1	3167.7	1543.0	4605.0
Input	Number of employees	18183.0	221.0	3361.8	410.0	7262.4
Output	Container (million TEU)	37.1	0.7	8.4	2.9	14.2
Output	Bulk (million tons)	147.0	8.9	40.3	13.0	54.6

*Std. Dev = Standard deviation

(Table by the authors based on data gathered from various publically available data sources related to ports listed in Table 6.2)

6.3.1.2 Container Terminal

To conduct the efficiency analysis at the terminal level, a typical container terminal from each of the sampled ports was selected. The sample of container terminals is shown in Table 6.4 and the characteristics of the variables used to estimate the relative efficiency of the sample container terminals are presented in Table 6.5.

Table 6.4 Sample of container terminals for efficiency comparison
(Table by the authors)

Country	Sample Port	Sample Container Terminal
Australia	Port of Melbourne, Melbourne	Swanson Dock
Australia	Port of Fremantle, (WA)	North quay terminal (Fremantle)
Australia	Port Botany (Sydney)	DP World Container Terminal
Indonesia	Tanjung Priok Port (Jakarta)	Jakarta International Container Terminal
Indonesia	Tanjung Perak Port (Surabaya)	TTL — Terminal Teluk Lamong
Indonesia	Tanjung Perak Port (Surabaya)	TPS — Terminal Petikemas
China	Port of Shanghai (Shanghai)	Pudong International Container Terminal

Table 6.5 Descriptive container terminal statistics for inputs and outputs
variables for DEA

	Variable	Max	Min	Mean	Medium	Std. Dev.
Input	Terminal area (hectares)	89.0	30.8	46.9	38.6	19.6
Input	Total Length of berths (km)	1.8	0.9	1.3	1.3	0.3
Input	Number of berths	9.0	3.0	5.9	7.0	2.3
Input	Number of cranes	79.0	7.0	35.0	30.0	24.6
Output	Container throughput (million TEU)	2.6	0.6	1.7	2.0	0.8
Output	Crane rate (TEU/hour)	35.0	22.0	28.2	28.0	4.1
Output	Ship rate (TEU/hour)	86.0	50.0	59.9	56.0	12.8

(Table by the authors, based on data gathered from various publically available
data sources related to ports listed in Table 6.4)

6.3.2 Efficiency Comparison Based on DEA Result

6.3.2.1 Port

The inputs and outputs shown in Table 6.5 were used for the DEA analysis to determine efficiency, while Table 6.6 shows the efficiency computed, based on these variables. This demonstrates that the Australian ports are more efficient than the Indonesian ports when comparing the *functional* input: land size, length of berths, number of berths and number of cranes. Port of Melbourne, Fremantle Port, Port Botany (Sydney) and Port of Shanghai are relatively efficient since the scale efficiency equals to 1 while Tanjung Perak Port (Surabaya) and Tanjung Priok Port (Jakarta) are relativity inefficient since their scale efficiencies are less than 1. The Surabaya port is less efficient than Jakarta port with scale efficiencies of 0.861 and 0.910 respectively (Table 6.6). Both these ports scored low efficiencies in the CCR and BCC models.

The Australian ports are relatively efficient when comparing the *operational* input: operating expense, net assets and number of employees (Table 6.7). On the other hand, Tanjung Perak Port (Surabaya) is relatively

Table 6.6 Port Efficiency score for functional inputs based on
DEA models (Table by authors)

Country	Port	CCR Efficiency	BCC Efficiency	Scale Efficiency
Australia	Port of Melbourne	1.000	1.000	1.000
Australia	Fremantle Port	1.000	1.000	1.000
Australia	Port Botany (Sydney)	1.000	1.000	1.000
Indonesia	Tanjung Perak Port (Surabaya)	0.488	0.567	0.861
Indonesia	Tanjung Priok Port (Jakarta)	0.598	0.657	0.910
China	Port of Shanghai	1.000	1.000	1.000

inefficient as scale efficiency is less than 1 (0.863), but Tanjung Priok Port (Jakarta) is relativity efficient as scale efficiency equals 1 when comparing operational inputs.

Generally, the Australian ports and the Chinese ports are relatively efficient compared to the Indonesian ports. Comparing Indonesian ports, Tanjung Priok Port (Jakarta) is more efficient than Tanjung Perak Port (Surabaya).

Table 6.7 Port Efficiency score for operational inputs based on
DEA models (Table by authors)

Country	Port	CCR Efficiency	BCC Efficiency	Scale Efficiency
Australia	Port of Melbourne	1.000	1.000	1.000
Australia	Fremantle Port (Perth)	1.000	1.000	1.000
Australia	Botany Port (Sydney)	1.000	1.000	1.000
Indonesia	Tanjung Perak Port (Surabaya)	0.807	0.935	0.863
Indonesia	Tanjung Priok Port (Jakarta)	1.000	1.000	1.000
China	Port of Shanghai	1.000	1.000	1.000

6.3.2.2 *Comparison of Container Terminals*

The major container terminals in each port were analysed for detailed study. The container terminal efficiency was calculated with the following inputs: terminal area, length of berths, number of berths and number of cranes with regard to different outputs (crane rate, ship rate and container throughput). As shown in Table 6.8, in terms of crane rate, Terminal Teluk Lamong (TTL), North Quay Terminal (Fremantle), DP World Container Terminal (Sydney) and Pudong International Container Terminal (Shanghai) are relativity efficient since the scale efficiency equals to 1 while Jakarta International Container Terminal (JICT), Terminal Petikemas (Surabaya) (TPS) and Swanson Dock (Melbourne) are relativity inefficient due to scale efficiency less than 1. Swanson Dock in Port of Melbourne is inefficient in the CCR model but efficient in the BCC model.

Table 6.8 Container terminal Efficiency in terms of Crane Rate
(Table by authors)

Container Terminal	CCR Efficiency	BCC Efficiency	Scale Efficiency
Jakarta International Container Terminal (Jakarta)	0.624	0.751	0.830
TPS — Terminal Petikemas (Surabaya)	0.971	0.999	0.973
TTL — Terminal Teluk Lamong (Surabaya)	1.000	1.000	1.000
Swanson Dock (Melbourne)	0.845	1.000	0.845
North Quay Terminal (Fremantle)	1.000	1.000	1.000
DP World Container Terminal (Sydney)	1.000	1.000	1.000
Pudong International Container Terminal (Shanghai)	1.000	1.000	1.000

In terms of ship rate, JICT, TPS, TTL and Swanson Dock (Melbourne) are relatively inefficient as scale efficiency is less than 1 (Table 6.9).

In terms of container throughput (Table 6.10), Swanson Dock (Melbourne), DP World Container Terminal (Sydney) and Pudong International Container Terminal (Shanghai) are relatively efficient as scale efficiency equals to 1. North Quay Terminal is inefficient in the CCR model but efficient in the BCC model.

Table 6.9 Container terminal Efficiency in terms of Ship Rate
(Table by authors)

Container Terminal	CCR Efficiency	BCC Efficiency	Scale Efficiency
Jakarta International Container Terminal (Jakarta)	0.767	0.794	0.966
TPS — Terminal Petikemas (Surabaya)	0.817	0.903	0.905
TTL — Terminal Teluk Lamong (Surabaya)	0.869	0.950	0.915
Swanson Dock (Melbourne)	0.858	1.000	0.858
North Quay Terminal (Fremantle)	1.000	1.000	1.000
DP World Container Terminal (Sydney)	0.988	1.000	0.988
Pudong International Container Terminal (Shanghai)	1.000	1.000	1.000

Table 6.10 Container terminal Efficiency in terms of Container
Throughput (Table by authors)

Container Terminal	CCR Efficiency	BCC Efficiency	Scale Efficiency
Jakarta International Container Terminal (Jakarta)	0.744	0.818	0.910
TPS — Terminal Petikemas (Surabaya)	0.661	0.960	0.689
TTL — Terminal Teluk Lamong (Surabaya)	0.348	0.950	0.367
Swanson Dock (Melbourne)	1.000	1.000	1.000
North Quay Terminal (Fremantle)	0.725	1.000	0.725
DP World Container Terminal (Sydney)	1.000	1.000	1.000
Pudong International Container Terminal (Shanghai)	1.000	1.000	1.000

From the above Tables 6.6 to 6.10, Australian container terminals are generally more efficient than Indonesian container terminals. Where Indonesian container terminals are concerned, JICT shows, on average, around 80%–90% efficency in each aspect. TPS and TTL have high efficiency scores in terms of crane rate and ship rate but relativity low scores in terms of container throughput. TTL in particular had a significantly lower efficiency score in terms of container throughput ability 36.7%, while the other container terminal TPS scored 68.9% efficiency (Table 6.10). For the sampled Australian container terminals, Swanson Dock in the Port of Melbourne is less efficient in terms of crane rate and ship rate with around 85% but very efficient in terms of container throughput. In contrast, North Quay Terminal in the Port of Fremantle is efficient in terms of crane rate and ship rate but inefficient in container throughput. As one of the top container terminals in China, Pudong International Container Terminal in the Port of Shanghai is relatively efficient and scored 100% effiency in all aspects, under both the CCR and BBC model.

Different port and terminal efficiency factors are discussed in the section below, where the framework presented by Cheon, Dowall and Song (2010) is used as a guideline. This report affirms their framework, using it to explain the areas of improvement required by ports, as explained in the section above with CCR model efficiency, BCC pure technical efficiency and scale efficiency.

Table 6.11 Sources of efficiency gains (after Cheon, Dowall and Song (2010))

Category (DEA models)	Areas of improvement
Technical efficiency	Improve utilization and optimisation of terminals
	Crane and facilities improvement
	Labour reforms
Overall progress efficiency	Container trade volume
Scale efficiency	Governing and managing structure reform
	Better decision making and investment climate

6.4 Discussion

The improvement percentage of inefficient units based on constant crane rate, ship rate and throughput are shown in Fig. 6.4.

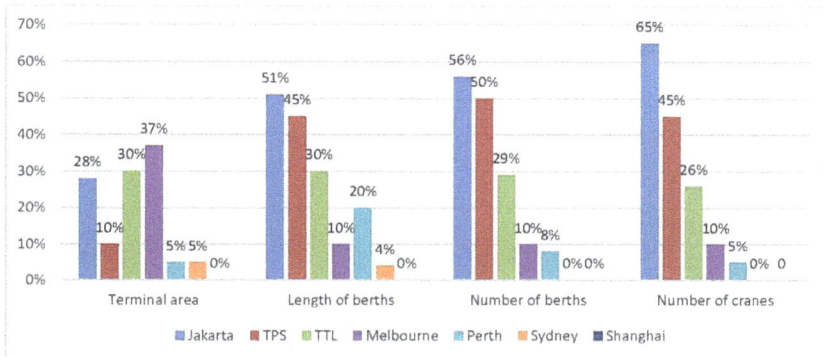

Fig. 6.4 Improvement percentage* of inefficient units based on constant crane rate, ship rate and throughput (Figure by authors)

*vertical axis % improvement in efficiency required. Also note that Shanghai is not depicted as Shanghai is relative efficient at 100%

From Fig. 6.4, JICT has the highest improvement rate required to match the optimal required efficiency score and improve its terminal operations. This figure is based on the percentage improvement of each inefficient unit of terminals on crane rate, ship rate and throughput efficiency. Sydney and Shanghai both performed relatively well with improvements of 4% and 0 % overall. Fremantle and Melbourne have a slack improvement of around 16% and 10 % respectively. The Indonesian terminals have the highest room for efficiency improvements with Jakarta (JICT) 50%, TPS 35% and TTL 30% overall. A summary of the container terminal efficiency scores is shown in Table 6.12.

6.4.1 Indonesia

Overall, from the port efficiency results shown in Tables 6.6 and 6.7, both of the Indonesian ports examined are ranked less efficient relative to the Australian and Chinese ports. The Port of Tanjung Perak in Surabaya, on the whole, had a lower efficiency score compared to the Port of Tanjung Priok in Jakarta. Andenoworih (2010) and Syafaaruddin

Table 6.12 Summary of Container Terminal Efficiency scores
(Table by authors)

Container Terminal	Efficiency Score		
	Crane rate	Ship rate	Container throughput
Jakarta International Container Terminal (Jakarta)	0.830	0.966	0.910
TPS — Terminal Petikemas (Surabaya)	0.973	0.905	0.689
TTL — Terminal Teluk Lamong (Surabaya)	1.000	0.915	0.367
Swanson Dock (Melbourne)	0.845	0.858	1.000
North Quay Terminal (Fremantle)	1.000	1.000	0.725
DP World Container Terminal (Sydney)	1.000	0.988	1.000
Pudong International Container Terminal (Shanghai)	1.000	1.000	1.000

(2015) both confirm that Jakarta is efficient overall in Indonesia due to its advantageous location within a high regional economic activity area. Based on the results, the major determinants of port efficiency are the following outputs: annual container throughput, and ship rate. This is where Tanjung Priok outperforms Surabaya with higher throughputs in both categories (see Fig. 6.12)

From the DEA results, it can be seen that JICT also has a better efficiency score using container throughput as the output. However, it has a lower crane rate within the terminal. This is supported by earlier research by Afriansyah et al. (2017) and Wiradanti et al. (2016), where slow landside customs handling as well as the poorly integrated information system of the port caused major congestion issues in the terminal. The DEA results shown in Tables 6.7 to 6.10 highlight that crane rate and the efficiency score at JICT is the lowest among terminals, suggesting a poor handling rate of containers when loading/unloading, which increases ship dwell time. The ship turnaround time at the terminal alone is ten hours more than the closest rival TPS and TTL. Low infrastructure expenditure and low quality of workers with high capital input are common issues in Indonesia (Firdausy 2005). The different models of DEA, BCC, CCR and

Scale model gave similar outputs, lending support to the finding from the literature review that Jakarta is inefficient in seaside and landside operations. The Port of Tanjung Priok in Jakarta has three times more cranes and employees than the Port of Melbourne, yet still ranks lower in efficiency. This is supported by the study from Wiradanti et al. (2016), which reported that the Indonesian government has approved funding for further expansion and upgrade of the port to improve the sea/land operations and ease congestion.

Both terminals in Surabaya have high efficiency in terms of sea-side crane operations. Because annual throughput data was not available for TTL, an estimation is used for the container TEU throughput at 40% capacity of its full capacity of 1.6 million annual TEU (Seatrade Maritime 2017). However, the DEA analysis showed TTL is inefficient as an overall terminal, since it had low container throughput. It also has a high net asset value, and this does not equate to the profits and expected throughput, due to low usage. Rahmanto (2016) confirms this, describing TTL as a low usage terminal with "state-of-art" facilities, but with poor road/rail infrastructure outside the terminal. The terminal needs to improve its container volume to achieve the desired efficiency score and improve its terminal usage capacity. Having its own gas-fired power plant in the terminal (Terminal Teluk Lamong 2015) did not help improve the issue in any way or help increase the business volume to the port corporation. Firdausy (2005) strongly suggests implementation of institutional reform to solve the poor governance and investment climate that could change the sustainability of the terminal business. It will also lead to better decision making in investments that the terminal desperately needs in terms of multimodal transport from the terminal to the outside world (Rahmanto 2016).

To validate our findings of inefficiency at TTL, a sensitivity analysis was done by introducing a new estimate for the annual throughput. It is expected that annual container throughput will increase by 0.4 million each year (Seatrade Maritime 2017), hence 60% capacity was used as the estimation (0.96 million). The sensitivity analysis results did not generate a huge difference to the earlier assumption with a new efficiency score of 0.522. This means that, with its expensive new equipment and facilities, the trade volume needs to increase for the port to reach its potential optimal efficiency. This in turn would increase the utilisation rate of the port capacity.

The findings from the TPS are consistent with the research findings of Groenveld and Wanders (2009). Table 6.12 shows that slight improvements are needed for crane rate, ship rate and landside operations in order to boost efficiency. Compared with TTL and Swanson Dock in Melbourne, TPS is doing quite well in terms of seaside operational function, where the crane rate in DEA Table 6.12 is higher than that of Melbourne's Swanson Terminal. However, the container throughput efficiency score is lower than that of Jakarta International Terminal, and the Australian and Chinese terminals. From the CCR model, it is ranked second, behind JICT, and in the BCC model it is ranked first, ahead of JICT. Research conducted by Syafaaruddin (2015) supports this finding that, overall, TPS has achieved near-full capacity of the terminal and has generated the second highest container volume behind JICT. It is placed behind Jakarta in the scale efficiency score, which is an aggregate of the pure technical efficiency and general efficiency. This indicates that TPS either has to improve the quality of its workers to improve crane rates, or decrease the trade volumes to match the ideal optimal efficiency level.

Surabaya's Tanjung Perak port as a whole did not achieve a good efficiency score, ranking last in the port ranking. Seo et al. (2012) used a similar DEA CCR model in their analysis with a larger sample size. This supports our DEA analysis for Tanjung Perak, where both the output and input-orientated model showed the lowest efficiency scores. It is suggested that port managers can mitigate this by improving port operations and management. An analysis of the relative efficiencies of the two major terminals in Tanjung Perak (TPS and TTL) indicates that both terminals contribute to the overall port performance with their relatively low crane rate and container output DEA efficiency scores.

Looking at ownership structures, JICT and TPS both have private sector involvement while TTL is wholly owned by a State Owned Enterprise. Our analysis shows that JICT and TPS are performing better in overall efficiency compared to TTL. Although TTL is better equipped with modern facilities, it is still outperformed by the two Indonesian terminal counterparts in overall performance. As stated by Tongzon and Heng (2005), government ports may gain benefits in allowing private sector participation, which may introduce better decision making in structural management and assist the port to become a more efficient performer and be more profitable.

Figures 6.5 and 6.6 show areas requiring improvements for the terminals. Port of Tanjung Priok in Jakarta requires moderate (yellow) improvement in all areas: seaside technical operations as well as landside, especially customs clearance (red). Tanjung Perak port needs a high (red) level of improvement in landside infrastructure development for optimal efficiency, predominantly caused by the inefficient performance of Teluk Lamong.

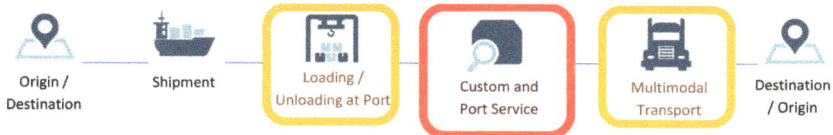

Fig. 6.5 Port of Tanjung Priok (Jakarta) logistics flow chart (Figure by authors)

Fig. 6.6 Port of Surabaya logistics flow chart (Figure by authors)

6.4.2 Australia

Due to inaccessibility of data, landside analysis of Melbourne's Swanson Dock could not be quantified. However, a study from Infrastructure Victoria (2017) shows that the landside multimodal infrastructure of Swanson Dock to outside destinations is efficient, and can sufficiently accommodate future population and demand growth in the long term. It has been suggested that rail transport of containers should be developed to share the logistics load, increasing from the current 10% rail usage (Infrastructure Victoria 2017). The focus for the terminal is still to upgrade the seaside technical facilities in order to improve crane rates. Efficiency scores of 0.84 crane rate and 0.86 ship rate (Table 6.12) are not sufficient for a port that handles 2.64 million TEU's annually. This finding confirms the conclusion of Lubulwa, Malarz and Wang (2011) and Ghaedhi, Cahoon and Nguyen (2016): that on-dock rail infrastructure and crane facilities are behind other advanced terminals in the world, especially TPS and TTL. The lack of connectivity between terminals and docks adds time and cost to the freight system, as trucks are needed to service the gap. Infrastructure Victoria (2017) also strengthens this view by stating the need to upgrade berth capacity and yard with on-dock rail to improve the crane rate. By increasing "rail's mode share of container haulage", it will have a positive improvement on the operational and management practice of the terminal.

In terms of operational efficiency, North Quay container terminal in Fremantle did not have an issue at terminal level analysis. It did however receive a score of 0.725 in overall container throughput efficiency (Table 6.12), lower than JICT, and other Australian and Chinese Terminals. Looking at the container throughput, North Quay has the lowest annual throughput. Although it is efficient in handling containers, the throughput result suggests that the size and the scale of the terminal may be insufficient when compared with larger terminals, in terms of the container throughput volume at terminal level. Cheon, Dowall and Song (2010) stressed that scale and size of ports may play a crucial role in determining the efficiency as the volume of trade does not meet up with other larger volume terminals. Volume throughput needs to increase by 15–20% to meet optimal efficiency.

Port Botany in Sydney is efficient in the DEA analysis, supporting the findings of Tongzon (2001). Slight improvement can be made in the handling of crane and ship rates, where they are just below the score of 1. DP World container terminal also achieved scores of 1 for crane rate, ship rate and overall throughput efficiency rate output. Zahran et al. (2015) confirms this finding that Sydney has a relatively good efficiency rating when they performed DEA against revenue and throughput in their study. The Port of Melbourne should upgrade and focus on investing in new cranes and on dock facilities (yellow), in order to improve seaside operations, as shown in Fig. 6.7.

Fig. 6.7 Port of Melbourne logistics flow chart (Figure by authors)

6.4.3 Opportunities for Future Research

Throughout the stages of acquiring data and performing DEA analysis, it was recognised that there were limitations in the completeness of the data collected on which to base the analysis. This data was mostly obtained from public sources. Future research into Australian and Indonesian port efficiency would benefit from sourcing data directly from the ports. The current DEA approach used in this study did not consider the temporal scale efficiency. It would be beneficial in future research to include datasets of various time periods to investigate temporal changes which can further strengthen the DEA results. This project mostly emphasised the seaside crane handling structure and overall container throughput rate. It is highly recommended that for a complete port operational review study, landside data from ports and terminals should be included in the analysis. Such considerations would improve the methodology and the expanded dataset would provide further insights into other issues, such as connectivity to the other terminals and inland ports.

6.5 Conclusion

Indonesian ports require more efficiency improvement, and this can be realised from improving the sea-side technical operations and quality of workers. Labour reform may be required in Jakarta's Port of Tanjung Priok, while Surabaya's Tanjung Perak Port may require better institutional and policy reform to improve the investment climate and raise throughput volume to achieve optimal efficiency. Indonesian ports and terminals, which are mostly State Owned Enterprises, may benefit more from private sector involvement. Here, a more transparent management structure and system could help improve overall port performance. In general, the efficiency of Indonesian port terminals is lower than that seen in Australian port terminals in all aspects — seaside and landside — although there is healthy competition within the terminal level.

References

Almawsheki, ES, Shah, MZ and Al-Iraqi, AS 2014. *Efficiency analysis of container ports: A review*, paper presented at the conference proceedings of 8th SEATUC Symposium, 4–5 March, Johor Bahru, Malaysia.

Andenoworih, TH 2010. *Measuring relative container terminal efficiency in Indonesia*, PhD Thesis, Erasmus University, Rotterdam, The Netherlands, thesis.eur.nl/pub/33240

Afriansyah, AR, Febriani, E, Fahmi, QA and Krismawanti, DD, n.d. *Online integration system as a solution of reducing dwelling time using management informations system approach.*

Chen, PSL, Pateman, H and Sakalayen, Q 2017. 'The latest trend in Australian port privatisation: Drivers, processes and impacts', *Research in Transportation Business and Management*, 22, pp. 201–13.

Cheon, S, Dowall, DE and Song, DW 2010. 'Evaluating impacts of institutional reforms on port efficiency changes: Ownership, corporate structure, and total factor productivity changes of world container ports', *Transportation Research Part E: Logistics and Transportation Review*, 46:4, pp. 546–61, https://doi.org/10.1016/j.tre.2009.04.001

Cullinane, K, Ji, P and Wang, TF 2005. 'The relationship between privatization and DEA estimates of efficiency in the container port industry', *Journal of economics and business*, 57:5, pp. 433–62, https://doi.org/10.1016/j.jeconbus.2005.02.007

Cullinane, K, Wang, TF, Song, DW and Ji, P 2006. 'The technical efficiency of container ports: comparing data envelopment analysis and stochastic frontier analysis', *Transportation research part A: Policy and practice*, 40:4, pp. 354–74, https://doi.org/10.1057/mel.2011.15

Chung, KC 1993. *Port Performance Indicators*, Transportation, Water and Urban Development Department, The World Bank, siteresources.worldbank.org/INTTRANSPORT/Resources/336291-1119275973157/td-ps6.pdf

Department of Foreign Affairs and Trade (DFAT) 2016. *Indonesia*, Australian Government, Australia, dfat.gov.au/trade/resources/documents/indo.pdf

Department of Foreign Affairs and Trade (DFAT) 2017. *Australia's trade at a glance*, Australian Government, Australia, dfat.gov.au/trade/resources/trade-at-a-glance/pages/asean.aspx

Department of Foreign Affairs and Trade (DFAT) 2019. *Indonesia-Australia comprehensive economic partnership agreement*, Australian Government, Australia, dfat.gov.au/trade/agreements/not-yet-in-force/iacepa/Pages/indonesia-australia-comprehensive-economic-partnership-agreement.aspx

Firdausy, CM 2005. *Productivity performance in developing countries, country case studies: Indonesia*, report for the United Nations Industrial Development Organisation (UNIDO), www. unido. org/file-storage/download

Fremantle Ports 2017. *Fremantle ports Western Australia*, www.fremantleports. com.au/About/Pages/default.aspx

Ghadehi, H., Cahoon, S and Nguyen, H 2016. 'The role of rail in the Australian port-based container market: challenges and opportunities', *Australian Journals of Maritime and Ocean Affairs*, 8–1, pp. 52–72, https://doi.org/10.108 0/18366503.2016.1173632

Groenveld, R and Wanders, S 2009. 'Computer simulation model International Container Terminal Tanjung Perak, Surabaya, Indonesia', in *Proceedings of the International Workshop Harbour, Maritime and Industrial Logistics, Modelling and Simulation*, Genoa, Italy: SCS European Publishing House.

Hill, H (Ed.) 2014. *Regional dynamics in a decentralized Indonesia*, Singapore: Institute of Southeast Asian Studies.

Hung, SW, Lu, WM and Wang, TP 2010. 'Benchmarking the operating efficiency of Asia container ports', *European Journal of Operational Research*, 203:3, pp. 706–13, https://doi.org/10.1007/s12544-015-0187-z

Infrastructure Victoria 2017. *Second container port advice — Evidence base discussion paper*, Victoria, Australia: Infrastructure Victoria.

IPC 2017. *KOJA Container Terminal*, www.indonesiaport.co.id/menu/koja-ct.html

JICT 2013. *JICT shareholder at glance*, www.jict.co.id/?x0=andx1=68andx2=article

Lam, JS and Yap, WY 2006. 'A measurement and comparison of cost competitiveness of container ports in Southeast Asia', *Transportation*, 33:6, pp. 641–54, https://doi.org/10.1007/s11116-006-7474-4

Lin, JY 2011. 'China and the global economy', *China Economic Journal*, 4:1, pp. 1–14, https://doi.org/10.1080/17538963.2011.609612

Logistics Capacity Assessment 2017. *Indonesian Surabaya Port of Tanjung Perak*.

Lubulwa, G, Malarz, A and Wang, SP 2011. *An investigation of best practice landside efficiency at Australian container ports*, proceedings of the Australasian Transport Research Forum, 29–30 September, Adelaide, Australia.

Ojala, L and Çelebi, D 2015. *The World Bank's Logistics Performance Index (LPI) and drivers of logistics performance*, prepared for the roundatable 'Logistics development strategies and their performance measurements' at the International Transport Forum, 9–10 March, Queretaro, Mexico, www.itf-oecd.org/sites/default/files/docs/ojala.pdf

Panayides, PM, Parola, F and Lam, JSL 2015. 'The effect of institutional factors on public–private partnership success in ports', *Transportation Research Part A: Policy and Practice*, 71:C, pp. 110–27, https://doi.org/10.1016/j.tra.2014.11.006

PR Newswire 2017. *Lonsdale Consortium comprises Future Fund, QIC, GIP and OMERSacquire 50-year lease of Port of Melbourne*, www.prnewswire.com/ news-releases/lonsdale-consortium-comprising-future-fund-qic-gip-and-omers-acquire-50-year-lease-of-port-of-melbourne-300330084.html

Rahmanto, WP 2016. *Kandangan dry port project: an option of solution for congestion: case of Lamong Bay Terminal*, Surabaya, Indonesia: World Maritime University Dissertations, 528, pdfs.semanticscholar.org/2ad6/2cb9138dee9bd957b0e5e9 eb83d840067837.pdf

Wee, V 2015. Indonesia awards concessions for Teluk Lamong, Makassar ports, *Seatrade Maritime News*, www.seatrade-maritime.com/news/asia/indonesia-awards-concessions-for-teluk-lamong-makassar-ports.html

Seo, YJ, Ryoo, DK and Aye, MN 2012. 'An analysis of container port efficiency in ASEAN', *Journal of Navigation and Port Research*, 36:7, pp. 535–44.

Syafaaruddin, DS 2015. *Evaluation of container terminal efficiency performance in Indonesia: Future investment*, Rotterdam, The Netherlands: Erasmus University.

Terminal Teluk Lamong 2015. *Terminal overview*.

Wanke, PF and Barros, CP 2015. 'Public-private partnerships and scale efficiency in Brazilian ports: Evidence from two-stage DEA analysis', *Socio-Economic Planning Sciences*, 51, pp. 13–22, https://doi.org/10.1016/j.seps.2015.06.002

Wiradanti, B, Pettit, S, Abouarghoub, W and Beresford, AKC 2016. *Trends in trade and port development of rising economies: Mexico and Indonesia*, paper presented at the Logistics Research Network Conference, The Chartered Institute of Logistics and Transport (CILT), Hull University, United Kingdom:

World Shipping Council 2017. *Top 50 world container ports*, www.worldshipping. org/about-the-industry/global-trade/top-50-world-container-ports

World Bank Group 2013, *Transport in Indonesia*.

World Bank 2016. *Connecting to Compete 2016 Trade Logistics in the Global Economy. The Logistics Performance Index and Its Indicators*, openknowledge.worldbank. org/bitstream/handle/10986/24598/Connecting0to00n0the0global0economy. pdf?sequence=1andisAllowed=y

Wu, YCJ and Goh, M 2010. 'Container port efficiency in emerging and more advanced markets', *Transportation Research Part E: Logistics and Transportation Review*, 46:6, pp. 1030–42, https://doi.org/10.1016/j.tre.2010.01.002

Tongzon, J 2001. 'Efficiency measurement of selected Australian and other international ports using data envelopment analysis', *Transportation Research Part A: Policy and Practice*, 35:2, pp. 107–22, https://doi.org/10.1016/S0965-8564(99)00049-X

Tongzon, J and Heng, W 2005. 'Port privatization, efficiency and competitiveness: Some empirical evidence from container ports (terminals)', *Transportation Research Part A: Policy and Practice*, 39:5, pp. 405–24, https://doi.org/10.1016/j. tra.2005.02.001

Yuen, ACL, Zhang, A and Cheung, W 2013. 'Foreign participation and competition: A way to improve the container port efficiency in China?',

Transportation Research Part A: *Policy and Practice*, 49:C, pp. 220–31, https://doi.org/10.1016/j.tra.2013.01.026

Zahran, SZ, Alam, JB, Al-Zahrani, AH, Smirlis, Y, Papadimitriou, S and Tsioumas, V 2015. 'Analysis of port authority efficiency using data envelopment analysis', *Maritime Economics and Logistics*, 19:3, pp. 518–37, https://doi.org/10.1057/mel.2015.33

7. Innovation in Port Development

The Quad Helix Model[1]

S. Wahyuni[2]

7.0 Introduction

A seaport is large infrastructure that is critical to a city's economy. Large port projects are normally planned and initiated by the government of the day. However, this planning and project initiation approach may not always be optimal, since it is usually driven top-down. The early involvement of other stakeholders at the port-city interface such as the private sector, academia and the wider community may be useful in collaboratively developing a port project. This paper provides a comprehensive case study on how an Academic-Business-Community-Government plus bank partnership can be nurtured to create innovation through direct observation method to TAMA (Technology Advanced Metropolitan Area) in Japan and an analysis of the port development of Shenzhen. To develop a successful port cluster, there is a need for a systematic cluster strategy that includes: the cultivation of key persons

---

1   Some parts of this article have been published in Chapter 7, 'Bagaimana Mmperkuat Kemitraan ABG: Studi Kasus Tama (Jepang)' in S. Wahyuni and Wahyuningsih, *Strategi Kawasan Ekonomi Khusus* (Salemba Empat: Jakarta, 2018), pp. 129-142.
2   Associate Professor, Dept. of Management, Faculty of Economics and Business, Universitas Indonesia.

https://doi.org/10.11647/OBP.0189.07

for local industrial vitalisation; analysis for new industries; any kind of supports for planning industrial vitalisation plan; supports for collaboration with other areas; and overseas marketing.

Many small and medium-sized enterprises (SMEs), as well as port management, are struggling with developing their businesses due to the limits of resources, capabilities and network/linkage. The mushrooming development of ports in the world does not guarantee that their competitiveness remains the same over the years. Some ports which previously ranked top in the world have now been replaced by other ports. For example, Rotterdam — once rated the busiest port in the world — was recently replaced by Shenzhen, a relative newcomer in the port industry. The rank is now reversed. The Port of Shenzhen is now ranked as the fourth busiest container port in the world in terms of container throughput, only slightly behind Hong Kong in third (McKinnon, 2011). Shenzhen has seen double digit growth rates in its containerized cargo throughput for a number of years. This achievement is the result of high speed foreign direct investment (FDI), quick development of Shenzhen as a special economic zone, and close coopetition between all stakeholders: academy, business, government and community. These stakeholders are not only located in Shenzhen, but also in Hongkong and in other cities across China.

Port competitiveness has been widely studied over the years. Interestingly, the nature of changes in and around ports is fundamentally different today: changes are often disruptive, and very often located outside the port area, and therefore often out of control of the pure port actors (Song, 2014). The challenge of the future development of seaports is the growing importance of hinterland connections, international logistics chains, the share of hinterland transportation and collaboration between ABCG (Academic-Business-Community-Government). A close partnership with all parties involved needs to be established to develop a successful port. To increase port competitiveness, there is a need to maintain both competition and cooperation among port management. As Notteboom, Ducruet and Langen (2009, p. 2) write:

> Adjacent ports are typically fierce competitors, a competition that often contributes to the strong market positions of the respective seaports. However, the relationship between adjacent ports has also grown stronger in the sense that port executives as well as the private sector

stress that, while maintaining a healthy competition, opportunities for cooperation and coordination can be further explored.

The aim of this chapter is to provide a comprehensive understanding on how to develop a successful cluster with the help of ABCG (Academic-Business-Community-Government) plus banks. This strategy should include engagement of key stakeholders for local industrial vitalization, analysis for new industries, any kind of supports for creating an industrial vitalization plan, and support for collaboration with other regions. As our case study, we use a company in Western Metropolitan Tokyo: the Greater Tokyo Initiative, Technology Advanced Metropolitan Area (TAMA) association. The background and strategic support content of the Greater Tokyo Initiative will be introduced and discussed. In addition, we will also link the analysis with the development of Singapore port.

7.1 Port Strategic Development

Whenever discussing port development, we cannot neglect the importance of co-operation: co-operation built between ports, and partnerships built between ports and other stakeholders (communities, universities etc.). Nevertheless, we should also take into serious consideration a new strategic approach — "coopetition", a term coined by Brandenburger and Nalebuff (1996). The term "coopetition" is a mixture of competition and co-operation, thus having a strategic implication that those engaged in the same or similar market should 'collaborate to compete' as a win–win strategy, rather than a win–lose one. Such is the inter-relationship between Hong Kong and South China ports, which ultimately increased Hong Kong's competitiveness and also helped other ports in South China. Instead of competing with Hong Kong, Shenzhen developed a strategic partnership with Hong Kong to provide complementary rather than competing services, so that competitiveness of both ports can be leveraged up. Brandenburger and Nalebuff (1996) name this group as 'complementors', a counterpart to the term 'competitors'. From this study it was revealed that there are several potential areas for collaboration. From Table 7.1 we can see that port competitiveness is not only dependent on maritime connectivity, efficiency and quality of port operations, but also highly dependent on hinterland connectivity and local goodwill. It is clear that a competitive port must create economic value not only for the direct port stakeholders, but also for the community.

Table 7.1 The determining factors of Port competitiveness

Determinant	Instrument	Examples
1) Maritime connectivity	Transhipment	Singapore
	Nautical access	Deep sea ports
	Internationalisation strategies	Rotterdam, Antwerp
2) Port operations		
Quality of inputs	Skills mapping and matching	New York/New Jersey
	Training and education	Singapore
	Social dialogue	Antwerp
	Upgrading equipment	Hamburg
	Land availability	
Quality of organisation	Port planning	Rotterdam
	Port information systems	Valencia
	Competition	Most large ports
	Coordination between ports	Copenhagen/Malmö
3) Hinterland	Links port with other transport modes	Rotterdam
	Dry ports and extended gates	Gothenburg
	Freight corridors	Betuwe-line
4) Local goodwill	Port centres	Genoa
	Port education	Long Beach
	Maritime museums	Antwerp
	Port events	Rotterdam
	Information and social media	Incheon
	Public access to port	Hamburg
	Other goodwill projects	Valparaíso

Source: Merck (2009).

In Figure 7.1, we can observe the maritime cluster composition of services that has been followed by many ports worldwide. The ports of London, Singapore and Rotterdam have the most complete composition: they are not only supported by hard infrastructure, but, most importantly, by soft infrastructure like research, education and training, ICT, maritime culture and heritage.

Despite the completeness of services, a high value creation port must consider the importance of building market power so that there will be economies of scale for cargo transshipment. The market power theory provides a useful tool by which we can explain the current situation and predict the future trend for container ports in the region. In a broad sense, market power is the ability of a market participant or group of participants (i.e. persons, firms and partnerships, etc.) to influence price, quality, and the nature of the product or service in the marketplace (Shepherd 1970). The fact that a terminal operator has a high degree of market power, by definition, means that the operator has a high degree of control over pricing and services decisions in a port service market

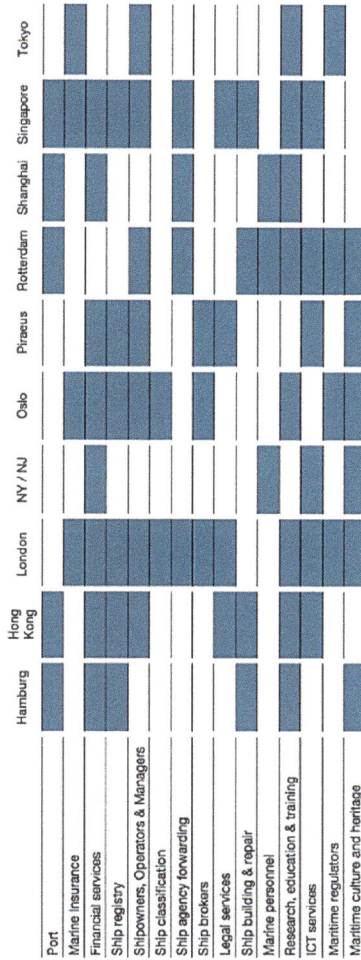

Fig. 7.1 Maritime Cluster composition of services in major port cities. Source: Lam and Zhang, (2011).

(Song 2002). Under the assumption that the container port operators in this region are profit maximisers, they will attempt to improve their competitiveness by securing stronger positions in their market, so that they can enhance their market power.

Figure 7.2 shows how market power can be increased significantly through joint venture, strategic alliances, merger or even acquisition. This model (which has been implemented in Hong Kong) threatens the profitability of the container ports and weakens the firm's market power. Co-operation between two firms apparently could enhance the

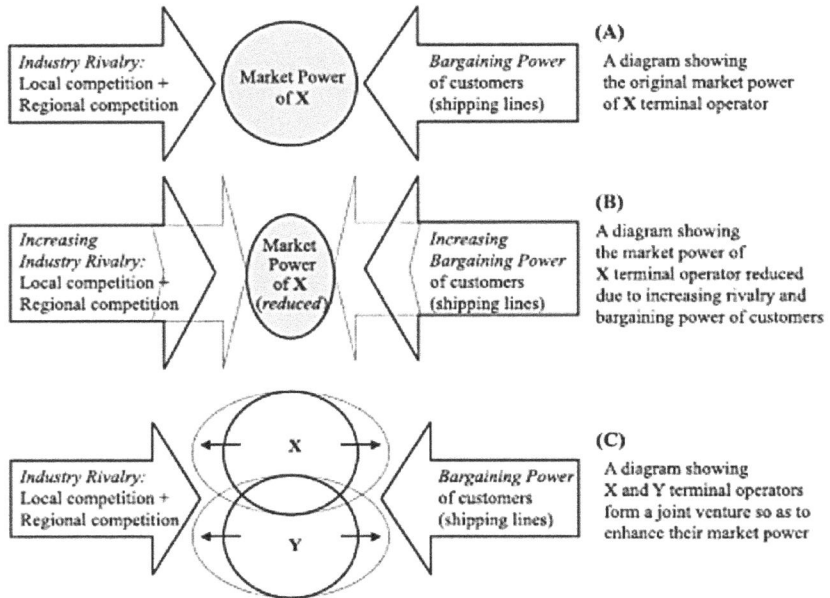

Fig. 7.2 Enhancement of market power through joint venture. Source: Song (2001).

competitiveness and market power of the firm. Rather than utilizing competitive strategies alone, the terminal operators may adopt a co-operative strategy as a useful option to develop a stronger position in their market. In other words, a co-operative strategy may offer a mutually beneficial opportunity for collaborating units to reshape their positions in the industry. Furthermore, it may allow them to increase their market power.

7.2 Case Study TAMA (Japan)

The TAMA-Greater Tokyo Initiative is a public-benefit association located at Hachioji City, Tokyo, Japan. It was created in 1998, with the aim of vitalising industries in TAMA through innovating collaborations among industries, universities, governments, and financial institutions. Geographically, it covers western parts of the Greater Tokyo Metropolis, including the Prefectures of Tokyo, Kanagawa, and Saitama.

The TAMA-Greater Tokyo Initiative is a cluster that consists of 602 affiliates, including 41 universities, 20 local governments, 36 chambers of commerce, and more industry groups, financial institutions, and industrial companies, since August 2014. Approximately 300 members of the cluster are companies focusing on innovation using advanced technologies.

To serve its role as a supporting association, the TAMA-Greater Tokyo Initiative promotes innovations and collaborations throughout a network of ABCG (Academic-Business-Community-Government) plus banks. Their unique aim is not only to develop the regional network so that some projects can run smoothly supported by ABCG, but also to create collaborations with other clusters in Japan and globally, in order to contribute to global innovations and strengthen their network. These aims and networks are illustrated in Figure 7.3.

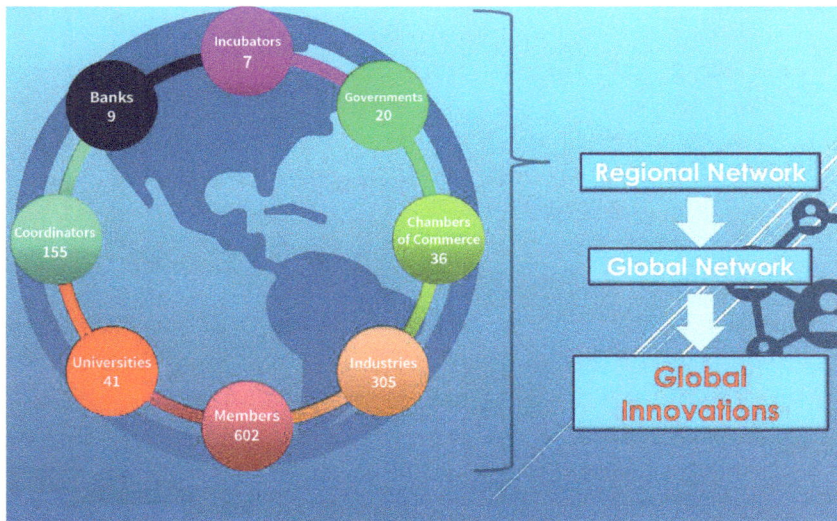

Fig. 7.3 TAMA's aims and networks. Source: adapted from TAMA-Greater Tokyo Initiative (2017).

Figure 7.4 shows that TAMA's primary concerns are not only to nurture collaboration, but also to generate networks and expand business. Due to this strong linkage, many Japanese SMEs have been able to expand their business abroad, ultimately becoming multinational companies all over the world.

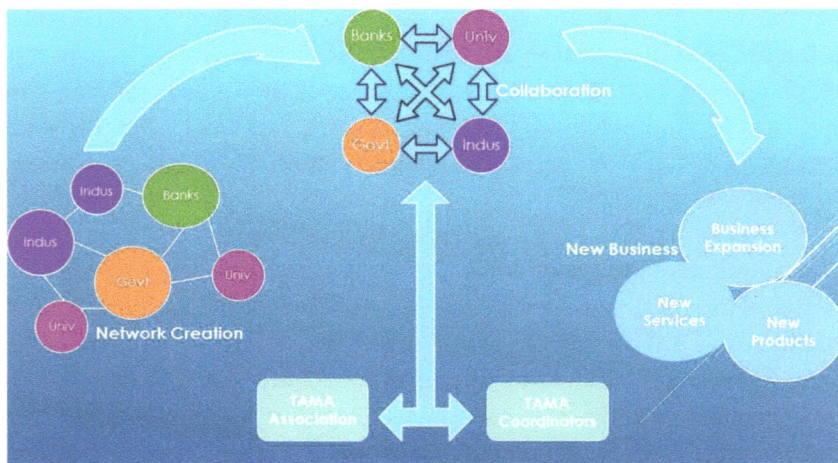

Fig. 7.4 Main Functions of TAMA. Source: adapted from Wahyuni and Wahyuningsih (2018).

The network generation from industry, university, government and bank provides a strong valuable linkage for any kind of collaboration and development of new business. As Douglas and Nancy (2008) observe, when collaborations work, they are synergistic in that they produce more than they cost. More specifically, like any asset, collaboration across organizational boundaries requires an investment by boundary spanners and their organizations. Both organizations must be willing to engage in some risk taking and invest some human, social, and financial capital. Maturing the asset requires patience, goodwill, and time. Yet even with these investments, the collaboration asset will not form in the absence of boundary spanners. They are the primary active ingredient that pulls people together; they instigate, manage, and grow the collaboration asset. For this reason, the principal boundary spanners of any collaboration must trust each other and be trusted by their respective organizations if the collaboration asset is to survive the process of cross-organizational learning.

7.2.1 Financial Resources

Since its establishment in 1998, the TAMA-Greater Tokyo Initiative has received large financial support from the Kanto bureau of the Ministry of Economy, Trade and Industry (METI). During the early stage of its operation, the association's supporting programs were mainly financed by grants from the Kanto METI, in addition to its membership fees.

Followed by the growth of its members and service menus, the TAMA-Greater Tokyo Initiative is in need of more grants to provide integrated support for its member companies. Besides funds from the METI, grants have also been obtained from both national and local authorities such as the Ministry of Education, Culture, Sports, Science and Technology (MEXT), the Ministry of Internal Affairs and Communications (MIC), the Small and Medium Enterprise Agency, Tokyo Metropolitan Governments, and other local governments.

7.2.2 Five-year Action Plans

A series of action plans have been carefully designed to accomplish the TAMA-Greater Tokyo Initiative's objectives, as well as to assist its member companies. Those action plans have been divided into four stages: networking; new research, development projects and business; eco-friendly manufacturing; and eco-clustering.

The first five-year action plan for the period of 1998 to 2002 focused on "networking". When the TAMA-Greater Tokyo Initiative was newly established, it did not possess enough solid fundamentals in terms of technologies, infrastructure, and partnership. In recognition of this, the TAMA-Greater Tokyo Initiative's first five-year action plan began with infrastructure development and network construction. Several activities that supported the construction of the network infrastructure were the development of an information network, meetings between academics and industry, exhibitions of TAMA technology, the development of search engines for academic and industry integration, business fairs, and the development of a virtual laboratory.

After constructing the network, the TAMA-Greater Tokyo Initiative concentrated on creating new research and development (R&D) projects by promoting academic and business partnerships in the second five-year action plan (2003 to 2007). This involved the invention of new technology, and the development of products that met market needs.

The TAMA-Greater Tokyo Initiative is currently under its fourth five-year action plan (2013–2017) and is focusing on "Eco-cluster in TAMA" (Figure 7.5). Besides continuing to develop the previous five-year action plans, it intends to promote TAMA globally by creating ten global niche top (GNT) companies — companies that possess high market shares in global niche markets.

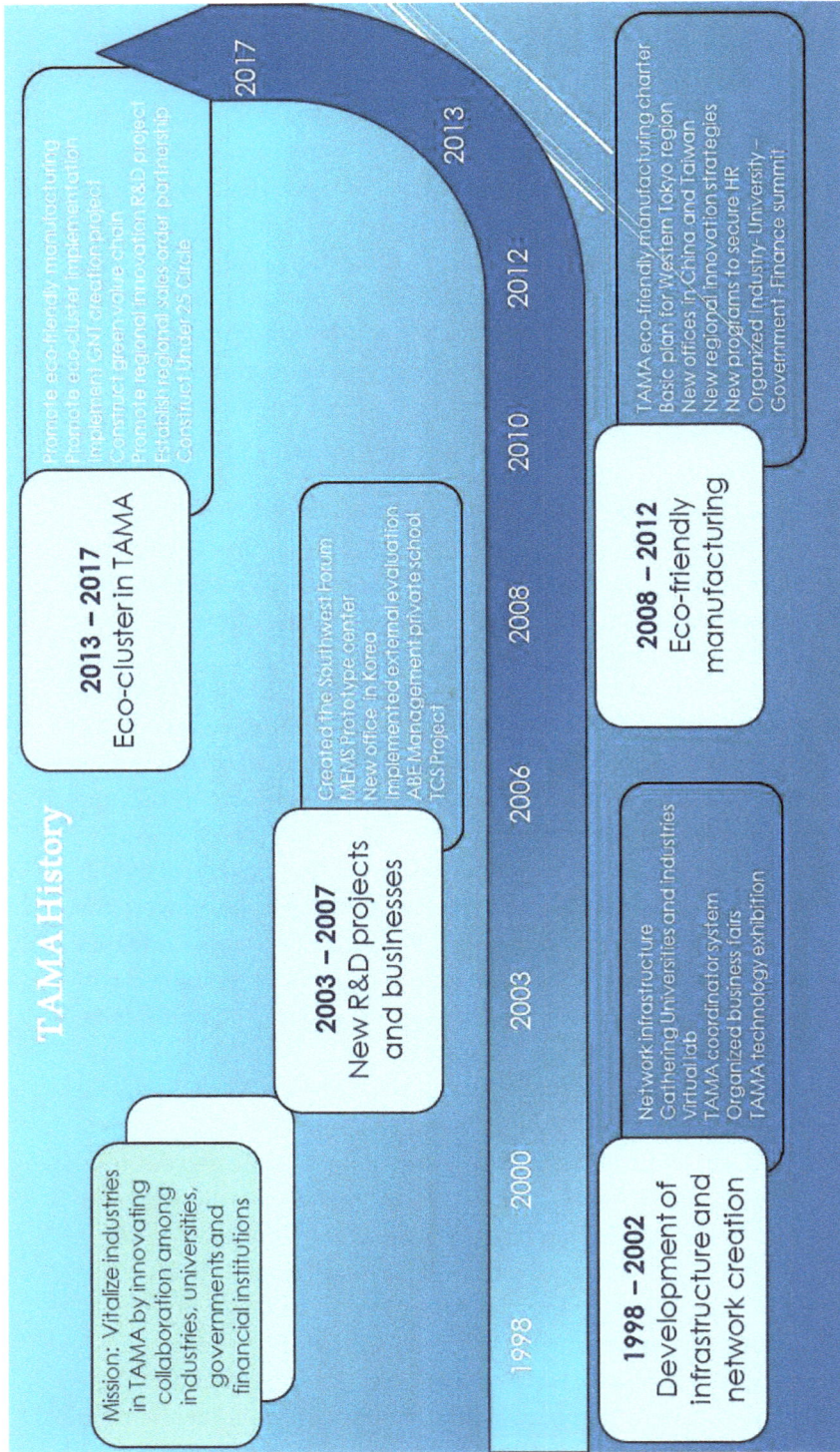

Fig. 7.5 TAMA-Greater Tokyo Initiative's Five-year Action Plans. Source: adapted from TAMA-Greater Tokyo Initiative (2017).

To realise the above five-year plan, TAMA developed an integrated strategy which is shown in Figure 7.6. First, the national government sets policies for industrial supports. Second, according to the policies, grant aid and supports from clustering policies are set for focused areas. This can be "high octane gas" for companies in the area of focus. Third, the cooperation amongst local supporting agencies, such as local governments, chambers of commerce, Kanto METI, and TAMA, offers support to the target industries. Fourth, this support vitalises the industry by accumulating industries and boosting networking. Fifth, this leads to increases in employment, and in tax revenue. Sixth, since the tax revenue increases, the government can therefore increase the amount of grant aid. This cycle acts as an engine for industrial vitalisation.

Figure 7.7 delineates the steps for business development from the earlier to the later stages, and shows how the TAMA association supports each step. In each stage, TAMA provides a variety of support menus from R&D by collaboration between industries and universities, to marketing by business fairs or investments (TAMA funds), and, additionally, human resources and training.

In implementing this strategy, TAMA provides the following support:

1. Cultivation of key persons for local industrial vitalization.

2. Supporting strategy formation and analysis for new industries.

3. Support for planning the industrial vitalization plan.

4. Projects for solving social issues in the region.

5. Support for collaboration with other areas.

6. Support for marketing in the Greater Tokyo Area.

7. Supports for overseas marketing.

From the above example, we can see that it is not enough to develop Tokyo solely through government initiatives. A comprehensive collaboration between ABCG and banks is ultimately needed. The same approach has been taken by the Port of Singapore (see Box 1), which has been able to maintain its competitive position through time. Singapore's high performance is not only due to its innovation policy, but to the existence of an epistemic community. Singapore shows the most rapid

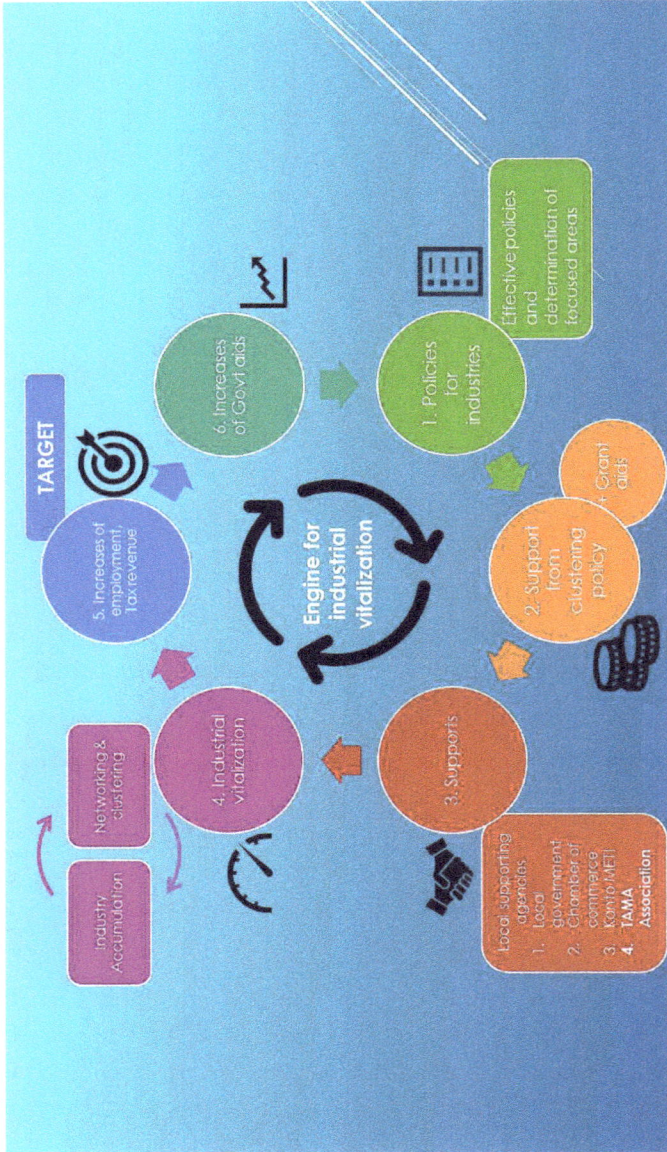

Fig. 7.6 TAMA strategy 1. Source: adapted from TAMA-Greater Tokyo Initiative (2017).

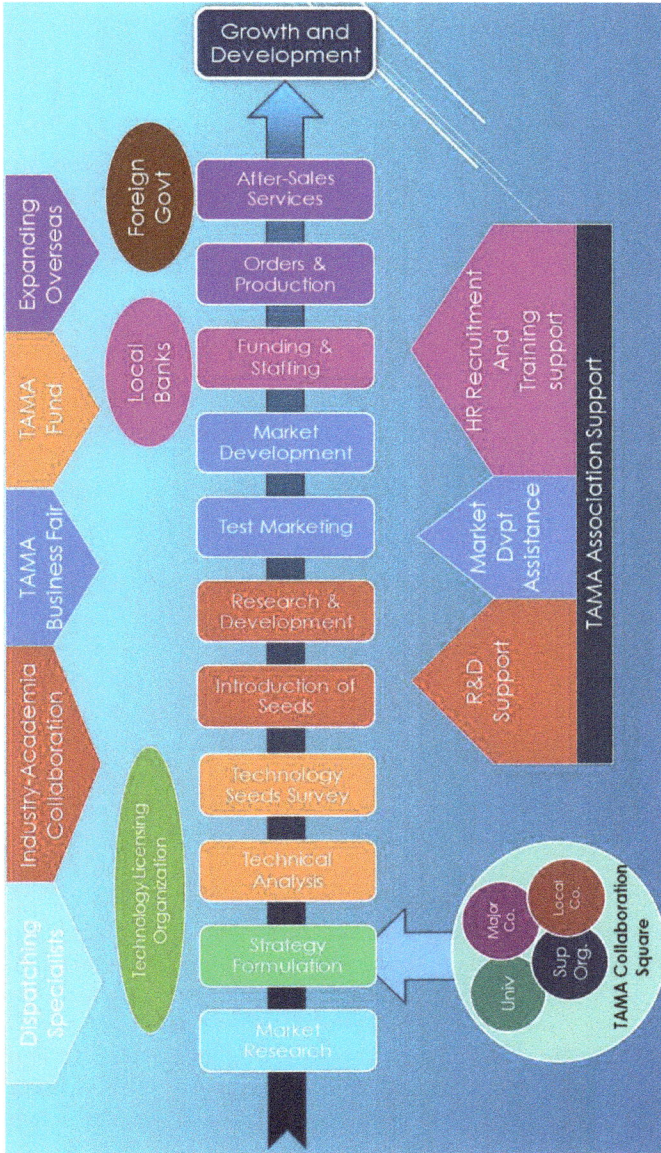

Fig. 7.7 Strategy 2: TAMA support measures. Source: adapted from Wahyuni and Wahyuningsih (2018).

growth in terms of generating local innovations. The Government has provided a set of grants to encourage enterprises to invest in local R&D (e.g. the Productivity and Innovation Credit (PIC) provides significant tax deductions or payouts for investments in research and development, innovation, automation and training).

The Maritime and Port Authority of Singapore (MPA) has established a SGD 250 million Maritime Innovation and Technology (MINT) fund (mpa.gov.sg/web/portal/home/maritime-companies/research-development/Funding-Schemes/mint-fund) to support their long-term vision to be a research-intensive, innovative and entrepreneurial economy.

Box 5. Maritime Cluster Building in Singapore

In the past, Singapore had been over-reliant on the conventional port functions of providing cargo handling, ship-related services and storage. However, in light of the need to diversify its business operations and thus maintain its position as a logistics hub, the government of Singapore has embarked on establishing Singapore as a maritime logistics hub. Singapore is now a home to more than 5,000 maritime establishments, with S$ 28 billion gross receipts, employing a workforce accounting for 5 per cent of Singapore's national employment and whose output account for 7 per cent of Singapore's GDP. Singapore has attracted a number of shipping groups to register in its Registry of Ships.

To increase the value-added of the port of Singapore, the Singapore government has undertaken a number of fiscal measures and other incentives to attract advanced logistics companies to locate around the port of Singapore and form a maritime cluster. The strategy is to build a maritime business cluster to enhance position as a logistics hub: a clustering of port and maritime-related activities complementary to the trade in goods and services (linking port Operations to international trade) and a one-stop service for customers by providing an integrated maritime logistics services and attaining the economies of scale and scope. Apart from maintaining transparency of regulations, provision of word class infrastructure, provision of adequate supply of skilled logistics professionals and provision of a foreign-friendly environment, fiscal measures and other generous incentives have played a major role towards attaining a maritime logistics hub status. The major tax incentives include the Approved International Shipping Enterprise (AISE)scheme, Approved Shipping Logistics Enterprise (ASLE) tax benefits for Ship Registration and Business Development Support. The AISE offers income tax exemption for 10 years for foreign flag ships provided that the owner or charterer controls a significant amount of ships and have a significant operation in Singapore. In the past only Singapore flag ships were given income tax exemption, and this exemption assisted in the substantial expansion of Singapore fleet in the 1970s and 1980s. However, in many cases there was very little further benefit for Singapore and its economy since a large of that fleet was operated, commercially and technically, outside Singapore. To increase the use of Singapore as a base for the management and control of their shipping operations, Singapore introduced in 1991 a tax incentive under the AIS incentive scheme to exempt shipping lines awarded a AISE status from tax on the income from vessels operated by them, whether registered under Singapore flag or elsewhere. The ASLE provides a concessionary income tax on qualifying incremental income for established ship management, ship agencies, freight forwarders and logistics operators. To encourage foreign vessels to register with Singapore's Registry of Ships, profits of a shipping enterprise derived from the operation of a Singapore-registered ship are income tax exempt. This applies to income derived from the carriage in international waters of passengers, mails, livestock or goods or from towing or salvage operations carried out in international waters by Singapore ships, and includes charter of Singapore ships. It also exempts shipping companies registered with Singapore from withholding tax on interest payments with respect to offshore loans to finance ships. Under this incentive scheme there is also no tax on gains from vessel sales. The government also extends business development support to ship-owners and maritime auxiliary service providers by providing grants and defraying expenses at initial development on reimbursement basis.

To foster innovation within the maritime industry, the government has established since 2003 the Maritime Innovation and Technology Fund (MITF) and to address the shortage of supply of skilled logistics professionals, the government has established since 2002 the Maritime Cluster Fund (MCF). The MITF includes the Maritime Industry Attachment Programme, the Joint Tertiary & Research Institutions and MPA R&D Programme, the Maritime Technology Professorships and the Platform for Test-bedding, Research, Innovation and Development for New-maritime Technologies (TRIDENT). The MCF was established by Singapore's Maritime and Port Authority to support the maritime industry's manpower and business development efforts.

Box 1 Source: Merck (2009).

7.3 Conclusion

This study demonstrates that, in order to develop a successful cluster, a systematic cluster strategy must incorporate the following: the banks, the cultivation of key persons for local industrial vitalisation, analysis for new industries, support for planning the industrial vitalisation plan, support for collaboration with other areas, and also overseas marketing, so that the port project not only runs smoothly but also creates collaboration with other clusters worldwide to strengthen their network.

In this chapter, we have demonstrated how the TAMA association helps businesses become internationally competitive by implementing a strong partnership between Academics, Business, Community and Government (ABCG). In doing so, we have illustrated the profile and support activities of the TAMA-Greater Tokyo Initiative, which include network generation, collaboration, and expansion of business, both domestically and overseas. The case study of Singapore port development highlights the importance of R&D and support from communities in providing value creation.

Because port-cities face common challenges, regions with many different neighbouring port-cities need to develop regional networking. Port-cities require large amounts of capital to finance state-of-the-art infrastructure and must increasingly compete for different sources of funding not only nationally, but even at regional or international levels. The economic benefits from ports are manifold: firstly, ports play an essential role in global supply chains, and, as such, act as facilitators of trade between port-regions and countries. Secondly, port competitiveness also depends on their network and market power. Thirdly, ports could provide value-added services through the economic activities stimulated by an ABCG partnership. Finally, ports are also spatial clusters for innovation, research and development.

References

Brandenburger AM and Nalebuff, BJ 1996. *Co-opetition*, New York, USA: Doubleday.

Connell, J, Voola, R 2013. 'Knowledge integration and competitiveness: a longitudinal study of an industry cluster', *Journal of Knowledge Management*, 17:2 , pp. 208–25, https://doi.org/10.1108/13673271311315178

Douglas, G and Wolf, N 2008. 'Working together: a corrections-academic partnership that works, *Equal Opportunities International*, 27:2 , pp. 148–60, https://doi.org/10.1108/02610150810853479

Fung, CK 1995. Hong Kong's territorial development strategy', in *Global Competitiveness, Working paper series*, Hong Kong, China: *City University of Hongkong.*

Jorde, TM and Teece, DJ 1989. 'Competition and co-operation: striking the right balance', *California Management Review*, 31:3, pp. 25–37, https://doi.org/10.2307/41166568

McKinnon, A 2011. *Hong Kong and Shenzhen ports: Challenges, opportunities and global competitiveness*, Hong Kong, China: Hong Kong Centre for Maritime and Transportation Law, City University of Hong Kong, businessdocbox.com/Logistics/69177456-Hong-kong-and-shenzhen-ports-challenges-opportunities-and-global-competitiveness.html

Merck, O 2014. *The Competitiveness of global port-cities: Synthesis Report*, OECD report, www.oecd.org/cfe/regional-policy/Competitiveness-of-Global-Port-Cities-Synthesis-Report.pdf

Nonaka, I 1994. 'A dynamic theory of organizational knowledge creation', *Organizational Science*, 5:1, pp. 14–37, www.svilendobrev.com/1/Nonaka_1994-Dynamic_theory_of_organiz_knowledge_creation.pdf

Notteboom, TE, Ducruet, C and Langen, PW 2009. *Competition and coordination among adjacent seaport*, Farnham, United Kingdom: Ashgate Publishing.

Notteboom, T and Rodrigue, JP 2005. 'Port regionalization: Towards a new phase in port development', *Maritime Policy And Management*, 32:3, pp. 297–313, https://doi.org/10.1080/03088830500139885

Notteboom, T and Winkelmans, W 2001. 'Structural changes in logistics: how will port authorities face the challenge?', *Maritime Policy and Management*, 28:1, pp. 71–89, https://doi.org/10.1080/03088830119197

Small and Medium Enterprise Agency 2014. '2014 White Paper on small and medium enterprises in Japan' pp. 295–369, www.chusho.meti.go.jp/pamflet/hakusyo/H26/download/2014hakusho_eng.pdf

Song D-W 2002. 'Regional container port competition and co-operation: the case of Hong Kong and South China', *Journal of Transport Geography*, 10:2, 99–110, https://doi.org/10.1016/S0966-6923(02)00003-0

TAMA-Greater Tokyo Initiative 2017. *Outline of the Greater Tokyo initiative.*

Wahyuni, S, Ghauri PN and Karsten, L 2007. 'Managing international strategic alliance relationships', *Thunderbird International Business Review*, 49:6, pp. 671–87, https://doi.org/10.1002/tie.20166

Wahyuni, S 2013. *Developing special economic zone: Benchmarking between Indonesia, Thailand, Malaysia and China, Indonesian Ministry of Trade*, Indonesia: University of Indonesia and Salemba Empat.

Wahyuni, S and Wahyuningsih 2018. *Strategi Kawasan Ekonomi Khusus,* Indonesia: University of Indonesia and Salemba Empat.

Yeh, GO, Mak, CK (eds.) n.d. *Chinese cities and China's development*: *A preview of the future role of Hong Kong,* Hong Kong, China: Centre of Urban Planning and Environmental Management, University of Hong Kong.

8. Revealing Indonesian Port Competitiveness
Challenge and Performance

S. Wahyuni,[1] *A. Azadi Taufik,*[2] *and F. K. P. Hui*[3]

8.0 Introduction

Port competitiveness is an important aspect that can boost national competitiveness. According to Merk (2013), ports are beneficial not only as trade facilitators, but also as providers of value-added activities. They boost port employment, and become places of innovation, research and development. Dwarakish and Salim (2015, p. 299) analysed various reports from ports around the world and concluded that "the growth and development of ports leads to greater trade activity, increased supply, greater foreign reserves, and reduced prices for commodities as a whole", and that the development of ports serves as "a good reflection of a country's economy."

Although Indonesia is a maritime country, its ports have not performed as expected by Joko Widodo, current President of Indonesia,

1   Associate Professor, Dept. of Management, Faculty of Economics and Business, Universitas Indonesia.
2   Former student in Dept. of Management, Faculty of Economics and Business, Universitas Indonesia.
3   Senior Lecturer and Academic Specialist, Dept. of Infrastructure Engineering, School of Engineering, The University of Melbourne.

who would like to establish a sea toll, and see Indonesia become a world class maritime player. Compared to the neighbouring countries in East Asia and the Pacific, Indonesia ranks 7th in container port traffic (Dappe and Suárez-Alemán 2016), while Malaysia and Singapore rank 4th and 2nd, respectively. According to the Global Competitiveness Report 2017–2018, Indonesia ranks 5th in the Association of Southeast Asian Nations (ASEAN) in overall infrastructure quality, below Singapore, Malaysia, Brunei Darussalam, and Thailand. In ASEAN, Indonesia's port infrastructure quality ranks 4th, below Singapore, Malaysia, and Thailand. In terms of the Logistics Performance Index in 2016, Indonesia ranks 4th again below Singapore, Malaysia, and Thailand, with infrastructure and international shipments receiving low scores (Table 8.1). Land and port bottlenecks in Indonesia's economic corridors result in logistical costs estimated to be 24–26% of the GDP (Carruthers 2016). In order to strengthen Indonesian port competitiveness, smart and strategic positioning, marketing and implementation need to be undertaken.

Indonesia is an archipelago, where efficient sea transportation between islands can potentially create a more efficient supply chain (Wiranta 2003) that would address the high costs of shipping within Indonesia (Sandee 2011). The emergence of the ASEAN Economic Community will also increase trade within the region and accelerate the need for Indonesian port competitiveness (van Dijk, van de Mheen, and Bloem 2015).

Research into Indonesian port competitiveness is limited. A search through the Scopus database (Elsevier) — which provides a searchable database of scientific journals, books, and conference proceedings — identifies only four articles about Indonesia from a total of 455 articles and reviews with titles, abstracts, or keywords consisting of either "competitiveness" or "selection" or "choice" or "performance" combined with the term "port" since 1980 to the present. That represents 0.9% of all articles compared to 10% of articles about China, 9% of articles about South Korea, and 8.8% of articles about the USA. This suggests that there are substantial gaps in the research into Indonesian port competitiveness.

The research reported in this chapter tries to fill this gap by identifying the position of Indonesian ports relative to other Asian

Table 8.1 Rank of ASEAN Logistics Performance Index

Country	ASEAN Rank	Global Rank	Total Score	Customs	Infra-structure	International Shipments	Logistics Competence	Tracking and Tracing	Timeliness
Singapore	1	5	4.14	4.18	4.20	3.96	4.09	4.05	4.40
Malaysia	2	32	3.43	3.17	3.45	3.48	3.34	3.46	3.65
Thailand	3	45	3.26	3.11	3.12	3.37	3.14	3.20	3.56
Indonesia	4	63	2.98	2.69	2.65	2.90	3.00	3.19	3.46
Viet Nam	5	64	2.98	2.75	2.70	3.12	2.88	2.84	3.50
Brunei	6	70	2.87	2.78	2.75	3.00	2.57	2.91	3.19
Philippines	7	71	2.86	2.61	2.55	3.01	2.70	2.86	3.35
Cambodia	8	73	2.80	2.62	2.36	3.11	2.60	2.70	3.30
Myanmar	9	113	2.46	2.43	2.33	2.23	2.36	2.57	2.85
Laos	10	152	2.33	1.85	1.76	2.18	2.10	1.76	2.68

Source: Arvis et al. (2016).

ports, and by engaging with the challenges faced by Indonesian ports. Findings from this study hopefully can help policy makers in crafting their strategy to boost Indonesian port performance through improved financing decisions for seaport projects. This chapter contributes to research and management practice by identifying important aspects of port competitiveness and encouraging investor interest by overcoming inefficiencies in government bureaucracy, customs clearance, and strategic decision making, energy infrastructure and road rail connectivity.

8.1 Literature Review

Currently, Indonesia has more than 2,000 ports and terminals (Ministry of Transportation, 2013), with 111 commercial ports, 1,129 non-commercial ports, and more than 800 special terminals for mining, oil, gas, and chemical industries.

There are four state-owned port companies that are major players in the Indonesian port industry. Known as PT Pelabuhan Indonesia (Pelindo) I, II, III and IV, the companies operate public ports within geographical regions as depicted in Figure 8.1. The four port corporations generated USD 130 million in 2017 (Maulana 2018), which accounts for 0.21% of Indonesia's GDP.

According to OECD (2012), although each Pelindo was designed as a limited liability, profit-making company, the government of Indonesia controls port tariffs at a national level to allow cross-subsidisation amongst them. With the Shipping Law of 2008, Pelindo's role has been limited to port operators and port service providers, and is no longer a port authority, allowing in theory for competition and greater participation of other operators from the private sector.

Lee, Song and Ducruet (2008) state that there is a common trend amongst Western port cities to shift port facilities towards outer areas of their metropolitan regions, whereas Asian ports have been shifting land-use activities towards creating Global Hub Cities, thereby responding to the demand for an integrated global logistical system to handle cargo import and export in Asia.

Merk (2013) states that large port-cities have gateway ports which serve port traffic to metropolitan areas and its hinterland. Hinterland

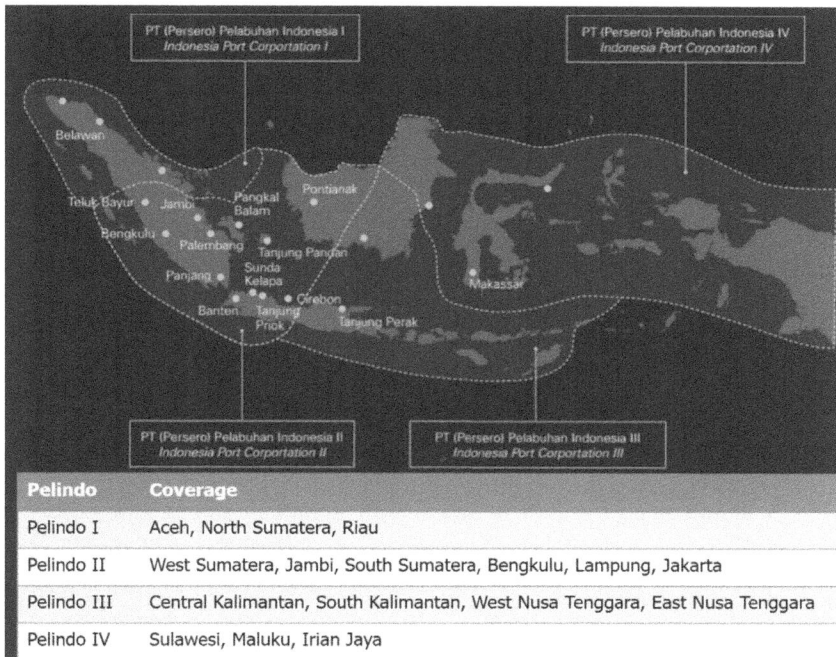

Pelindo	Coverage
Pelindo I	Aceh, North Sumatera, Riau
Pelindo II	West Sumatera, Jambi, South Sumatera, Bengkulu, Lampung, Jakarta
Pelindo III	Central Kalimantan, South Kalimantan, West Nusa Tenggara, East Nusa Tenggara
Pelindo IV	Sulawesi, Maluku, Irian Jaya

Fig. 8.1 Coverage of Pelindo I, II, III, and IV. Source: adapted from Sheng (2015).

proximity refers to the geographical proximity between industrial zones and ports. Hinterland connectivity refers to the transportation systems and links between industrial zones and ports, such as roads, railways, and the transport cost and travel times. Kim (2014) found that amongst service-oriented, cost-saving oriented, task-achiever oriented, and infrastructure-oriented actors, inter-modal links and land transport systems are important elements of port choice behaviour. Tang, Low and Lam (2011), state that availability of inter-modal transport facilities allows for easier handling of containers being imported or exported. Walter and Poist (2003) reinforce the point that inter-modal transport facilities allow for easier local and regional deliveries.

Port infrastructure and facilities are also an important factor in the determination of port competitiveness (Lin and Tseng 2007). Based on the work of De Martino and Morvillo (2008), infrastructure can be categorised into hard and soft components. Hard components include infrastructure, supra-structures, equipment, geographical location, and inland logistics platforms whilst soft components include supplied services, interfirm ties, ICT systems, and safety and security. Other researchers focused on measurable port facilities instead of physical objects, such as handling efficiency (Lirn, Thanopoulou, Beynon and Beresford 2004; Cullinane, Fei and Cullinane 2004), and reliability of facilities, and storage capacity (Grosso and Monteiro 2009; Yuen, Zhang and Chueng 2012).

Operational efficiency and port service quality are important factors in port competitiveness. Operational efficiency is the ability of the port to use its resources to deliver high operational performance efficiently (Parola, Risitano, Ferretti and Panetti 2016). This can be measured in numerous ways, including: throughput; ship turnover time; cargo handling productivity; capacity utilisation; and other measurements used to indicate operational performance and resource utilization (Steven and Corsi, 2012).

Yen, Zhang and Chueng (2012) outline how customs procedures and government regulator administrative procedures are also important factors that determine port competitiveness. De Langen (2004) includes governance alongside maritime accessibility and hinterland infrastructure, as important determinants of the seaport performance.

Other research focuses on the competitiveness of major ports in Southeast Asia (Kutin, Nguyen and Vallée 2017; Dang and Yeo 2017; Cheong and Suthiwartnarueput 2015). There are several possible reasons for the lack of port development in Indonesia. An internal analysis conducted by Bank Mandiri (Nirwan 2017) concluded that the general obstacles for project development in Indonesia also occur in port infrastructure development, namely land acquisition, construction issues, financing issues, planning and preparation issues, and permit issues. Figure 8.2 shows that corruption, inefficient government bureaucracy, lack of access to financing, inadequate supply of supporting infrastructure, and policy instability are the most problematic factors of doing business in Indonesia.

Improving Indonesian port competitiveness is crucial for the national economic development of the country. The government claims that improving the seaport transportation in Indonesia can help overcome disparity in local economic development in the western and eastern regions of the vast archipelago nation (Ministry of National Development Planning, 2014). The Ministry of Transportation is even more ambitious, viewing the development of seaport transportation in

Corruption	13.8
Inefficient government bureaucracy	11.1
Access to financing	9.2
Inadequate supply of infrastructure	8.8
Policy instability	8.6
Government instability/coups	6.5
Tax rates	6.4
Poor work ethic in national labor force	5.8
Tax regulations	5.2
Inflation	4.7
Inadequately educated workforce	4.3
Crime and theft	4.0
Restrictive labor regulations	4.0
Foreign currency regulations	3.3
Insufficient capacity to innovate	2.5
Poor public health	1.8

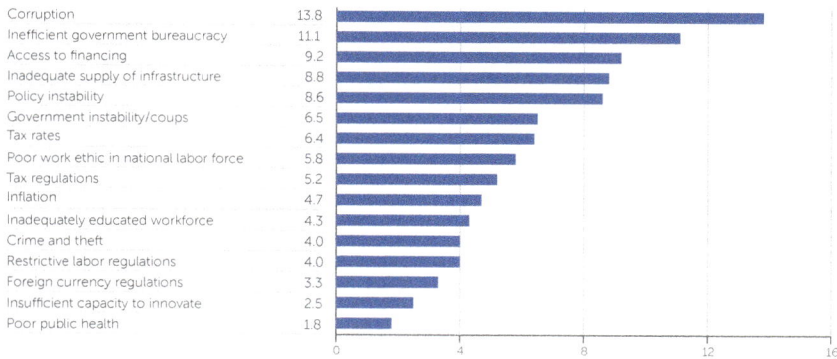

Fig. 8.2 Most Problematic Factors of Doing Business in Indonesia.
Source: Schwab (2017).

Indonesia as having the potential to transform Indonesia into a global maritime power in an increasingly Asian-centric global economy (Ministry of Transportation, 2015). Leinbach (1995) argues that transportation infrastructure is particularly critical for development in developing countries. This argument is supported by Kamaluddin (2003) who conducted a study on the importance of transportation infrastructure to Indonesia's development. As an archipelago, Wiranta (2003) suggests that the development of sea transportation between islands in Indonesia can create a more efficient supply chain that solves what Sandee (2011) — a World Bank trade specialist — reports as the high costs of shipping: it is currently more expensive to ship from Padang to Jakarta than from Jakarta to Singapore. In the near future, the importance of port competitiveness will continue to increase with the emergence of the ASEAN Economic Community, where trade is expected to intensify (van Dijk, van de Mheen and Bloem 2015).

Responding to the need to improve Indonesian port competitiveness, the Indonesian government is in the midst of planning and implementing broad policies and strategies concerning maritime and port development. President Widodo envisions Indonesia as a Global Maritime Nexus, involving 34 ministries and 425 policies which range from maritime diplomacy, maritime connectivity, marine industry, maritime security, and nautical cultural. The National Development Plan and the Ministry of Transportation Strategic Planning for 2015–2019 outline the ways in which policies and strategies for the port sector focus on increasing private investment for port services, and on the development of twenty-four strategic ports to create a maritime highway (dubbed Indonesia's Sea Toll Project) that would act as a transportation network amongst all regions of Indonesia. Other policies include a reform package to improve logistics in the country through transportation insurance, logistics cost reduction, strengthening the Indonesian National Single Window, and reducing the number of prohibited goods. Whether these policies have or will increase port competitiveness is yet to be evaluated.

8.2 Methodology

The study reported in this chapter is part of a research project into the Efficient Facilitation of Major Infrastructure Projects with a focus on ports, where an online survey, focus group discussions (FGD), and in-depth interviews were conducted with key port stakeholders in Indonesia and Australia in 2017/18. The research is a collaboration between The University of Melbourne in Australia and the Universitas Indonesia, Universitas Gadjah Mada and Institut Teknologi Sepuluh Nopember in Indonesia as part of research funded by the Australia-Indonesia Centre Infrastructure Cluster Research Group. The methodology associated with the Efficient Facilitation of Major Infrastructure Projects study is described in full in Appendix 1. This chapter focuses exclusively on the results from the online port survey, FGD, and in-depth interviews from Indonesia.

The online survey into port planning and development explored investment decisions, port/city performance, barriers to doing business, funding and financing decisions, port sustainability, procurement and capacity building. The online survey targeted port authorities, policy-makers related to ports, and other port actors in Indonesia. The key port stakeholders were also approached to take part in the FGD and in the in-depth interviews.

The online port survey included a question asking participants to indicate from a list of twenty-nine factors provided, how problematic these factors are to doing business in Indonesia. Respondents were required to indicate how problematic the factors are on a scale of 1 to 5, where 1 is the most problematic, and 5 least problematic. The list comprised the sixteen factors that the World Economic Forum (WEF) uses in their Executive Opinion Survey, the ten indicators used by the World Bank for their 'Doing Business' rankings (WB), and three additional factors that were identified as issues in Indonesia: affordable energy availability, land acquisition and regulatory uncertainty.

8.2.1 Focus Group Discussions and In-Depth Interviews

On the 25 September 2017, FGD were held at the Ministry of Transportation office in Jakarta with port experts and authorities to obtain a deeper understanding of Indonesian port planning, development, and financing. The FGD were structured into two sessions: the first session focused on Indonesian port planning and development, while the second session focused on Indonesian ports financing. Each session began with a presentation from invited speakers, followed by a panel discussion. The FGD session was attended by more than thirty-six high-ranking officials and representatives of the government, major corporations in logistics and development, banks, associations, universities, and other experts.

In-depth interviews were also conducted to uncover specific expert insights into Indonesian port competitiveness. To find information about the strategic direction of Indonesian port development we interviewed senior representatives from Pelindo II's Strategic Bureau. For information on the operational performance we interviewed the executive team members from Pelindo II's Operations and Information System Division. Finally, we interviewed the managers at the Jakarta International Container Terminal to obtain details on competitiveness regarding one of Indonesia's growing and highest potential terminals.

8.3 Results and Discussion

There were fifty-nine respondents to the online Indonesian port survey in total. The specialisation of our respondents varies, with a total of twenty different specialisations (see Figure 8.3). Most of them specialise in port management (n = 15, 25%), engineering (n = 14, 24%), and investment management (n = 5, 8%). This specialisation indicates enough knowledge on port operations and business-related activities such as financing, operations, etc. Lastly, 49% of our respondents work for or with port operators (n = 29), 42% work for or with government departments (n = 25), 36%, work for or with terminal operators (n = 21), 10% work for or with logistics service providers (n = 6), and 15% in other areas (n = 9). These are all important aspects of port operations.

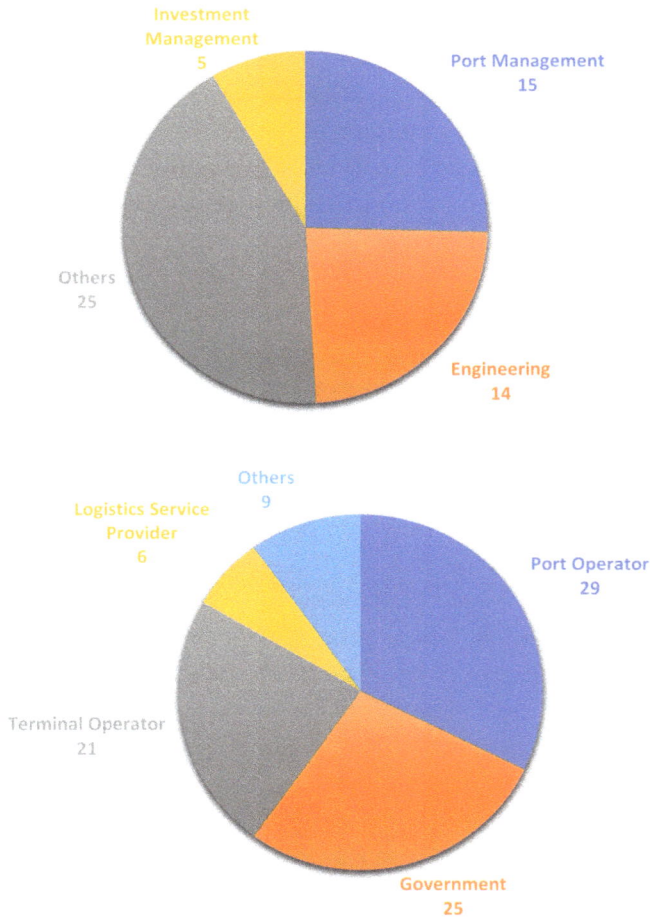

Fig. 8.3 Respondent Data: (Top) Respondent's Specialisation and number of respondents, (Bottom) Respondents' association/working for or with, in the ports and number of respondents (Figure by the authors)

Due to the dominant role of the state-owned corporations Pelindo I, II, III, and IV, this discussion further investigates the leadership and decision making of the Indonesian government, and its impact/influence on port competitiveness. We explore the role of the government and State Owned Enterprises (SOEs) by analysing the administration, bureaucracy, policy, and regulations taken by the government that influence the performance of infrastructure sectors, such as ports. Since many of the investment decisions for ports are still controlled by the government, the level of investment facilitation accommodated by the government will be a good determinant to evaluate port competitiveness. Lastly, evaluating the usefulness of past reform packages — and the level of approval towards investment facilitation for port performance — will also indicate the success of the government in improving Indonesian port competitiveness.

A summary of the Indonesia port problems identified from the research conducted is shown in Figure 8.4.

Indonesian Port Problems

Government Support

- Corruption and bribery
- Inefficient government bureaucracy in customs and decision making
- Policy instability in consistency and commitment
- Gap between policy expectation and policy realization

Business Support

- Inadequate supply of infrastructure, especially in transportation and energy
- Problems of prolonged and uncertain land acquisition
- Poor work ethic in national labor workforce, especially in professionalism and forward-looking

Operational Performance

- Lack of road connectivity
- Lack of transport infrastructure
- Inadequate channel depth
- Management inefficiency
- Lack of energy infrastructure
- Problems with custom clearance

Fig. 8.4 Summary of Indonesian port problem (Figure by authors)

Results from this study show that there are ten most problematic factors for doing business in Indonesia, from the perspective of the survey respondents as shown in Figure 8.5. Corruption, followed by government bureaucracy, are the most problematic.

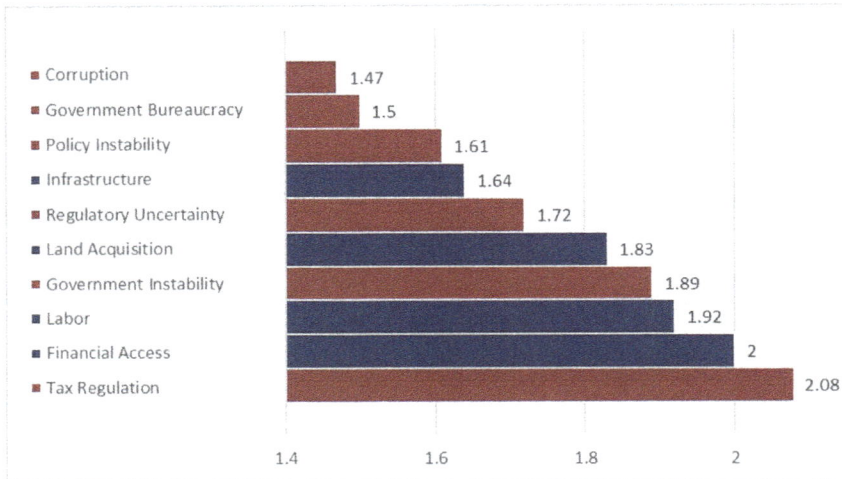

Fig. 8.5 The Most Problematic Factors for Doing Port Business in Indonesia.
(Figure by authors). Red (Government Related Variables), Blue (Business
Related Variables) 1 (Most Problematic-Major Effect), 3 (Neutral), 5 (Least
Problematic-Minimal/No Effect)

Figure 8.5 highlights the severity of corruption as a problematic factor. In terms of infrastructure projects, many respondents claim that "there are many stakeholders that try to obtain profit illegally which result in the value of the project being marked-up" or that there are "too many interest[ed] parties wanting a slice of the action". These stakeholders are called "legal premans within the government process" by another respondent. "Preman" is a derogatory word to describe hooligans or delinquents. The problem of corruption is not only a government problem: one respondent claimed that "development funds must be ensuring that all process is honest and that [corporations] fulfil Good Corporate Governance". One respondent boldly includes port operators as one of the actors involved in political interference and corruption, and identified lack of policy as the main obstacle in advancing infrastructure projects.

Of course, there is no implication that all government policies are futile. Recently, the Joko Widodo administration has provided a reform package intended to reduce the high logistics and high freight costs to improve the supply chain. The previous President, Susilo Bambang Yudhoyono, enacted a reform program consisting of the 2008 Shipping

Law which opened competition of port operations between Pelindo I, II, III, and IV with private sectors, and the Indonesia National Single Window (INSW). As the former policy received resistance from Pelindo I–IV, Widodo's administration further relaxed restrictions on logistics service providers, including freight forwarders, storage providers, distribution providers, transport providers, and cargo handlers. The INSW was strengthened through increased integration between the Ministry of Transport, Ministry of Trade, and the Ministry of Finance. In addition, the 15th Economic Reform Package in June 2017 enacted the following policies: to enhance transportation insurance; to reduce costs for logistics service providers by decreasing transportation operating costs; to eliminate requirements for cargo transportation permit; to decrease port investment cost; to standardize documents; to develop regional distribution centres; to ease procurements, reducing the number of restricted goods; and to strengthen the Indonesia National Single Window (Figure 8.6).

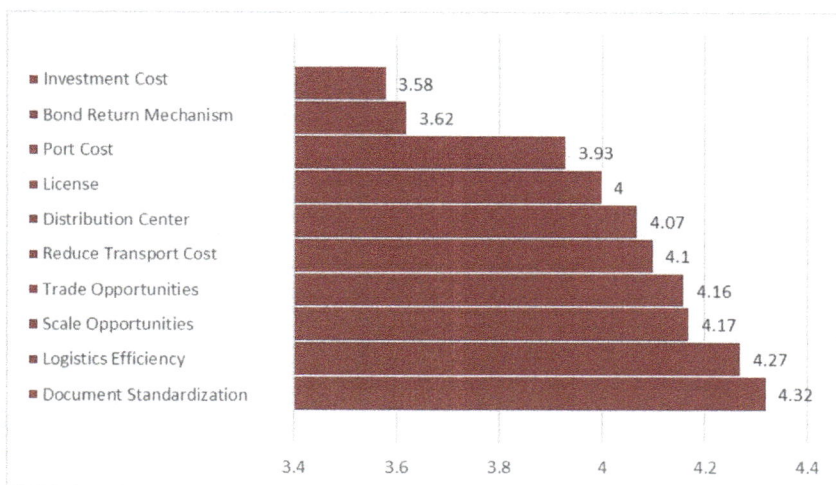

Fig. 8.6 Government Reform Package Usefulness Score (mean) (Figure by the authors). 1 (Very Unhelpful), 3 (Neither Unhelpful or Useful), 5 (Very Helpful)

Document standardisation was perceived by respondents to be one of the most useful initiatives within the reform packages, receiving a score of 4.32 (Fig. 8.6). One of the interviewees, a senior port executive indicated that the flow of documents used to be a problem that contributed to long dwell times in Indonesian ports, as it still required human interaction to receive and approve documents. A recent E-Service technology has also been implemented in Tanjung Priok, which provides electronic features for booking, tracking and tracing, billing, payment, delivery, and loading cancel. These electronic features increase procedural clarity for customers.

The World Bank Representative Head for Indonesia explains that the reform package is expected to overcome Indonesia's logistics bottleneck, resulting in a more efficient economy. The Indonesia National Shipowners' Association (INSA) says that the package will increase the role of national shipping lines, thereby encouraging the shipping competitiveness towards the global market. The Indonesian Logistics Association (ALI) asserts that the package will smooth the flow of cargoes and cut logistics cost. The reform addresses a logistical problem outlined by a leader in Pelindo II, who reports that most of the costs incurred by customers are from external logistic players:

> The internal analysis that we conducted found that only 20% to 30% of cost that is incurred by port customers are from the port itself, the rest are incurred by external logistic players outside the port. (Stakeholder in Pelindo II)

We proceed now in analysing the business-related factors that impact on Indonesian port competitiveness. As shown previously, the results of our survey indicate that the three most problematic business factors are an inadequate supply of infrastructure, land acquisition, and poor work ethics in the national workforce. In terms of infrastructure, one respondent stated that "in Jokowi's Presidency with the tagline 'Indonesia as a World Maritime Fulcrum', is actually very great. But it needs more support with real actionable programs, in terms of infrastructural improvements, accessibility, and connectivity of ports in Indonesia". Many other respondents agree that infrastructure is highly important to develop ports in Indonesia, saying that "ports are not able to operate in solo and will require all supporting infrastructure to ensure the sustainability of port operations".

The condition of infrastructure that supports ports is currently very poor. As one respondent said: "hard accessibility to ports makes [the ports] worthless. For so long, Indonesia has had problems of accessibility, either be it by sea or by land". Another respondent, echoing the conditions outlined in our introduction, stated that "the development of transportation and energy in Indonesia is far behind our neighbouring countries, both in South East Asia and the world."

The forms of infrastructure that our respondents are referring to are transportation infrastructure and energy infrastructure. Questions about operational efficiency are relevant here, with the survey showing that road connectivity, transport, and energy require operational improvements, scoring 1.11, 1.31, and 1.5 respectively. Indonesia's transportation infrastructure is underperforming. According to our resource person in Pelindo II,

> The government's road connectivity masterplan for Indonesia constantly changes and doesn't focus on integrated urban mass transportation. (Stakeholder in Pelindo II)

There were many comments made by survey respondents which concerned Indonesia's transportation infrastructure, and questioned why transportation infrastructure in Indonesia is still causing logistical problems. One survey respondent said that "transportation infrastructure and roads hold an important role in goods and service distribution. The delay of distribution paths has caused economic losses from other sectors". The inefficient flow of goods between Indonesian hinterlands and the ports constitutes the major loss felt by the port sector as a result of poor transportation infrastructure. Resource persons expressed that Indonesia's transportation infrastructure is well behind other Southeast Asian countries. Another respondent indicated that transportation is one of the reasons for the high price in many Indonesian regions, stating that "the delay in the distribution path can result in economic loss" since the inefficient distribution of goods causes losses in other economic sectors. The concern is that transportation is especially important to enhance economic equality and growth in other regions of Indonesia. Integration of ports with industrial parks, production centres, and distribution centres was noted as a prerequisite for improvement because, irrespective of how great ports are implemented, it becomes less useful if access to those ports is difficult.

Many respondents to the survey noted the importance of an integrated intermodal transportation system as a way of improving

Indonesia's adequate transportation infrastructure. One individual wrote that "the existence of ports and terminals must be supported with good integrated intermodal [transportation]. Access to the port from the sea and from land must be good for trucking and large ships. Then, intermodal integration, such as trains, must be a main alternative." However, the solution to Indonesia's transportation infrastructure is not that simple. Other respondents countered arguments that Indonesian ports require the further development of railways. Interestingly, the Indonesian condition is an anomaly compared to other international ports, where trains have become cost effective for delivery to and from ports. A leader of the Indonesian Railway Company explained that Indonesian ports cannot rely on railways because they are not a cost-effective mode of transporting freight:

> Railway is usually used in Java mostly; Nevertheless, in Indonesia railways cannot compete with trucking. Railway transport cost is almost three times more than trucking. Because we have to pay maintenance fee for trains, while this does not occur in trucking. Government policy needs to help this situation. (Stakeholder of Indonesian Railway Company)

One of the current plans to improve the competitiveness of Tanjung Priok port is through intermodal connectiveness with the construction of a Cikarang-Bekasi waterway canal. This waterway canal cuts through the problem of Jakarta's infamous congested roads and the high cost of using railways to transport goods. The government hopes to connect the Cikarang industrial zones with port terminals in Jakarta directly, increasing the effective proximity of Jakarta with its industrial hinterlands.

In terms of energy, one respondent described that "there is unequal distribution of electricity and water to support port activities". This is especially prevalent in less developed regions of Indonesia, where electricity supply is uncertain and there are many power shortages.

The problem of inadequate access to infrastructure may stem from the ways in which Indonesia plans its infrastructural projects. As explained by a leader in the National Development Planning Body,

> In terms of infrastructure in general, Indonesia is different from other countries. Other countries do feasibility studies before deciding on the financing scheme. In Indonesia the process is reversed. In Indonesia we determine the financing scheme, either assigning it to SOE, finance

through PPP, or through loan, before any feasibility study is conducted. (Stakeholder in the National Development Planning Body)

Respondents claim that "the government needs to improve its analysis on infrastructure development so that it is suitable with the level of development in the economic area". One respondent went to the extent of explaining that the main obstacle for obtaining a project infrastructure permit is "uncertainty that a project is feasible from a commercial side or whether it drives social and economic improvement". The primary suggestion for the government to overcome this problem is to establish a "development bureau and masterplan in each city to prevent late development. This biro (bureau) has to use a creative process and innovation in each area should be given to a professional team".

After infrastructure, land acquisition is the next most problematic business-related variable for port competitiveness. During the FGD sessions, we found that land acquisition conducted by the government still requires an unacceptably long period of time. This creates a problem whereby foreign investors become more hesitant to be part of port infrastructure developments due to the long time required to start construction. We discovered from managers at Jakarta International Container Terminal that the construction of the New Priok Container Terminal One (NPCT1) — a brand-new PPP funded terminal in Tanjung Priok Port off the coastline of the Jakarta Bay — faced a land-acquisition issue with residents. The residents refused to have their houses compulsorily acquired for the construction of a new terminal road. Due to this refusal, the road construction project was forced to change route and be re-designed, to account for the land that it was unable to obtain because of the residents' refusal to sell.

Where the port workforce is concerned, problematic factors include national work ethic, and lack of education. Interviews indicate that there is a lack of professionalism amongst port staff. Port operator employees are often ill equipped and inexperienced to interact with foreign players due to lack of training provided by the corporation for communication and interaction with foreigners. This lack of experience to interact with foreign players was described in terms of language barriers, feelings of inferiority towards foreigners, and a lack of understanding of foreign work standards such as timeliness and punctuality. Many employees and managers display a lack of trustworthiness and integrity, especially in dealings with foreign players. This adverse attitude to the involvement of foreign players is justified as being a disturbance to local uniqueness.

Interviewees indicated that, within Pelindo I, II, III and IV, many employees were not "forward-looking". Many of them had been habituated to feel comfortable with the corporation's current standings and already feel they are accomplished within domestic markets. This mindset leads to unwillingness to involve foreign investors or experts. Along with that, many employees have a pessimistic view towards the vision of new programs, calling them "only dreams" instead of discussing necessary actions to achieve new visions. This is perpetuated by a system of seniority and rigid chain of command amongst the corporation's organisational structure. This also inhibits the promotion of younger-generation staff into important positions of responsibility, even when those individuals are more open, adaptive, and tech-savvy.

Management inefficiencies still exist. Many of the basic port technologies that we would expect of large ports have only recently been implemented in Tanjung Priok. It is a good sign that representatives in Pelindo recognize the problem of management inefficiency and are implementing technologies such as VTS (Vessel Traffic Service) — the equivalent of Air Traffic Control for ships — MOS (Marine Operating Systems), which allows for port ship communication and planning, TOS (Terminal Operating Systems), which follows terminal cargo, and Container Freight Service Center, which allows customers to electronically track containers. E-Services and Gate Systems have been implemented only since 2015. This shows a lack of capacity to integrate technology into port management systems. Interviews indicate that the two factors preventing early implementation of technologies are the cost of innovations, and the unwillingness of corporate employees to adopt such innovations. Extensive change management is required to introduce and habituate corporate employees, and other stakeholders, to system improvements such as introducing state-of-the-art technologies.

One other point raised by a respondent was that there is "too much bureaucracy in the port, starting for quarantines, customs, and managing permits in government institutions cause the long dwelling time in Indonesia". Other responses to the survey question concerning operational improvement indicate that improvements are needed in customs clearance.

The last factor that determines Indonesian port competitiveness is business support (Figure 8.4). As a developing country with multiple economic, financial, and technological constraints, business support is an important determinant in deciding the level of accommodation required in Indonesia's current business-related climate to support port competitiveness. The business-support factors include general macroeconomic factors and infrastructure, and technology that influences business performance and investor willingness. The finance factor includes access to finance and protection, while the business-activities factor includes aspects related to the ease of doing port business.

8.4 Conclusions

The results from this research have identified that the factors influencing Indonesian port competitiveness are numerous. The three distinct factors identified are government support, business support, and operational performance. Both operational performance and business support have been extensively researched and reported on as important factors in existing literature. Government support was developed as another factor that impacts port competitiveness, wherein the government and Pelindo I–IV play an active and dominant role in shaping Indonesia's port industry.

We found that, even though there is general support towards the government policies in facilitating port investment, there seems to be a substantial gap between policy expectation and policy realisation. This gap is caused by inefficient government bureaucracy, especially in customs clearance and the strategic decision making of dominant port actors such as Pelindo I, II, III and IV. Investors and developers are also deterred by the inconsistent application of policies and the lack of commitment from the government, which causes policy instability and uncertainty. Slow and uncertain land acquisition remains a prevalent problem.

Despite the lack of connectivity, a transparent and a quick process of investment apparently becomes the main agenda of port reformation. Hopefully this self-reflection could help policy makers and port stakeholders in designing a grounded strategy that can boost Indonesian port competitiveness. All these factors work together to impede investor willingness to participate in infrastructure projects.

References

Arvis, J, Saslavsky, D, Ojala, L, Shepherd, B, Busch, C, Raj, A, and Naula, T 2016. *Connecting to compete 2016*: *Trade logistics in the global economy*: *The Logistics Performance Index and its indicators*, Washington D.C., USA: The World Bank, wb-lpi-media.s3.amazonaws.com/LPI_Report_2016.pdf

Carruthers, AM 2016. *Developing Indonesia's maritime infrastructure*: *The view from Makassar*, ISEAS Yusok Ishak Institute, 49, www.iseas.edu.sg/images/pdf/ISEAS_Perspective_2016_49.pdf>

Cheong, I and Suthiwartnarueput, K 2015. 'ASEAN's initiatives for regional economic integration and the implications for maritime logistics reforms', *The International Journal of Logistics Management*, 26:3, pp. 479–93, https://doi.org/10.1108/IJLM-08-2013-0092

Cullinane, K, Fei, WT and Cullinane, S 2004. 'Container terminal development in Mainland China and its impact on the competitiveness of the port of Hong Kong', *Transport Reviews*,24:1, pp. 33–56, https://doi.org/10.1080/0144164032000122334

Dang, VL and Yeo, GT 2017. 'A competitive strategic position analysis of major container ports in Southeast Asia', *The Asian Journal of Shipping and Logistics*, 33:1, pp. 19–25, https://doi.org/10.1016/j.ajsl.2017.03.003

Dappe, MH and Suárez-Alemán, A 2016. *Competitiveness of South Asia's container ports*: *A comprehensive assessment of performance, drivers, and costs*, Washington D.C., USA: The World Bank, www.worldbank.org/en/news/press-release/2017/04/27/port-performance-south-asia-better-still-expensive-slow-report

De Martino, M and Morvillo, A 2008. 'Activities, resources and inter-organizational relationships: Key factors in port competitiveness', *Maritime Policy and Management*, 35:6, pp. 571–89, https://doi.org/10.1080/03088830802469477

De Langen, P 2004. 'Governance in Seaport Clusters', *Maritime Economics and Logistics*, 6:2, pp. 141–56, https://doi.org/10.1057/palgrave.mel.9100100>

Dwarakish, GS and Salim, AM 2015. 'Review on the role of ports in the development of a nation', *Aquatic Procedia*, 4, pp. 295–301, https://doi.org/10.1016/j.aqpro.2015.02.040

Grosso, M and Monteiro, F 2009. 'Relevant strategic criteria when choosing a container port — The case of the port of Genoa', *European Transport Conference*, 3:4, pp. 299–306.

Kamaluddin, R 2003. *Ekonomi transportasi: Karakteristik, teori, dan kebijakan*, Jakarta, Indonesia: Ghalia Indonesia.

Kim, JY 2014. 'Port user typology and representations of port choice behavior: A Q-methodological study', *Maritime Economics and Logistics*, 16:2, pp. 165–87, https://doi.org/10.1057/mel.2013.26

Kutin, N, Nguyen, TT and Vallée, T 2017. 'Relative efficiencies of ASEAN container ports based on data envelopment analysis', *The ASIAN Journal of Shipping and Logistics*, 33:2, pp. 67–77, https://doi.org/10.1016/j.ajsl.2017.06.004

Lee, S, Song, D and Ducruet, C 2008. 'A Tale of Asia's world ports: The spatial evolution in global hub port cities', *Geoforum*, 39:1, pp. 372–85, https://doi.org/10.1016/j.geoforum.2007.07.010

Leinbach, TR 1995. 'Transport and Third World development: review, issues, and prescription', *Transportation Research Part A: Policy and Practice*, 29:5, pp. 337–44, https://doi.org/10.1016/0965-8564(94)00035-9

Lin, LC and Tseng, CC 2007. 'Operational performance evaluation of major container ports in the Asia-Pacific region', *Maritime Policy and Management*, 34:6, pp. 535–51, https://doi.org/10.1080/03088830701695248

Lirn, TC, Thanopoulou, HA, Beynon, MJ and Beresford, AKC 2004. 'An application of AHP on transhipment port selection: A global perspective', *Maritime Economics and Logistics*, 6:1, pp. 70–91, https://doi.org/10.1057/palgrave.mel.9100093

Maulana, R 2018. 'Pendapatan Pelindo I–IV Tahun Lalu Tembus Rp24 Triliun', *Bisnis Indonesia*, industri.bisnis.com/read/20180122/98/729300/pendapatan-pelindo-i-iv-tahun-lalu-tembus-rp24-triliun

Merk, O 2013. 'The competitiveness of global port-cities: Synthesis Report', in *OECD Regional Development Working Papers, no. 2013/13*, Paris, France: OECD Publishing, https://doi.org/10.1787/5k40hdhp6t8s-en

Ministry of National Development Planning 2014. *Rencana Pembangunan Jangka Menengah Nasional (RPJMN) 2015–2019: Buku I: Agenda Pembangunan Nasional*, www.bappenas.go.id/id/data-dan-informasi-utama/dokumen-perencanaan-dan-pelaksanaan/dokumen-rencana-pembangunan-nasional/rpjp-2005-2025/rpjmn-2015-2019/

Ministry of Transportation 2013. 'The future of Indonesia's port system', paper presented at the Port Development and Expansion Asia 2013 Conference, November, Jakarta, Indonesia, www.iqpc.com/media/1000519/29609.pdf

Ministry of Transportation Directorate General of Sea Transportation 2015. *Keputusan Direktur Jenderal Perhubungan Laut Nomor UM.008/100/19/DJPL-15 Tentang Rencana Strategis (RENSTRA) Direktorat Jenderal Perhubungan Laut Tahun 2015-2019*, hubla.dephub.go.id/kebijakan/Rencana%20Strategis/RENSTRA%20DJPL%202015%20-%202019.pdf

Nirwan, E 2017. *Financing solution for port sector*, unpublished paper, Jakarta, Indonesia: PT Bank Mandiri.

Parola, F, Risitano, M, Ferretti, M and Panetti, E 2016. 'The drivers of port competitiveness: A critical review', *Transport Reviews*, 37:1, pp. 116–38, https://doi.org/10.1080/01441647.2016.1231232

Sandee, H 2011. 'Promoting regional development in Indonesia through better connectivity', *World Bank News*, www.worldbank.org/en/news/opinion/2011/03/13/promoting-regional-development-indonesia-through-better-connectivity

Schwab, K 2017. *The global competitiveness report 2017–2018*, World Economic Forum Reports, www.weforum.org/reports/the-global-competitiveness-report-2017-2018

Sheng, LJ 2015. *Indonesia's new administration: Infrastructure and manufacturing opportunities*, IE Insights, 21, www.iesingapore.gov.sg/-/media/IE-Singapore/Files/Publications/IE-Insights/Vol-21-Indonesia-New-Administration-Infrastructure-and-Manufacturing-Opportunities.ashx

Steven, AB and Corsi, TM 2012. 'Choosing a port: An analysis of containerized imports into the US', *Transportation Research Part E: Logistics and Transportation Review*, 48:4, pp. 881–95, https://doi.org/10.1016/j.tre.2012.02.003

Tang, LC, Low, JMW and Lam, SW 2008. 'Understanding port choice behaviour — A network perspective', *Network and Spatial Economics*, 11:1, pp. 65–82, https://doi.org/10.1007/s11067-008-9081-8

Van Dijk, C, van de Mheen, P and Bloem, M 2015. *Indonesia maritime hotspot*, Rotterdam, The Netherlands: Nederland Maritiem Land, www.maritiemland.nl/wp-content/uploads/2015/09/NML-serie-44-Indonesia-Maritime-Hotspot.pdf

Walter, CK and Poist, RF 2003. 'Desired attributes of an inland port: Shipper vs. carrier perspectives', *Transportation Journal*, 42:5, pp. 42–55, www.jstor.org/stable/20713548

Wiranta, S 2003. *Pengembangan Jasa Transporatasi Laut dalam Rekonstruksi Ekonomi*, Jakarta, Indonesia: Pusat Penelitian Ekonomi Lembaga Ilmu Pengetahuan Indonesia.

World Bank n.d. *World development indicators*, databank.worldbank.org/data/reports.aspx?source=2andseries=IS.SHP.GOOD.TUandcountry

Yuen, CA, Zhang, A and Cheung, W 2012. 'Port competitiveness from the users' perspective: An analysis of major container ports in China and its neighboring countries', *Research in Transportation Economics*, 35:1, pp. 34–40, https://doi.org/10.1016/j.retrec.2011.11.005

9. Initial Investigation into the Effectiveness of Australian Ports' Governance and Management Structures

H. Al-Daghlas,[1] F. K. P. Hui,[2] and C. F. Duffield[3]

9.0 Introduction

The Australian Government has used asset recycling of major ports as a source of funds since the early nineties. The theory is that the capital gained through the long-term leasing or sale of such facilities can be repurposed as a stimulus to build new infrastructure facilities and thus leverage the economic return from the capital rather than having it locked away in a specific long-term asset. According to the government of New South Wales, asset recycling or (capital recycling) is defined as "the sale of underperforming or surplus assets to return the capital to invest in new assets or revitalise existing assets" (Baird 1995; NSW Property 2016). Policymakers should first decide if the service delivered by the underperforming or surplus asset is best done by the government

1   PhD Candidate, Dept. of Infrastructure Engineering, The University of Melbourne.
2   Senior Lecturer and Academic Specialist, Dept. of Infrastructure Engineering, The University of Melbourne.
3   Professor of Engineering Management, Deputy Head of Department (Academic), Dept. of Infrastructure Engineering, The University of Melbourne.

or the private sector (SMART Infrastructure Group 2015). As a result, the control and possibly ownership of the asset will change, and the government must decide on how to re-invest the proceeds from the lease or sale.

Investing in Australian ports has been attractive to both local private investors and international investors, who look at Australian ports as an attractive long-term cash generator and thus a worthwhile addition to their portfolio. The purpose of this chapter is to investigate the effectiveness of the Australian Ports' Governance and management structures. The research methodology uses thematic analysis of focus group discussions involving port stakeholders in Melbourne.

The next section provides a detailed review of the literature focused on three topics related to asset recycling of Australian ports: Australian Ports Reform, Private Investments in Australia, and Critical Assessment of Australian Asset Recycling. Section three presents a brief description of the research and findings from the thematic analysis of the focus group discussions on port governance and management structures. The final section presents the concluding remarks and discusses the future directions for this research.

9.1 Literature Review

9.1.1 Australian Ports Reform

Since 2010, Australian state governments have used asset recycling to offer long-term leaseholds to port operators in several major city-ports. The Government considers this asset recycling as a ready source of funds for other infrastructure projects, and a tool to reduce the state's debt (Chen, Pateman and Sakalayen 2017). Such schemes have also been encouraged by the Australian Government who until recently would provide a 15% bonus of the sale price to a state or Territory if they were prepared to recycle an asset. Australian ports first experienced restructuring more than 25 years ago, in the form of corporatisation and privatisation, when government-owned-businesses (State-Owned Enterprises run like private companies) started to operate the ports. This was done with the aim of improving the efficiency of the ports by setting government interference away from daily activities (Everett 2003). Since then, all Australian state governments have reformed their ports through corporatisation and privatisation (Everett and Pettitt 2006).

In 2003, Everett (2003) reports that the government and political interface continue to have an impact on the commercial activities of the ports. He argues that once the cause of this intervention is treated, the ports will be able to operate freely. Three years later, Everett and Pettitt (2006) re-reported that after a decade of port corporatisation, the main goals were not met and this was due to continuous political interference. Everett and Pettit led the discussion towards privatisation, by highlighting the issues associated with maintaining public ownership of Victoria's main port (the Port of Melbourne), while two other ports in Victoria had already been privatised (Geelong Port and the Port of Portland). They debated how, given the high degree of political interference, the main Victorian port would not be competitive with the two privatised ports.

It took the Australian government over a decade to recognise that the initial goals of port reform via corporatisation were not met (Everett and Robinson 2006). Subsequently, state governments embraced the privatisation of ports using the asset recycling model, starting with South Australia Ports in 2001, to the latest fifty-year lease of the Port of Melbourne at a sum of AUD 9.7 billion (Chen, Pateman and Sakalayen 2017).

While the private owner becomes the landlord and the operator of the port, the government remains the regulator and maintains the right of land after the end of the lease (Chen, Pateman and Sakalayen 2017). The Australian Ports are leased under the private/public model as per the Four Models of port administration developed by (Baird 1995). This model is shown in Table 9.1 Four Models of port administration.

Table 9.1 Four Models of port administration

Models	Port Functions		
	Landowner	Regulator	Utility
1 Pure public sector	Public sector	Public sector	Public sector
2 Public / private	Public sector	Public sector	Private sector
3 Private / public	Private sector	Public sector	Private sector
4 Pure private sector	Private sector	Private sector	Private sector

Source: Baird (1995).

While Everett and Pettitt (2006) suggest that port privatisation could be the solution to achieving commercial goals, Chen, Pateman and Sakalayen (2017) have raised concerns about the risks associated with long-term leases, including: "The risk of undervaluing port assets, increased charges, impeded competition, decreased long-term port investment, and other issues affecting public interests". Conversely, during the Australian Port Privatisation Forum held in 2015, Mr Pallas the Victorian Government Treasurer assured that the port resale would be conducted in a positive climate and with the community interest as a priority. He added that the money would be used for fifty level crossing removals, agricultural projects, and other transport infrastructure (Institute for Supply Chain and Logistics 2015).

Chen and Everett (2013) view port privatisation as an indicator of a change in the governing philosophy: a movement away from inefficient port authorities, and the elimination of political interference. However, Chen and Everett (Chen and Everett 2013) also cite work from Wang, Knox and Lee (2013), where Wang et al. (2013) expressed concerns over social and environmental issues of public interest, impacted by the private owner decisions.

It can be observed from the review of the existing literature that asset recycling can keep political intervention away from daily port operations. However, the process of asset recycling itself has raised several concerns. These concerns create the need to produce an overall framework that regulates and facilitates the leasing of ports and other critical government-owned infrastructure. They further create the need to form a robust risk evaluation associated with long-term leaseholds.

9.1.2 International Private Investment in Australia

Private, local and international investments in Australian ports are detailed in Table 9.2.

Iyer, Rambaldi and Tang (2009) do not see Australia as an attractive investment market. Rather, they described the Australian economy as one of the most closed economies in the Organization for Economic Co-operation and Development (OECD). By studying foreign investments from 1988 to 2003, Iyer, Rambaldi and Tang (2009) found that among the OECD countries, Australia had an excellent economic

Table 9.2 The transaction details and investors in major city ports in
Australia. (Table compiled by the authors)

Port	State	Duration of the Lease	Year the lease commenced	Investors
Port of Brisbane	Queensland	99-year	2010	Global Infrastructure Partners (GIP) 27% until 2013.Caisse de dépôt et placement du Québec.
				Queensland Investment Corporation (QIC) 27%
				Industry Funds Management (IFM) 27%
				Tawreed 19%
Port of Botany and Port Kembla	New South Wales	99-year	2013	Industry Funds Management (IFM) 45%
				Australian Super 20%
				Tawreed 20%
				Qsuper15%
Port of Melbourne	Victoria	50-year	2016	Global Infrastructure Partners (GIP) 40% (GIP, China Investment Corporation CIC, Korea's National Pension Service NPS)
				OMERS 20%
				Future Fund 20%
				Queensland Investment Corporation (QIC) 20%

> Lattin (2017) reflects that ports are considered critical state-owned infrastructure and the Foreign Investment Review Board is required to assess the sale of such assets carefully. Lattin (2017) also emphasises the need for early engagement of foreign investors with the Review Board to ascertain the terms and conditions that need to be fulfilled before proceeding with the investment. Earlier, Bergin (2015) raised a similar concern following the ninety-nine-year lease of the Port of Darwin to Chinese firm Landbridge Group, taking into consideration the status of ports as a national security infrastructure, and identifying the need for a proper approach and policies for such transactions.

growth record but a relatively low foreign investment and trade openness.

In a detailed analysis of what affects foreign investment in Australia, Sadleir and Mahony (2009) observe that the review of policies and regulation in regard to foreign investment is often triggered by circumstances facing Australia. For example, in 2007 the commodity prices witnessed a rapid increase, which sparked the question of whether to restrict or otherwise control foreign investment. Sadleir and Mahony (2009) continued to study how institutional factors and public policies affected foreign investment and suggest that more analysis of regulatory regimes and foreign investment is needed.

Sun, Zhang and Chen (2013) subsequently investigated the challenges of Chinese investment in an iron project in Australia as a case study. They argue that the difference in the institutional environment between China and Australia creates institutional distance, which can result in additional operational costs and difficulties in business operations. Sun, Zhang and Chen (2013) suggest that Chinese foreign investors need to choose a country of similar institutional background or adapt to the globalisation strategy.

In a recent Treasury working paper McKissack and Xu (2016) conclude that foreign investors and their portfolio equity investment are important in helping to finance major Australian projects, supplementing Australia's national savings, which ultimately results in higher living standards. However, McKissack and Xu (2016) emphasise the importance of a comprehensive understanding of the changing environment of foreign investment in Australia, and the need for business, academia, and policymakers to work together to understand the trends in investments.

In conclusion, it is imperative to carefully assess foreign investments in critical infrastructure such as ports as these kinds of projects involve many stakeholders. The mechanisms for reviewing such proposals from foreign investors must be effective in ascertain the economic and other flow-on effects from the business proposal.

9.1.3 Factors Influencing Asset Recycling in Australia

The sale of an income-earning asset, whether a government-owned asset or a privately-owned asset is generally determined by its market value which will be the risk-adjusted net present value of the anticipated flow of future earnings (Quiggin 2010). However, this is not a straight-forward computation, and the process of arriving at a final value is influenced by numerous factors. In the case of government-owned assets, the fiscal case must be considered. Three issues were observed in the case of recycling government-owned assets.

In the political economy, politicians have the power to use resources to maximise their chances of re-election, strengthening their political base or furthering their political ambitions or goals (Buchanan and Tullock 1962; Dixit and Londregan 1995; Downs 1957). This may conflict with the goal of obtaining the best possible deal, as politicians may be willing to forego a better deal, i.e. selling at below-market value to further political ambitions or political goals (Laurin 2004).

Ports are generally monopolies or monopolistic competitions where the owner has a certain degree of power in setting prices. When the government cedes control of port operations to the private operator, the pricing decisions are left to the private sector. Private operators have a goal to maximise profits or seek the highest economic rent from consumers (Quiggin 2010) which in turn may bring about political pains to the government in power.

Lastly, infrastructure investments such as ports provide an essential service to the community that also generates revenues. In most cases, this revenue is likely to exceed the cost of capital. However, as infrastructure projects have extremely long life-cycles, the analysis around the anticipated revenues can be highly speculative, taking into consideration things that may be planned or anticipated in the future. This is even more so when the infrastructure asset is to be sold. The high degree of uncertainty adds significant risk, and this is compounded by the potential for political influence in the formulation of the proposed sale and the resultant price obtained for the community (Quiggin 2010).

9.1.4 Typical Management Structure

A range of port management structures exist. Each approach seeks differing levels of private sector involvement and regulation (see Fig. 9.1 Port management — the balance between public and private (World Bank 2007)).

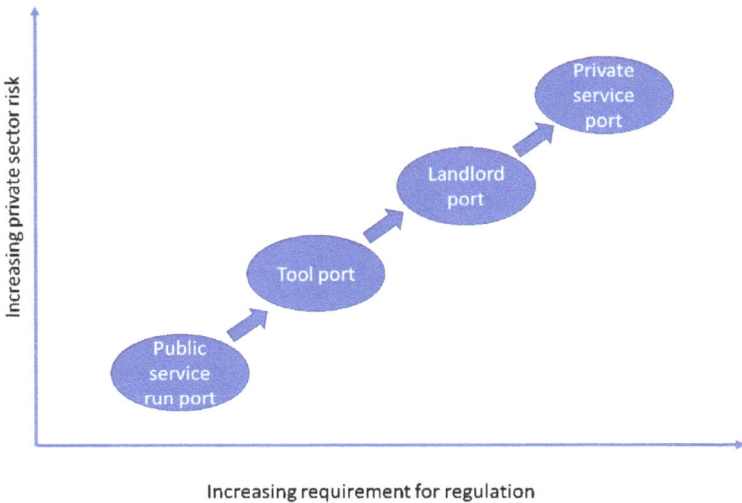

Fig. 9.1 Port management — the balance between public and private
(World Bank 2007)

The general management structure adopted in Australia is that defined by the World Bank as the PPP landlord model (Delmon 2009) (see Fig. 9.2 Landlord port management structure (AIC 2018); Fig. 9.1 Port management — the balance between public and private (World Bank 2007). In this model, the government enters a long-term lease to the private sector; in the case of the Port of Melbourne, this concession is with investors who in turn lease parcels of the port to different operators.

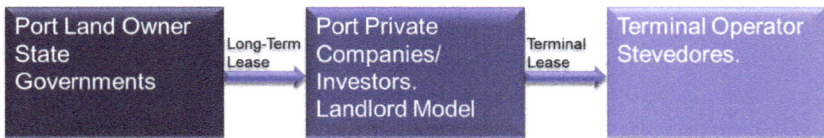

Fig. 9.2 Landlord port management structure (AIC 2018)

9.2 Methodology, Results and Discussion

This investigation into Australian port governance and management structures is part of a larger research project that examines the Efficient Facilitation of Major Infrastructure Projects in Australia. The research was conducted in accordance with the Engineering Human Ethics Advisory Group guidelines at The University of Melbourne and had ethics approval. The details of the methodology used in the research project are in Appendix 1.

A focus group discussion (FGD) was conducted with senior government officials, financiers, industry representatives and terminal/port operators associated with ports in Australia. Survey respondents were asked to indicate their willingness to participate in an FGD, and accordingly, they received an invitation to take part in the FGD. The de-identified general profile of the participants who took part in the FGD is shown in Appendix 1.

The participants were engaged in an informal discussion on governance, policy, and management structure in ports using the questions listed in Appendix 1. The FGD was recorded and then transcribed verbatim. Using NVivo, a qualitative analysis software, FGD data were coded by the first author using thematic analysis. Figure 9.1 shows diagrammatically the results of themes observed from the thematic analysis.

9.2.1 Factors Which Bring Improvement to Governance/ Policy in Ports

When participants from the two focus groups discussed what factors brought an improvement to governance/policy in ports, numerous themes emerged: government is a key player; importance of regulation and policy-making; the need to understand drivers for each port; clarity of vision for port governance and policy-making, taking into consideration lead time, importance of planning and some other factors. We look at these themes briefly in the bullet points below (and summarised in Table 9.3):

- **Government is a key player:** One of the most important factors which repeatedly came up in both group discussions was the

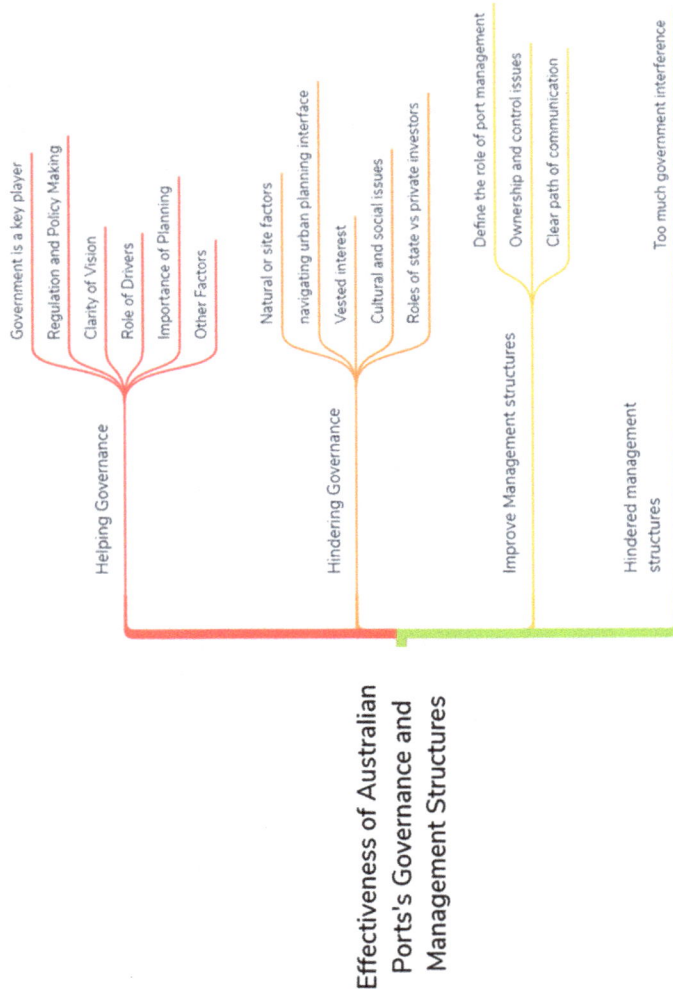

Fig. 9.3 Themes observed from the thematic analysis of the FGD discussions (Figure by the authors)

role of the government in improving governance/policy at the ports. Participants of the focus group felt that the government had a key role in terms of making major decisions concerning investments. The government is also responsible for setting the scene in developing a good relationship with the ports. In this respect, the government makes centralised decisions and is required to take into consideration the constraints faced by ports.

- **Regulation and Policy Making:** Another important theme that emerged was that regulation and policy-making need to go hand in hand. Existing policies or regulations need to be regularly reviewed with a good line of communication with all stakeholders. Decisions on regulations and policies need to be made with an understanding of how things should be prioritised at various ports.

- **Role of Drivers:** Several participants mentioned that it was important to acknowledge that no two ports were the same and each had their own set of strengths and weaknesses. In addition, there was a dire need to understand what the drivers were for each of the ports. Governance and policy, therefore, must be able to cater to, and allow regulators to consider, the different needs in different ports.

- **Clarity of Vision** Another important theme which emerged during the discussion was the importance of having clarity of vision. A clarity of vision enables stakeholders to be aligned when it comes to expectations on returns on investment, timelines and even service quality level. The discussions among both groups pointed out numerous occasions where there was a lack of clarity in vision regarding port development at various ports across Australia.

- **Importance of Planning:** The importance of planning was also mentioned by one or two participants who mentioned the importance of strategic port plans and national port strategies. This is in line with the clarity of vision mentioned earlier. A long-term or strategic plan ensures that subordinate plans work in congruence with higher-level plans.

- **Other Factors:** A few other factors are worthy of mention as they have been observed as influencing the governance process. One participant mentioned the importance of factoring in lead time for planning and development. Another participant also mentioned that autonomy, competitiveness and being able to work and develop projects helped improve governance/policy in ports.

Table 9.3 Factors Helping to Improve Governance/Policy in Ports
(Table by the authors)

Factors That Help Improve Governance/Policy in Ports
1. Government is a key player
The government has a key role
Good working relationship with the port authorities
Centralised decision making such as in China
Understanding the constraints
2. Regulation and Policy Making
Regulation and policy-making goes hand in hand
Review the relevance of policy making
Communication with stakeholders
Understanding what to prioritise
3. Understanding Port Drivers
Understanding that no two parts are alike
Understanding port drivers
4. Clarity of Vision
Clarity from government
Clarity about policies
Clarity about complaints
Clarity about timelines
5. Factoring in Lead Time
Lead time for infrastructure
Lead time for planning
Importance of planning
6. Importance of Planning
Importance of strategic port plan
National Port strategy

Factors That Help Improve Governance/Policy in Ports
7. Others
Autonomy
Competitiveness
Able to work and develop

9.2.2 Factors Acting as Obstacles to Governance/Policy in Ports

It emerged during the course of the two focus discussion groups that some factors acted as obstacles or hindrances to improving the governance/policy of ports (See Table 9.4):

- **Natural or Site Factors:** Among the first factors to be identified during the group discussions were natural factors, such as environmental limitations, geographical limitation, swing basin related issues and expansion capabilities. These were factors which could not be changed, either due to the geographical location of the port, the proximity to an urban area, or because of the natural design of the port.

- **Navigating Urban Planning Interface:** The second factor which participants felt could act as a hindrance was the complex and regulation-ridden navigation of the urban planning interface where issues such as land use, social and environmental impact, and urban interface were raised in group discussions. Furthermore, many examples were provided by the participants to illustrate this particular theme. It is noteworthy that this issue is not faced by Australia alone. In Jakarta, port expansion near the ports is also likened to be a land reform exercise.

- **Vested Interests:** The third factor discussed during the focus group discussions was how vested interests of different stakeholders in the port created obstacles for governance and policy-making. Some of the sub-themes to emerge from the groups were: self-interest, greed and power, the role of bureaucracy/red tape, divested interests and how decentralised decision-making could all cause problems.

- **Cultural/Social/Historical Practices:** The fourth issue to emerge from the groups was how cultural, social and historical practices embedded within port-related organisations often made change difficult and brought in a sense of inertia. Long-standing traditions, cultural aspects, historical aspects of operating a port also stopped change from being introduction as people are generally resistant to changes and are suspicious of any moves to upset the status quo. Sometimes, regulators need to understand that change takes time and there is a need to convince stakeholders of the benefits of changes.

- **State Versus Privatized Running of Ports:** There was also a mention of the different roles of the state versus private investors in the running of the port. A discussion on the side was also taking place regarding how the different roles played out by the state and private investors may either improve or hinder governance/policy making of ports. Some participants felt that a 'parent-child' relationship between, on the one hand, the government and private investors, and, on the other hand, the port operators existed and this was stifling the port operations.

The factors identified during the FGD as obstacles or hindrances to governance/policy of ports are summarised in Table 9.4.

9.2.3 Factors Which Help Improve Management Structures in Ports

Participants in the FGD identified several factors that could help improve management structures in ports and further summarised in Table 9.5:

- **Defining Port Management:** Some participants felt that when defining governance structure or policies, it would help to first define which organisations were being targeted as there were many different types of organisations present

Table 9.4 Factors Acting as Obstacles to Governance/Policy of Ports
(Table by the authors)

Obstacles to Governance/Policy of Ports
Natural Factors
Environmental Limitations
Geographical Limitations
Swing Basin
Expansion Capacity
2. Navigating Urban Landscape
Urban land use
Social and environmental impact
Urban interface
3. Vested Interests
Self Interest
Greed and Power
Divested interests
Bureaucracy
Decentralised decision-making
4. Cultural/Social/Historical Factors
Cultural/social factors
Historical factors
Inertia stopping change.
5. State-Owned vs. Privatized Ports
Landlord ports are like cash cows
State-owned ports are often held back
6. Adverse Impact of Regulation
Regulation strangles innovation

at the ports. These organisations come with different types of management and reporting structures. Furthermore, one or two participants felt that there was no clear line of sight of operational management in the governance structure of the ports post private sector engagement and that was an issue.

- **State Versus Private Ownership of Ports:** In addition, there was also a discussion held about how ports operated under state versus private ownership. One participant felt that in some cases the government was ceding control to private investors. However, other participants felt that private investment coming in helped improve management structures and processes. This, in turn, is likely to result in improvement to and efficiency of ports.

- **Clear Path of Communication:** One participant also felt that a clear path of communication with all stakeholders was also needed to improve management structures and processes in ports.

Table 9.5 Factors Which Help Improve Management Structures in Ports
(Table by the authors)

Factors Considered to Help Improve Management Structures in Ports
1. Private Versus State Ownership
In some cases, government cedes control to private investors
Private investment comes in and improves management structures
Privatisation of ports brings in improvement and efficiency
2. Define Management
Need to clarify which aspect of management is being targeted
Involvement of management as there is currently a lack of representation
3. Clear Communication
A clear path of communication is required.

9.2.4 Factors Which Hindered Improvement of Management Structures in Ports

The participants of the FGD also identified too much government interference as a factor that hindered improvement of management structures in ports:

- **Too Much Government Interference:** There was also a discussion about what hindered any improvement in management structures in ports. This discussion investigated the role of the private sector and the state in port management. While too much state involvement was not liked by participants, they also were not in favour of the idea of port management acting like landlords and considering ports to be cash cows. In addition, participants also felt that often the state and private investors were not on the same page.

9.2.5 Significance and Future Research

Private sector investments in Australian ports may seem like a viable option for raising revenues for the government. However, as ports are considered critical assets of the government, it raises issues of how ports should be governed and managed if the private sector were to be involved in the ownership and running of the ports. These issues are extremely important in not only helping the government understand how best to run the port, but also in helping the private sector to understand the stakeholders' expectations when they are running the ports. In turn, governance and management structures developed after privatisation are vital in influencing how well the port will be able to add value to the economy. Future research should investigate each of these themes and factors in greater depth from both government and private investors' perspectives. An in-depth case study analysis of ports is likely to highlight different situations and challenges.

9.3 Conclusion

In this study, our findings from two focus group discussion showed that to improve the governance and policy in ports in Australia, the government needs to reclaim its role as a key player and provide regulations that coordinate the work of the relevant port stakeholders. In addition, port stakeholders need to work together to create a clear vision and better planning for the port's future and strategies. However, there are also factors that are hindering governance improvement, such as environmental limitations, navigation of urban planning requirements and catering to the vested interests of different stakeholders.

Our study also found factors that helped improve management structures and processes in ports. The following factors were suggested to facilitate the management structure improvement: port management needs to be clearly defined under the landlord model; state government involvement under the new management structure needs to be clearly defined; and clear communication paths need to be developed to improve effectiveness of ports.

References

Australia-Indonesia Centre (AIC) 2018, 'The Australia-Indonesia Centre Infrastructure Cluster Conference, 'Building Sustainable and Resilient Portal Cities' Surabaya, Indonesia. Proceedings and extended abstracts, May 2018', p. 17, https://doi.org/10.4225/03/5b0cf3ab65a48

Baird, AJ 1995. 'Privatisation of trust ports in the United Kingdom: Review and analysis of the first sales', *Transport Policy*, 2, pp. 135–43.

Buchanan, J and Tullock, G 1962. *The Calculus of Consent: Logical Foundations of Constitutional Democracy, Vol. 3*, Indianapolis, USA: Liberty Fund, files. libertyfund.org/files/1063/Buchanan_0102-03_EBk_v6.0.pdf

Chen, S-L and Everett, S 2013. 'The dynamics of port reform: different contexts, similar strategies', *Maritime Policy and Management*, 41:3, pp. 288–301, https://doi.org/10.1080/03088839.2013.839513

Chen, S-L, Pateman, H and Sakalayen, Q 2017. 'The latest trend in Australian port privatisation: Drivers, processes and impacts', *Research in Transportation Business and Management*, 22, pp. 201–13, https://doi.org/10.1016/j.rtbm.2016.10.005

Delmon, VR 2009. *Landlord port structure graph — Public private partnership*, World Bank, PPP in Infrastructure Resource Center for Contracts, Laws and Regulations (PPPIRC), ppp.worldbank.org/public-private-partnership/library/landlord-port-structure-graph-pdf

Dixit, A and Londregan, J 1995. 'Redistributive politics and economic efficiency', *Political Science Review*, pp. 856–66.

Downs, A 1957. 'An Economic Theory of Political Action in a Democracy', *Journal of Political Economy*, 65:2, pp. 135–50, https://doi.org/10.1086/257897

Duffield C, Peng Hui FK, Wilson S, Wisesa H, Anhistry L, Wahyuni S, Taufik AA, Prijadi R, Galih W and Daghlas H 2018. *Efficient facilitation of major infrastructure project*, proceedings presented at The Australia-Indonesia

Centre's Infrastructure Cluster Conference 'Building Sustainable and Resilient Portal Cities', 8–9 May, Melbourne, Australia, p. 17, https://doi.org/10.4225/03/5b0cf3ab65a48

Everett, S 2003. 'Corporatization: a legislative framework for port inefficiencies', *Maritime Policy and Management*, 30:3, pp. 211–19, https://doi.org/10.1080/0308883032000113433

Everett, S and Pettitt, T 2006. 'Effective corporatization of ports is a function of effective legislation: legal issues in the existing paradigm', *Maritime Policy and Management*, 33:3, pp. 219–32, https://doi.org/10.1080/03088830600783137

Everett, S and Robinson, R 2006. 'Port reform: The Australian experience', *Research in Transportation Economics*, 17, pp. 259–84.

Institute for Supply Chain and Logistics 2015. *Port Privatisation in Australia Forum*, Melbourne, Australia: Victoria University, www.vu.edu.au/sites/default/files/iscl/pdfs/port-privatisation-synopsis.pdf

Iyer, KG, Rambaldi, AN and Tang, KK 2009. 'How trade and foreign investment affect the growth of a small but not so open economy: Australia?', *Applied Economics*, 41:12, pp. 1525–32.

Lattin, A 2017. 'Trends in foreign investment in Australia', *Clyde and Co*, www.mondaq.com/australia/x/557328/Inward+Foreign+Investment/Trends+in+foreign+investment+in+Australia

McKissack, A and Xu, J 2016. *Foreign investment into Australia*: *Foreign investment and trade policy division*, Parkes, Australia: Australian Government, The Treasury, static.treasury.gov.au/uploads/sites/1/2017/06/TWP_201601_Foreign_Investment.pdf

NSW Property 2016. *'Asset recycling — Insight report'*, The Government of New South Wales, Australia, www.property.nsw.gov.au/sites/default/files/Asset%20recycling%20insight%20report.pdf

Sadleir, C and Mahony, G 2009. 'Institutional challenges and response in regulating foreign direct investment to Australia', *Economic Papers*: *A journal of applied economics and policy*, 28:4, pp. 337–45, https://doi.org/10.1111/j.1759-3441.2010.00041.x

SMART Infrastructure Group 2015. *Asset recycling a smarter way for Australia?*, smart.uow.edu.au/content/groups/public/@web/@qa/documents/doc/uow189689.pdf

Sun, SL, Zhang, Y and Chen, Z 2013. 'The challenges of Chinese outward investment in developed countries: The case of CITIC Pacific's Sino Iron project in Australia', *Thunderbird International Business Review*, 55:3, pp. 313–22.

World Bank 2007. *Port reform toolkit*, ppp.worldbank.org/public-private-partnership/library/port-reform-toolkit-ppiaf-world-bank-2nd-edition

10. Alternative Ways to Finance Major Port Projects

Seaports in Indonesia

W. W. Galih[1] and R. Prijadi[2]

10.0 Introduction

Currently, the Government of Indonesia is engaged in a mission to develop the nation's physical connectivity. As stated in the National Development Planning Agenda 2015–2019, the mission has general objectives such as enhancing the quality and capacity of infrastructure, increasing mobility and national and regional connectivity. The Ministry of Transportation's decision no. 414/2014 envisions 1,240 port projects with 33 of these projects being major port developments. The strategic plan is part of President Joko Widodo's vision of a "sea toll road".

Based on the National Development Planning Agenda 2015–2019, sea transport infrastructure development alone would need an investment of about IDR 900 trillion. The estimated investment will be used to finance the activities to build, improve and extended the

1   Masters candidate (Magister of Management), Universitas Indonesia, 10430, Jakarta Pusat, Indonesia.
2   Associate Professor, Dept. of Management, Universitas Indonesia,16424, Depok, Indonesia.

twenty-four selected seaports (five main seaports and nineteen feeder seaports, including supporting facilities). This plan would include major developments of Kalibaru (The New Priok) Port, Cilamaya Port, Makassar New Port, Port of Kuala Tanjung, and Port of Bitung (Bappenas 2014). These projects will require considerably more funds than the government can provide. The government is attempting to boost the support for their development through State Owned Enterprises (SOEs), by incentivising the private sector through Public Private Partnership (PPP) schemes, and investment in other state-of-the-art and creative financing schemes. However, the implementation of this type of private financing is not simple. The complex nature of infrastructure projects revolves around two decision-making perspectives: the perspective of the public procurer, and the perspective of the private sponsors. In essence, the public procurer has two general alternatives to finance infrastructure projects: with or without private partnerships.

The aim of this paper is to explore various alternatives of port infrastructure project financing and to explain the underlying motives to utilise those alternatives from the two different perspectives. A case study of the New Priok Container Terminal One (NPCT-1) is provided to illustrate how different scenarios of financing schemes would affect the project risks allocation, and, in the end, the project value itself. The NPCT-1 is part of the first stage of the North Kalibaru Terminal development. The project includes the construction of a 32-hectare facility space, an 850 m container quay with a pool depth of -16 m LWS and a capacity of 1.5 million TEU. The NPCT-1 project construction started in 2013 and its commercial operation commenced in August 2016. The case study identifies and assesses the existing vehicle utilised to finance the NPCT-1 project, and then compares the existing vehicle with the Public Private Partnership framework and project finance alternatives.

This paper is structured as follows. The next section (literature review) discusses the two different perspectives of the public procurer and the private sponsors in an arrangement of infrastructure provision. This is followed by a discussion of risk allocation preferences in Public Private Partnership projects. Section three presents the methodology used to gain different opinions and insights from various Indonesian seaport industry stakeholders through a survey, a focus group discussion (FGD), and several in-depth interviews. Section four explores the insights from the survey and confirms them with a case study which is cash flow simulation scenarios to illustrate how different financing scenarios would affect the seaport project value. The implications for future seaport infrastructure project financing and concluding remarks are discussed in Section five.

10.1 Literature Review

In this section, we discuss two perspectives that usually occur in infrastructure project financing structures. We consider the discussion of infrastructure financing from the perspectives of public procurers, and subsequently, the perspectives of private sponsors.

10.1.1 The Public Procurer Perspective: Public Private Partnerships vs. Traditional Procurement

While value-for-money should be the main objective of the public procurer, Burger and Hawkesworth (2011)value for money is (or at least, should be explore the non-value-for-money factors that may influence the public procurer decision to utilise traditional procurement or PPP to finance infrastructure projects. Their survey-based study revealed that in many countries, traditional procurement is set to be the default option, while PPP is only utilised when "there is someone acting as a champion for setting up the project as a PPP". The "champion" can be interpreted at the discretion of the project's government contracting agency (GCA). Therefore, by creating incentives to prefer traditional infrastructure procurement to PPPs the rules in place interfere with the objectives to maximise value for money. These incentives in PPPs often drive enhanced service outcomes which is beyond the scope of traditional infrastructure procurement. The use of incentives is complex and does not always lead to perfect outcomes.

A competitive benchmark study of the outcomes of Indonesian power projects by Atmo et al. (2017) provides empirical evidence that projects with PPPs had better time performance and better operational availability than projects that utilised traditional procurement methods.

Nevertheless, there was no significant cost difference between the two procurement approaches. In order to resolve the problems with budgetary constraints and still maximise value for money, Atmo and Duffield (2015) propose implementation strategies based on their study of Indonesian PPP power projects post the 2008 global financial crisis. The study highlights the importance of regional export credit agencies to support Indonesian PPP power projects and the development of local manufacturing capabilities to reduce the projects' currency exchange risk. These case studies reveal that PPP arrangements need effective strategies to ensure better project deliveries.

The effectiveness of PPP project deliveries relies on several factors. Osei-Kyei and Chan (2015) reviewed academic journals, from 1990 to 2013, on the critical success factors (CSF) for implementing PPPs to compare the findings from these studies. The five most reported CSFs over the past 23 years are: risk allocation and sharing; strong private consortium; political support; community or public support; and transparent procurement. Chan, Lam, Chan, Cheung, and Ke (2010) group critical success factors for Chinese infrastructure PPPs into five underlying factors:

1. Stable macroeconomic environment
2. Shared responsibility
3. Transparent and efficient procurement process
4. Stable political and social environment
5. Judicious government control.

While the use of PPPs provides certain incentives for the public procurer, such as better project performance and risk allocation, PPP utilisation in seaport-related infrastructure in Indonesia is still limited. Most of the private financing involvement occurs under sub-concession contracts through the Indonesia seaport Corporations (IPCs), the State Owned Enterprises that are seaport operators, and creating joint-venture project companies to operate container terminals. This situation requires more study to explore alternate procurement strategies such as PPP or procurement improvement that can be implemented by the public procurer.

10.1.2 The Private Sponsor Perspective: Corporate Finance vs. Project Finance

Fundamentally, a company may choose to finance its activities through internal and external financing. There are two main external financing sources: equity and debt. Project finance is one aspect of corporate finance. To finance a project, the sponsor may choose to use corporate finance or project finance (Gatti 2008). The difference lies in whether the financing is done on the balance sheet or off the balance sheet. If a company chooses to finance its project with corporate finance, the financing is done with on-balance sheet financing, meaning that the company is liable to the creditors for the debt payments used to finance the project in the event of a failure to repay the debt credits. Companies with on-balance sheet financing must bear corporate debt and project debt with the cash flows and assets of the company itself.

Conversely, if a company chooses to finance its project with project finance, the financing is off-balance sheet financing, so the loan is a no recourse or a limited recourse. Debt payments are solely derived from the cash flows and assets of a special purpose vehicle (SPV) company established for the benefit of the project (Gatti 2008). While project finance is a common practice in PPP arrangements, there are many cases where a corporate-finance approach prevails as a suitable alternative (Yescombe 2007)private-sector financing through public-private partnerships (PPPs. In a corporate-finance structure for infrastructure financing, the project company is usually a wholly-owned subsidiary of the project sponsor or the infrastructure project is recorded as the sponsor's asset. The latter case means that the sponsor may enter directly into a PPP scheme with the public procurer. Compared with the project finance structure, the cost of finance and ancillary cost may be lower in the case of the corporate finance structure. This lower financing and ancillary cost will result in a lower cost for the public procurer. However, a corporate finance structure is reliant on the financial capacity of the project sponsor and its balance sheet soundness.

The use of project finance supports the idea that financing decisions affect a firm's value under certain circumstances (Esty 2003). One of the important characteristics of project finance is that there is a decision to finance assets separately, therefore allowing the project company to have highly leveraged capital structures (Esty 2004). The average project company has a debt to total capitalisation ratio of 70% (compared to 35% for public companies), concentrated equity ownership, and concentrated debt ownership (Esty 2003).

The main purpose of the project finance approach itself is the project risk allocation. Project finance is a way to distribute project risk amongst the parties involved in the arrangement to minimise the volatility of cash flows generated by the project (Gatti 2008). There are three basic strategies to mitigate the impact of project risk borne by the project company (Gatti 2008):

1. Retain the risk.

2. Transfer the risk by allocating it to key partners.

3. Transfer the risk to risk management professionals (insurers).

The internationally accepted practice is to use Abraham's principle of allocating risk to the party that is best able to manage the risk. In reality, the risk allocation gravitates towards those who have a higher risk tolerance. However, the allocation of risk is the subject of constant negotiation as participants often want to assume as little risk as possible. In an example of cost overrun in a turnkey contract situation between the project company and the project construction contractor, the determination of project cost by the contractor includes the normal profit, the assumed risk for project completion, the risk of cost overrun, and the risk premium caused by uncertainty during the project construction phase (Shen-fa and Xiao-ping, 2009).

Project finance allows sponsors to mitigate the risks that originate from the fact that the project company's managers' efforts have little impact on market outcomes. A model proposed by An and Cheung (2010) argues that "companies tend to prefer corporate financing of investment when effort has a significant impact on the magnitude and likelihood of favorable outcomes" and vice versa. When projects become very large and require a commensurate large capital budget it is less likely that companies can manage the risk and associated expenditure from normal operations. In such situations project finance or financing structures become a viable approach to manage cash flow requirements. Governments have a preference to be at arms length from such arrangements if at all possible as this creates a structured mechanism to manage their risk and to give confidence of the required budget envelope. Project creditors also benefit from project finance arrangements that provide legal protection against insider stealing and weak creditor protection laws. Subramanian and Tung (2016) explain that separate legal incorporation of the project company, combined with the fact that the project company only operates a single and discrete project, allows transparent cash flow separation.

Investors in PPPs typically require a minimum equity return (Yescombe 2007)private-sector financing through public-private partnerships (PPPs. With the debt management of the project finance approach, the higher the financial leverage for the project, the easier it is to earn a high level of return on equity (ROE). Table 10.1 illustrates a very simplified example of the benefit of leverage in two different scenarios of project's leverage.

Table 10.1 Impact of project finance structure to the sponsor's return (Yescombe 2007) private-sector financing through public-private partnerships (PPPs).

	Low leverage	High leverage
Project cost	1,000	1,000
Debt	500	900
Equity	500	100
Project Revenue (annually)	75	75
Interest rate on debt (annually)	5%	6%
Interest payable	5% x 500 = 25	6% x 900 = 54
Profit	75 - 25 = 50	75 - 54 = 21
Return on equity	50 ÷ 500 = 10%	21 ÷ 100 = 21%

As illustrated in the above table, if the project is financed with 50% debt, the ROE is 10%. Alternatively, if it is financed with a high leverage of 90% debt, the ROE is 21%, despite the fact that there is an increase in the cost of debt that reflects a higher risk for lenders. This simplified example illustrates how project finance arrangements can be a vehicle for risk transfer between project equity sponsors and lenders and may increase the sponsors' return. Risk allocation in a project finance scheme can also occur among the project sponsors. Project finance allows project sponsors to form a partnership, starting from the project bidding stage to the project commercial operation stage, with each bringing particular capabilities from their specific competencies to manage the project risks (Yescombe 2007)private-sector financing through public-private partnerships (PPPs.

Figure 10.1 summarises three different combinations of financing arrangement from the perspective of the public procurer and the private sponsor.

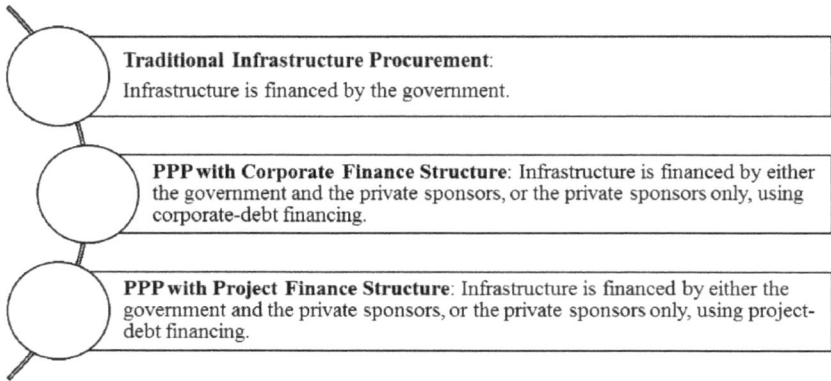

Traditional Infrastructure Procurement: Infrastructure is financed by the government.

PPP with Corporate Finance Structure: Infrastructure is financed by either the government and the private sponsors, or the private sponsors only, using corporate-debt financing.

PPP with Project Finance Structure: Infrastructure is financed by either the government and the private sponsors, or the private sponsors only, using project-debt financing.

Fig. 10.1 Infrastructure financing options. (Figure by the authors from Hui, Duffield, Wilson, 2018)

While there is a relatively large literature on the effectiveness of each financing option, limited research has been conducted into the industry stakeholders' insights and opinions on those options. This is especially important for Indonesia, as a developing country that is currently undergoing massive infrastructure development, because the Indonesian government is trying to encourage more private investors to put their money into these massive projects.

The research presented in this chapter explores insights and perspectives from various Indonesian seaport industry stakeholders related to financing of infrastructure projects via an online survey, focus group discussions and in-depth interviews conducted in Indonesia in 2017. It also uses a case study of a seaport infrastructure project financing strategy using a cash flow simulation model based on different financing scenarios to illustrate the effectiveness of the various ways to finance seaport projects. The case study is an empirical investigation conducted within a real-life context, "especially when the boundaries between phenomenon and context are not clearly evident" (Yin 2006). The case study strategy focuses on understanding the development present within single settings, combining "data collection methods such as archives, interviews, questionnaires, and observations" (Eisenhardt 1989).

10.2 Research Methodology

This paper reports on results from a study into Efficient Facilitation of Major Infrastructure Projects with a focus on Ports which utilised a combination of qualitative and quantitative research methodological approaches. The methodology associated with the Efficient Facilitation of Major Infrastructure Projects study is described in full in the Appendix. The qualitative approach included text responses from an online survey questionnaire, focus group discussions, and in-depth interviews. Quantitative data was also collected in the survey. The online survey was conducted to gain insight into the most effective financing vehicle for seaport infrastructure from the perspective of various Indonesian seaport industry stakeholders. In this questionnaire, each of the financing vehicle alternatives considered were given a Likert-scale based value, ranging from (1) "Not at all effective", (2) "Ineffective", (3) "Neither effective or ineffective", (4) "Effective", and (5) "Highly effective", to reflect how effective a method of financing is from the perspective of the survey participants. The scale also provided a sixth response option: "Don't know", for respondents who were not familiar or did not have experience with the financing vehicle alternatives that were considered. The questionnaire also included open ended questions. The respondents were also asked how the decision-making process for infrastructure projects could be improved, the major barriers to gaining project approval, and about major development that their port had attempted to undertake or had achieved using international providers. The findings from the survey were confirmed with the results from the focus group discussion (FGD) that we conducted in Jakarta in September 2017. Then, several in-depth interview sessions were conducted to follow up and confirm the information collected in the survey and the FGD.

Separate to the FGD, questionnaire, and interview results, the research utilised another quantitative method with a case study of the project of the New Priok Container Terminal 1 (NPCT-1) by investigating financing of seaport infrastructure to demonstrate how financing decisions can affect project performance and, therefore, its value. The case study of NPCT-1 is used in this study due to its prototypical value as a project (Flvvberg 2004). We highlight the more general aspects of the project, so that what we conclude from the NPCT-1 case can be used as a reference point for other cases of port infrastructure development in Indonesia.

This research builds cash flow simulations under the existing scenario, project agreements and assumptions, and compares it with an alternative scenario with different project capital structures, i.e. the ratio of project long-term debt compared to total project initial investment.

The simulations are built under capital budgeting principles. The project value is derived from a net present value (NPV) analysis, where project cash flows are discounted with a risk-adjusted discount rate. This paper does not utilise an advanced approach, such as real option analysis or probability simulation, as our purpose here is only to illustrate how different financing decision — i.e. the capital structure, which is set at the project initiation — might affect the project value to the sponsors.

The research methodology can be illustrated in Figure 10.2.

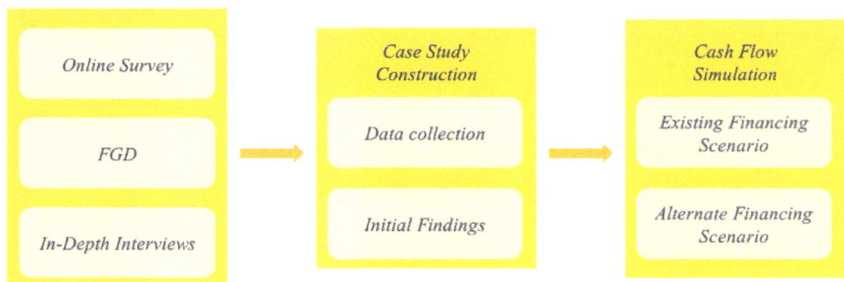

Fig. 10.2 Research flowchart (Figure by the authors from Hui, Duffield and Wilson 2018)

10.3 Results and Case Study

10.3.1 Survey Results

In total, thirty-four relevant finance-related responses were complete and included in the analysis. Half of these respondents were associated with State Owned Enterprises and 24% associated with the government at central agencies level. This is consistent with the fact that the Indonesian seaport industry is highly controlled by the government. The majority of the respondents have had experience in the Indonesian seaport industry (76%). The respondents' area of specialisation were diverse, such as engineering, seaport management, investment, finance, and legal. Not all respondents were port operators or terminal operators; some of them were from government departments or organisations and logistic service providers. In terms of years of experience, more than half of the respondents (53%) have had more than 10 years of specialisation experience, whilst most of them (79%) have 0–10 years of experience in the port industry (Fig. 10.3). This situation may explain why some of the respondents have extensive experience in their specialisation area (such as banking, consulting, or energy), but not necessarily in the port-specific area.

In the survey, respondents were asked their opinion on the most effective vehicle or method of financing seaport infrastructure development, and to indicate the relative effectiveness of the financing methods that were listed using a five-point Likert scale (1= not at all effective, 5 = highly effective), as shown in Table 10.2. The financing methods are ranked based on their mean scores. The PPP-related methods dominate the top-five financing vehicles or methods of financing. These PPP-related methods are the government-guaranteed PPP, PPPs, Availability Funding, and PPP with construction support. PPP with government guarantee has the highest mean score, whilst the Indonesian bank finance has the highest number of respondents who indicated it is either an effective or highly effective vehicle.

The arrangement of attractive incentives for investment, such as Special Economic Zones (SEZs), is indicated as either effective or highly effective by 62% of respondents (Table 10.2). Some of the Indonesian green-field port projects have included the development of an integrated SEZ or industrial zones as their hinterlands' economic growth strategy,

Associated Industry/Organisation (number of respondents)

State Owned Enterprise	17
Government – Central Agencies Level	8
Terminal Operations	7
Consultant	6
Others	15

Country of Experience (number of respondents)

Indonesia	26
Australia	5
The Netherlands	3
Singapore	3
Germany	2
United Arab Emirates	2
Others	8

Area of Specialisation

Engineering	7
Port Management	7
Investment	5
Finance	4
Legal	3
Others	13

Work Area at the Port

Port Operator/Owner	15
Government Department/Organization	14
Terminal Operator	11
Logistics Service Provider	3
Others	8

Years of Experience

	0-10 years	11-20 years	21-30 years	30+ years
Specialization years of experience	16	12	5	1
Work with ports years of experience	27	5	1	1

■ Specialization years of experience ■ Work with ports years of experience

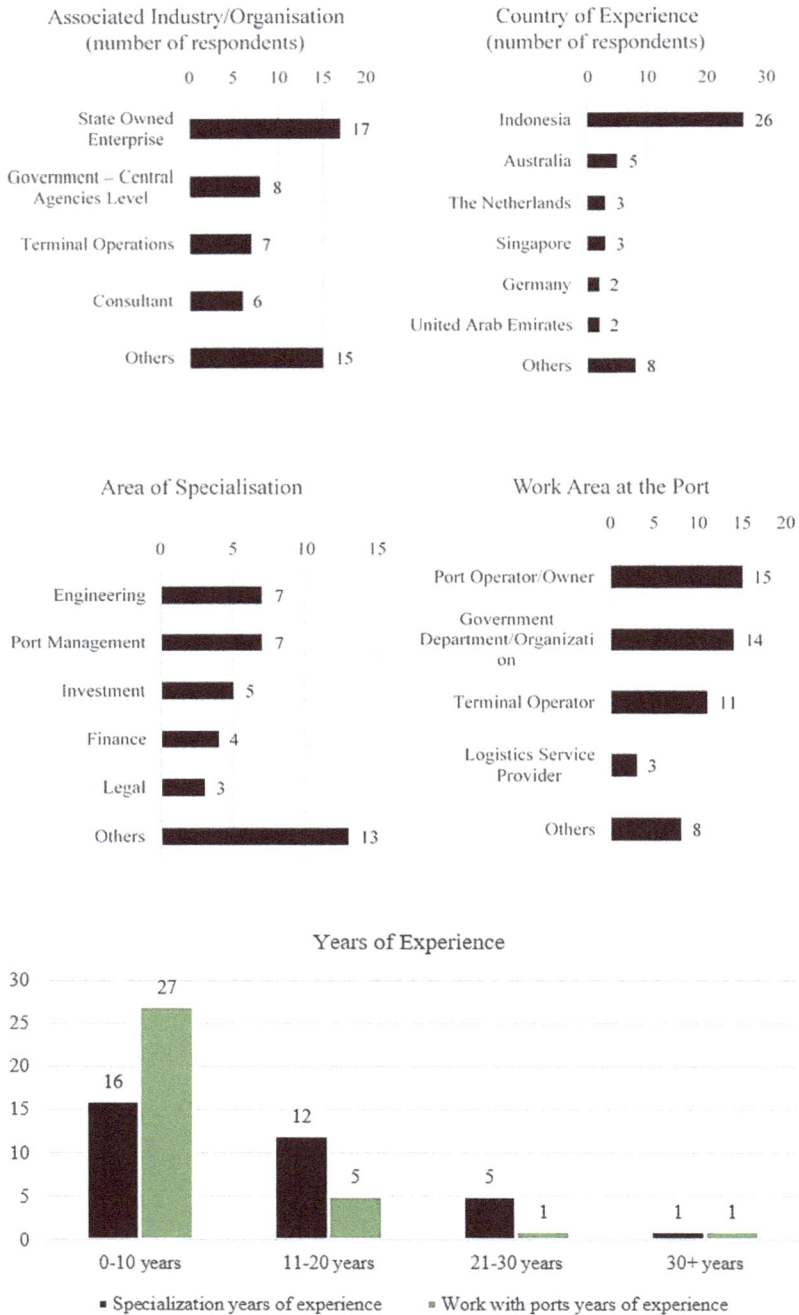

Fig. 10.3 Respondents' characteristics (n=34) (Figure by the authors)

Table 10.2 Financing vehicle/method effectiveness (Top-10 choices).

Rank	Financing Vehicles (FV)	% Agree that FV is Either Effective or Highly Effective	Mean Score	SD of Score	Don't Know	No Answer
1	PPP Government guaranteed	65%	4.1	0.8	3	4
2	Indonesian bank finance	71%	4.0	0.8	1	2
3	Public private partnerships	62%	4.0	0.9	1	4
4	Availability funding	65%	3.9	0.9	1	2
5	PPP with 'in kind' — construction support	62%	3.8	0.8	2	3
6	Arrangement of incentives to attract investment e.g. SEZ	62%	3.8	0.7	3	4
7	Direct company facilitation	59%	3.8	0.9	1	2
8	World bank	56%	3.8	0.9	2	3
9	Private seaport operator finance	56%	3.8	0.7	2	3
10	Viability gap funding	53%	3.7	0.7	3	4

thereby improving both cargo traffic and inland connectivity, for example the Port of Kuala Tanjung and the Kijing Terminal. The online questionnaire also provided the respondents with an option to choose a financing combination. Thirteen respondents to this question indicated that a combination of financing vehicles is either effective or highly effective. Some of the combinations mentioned by the respondents were "a mix of domestic bank loan and international loan", and a combination of "the government budget with the international finance organisation". One of the respondents also explained that while PPP should be a solution to financing issues, it is yet to be effective due to current restrictions on private ownership of port projects; investors are unlikely to invest their money if they are not gaining control over the business.

The next question in the survey asked the respondents their opinion on the major barriers to gaining approval for infrastructure projects in Indonesia. We conducted content analysis by categorizing respondents' responses into several categories. Figure 10.4 summarises the respondents' responses.

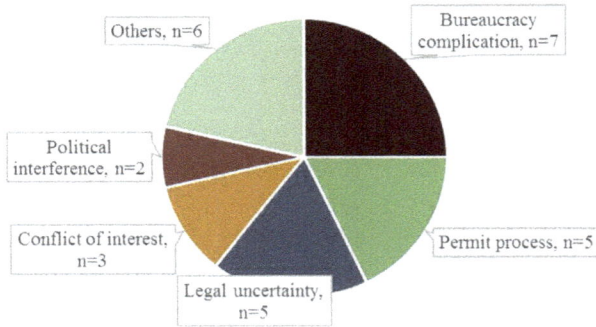

Fig. 10.4 Responses on the major barriers to gaining approval for infrastructure projects in Indonesia (Figure by the authors)

The top-five major barriers are related to the government's institutional practices, such as bureaucracy complication, permit process, legal uncertainty, conflict of interest, and political interference. Other respondents mentioned other factors such as capital expenditure, investment-inhibiting policies, land acquisition, limited time for project preparation, project financial viability, and the dominance of the state-owned port operators.

The next question asked respondents their opinion on how the decision making process for infrastructure projects could be improved in Indonesia. We conducted a qualitative content analysis on the text responses by categorising the responses into several categories, which is summarized in Figure 10.5.

The responses to this question are quite consistent with those given for the previous question. The top ways to improve the Indonesian decision-making process for infrastructure projects are all institutional: better project preparation; bureaucracy simplicity; transparency; permit support; legal certainty; and better coordination. Other responses suggest Public Private Partnership, deregulation, centralisation, better governance, land acquisition support, etc.

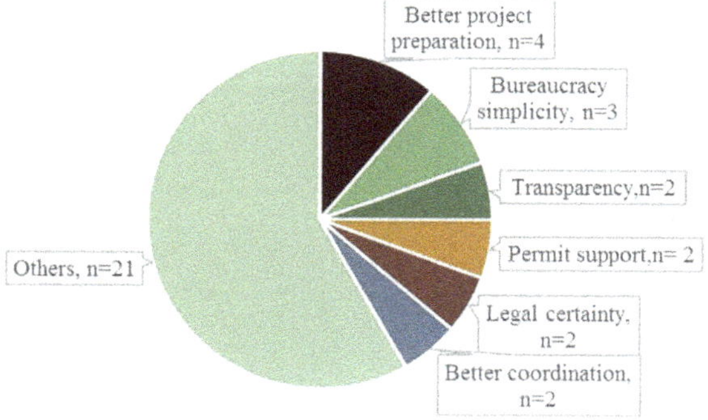

Fig. 10.5 The respondents' suggestions on ways to improve the decision-making process for infrastructure projects in Indonesia (Figure by the authors)

We asked the respondents whether their ports have attempted to undertake major development using international providers. More than half of the responses confirmed that they have made an effort to use international providers for major development of their ports, as shown in Figure 10.6.

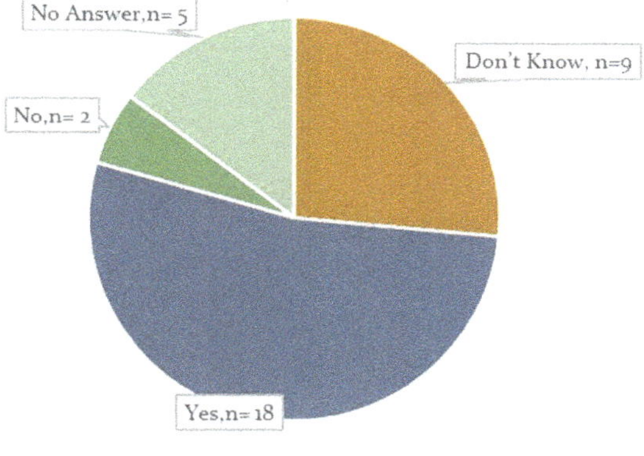

Fig. 10.6 Responses to the question "Has your port either attempted to undertake major development (or achieved major development) using international providers — including finance?" (Figure by the authors)

Following on from the previous question, respondents who answered "yes" were asked what kind of facilities were provided by the international providers. The global bond that was issued by PT Pelabuhan Indonesia II was mentioned by respondents, as was Public Private Partnerships (PPP), international direct investments and cooperation among the State

Owned Enterprises (SOEs). It is becoming more common that SOEs form joint ventures, with or without support from international providers, to finance infrastructure projects, including port infrastructure. The range of responses are shown in Figure 10.7.

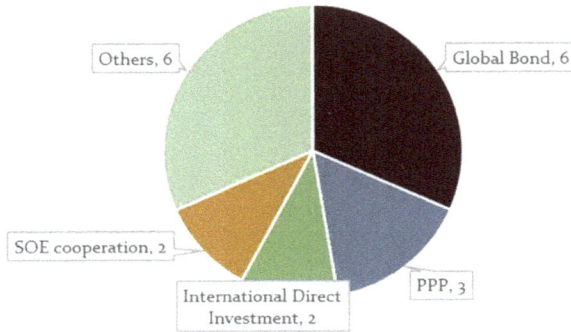

Fig. 10.7 Responses to the question on the different kinds of facilitations by international providers (Figure by the authors)

In the next section, we construct a case study on a container terminal project — the New Priok Container Terminal One (NPCT-1). This case study is conducted to illustrate how the use of project finance (instead of corporate-debt finance) and the use of PPP incentives would affect the project value, viewed from the perspective of PT Pelabuhan Indonesia II (IPC 2), the state-owned port operator acting as both the project sponsor and the government's contracting agency.

10.3.2 Case Study of NPCT-1

A case study is constructed by having project cash flow simulations under two different scenarios. We use the New Priok Container Terminal One (NPCT-1) project in this case study. The first scenario examines the NPCT-1 project's current financing structure — the contractual relationships between the project company, its sponsors, lenders and the government. The second scenario is built under a what-if assumption where the project is assumed to be financed under a PPP scheme with an annuity availability payments feature. The aim of this case study is to illustrate how the different financing methods might affect the project value and offer different features to the project sponsor. The analysis is viewed from the perspective of PT Pelabuhan Indonesia II (IPC 2), because IPC 2 stands in a quite unique position. On one hand, IPC 2 is a port operator company that holds ownership in several joint venture companies, including NPCT-1. On the other hand, IPC 2 is owned by the state. Therefore, it is possible to make IPC 2 the contracting agency of the NPCT-1 project, if the project is structured under a PPP-based financing method.

On April 5 2012, President SB Yudhoyono issued a presidential regulation to appoint PT Pelabuhan Indonesia II (Indonesia Port Corporation/IPC) to build, finance, and operate the NPCT-1 project (Kalibaru terminal project at the time). The presidential regulation was issued while a PPP-based tender was held to select the private sponsor for the project. The tender was immediately called off after the issuance of the presidential regulation, even though five consortiums were already selected for the qualification stage of the tender. The Ministry of Transport (MoT), as the government's contracting agency (CA), released a statement for the tender cancellation, stating:

> This (cancellation) is undertaken because the government does not have sufficient funds to build the project that worth IDR 8 trillion, including the infrastructure of bridges, dredging, and access road, which are valued at IDR 3 trillion. In addition to the absence of funds, according to Leon Muhamad, the Director General of Sea Transportation of the Ministry of Transportation, there was a quay owned by PT Pertamina on the right side of the access road to the Kalibaru project, which was not under consideration in the initial design of the container terminal. (Nugroho 2012)

This sudden change in the government's decision (from the initial decision to finance the project under a PPP-based scheme to then cancel this decision and appoint a State Owned Enterprise instead) caused a disappointment among the five consortium bidders who had already qualified to enter the next stage of the tender. After the cancellation, the President Director of IPC, immediately took the initiative to submit a proposal for the development of Kalibaru, the IPC version (Nugroho 2012). The situation was an example of the main issues related to infrastructure project initiation in Indonesia that we highlighted earlier in the discussion of survey results: the lack of project preparation, and institutional issues.

10.3.2.1 The Existing Financing Arrangement Overview

IPC signed a memorandum of understanding (MoU) with Mitsui Co. Ltd. (Mitsui) on February 25 2014, in Tokyo. Together with NYK Line, a Japanese shipping and logistic company, and PSA International Pte. Ltd. (PSA), a Singaporean seaport operator, Mitsui formed a consortium called the Sea Terminal Management and Service Pte. Ltd. (STMS, a Singaporean-registered company). On April 19 2014, PT IPC Terminal Petikemas (IPC TPK), a subsidiary of IPC, together with STMS, signed a shareholder agreement for the NPCT-1 project company. IPC, through IPC TPK, owns 51% of the NPCT-1 project company, while STMS owns 49%. The authorised capital of NPCT-1 amounted to USD 30 million. However, even though IPC owns 51% of NPCT-1, STMS provided the whole USD 30 million capital.

The way that IPC and STMS distributed the capital is that STMS made a payment of the 51% of the capital to IPC TPK, and this payment was recorded as IPC's liability with 0% interest (initially, the interest was at 7%, but the facility was renegotiated) (PT Pelabuhan Indonesia II (IPC) 2016). Then, IPC TPK placed the capital as an equity contribution to NPCT-1.

As stipulated in the shareholder agreement, STMS has the sole obligation and responsibility to provide funding for NPCT-1. There is one unique feature of the shareholder agreement: namely the Permitted Equity Return (PER) clause. This clause would inhibit IPC to receive any dividend payment from NPCT-1 before STMS achieves a certain rate of return from the project. In other words, STMS will receive all of the NPCT-1 dividend until the PER is achieved and IPC will receive the dividends only after the PER is achieved. The PER is calculated as an internal rate of return of the project's cash flow to equity (IRRequity). The terminal operation agreement of NPCT-1 expires within 25 years from the date of commencement of commercial operation of the terminal. If the PER is not achieved, the agreement will be extended until the PER is achieved but with a maximum term extension of 5 years (total maximum agreement term is 30 years).

There are two sources of return from NPCT-1 for IPC that are fixed, regardless of the terminal operating outcome. The first one is the USD 100 million advanced payment NPCT-1 had to pay to IPC after the 850 m quay construction was completed. Second, NPCT-1 has to pay IPC the fixed site quarterly rent, amounting to USD 14 million, or USD 56 million per annum. The overall contractual relationship that revolves around the NPCT-1 project can be summarised in Figure 10.8 below.

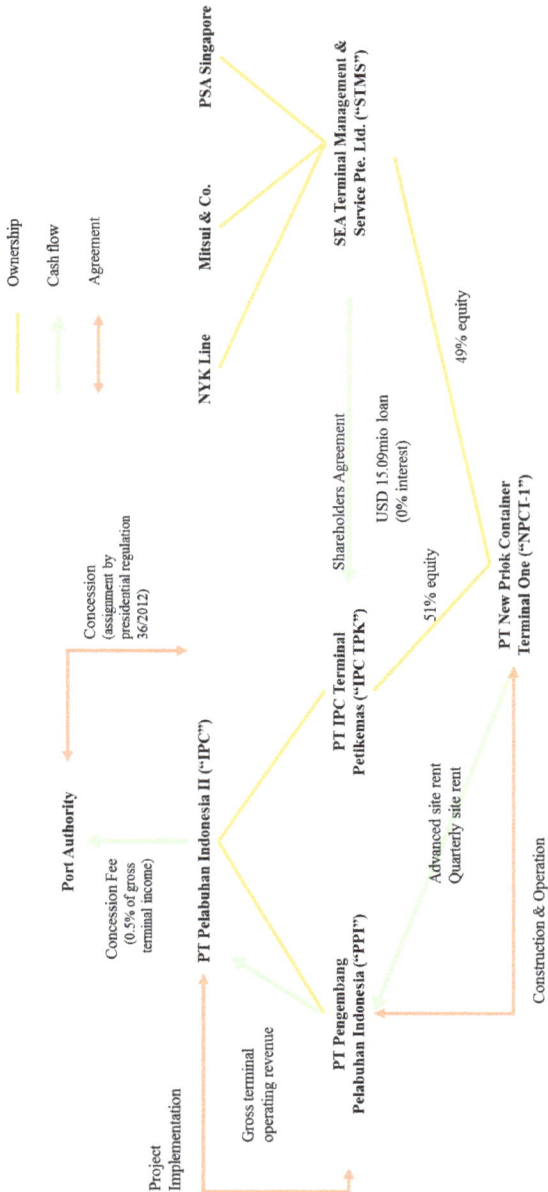

Fig. 10.8 The contractual relationship and project cash flows around the NPCT-1 project (Figure by authors based on data from IPC)

10.3.2.2 Existing Scenario Simulation Under Different PER Rates and Capital Structures

In this section, we construct the cash flow simulation model under the existing financing structure of NPCT-1. First, we create a projection of the terminal's annual throughput. On March 2018, less than one-and-a-half years since the terminal commenced operation (August 2016), NPCT-1 had already recorded its 1 million TEU throughput (Kurniawan 2018). This is quite remarkable, as Indonesian container terminals would typically fill up half of their capacity in two years. One consideration for the projection is that the throughput cannot be as high as the full 100% terminal capacity, as such a condition would cause operational congestion inside the terminal. Then, the revenue per unit TEU is projected using the average revenue per TEU of PT Pelabuhan Tanjung Priok (PTP), a subsidiary of IPC that also operates terminals in Tanjung Priok Terminal. The average TEU per unit from the 2015 and 2016 data is USD 140 per TEU. We then simulate the project's income statement using the information that we have discussed earlier (the ownership structure, PER, upfront payment, quarterly site rent, authorized capital, contract term, etc.), added with some assumptions.

These simplifying assumptions may not be entirely accurate. This simulation is not aimed to decide whether the project is feasible financially; rather it is to illustrate how different PER rates and capital structures might affect the project value for IPC. In order to simulate the NPCT-1 project's net present value (NPV) to IPC, we need to discount the cash flow received from NPCT-1 with a discount rate. In this simulation, we assume that IPC financed the infrastructure investment using debt, in this case the 2015 global bond proceed, as the internal cash of IPC was not sufficient.

However, the construction started in 2013. Therefore, we simulate the cost of debt from previous debt facilities that IPC has had since 2013 (PT Pelabuhan Indonesia II (IPC) 2016). Prior to the global bond issuance, IPC had two different debt facilities. In 2013, the syndicate of Bank Mandiri and BNI gave a short-term loan facility to IPC with a floating rate at average time deposit rate +3.650% spread. The next year, this facility was refinanced using a loan facility from the syndication led by Deutsche Bank AG with a maximum facility which amounted to USD 1 billion that bears a floating interest at LIBOR +2.200%. Finally, in 2015, the loan facility was refinanced with the proceeds from the global bonds that bear 4.250% and

5.375% coupon rate for the ten-years and the thirty-years maturity bonds, respectively. The historical data of the loan facilities received by IPC has shown that domestic bank finance may not be the best option, as it might be much more costly than the other alternatives. The summary of the interest borne by the loan facilities is shown in Table 10.3 below.

Table 10.3 Loan facilities received by IPC from 2013 to 2015

Year	Loan facilities	Interest types	Interest rate (p.a.)		
			Floating	+Spread	Total
2013	Bank Mandiri and BNI syndicate	Floating	Time deposit rate: 5.500%	3.650%	9.150%
2014	Deutsche Bank AG syndicate	Floating	LIBOR: 0.939%	2.200%	3.139%
2015	Global bond	Fixed Coupon	4.250% (10-years maturity) and 5.375% (15-years maturity)		

Source: IPC annual reports 2013–2016.

As we simulate the debt proceeds and payments schedule, we can obtain a cost of debt (IRR_{debt}) of 5.669% per annum.

After we build the cash flow simulation under the existing structure, we then simulate the project value under different capital structures. In other words, we simulate the project value if NPCT-1 were to be financed with a project finance structure, instead of using the current structure of corporate-debt. Figure 10.9 illustrates the simulation result.

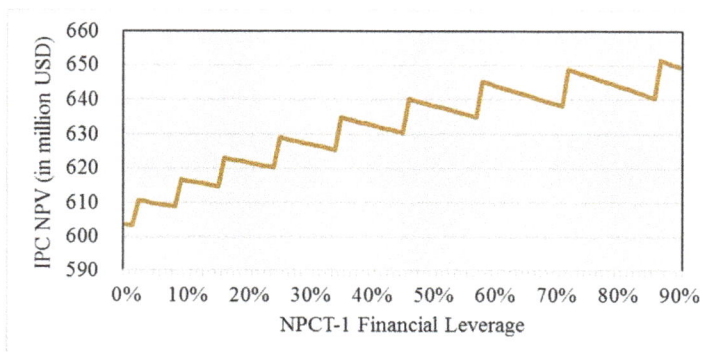

Fig. 10.9 The effect of the different NPCT-1 financial leverage levels on the project value with a certain target of IRR_{equity}/Permitted Equity Return (PER) (Figure by authors)

The more leveraged the project company, the higher value it can offer to IPC. The rationale is that if the project company is leveraged, then STMS would need so much equity that a higher IRR_{equity} could be achieved at an earlier point in time. The earlier the target IRR_{equity} can be achieved, the more dividend payments are made to IPC. Furthermore, the shape of the graph in Figure 10.9 shows a staged increase. This means that the project value will decrease at certain ranges of the project company's financial leverage levels because the project is required to pay a higher debt repayment. Then the value will increase significantly at some levels of leverage because of the extra dividend payment.

In order to better illustrate how different levels of project company leverage may affect the project value, we simulate the NPCT-1 value under different IRR_{equity} thresholds and compare the results between the unlevered and the levered project company.

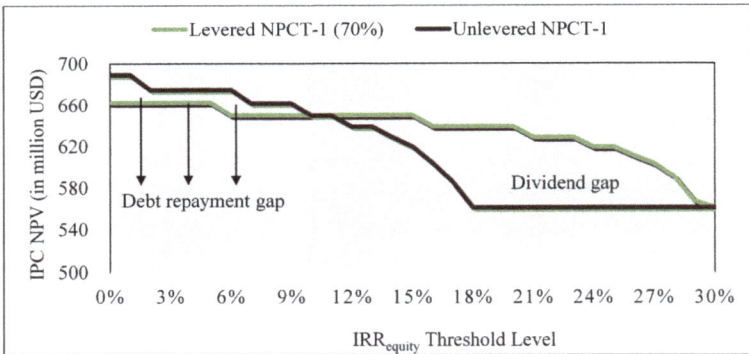

Fig. 10.10 The project value under different IRR_{equity} thresholds
(Figure by authors)

Figure 10.10 shows that at a lower IRR_{equity} threshold, the unlevered NPCT-1 may offer a higher project value to IPC. This is because at lower IRR_{equity} thresholds, the unlevered NPCT-1 can receive the same level of dividend payment as the levered NPCT-1, but the latter has to make the debt repayments, hence the debt repayment gap. However, at higher levels of IRR_{equity} threshold, the dividend payments received by the unlevered project company diminishes earlier than the levered project company. The levered project company would achieve a higher IRR at earlier periods, creating a gap that we call the "dividend gap".

Furthermore, as simulated in Figure 10.10 when the IRR_{equity} threshold level is at 10–11%, both the levered and the unlevered project company offer more or less the same level of NPV to IPC.

10.3.2.3 Alternative Scenario Overview

The second alternative scenario is provided here to confirm what the survey respondents suggested: that the PPP may be an effective financing vehicle for port infrastructure projects. In this scenario, we also use several assumptions as an addition to the information provided in the previous sections. The assumptions are as follows.

1. The project tender is assumed to be won by IPC.

2. However, a two-year delay is also assumed since a PPP structure may require a more complex preparation and coordination between IPC and the government and amongst the government agencies themselves.

3. A less favorable operating outcome is also assumed because the equity partner(s) is/are not certain whether the partner(s) has the capabilities to operate the terminal more efficiently (such as Public Service Authority) or offer favourable throughput volumes (such as Mitsui and NYK Line), or to add any other value to the project.

4. IPC bears the obligation and the responsibility to build the infrastructure, the superstructure, and to provide funding for the project company.

5. The shareholder agreement does not enclose the PER or IRR_{equity} threshold clause.

6. An availability-based payment by the government is provided to supplement the user-based charges. The availability-based payment used in this scenario is 'modified' in the sense that it is an annuity payment that may be made by the government throughout the project's operational term to 'guarantee' a certain level of the project's IRR_{equity}.

The contractual relationships amongst parties in alternative scenario is illustrated in Figure 10.11.

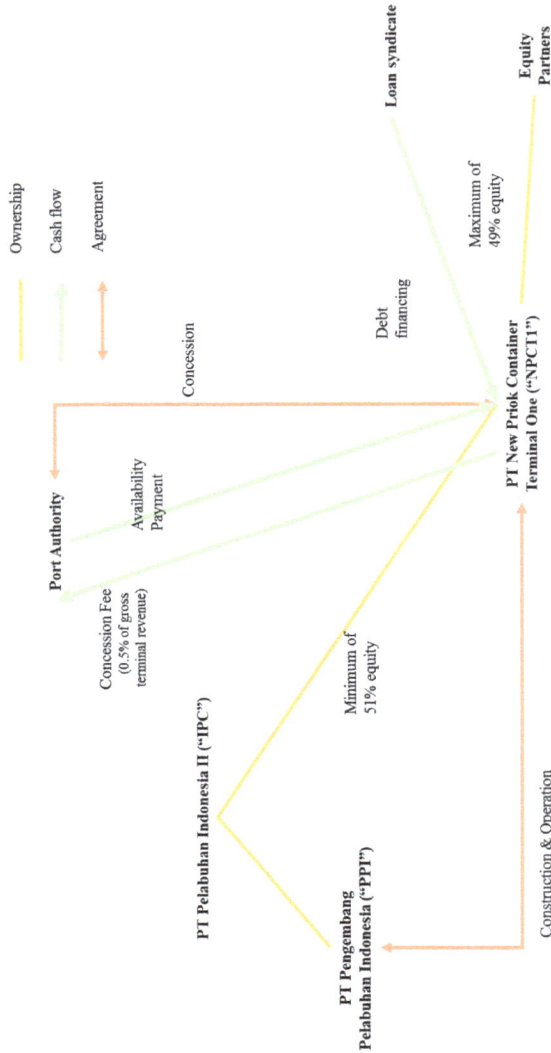

Fig. 10.11   The NPCT-1 project under a PPP-based structure with availability payment (Figure by authors)

10.3.2.4 *Alternative scenario simulation under different capital structures*

Without the PER clause the effect of the project company financial leverage is completely different in this scenario compared to the previous one. The higher level of the project company financial leverage would only diminish the NPV to IPC. At a lower leverage level, because of the lower IRR$_{equity}$, the project value will benefit from the availability payment that would keep the IRR$_{equity}$ at a certain level. Figure 10.12 illustrates this simulation outcome.

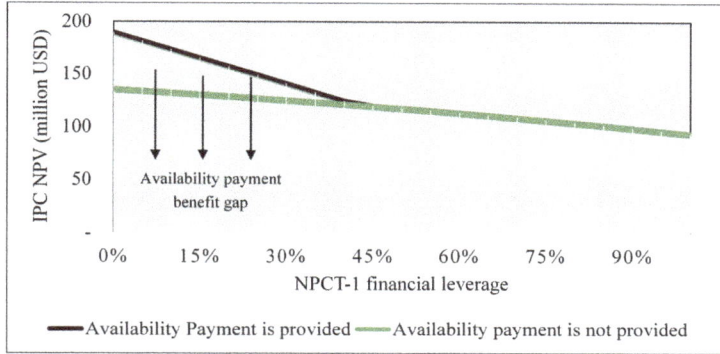

Fig. 10.12 The NPCT-1 project value to IPC under different project company financial leverage level (Figure by the authors)

We can see that in Figure 10.12 the availability payment feature offers some added value for the project only if it were funded with less than 45% financial leverage. At the 45% financial leverage level, or higher, the target IRR$_{equity}$ level may be achieved without the availability payment. Therefore, there is no added benefit from the availability payment. This is a pitfall of using IRR$_{equity}$ as a basis, or a threshold, for a dividend payment clause. IRR$_{equity}$ ignores the scale of the investment and the NPV. A higher IRR$_{equity}$ does not simply mean a higher NPV.

This reasoning is more clearly illustrated in Figure 10.13, where we simulate the project value under different IRR$_{equity}$ levels to be covered by the availability payment (AP) and we then compare the levered and the unlevered NPCT-1. Again, we show that the levered structure of the project company would not create additional value under this scenario. On the other hand, the levered NPCT-1 would benefit from the AP because of its lower IRR$_{equity}$ that would be covered by the AP, thus adding more value to the project.

However, the benefit received by IPC out of the AP might be offset by what the government has to sacrifice. Under this scenario, the government has to make larger payments when the project IRR$_{equity}$ is lower. Therefore, from the public-sector perspective, it is better if the project company has a higher financial leverage level, as a higher level of leverage would increase the project's IRR$_{equity}$. At a certain level of

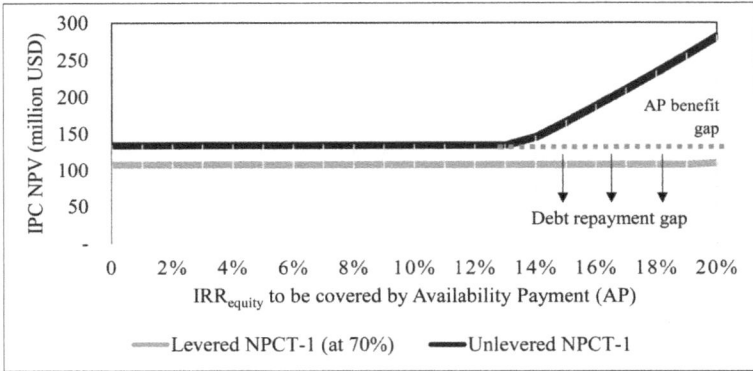

Fig. 10.13 The NPCT-1 project value to IPC under different level of IRRequity to be covered by the availability payment (Figure by the authors)

the project company financial leverage, there would be no availability payment required, as illustrated by Figure 10.14 below.

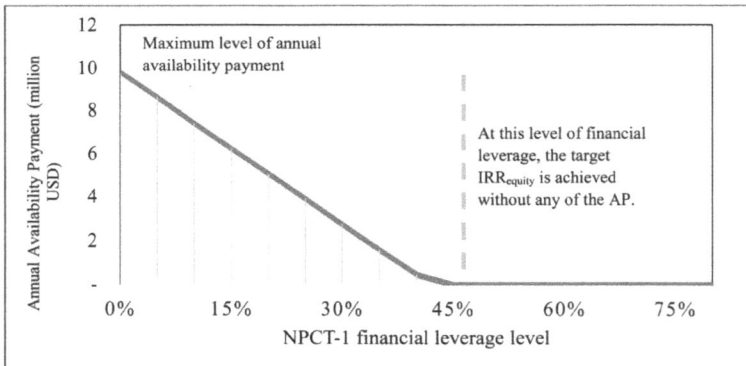

Fig. 10.14 The availability payment requirements that the government must pay at a certain level of target IRR_{equity} under different project company capital structure (Figure by the authors)

10.4 Discussion

The top-five financing schemes that were deemed effective by the respondents to the survey as shown in Table 10.2 are now discussed more closely.

10.4.1 Indonesian Domestic Banking Finance for Port Infrastructure Projects

One of the top-picked financing schemes is unsurprisingly the financing capacity from the domestic banking sector. Based on the data from Nirwan (2017), the financing facilities from the Indonesian banking sector are growing year-on-year, and they are projected to grow more in the future, as shown in Figure 10.14.

**Banking Financing on Logistic Infrastructure
(in trillion Rupiah)**

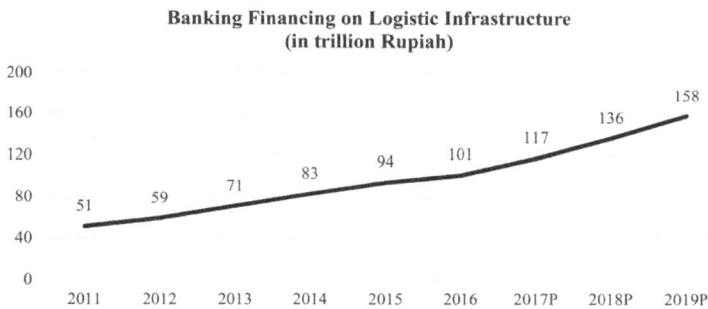

Fig. 10.15 Banking financing allocated to logistic infrastructure (road, railway, port, airport, information and communication technology, warehouse) in trillion Rupiah. Source: Nirwan (2017).

However, the domestic banking sector is faced with obstacles in allocating loans to infrastructure projects (Nirwan 2017). The main obstacle is the problematic source of funds. Generally, banks have two choices to fund their loans: either by emitting deposits, or by selling the loans to investors. In a situation where deposits are uninsured and unregulated, but with asymmetric information regarding asset quality, Greenbaum and Thakor (1987) found that banks would securitise better quality assets and finance the poorer quality assets with deposits. In the case of loan facilities that are provided to infrastructure projects, liquidity becomes an important issue. There are potential liquidity mismatch constraints with already high Loan to Deposit Ratio (LDR) of the domestic banks.

The second obstacle is the domestic bank loan pricing. For developing countries like Indonesia, political risk is a crucial determinant for loan pricing (Girardone and Snaith 2011). As a result, lenders would take into account whether the project's geographic location is in a country with low political risk, and, if not, whether the project is guaranteed by the government. A senior finance executive stated in his presentation at the focus group discussion in Indonesia that

> The lending rate of domestic banks is much higher than of external sources of funds, such as from development banks (ADB, World Bank, JBIC, and others), implying that bank financing is not firstly preferable.

However, Kleimeier and Megginson (2000) found that floating-rate project finance loans have lower credit spreads compared with non-project finance loans. It is interesting, considering the non-recourse nature of project finance loans. Nevertheless, the authors explained that a project finance structure is an effective monitoring tools because it may provide relatively transparent project cash flows that are separated from the sponsor's cash flows. Careful contract designs in project finance structures may provide a monitoring tool which mitigates potential agency problems, reduces the credit risks and lowers the loan spread (Corielli, Gatti, and Steffanoni 2010).

The third obstacle is the macroeconomic situation of the country where projects take place. Nirwan (2017) also stated that when the government budget deficit is high, as the infrastructure spending increases, the government may decide to issue more government bonds. This is not ideal for the domestic banks, as these government bonds will reduce the banks' funds.

Indonesian infrastructure projects — especially port projects — are still highly reliant on the support of the state-owned domestic banks, namely Bank Mandiri, Bank BNI and Bank BRI. Recently, the three banks formed a syndicate that provides the Kuala Tanjung Port project company (PT Prima Multi Terminal) an IDR 2.1 trillion loan facility from the total project investment of IDR 4 trillion (Alaydrus 2016). Even though financing support from the domestic banking sector is still very much expected, the sector is not without constraints, as discussed above. The government needs to provide further support for infrastructure projects to promote alternate financing vehicles. As shown in the survey results, the PPP-based financing methods are highly expected by our survey respondents, even though the use of PPP financing is still limited in the port sector. The next section discusses what the government has to offer in order to promote PPP financing schemes.

10.4.2 Government Fiscal Support for Public Private Partnership Projects

There are at least three main fiscal support forms for PPP projects provided by the Indonesian Government: the availability-based payments; the viability gap fund; and the government guarantee.

10.4.2.1 Availability Payment

Availability payments are payments made by the public sector to the project companies for the provision of the asset (Li 2003). According to the UK's Treasury Task Force (TTF 2001), the main features of these payments are as follows:

1. These payments should not be made until the service is available.

2. There should be a single unitary charge that excludes separate independent elements relating to availability or performance.

3. Payment is based on availability or performance.

4. The payment mechanism should include payment reduction for insufficient performance (Li 2003).

The crucial issue of unavailability as an aspect of availability payment features is how to incentivise the project company to not merely operate so as to avoid payment deductions, but to offer improvements in service. Bonus schemes should therefore be considered when better performance is self-funding in some way (Yescombe 2007)private-sector financing through public-private partnerships (PPPs. Availability payments can be the key mechanism for market risk allocation between the project company and the public procurer when the total income generated from service provision and commercial activities is insufficient to generate an acceptable level of equity return to the project sponsors (Gatti 2008). Availability payments convert revenue risk into public procurer default risk that can be considered as either political or regulatory risk or sovereign default risk (Roumboutsos and Pantelias 2015).

In October 2015, the Indonesian Ministry of Finance issued the Ministerial Regulation on Finance Number 190 Year 2015 Regarding Availability Payment on PPP in Infrastructure Provision. This gives the legal basis for availability payment schemes in Indonesian PPPs. Several projects have been proposed for the schemes, including the Urban Railway City of Medan, North Sumatera. The availability payment model is proposed for the initial 10–15 years of operation before full reliance on the end user tariff scheme afterwards (Bappenas, 2017).

10.4.2.2 Viability Gap Fund

Another form of government fiscal support for infrastructure projects is the viability gap fund (VGF) as regulated in the Ministerial Regulation of Finance Number 23 Year 2012. The VGF is the last resort to make economically-viable PPP projects becomes financially-viable. The Indonesian VGF can give support to the construction costs of up to one half of the total construction costs. For example, The Bandar Lampung Water Supply project is projected to receive VGF from the Ministry of Finance, with the estimated project cost of USD 81.48 million (Bappenas, 2017).

10.4.2.3 Government Guarantee

On December 30 2009, the Ministry of Finance of the Republic of Indonesia (MoF) established the Indonesia Infrastructure Guarantee Fund (IIGF), as a State Owned Enterprise, to address the three issues related to the government guarantee above. The guarantee provided by the IIGF is offered to improve projects' bankability and therefore giving assurance to the private sponsors of infrastructure projects under PPP schemes. By the end of 2016, the IIGF portfolio consisted of sixteen infrastructure projects that are dominated by toll road projects (eight projects) (IIGF 2016).

In general, although the reliance on domestic bank financing is still apparent, the constraints that limit the domestic banking sector have made the use of project finance and the PPP-based financing methods which are very much anticipated by the majority of our respondents.

10.5 Conclusion

Indonesia is one of the countries that is currently witnessing a rise in infrastructure development, especially in its transport infrastructure.

The government does not have enough funds available to build all of the necessary projects. This financing gap, common to many countries, makes private funding indispensable for infrastructure projects. On the other hand, the private sponsors would expect a high return for such long-term and irreversible investments. There are alternative financing methods that have been developed to achieve more bankable infrastructure projects. The purpose of this paper has been to understand these alternatives and what they can offer to attract more investments in port infrastructure projects development.

A survey of Indonesian seaport industry stakeholders found that the respondents perceive domestic banking as one of the main financing sources of port infrastructure investments. However, the domestic banking sector is not without constraints: the need to match the banking source of fund liquidity; the loan pricing in countries with high level of political risks; and unaccommodating macroeconomic policies by the government. Taking into account these constraints, alternative ways to finance port infrastructure projects have been considered. The respondents in our survey reported that a Public Private Partnership (PPP)-based financing structure could be effective for port investments. These views might come from the incentives arising from the government fiscal supports related to PPP deals. There are at least three main fiscal support forms: the availability-based payments; the viability gap fund; and the government guarantee.

A case study of the New Priok Container Terminal One (NPCT1) was conducted with IRR_{equity} as the basis of dividend distribution between the shareholders, PT Pelabuhan Indonesia (IPC) and its consortium partner, STMS. We simulated the project value from the perspective of IPC, as the project sponsor, under different scenario and assumptions. The first scenario is the existing financing structure of the project. The other scenario is the PPP-based scenario. In the first scenario, IPC bears the responsibility to fund the terminal's infrastructure investment only, such as reclamation, access roads, dredging, etc. Meanwhile, in the second scenario, IPC is assumed to be responsible for providing 51% of the total project initial outlay, both the infrastructure and the superstructure investment.

Both scenarios have a "guarantee" scheme for the private sponsor, STMS. In the first scenario, the guarantee is structured as a permitted equity return (PER), while in the second scenario, an availability payment is designed to guarantee a certain level of IRR$_{equity}$ to the sponsors. Under the first scenario, the simulation model illustrates how a project finance structure might add value to the existing financing arrangement. A higher project leverage would lower the total equity contribution. A lower equity contribution means that a higher IRR$_{equity}$ can be achieved at an earlier period of time than if the project company is unlevered. An unlevered project company would add more value than a levered one, under the second scenario.

There are two main limitations of this research. The first limitation, regarding the survey analysis, is the small number of respondents. Second, the simulation model that we developed is built upon some simple assumptions. There are possible future research topics. For example, to test whether the respondents' background (such as industry, private or public sector, education, experience) would affect their views on the various financing methods. Future research could also benefit from utilising more advanced analyses, such as real-option analysis, to illustrate how project management decisions during the project operation may provide significant benefits for the project sponsors.

References

Alaydrus, H 2016. 'Prima Multi Terminal Terima Kredit Sindikasi Rp2,1 Triliun', *Bisnis,* industri.bisnis.com/read/20160329/98/532433/prima-multi-terminal-terima-kredit-sindikasi-rp21-triliun

An, Y and Cheung, K 2010. 'Project financing: Deal or no deal', *Review of Financial Economics*, 19:2, pp. 72–77, https://doi.org/10.1016/j.rfe.2009.02.002

Atmo, G and Duffield, C 2015. 'Attaining value from private investment in power generation projects in Indonesia: an empirical study', *Journal of Sustainable Infrastructure Development*, 1:4, pp. 65–79.

Atmo, GU, Duffield, C, Zhang, L and Wilson, DI 2017. 'Comparative performance of PPPs and traditional procurement projects in Indonesia', *International Journal of Public Sector Management*, 30:2, pp. 118–36, https://doi.org/10.1108/IJPSM-02-2016-0047

Bappenas 2014. *Rencana Pembangunan Jangka Menengah Nasional 2015–19*, https://www.bappenas.go.id/id/data-dan-informasi-utama/dokumen-perencanaan-dan-pelaksanaan/dokumen-rencana-pembangunan-nasional/rpjp-2005-2025/rpjmn-2015-2019/

Bappenas 2017. *Public Private Partnerships: Infrastructure projects plan in Indonesia*.

Burger, P and Hawkesworth, I 2011. 'How to attain value for money: Comparing PPP and traditional infrastructure public procurement', *OECD Journal on Budgeting*, 2011:1, pp. 1–56, www.oecd.org/governance/budgeting/49070709.pdf

Chan, APC, Lam, PTI, Chan, DWM, Cheung, E and Ke, Y 2010. 'Critical success factors for PPPs in infrastructure developments: Chinese perspective', *Journal of Construction Engineering and Management*, 136:5, pp. 484–94, https://doi.org/10.1061/(ASCE)CO.1943-7862.0000152

Corielli, F, Gatti, S and Steffanoni, A 2010. 'Risk shifting through nonfinancial contracts: Effects on loan spreads and capital structure of project finance deals', *Journal of Money, Credit and Banking*, 42:7, pp. 1295–320, https://doi.org/10.1111/j.1538-4616.2010.00342.x

Eisenhardt, KM 1989. 'Building theories from case study research', *The Academy of Management Review*, 14:4, p. 532, https://doi.org/10.2307/258557

Esty, BC 2003. 'The economic motivations for using project finance', *Harvard Business School*, pp. 1–44, www.people.hbs.edu/besty/esty%20foreign%20banks%203-9-03.pdf

Esty, BC 2004. 'Why study large projects? An introduction to research on project finance', *European Financial Management*, 10:2, pp. 213–24, https://doi.org/10.1111/j.1354-7798.2004.00247.x

Flvvbjerg, B 2004. 'Five misunderstandings about case-study research', in *Qualitative Research Practice*, Seale, FC, Gobo, G, Gubrium, JF and Silverman, D (eds.), California, USA: SAGE Publications Ltd, pp. 420–34, https://doi.org/10.1177/1077800405284363

Gatti, S 2008. *Project finance in theory and practice*, Amsterdam, The Netherlands: Elsevier, https://doi.org/10.1016/B978-0-12-391946-5.00001-3

Girardone, C and Snaith, S 2011. 'Project finance loan spreads and disaggregated political risk', *Applied Financial Economics*, 21:23, pp. 1725–34, https://doi.org/10.1080/09603107.2011.577006

Greenbaum, SI and Thakor. AV, 1987. 'Bank funding modes: Securitization versus deposits'. *Journal of Banking and Finance*, 11:3, pp. 379–401, https://doi.org/10.1016/0378-4266(87)90040-9

Hui, KP, Duffield, CF, and Wilson, S (eds.) 2018. Port Competitiveness and Financing Research, Workshop 4 April 2018, ISBN No 978 0 7340 5431 9

IIGF 2016. *Indonesia Infrastructure Guarantee Fund (IIGF) Annual Report.*

Kleimeier, S and Megginson, W L 2000. 'Are project finance loans different from other syndicated credits?', *Journal of Applied Corporate Finance*, 13:1, pp. 75–87, https://doi.org/10.1111/j.1745-6622.2000.tb00043.x

Kurniawan, D 2018. 'NPCT1 Berhasil Bongkar Muat 1 Juta TEU' (NPCT1 successfully unloaded 1 Million TEU), *Gatra*, www.gatra.com/rubrik/ekonomi/312333-NPCT1-Berhasil-Bongkar-Muat-1-Juta-TEU

Li, B 2003. Risk management of construction Public Private Partnership projects, (May), PhD thesis, Glasgow, Scotland: Glasgow Caledonian University.

Nirwan, E 2017. *Financing solution for port sector*, Jakarta, Indonesia: PT Bank Mandiri (Persero) Tbk.

Nugroho, R 2012. 'Tender Kalibaru Batal, Konsorsium Kecewa', *Kompas*, ekonomi.kompas.com/read/2012/01/26/1024160/tender.kalibaru.batal. konsorsium.kecewa

Osei-Kyei, R and Chan, APC 2015. 'Review of studies on the critical success factors for public-private partnership (PPP) projects from 1990 to 2013', *International Journal of Project Management*, 33:6, pp. 1335–46, https://doi. org/10.1016/j.ijproman.2015.02.008>

PT Pelabuhan Indonesia II (IPC). 2016, *Annual Report IPC*.

Roumboutsos, A and Pantelias. A 2015, 'Allocating revenue risk in transport infrastructure Public Private Partnership Projects: How it matters', *Transport Reviews*, vol. 35:2, pp. 183–203, https://doi.org/10.1080/01441647.2014.988306

Shen-fa, W, and Xiao-ping, W 2009. 'The rule and method of risk allocation in project finance', *Procedia Earth and Planetary Science*, 1:1, pp. 1757–63, https:// doi.org/10.1016/j.proeps.2009.09.269

Subramanian, K V and Tung, F 2016. 'Law and project finance', *Journal of Financial Intermediation*, 25, pp. 154–77, https://doi.org/10.1016/j.jfi.2014.01.001

Yescombe, ER 2007. *Public-Private Partnerships. Public-Private Partnerships*, Amsterdam, The Netherlands: Elsevier, https://doi.org/10.1016/B978-0-7506-8054-7.X5022-9

Yin, RK,2006. *Case study research — Design and methods. Clinical Research*, California, USA: SAGE Publications Inc, pp. 8–13, https://doi.org/10.1016/j. jada.2010.09.005

11. The Critical Importance of Land Transport when Considering Port Development

The Case of Three Indonesian Ports

D. Parikesit,[1] S. Basalim,[2] and W. W. Wibowo[3]

11.0 Introduction

Over the years, academic and policy discussions on ports have moved from a traditionally single mode infrastructure analysis, to a more complex supply chain system of moving goods. The term "hinterland", often used in relation to the areas served by seaports or river ports, derives from the German words of "hinter" or behind, and "land" or land. Hence the word hinterland loosely means an area or areas behind the urban area or a port or a major economic centre. The relationship between ports and their hinterland has become apparent since early times, when ports were a means by which to carry agricultural produce,

---

[1] Professor of Transporation Engineering, Dept. of Civil and Environmental Engineering, Universitas Gadjah Mada.
[2] PhD Candidate, Dept. of Civil and Environmental Engineering, Universitas Gadjah Mada.
[3] Researcher at the Centre for Transportation and Logistics Studies, Universitas Gadjah Mada.

and products from the industry sectors, and transport them outside the region. Conversely, inputs of production were required to be imported through a port and sent to cities and their hinterland to ensure efficient production of farming and manufacturing commodities.

The role of ports, and the relationship between ports and their hinterlands, has substantially evolved, with many ports (especially large, regional ports) now serving as transit ports or hub ports. The emergence of Singapore and Dubai as international hub ports has changed the economic landscape of port development. Transit or hub ports are focusing their activities as a transfer point between mother vessels serving different regions, or between a mother vessel and a smaller connecting vessel, to the cargo sending or receiving regions. This type of port has little to do with activities inland. A typical example is the Port of Singapore, which had a throughput of 30.9 million TEU in 2016,[4] where 85% of its traffic is actually transshipment cargo,[5] leaving only a small percentage of its traffic serving the Singapore region.

On the other hand, the Ports of Antwerp and Rotterdam have 40% of traffic generated within a 40 km and 150–200 km radius from the respective ports (Notteboom 2008), making them hinterland-serving ports with a strong manufacturing base. In the case of US Ports, container imbalance (i.e. more imports than exports) have also caused a complexity in traffic and truck management (Chen et al. 2013). This is also the case observed in the Port of Melbourne in Australia. China, on the other hand, has more exports than imports, and approximately 85% of the containers are delivered by trucks (Guan and Liu 2009, quoted in Chen et al. 2013).

In recent years, we have witnessed the emergence of a new term — "self-generating port" — which refers to an integration between a port and an industrial area, often developed as a single or joint investment. The idea of the self-generating port emerged because the business risk associated with the traffic coming from and going to its hinterland is too complicated to be mitigated by the port operator. Ports can no longer rely on the traffic generated by their hinterland but need to produce their own traffic by having manufacturing industries

---

4   Singapore's 2016 Maritime Performance, published 11 January 2017. Accessed
     through www.mpa.gov.sg
5   Data taken from www.singaporepsa.com.

inside the port area supplying cargos and bulk commodities, as well as receiving them.

Whilst the ideas of regional or international hub ports and self-generating ports are appealing for both policy makers and investors, most ports still rely on their hinterland. This is due to several factors: firstly, these new types of ports are costly; and secondly, these ports require delicate coordination efforts not only between national and sub-national governments, but between governments and the private sector, especially the main industry players. Small ports in a country like Indonesia are likely to serve as hinterland ports, facilitating economic development of the region, far more than ensuring financial sustainability of those ports. The national and sub-national governments provide a large amount of subsidies to fill in the financing gap between the revenue and income from port operations. Many of the ports in Eastern Indonesia are, for instance, fully financed by the national government and treated as Public Service Agencies.[6]

This chapter will discuss the intricate relationship between ports and their hinterland, focusing on their transport activities. Multimodal operation of international ports will first be discussed in this chapter in the literature review, which will then be followed by an example of three ports in Indonesia namely: Belawan Port in Medan, North Sumatera; Tanjung Priok Port in Jakarta; and Tanjung Perak/Teluk Lamong Port Terminal in Surabaya.

11.1 Land Transport and Port Access: International Literature

The increasing importance of ports in regional and national development has been embedded in almost every developing and developed country's strategy. During the cold war era, the former USSR's strategy was to look

---

6   A Public Service Agency or "Badan Layanan Umum" (BLU in Indonesian language) is an agency within the government department providing public service. One of the features is that it can manage their own financial affairs. It can receive payment from the user and directly use/expedite their expenses without going through the consolidated revenue in the government treasury/Ministry of Finance. BLU is required to report their net income and account statement at the end of the fiscal year. The establishment of Indonesian BLU is stipulated by the Government Regulation No 74/2012.

for "warm water ports" or ports that can be accessed throughout the year. This has been the cause of conflicts and wars amongst the nations and countries in the European region. The combination of economic, socio-political, and security/defence aspects are often all amalgamated into a decision to develop and operate seaports.

China's Maritime Silk Road policy has also opened a large debate on port geography and how countries react to the global economic expansion of a particular country (Fig. 11.1). It also allows a new player, such as a big data company (in this case is IZP), to utilise its expertise to help manage global logistics movements. The main player is no longer monopolised by port operating companies or shipping lines. Another example informed by a conventional approach is the global port network of Dubai Port (DP) World shown in Figure 11.2, which has a portfolio of seventy-seven operating marine and inland terminals supported by over fifty related businesses in forty countries across six continents with a significant presence in both high-growth and mature markets. Container handling is the company's core business and generates more than three quarters of its revenue. In 2015, DP World handled 61.7 million TEU (twenty-foot equivalent units).

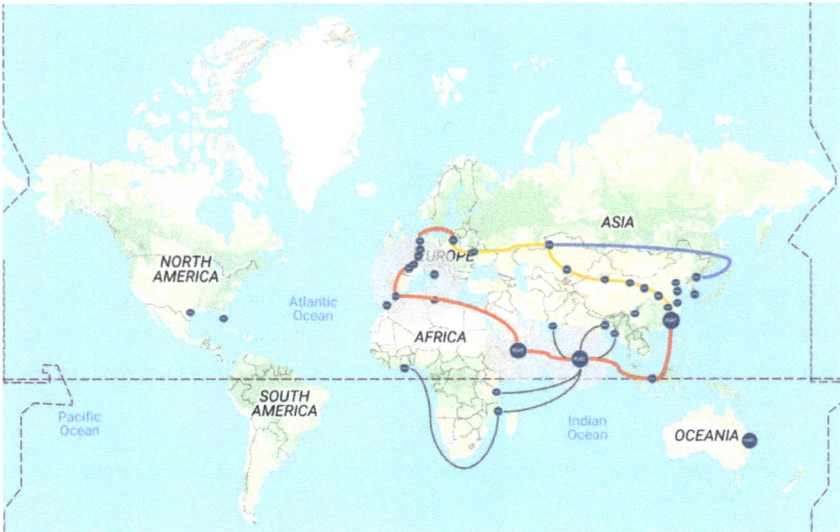

Fig. 11.1 Global Port Network of IZP and China Merchant Group.
Source: adapted from http://www.izptec.com, 11 September 2019.

Fig. 11.2 Dubai Ports global network. Source: adapted from
http://web.dpworld.com, 11 September 2019.

De Borger and de Bryune (2011) report that consolidation of ports around the world has resulted in 40% of the global market value and size represented by the "big four" terminal operators: Hutchinson, APM, PSA and P&O. This phenomena is best reflected by Notteboom (2008), who states "Port choice becomes more a function of network costs. Port selection criteria are related to the entire network in which the port is just one node. The ports that are being chosen are those that will help to minimize the sum of sea, port and inland costs, including inventory considerations of shippers" (Notteboom 2008, p. 6).

Land transport is known to operate under a less-than-equilibrium situation where many risks and uncertainties are not factored-in by both operators and regulators. The uneven level playing field between road and rail has in many countries, including in Australia, prevented the creation of a transparent market mechanism for different modes of transport to carry goods. This is where the advantage of port-to-port transport would offset the high land transport cost.

Rodrigue and Monios (in Ng et al. 2014) have indicated that the decreasing cost of ocean shipping has to some degree cross-subsidised the cost of overland transport, allowing regions distant from ports, or in countries without their own ports, to access global trade routes through intermodal links. Developments in the maritime sector influence the geography of hinterland transport in several ways: through competition for overlapping hinterlands; through attempts to improve efficiency of inland transport modes through large intermodal corridors; and through efforts to integrate supply chains by the setting of inland ports.

Table 11.1 below summarises the differences between road and rail in terms of their respective advantages and the issues related to their use.

Table 11.1 Comparisons of Advantages and Disadvantages of Road and Rail Modes

	Pros	Cons
Road	Freight can be delivered quickly as per a set schedule	Limitations such as cargo size and weights may be applicable for road weight across various states
	Cost-effective and economical, especially over short distances	May not be a cost-effective option across longer distances
	Full door to door movement	Limitations due to weather and road conditions
	Easier option to door movement	Not as environmentally friendly as rail
Rail	Greener option for transport as trains burn less fuel per ton mile than road vehicles	Additional costs to move a container from railhead to final destination, mostly using road freight.
	Freight trains carry more freight at the same time compared to road transport	Possible delays in cross-border movement due to change of train operators
	On average, long distance freight movement is cheaper and quicker by rail	Not economically viable across shorter distances
	Freight trains have proven to be transit sensitive even more than ocean freight delivering cargo from China to Europe in as little as eighteen days, compared to forty-four days by sea.	Abnormal cargoes cannot be moved in normal rail wagons

Source: Freightera (2017).

The table demonstrates that the choice for road and rail is complicated and requires thorough consideration, both from the transport authorities as well as from transport operators and freight forwarders. In many instances, the solution lies in the combination of both modes.

The development of networks of ports and their associated business model has been relatively new to transport and port researchers. An extensive critical review by Ng et al. (2014) indicated that throughout the period of 1950 until 2014, researchers in transport geography have concentrated their efforts at the national and local levels. Less attention has been given to trans-national economic and political interests on port development.

While the clusters of port research are derived mostly from the discipline of transport geography, other researchers are concentrating on the following areas: the business model; the relationship between port activities and the surrounding traffic; and the ways in which interaction between those two components often results in congestion and delays in the overall port logistics. An extensive literature on port business and port operations has also appeared in discussions amongst supply chain practitioners which focus on efficiency improvement through a better financing model, simulation techniques to improve pick-up or delivery time/costs, or business integration (merger and acquisition). Another large body of research concentrates on a micro-level analysis of traffic in and around ports. In the later section of this chapter we will highlight several findings and case studies of ports and how traffic simulation can reduce the congestion in port areas.

The review of international literature in this chapter falls under three discussion topics:

1. Regionalisation and spatial control.

2. Structural and organisational challenges of multi-mode port operation.

3. Disruption of land access to ports.

11.1.1 Regionalisation, Vertical Integration and Spatial Control of Commodities' Flow

As ports become financially independent from the government, they need to find a solution for business sustainability. Port operators are becoming active in searching for commodities and inbound as well as outbound traffic, to ensure enough demand to fill in the capacity they provide. Competition amongst ports is another reason for operators to seek innovative ways to manage their port business. Competition brings both business opportunity and lower profit margins. The only way to survive in this kind of business environment is to position and structure the port operation so that it becomes simultaneously creative and prudent.

Wilmsmaier et al. (2011, 2014) and Monios and Wilmsmaier (2012) state that ports are required to drive as well as react to developments in both land and water spheres, but they have lost the means to influence events to the degree they once could. The extension of a port's influence into the hinterland is one opportunity for port authorities to intervene and better influence the future. By allowing this to happen, two strategies are usually adopted: vertical and horizontal; and spatial integration.

The most common practice of control over spatial movement takes the form of an inland port, ICD (inland container depot, inland clearance depot, inland custom depot), or dry port.[7] These terminologies are often used interchangeably, but all represent the "port away from port" — a facility created and managed by a port operator, served by a port operator, and, in most cases, needing to comply with port regulations. The only difference is that this facility is not near water. The inbound and outbound cargos are processed using the same protocol as for the 'sea' port. Thus. when goods are transported to or received from the ports, the processing time is significantly reduced, the (sea) port productivity increases and the dwell time often increases. Proponents of this concept include Roso (2007) who argued that "with dry port implementation CO_2 emissions should decrease, queues at seaport terminals should be avoided, and the risk of road accidents reduced" (p. 527).

Wilmsmaier et al. (2011), however, differentiated the relationship between seaport and inland port into two types of development:

---

7   Nguyen and Notteboom (2016) classify dry ports into three categories. Close dry ports or satellite terminals are located in the proximity of seaports with strong connections to seaports by rail, barge and or trucks. Mid-range dry ports work as intermodal hubs to consolidate or deconsolidate cargo from shippers. The distant dry port is situated in the vicinity of the market, which might be the consuming area in import-based supply chains, or a core production location in export-based supply chains.

Inside-Out and Outside-In. Inside-Out describes a situation where the development of the inland facility may be driven by an inland carriage company (e.g. railroad, barge, logistics service provider) or a public body (more on this below), whereas an Outside-In arrangement may be developed by port authorities, port terminal operators or ocean carriers. In practice, many of the successful projects are those following Outside-In arrangement where the port operators are the main sponsors of the initiative. The proponents of Inside-Out arrangements usually hope to achieve twin aims: increasing modal shift (thus benefitting the environment), and increased attractiveness for businesses to locate in the area (thus creating jobs and economic development in the municipality and region). Wilmsmaier's analysis of Sweden's Inside-Out case study shows that in the absence, or limited, interest of the Port of Gothenburg, the initiative cannot be sustainably managed. They also looked into case studies from Scotland and the USA and suggested that while new Inside-Out projects are mostly promoted by national or sub-national governments, their success will depend on the buy-in of the port operators. This prerequisite is important, as many port operators are more interested in cooperation amongst the existing inland ports than new inland ports, because inland ports are exposing commercial revenue risks of a new untested project development.

Further study by Wilmsmaier et al. (2014) identify that it is not only the relationship between inland ports and seaports that is important in this matter: it is also important to understand how the group of ports behave, since they usually respond to the market. Their work on Latin American and Caribbean (LAC) ports indicates, "It is interesting to observe that each international operator shows specific geographical specialisation strategies" (p. 217).

Dry ports in developing countries are likely to be located close to large production bases, or even inside industrial zones; and usually situated in the middle of the chain for transloading between two transport modes. (Nguyen and Notteboom 2016, p. 4). They cite the examples of Lao Chai ICD in Vietnam, and another similar case Lat Krabang in Thailand. This is slightly different than what we find in the European Union (EU), where they have established European Distribution Centres (EDC), which take care of different products with different arrangements.

11.1.2 Intermodalities and Multi-Mode Operation of Ports: Organisational and Structural Linkage between a Port and its Hinterland

Under the assumption that firms will maximise their profit and provide the best service to customers, port operators are likely to exploit the economies of scale and scope. In addition to that, ports should be strategically located in a high and balanced demand area, both in terms of inbound and outbound traffic, while continuing to invest in better technology. As pointed out by Bomba et al. (2006, p. 1):

> Port users will continue to face pressure to lower production and shipping costs to remain competitive. To maintain the economic viability of their facilities, port authorities must consider improving landside linkages, as well as dockside improvements, and determine the optimal set of investments for ensuring efficiency and preventing bottlenecks.

They also argue that the important factor ensuring the success of the integration is the presence of an appropriate plan. However, in reality, efficiency needs to be gained through the private companies doing business along the supply chain. Operationally, the integration between port operations and the operation on its hinterland will be taken in the form of the business deal. Companies will take corporate actions through mergers, acquisition, alliance, joint venture or other forms of business arrangements. The ultimate functional integration will create a mega carrier. This is not a new idea.

Figure 11.3 presents an idea proposed by Robinson (2002), some fifteen years ago. Subsequently, Notteboom and Rodrigue (2005, p. 310) have systematically structured the level of integration and further predicted that:

> With an increasing level of functional integration many intermediate steps in the transport chain have been removed. Mergers and acquisitions have permitted the emergence of large logistics operators that control many segments of the supply chain (mega-carriers). Technology has played a particular role in this process namely in terms of IT (information technology), control of the process, and intermodal integration (control of the flows).

In turn, it is obvious that:

> The success of the port is strongly affected by the ability of the port community to fully exploit synergies with other transport nodes and other players within the logistics networks of which they are part. This observation demands closer co-ordination with logistics actors outside the port perimeter and a more integrated approach to port infrastructure planning. (Notteboom 2008, p. 37)

This raises the question whether this would be possible in the current governance and regulatory context; and how difficult it is for such complex integration to be implemented.

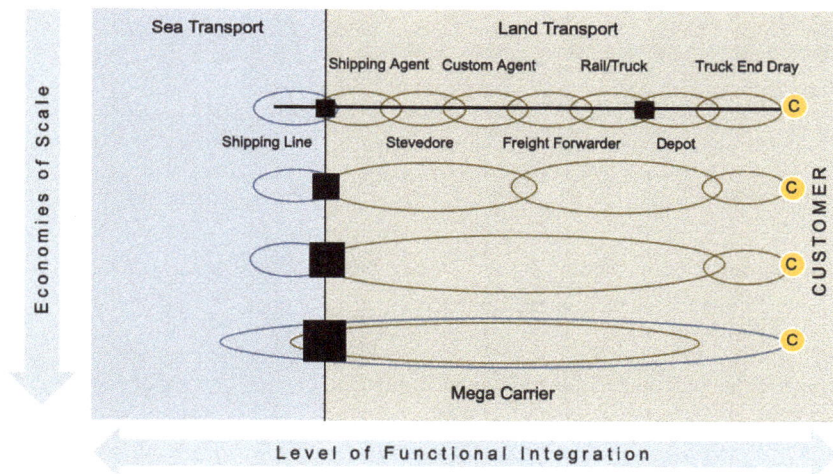

Fig. 11.3 Functional integration and exploitation of scale economies of logistics operation. Source: adapted from Robinson (2002) and Rodrigue (2006).

According to de Borger and de Bruyne (2011), the structural vertical integration of ports and transport firms will be "welfare-improving" (p. 269), only if government policies are optimal with respect to congestion tolls and port access. This implies that the private initiative for developing vertical integration will benefit both public and private sectors, but should be done in a proper and transparent manner, so that each party is aware of the price-correction policy to eliminate the imperfect market mechanism experienced in the land transport sectors. In other words, by failing to meet these criteria, either the public or the private sector will bear the risk of higher costs (i.e. lower charges will create congestion in the port periphery shouldered by the local traffic).

Other researchers argue, however, that such a simplistic approach is not useful when it comes to measuring port performance, since different ports may serve different combinations of commodities while producing the same throughput (de Langen and Sharypova 2013). Institutional barriers prevent the efficient and effective operation of an integrated port-inland system (Monios and Wilmsmeier 2012) and coordination amongst transport modes (Álvarez-SanJaime et al. 2015).

In fact, several ports investigated by de Langen and Sharypova (2013) use different PPI (port performance indicators) to reflect their productivity. To capture the land-and-seaside components of the operation, they are proposing the use of intermodal connectivity, arguing that:

> Intermodal connectivity is relevant, as many ports are confronted with growth prospects while the highway infrastructure around many port areas is congested. Thus, many ports, as well as policymakers have the ambition to handle a larger share of the volumes with intermodal transport and … Many port authorities also use intermodal connections in marketing efforts for attracting customers. (Langen and Sharypova 2013, p. 99)

What was realised, but not clearly discussed and understood, is that innovation in multi modal or intermodal operation is often hampered by regulations, leaving the sector as a fragmented business. This fragmentation has often resulted in a high logistic cost.[8] The mode integration alone is a challenge. OECD data on the modal split on various EU ports (quoted in Merk and Notteboom 2015) show the different combinations of road-rail-inland water transport for different ports. This suggests that different ports should have different business arrangements only from designing their mode split and should simulate

---

8   The World Bank indicated that Indonesia has a logistic cost of 25% of the manufacturing sales, whereas Thailand is 15% and Malaysia 15% (source: http://www.worldbank.org/en/news/press-release/2016/11/02/indonesia-400-million-approved-for-logistics-reform). Global average is believed to be between 9% and 14% depending on the industry sector. Notteboom and Rodrigue (2007) identified that "Globally, inland access costs account for 18% of the total logistics costs, and could be reduced by one third with appropriate regionalisation strategies" (p. 301).

the impact of that decision on the overall logistic costs or recommended port charges. Further, Merk and Notteboom (2015) identified five conditions to meet a better hinterland connection, as follows (pp. 17–18):

1. Provide sufficient capacity of hinterland infrastructure and in the interface between port and hinterland infrastructure: this condition links to the infrastructural layer.

2. Guarantee the efficient use of hinterland infrastructure: this condition links to the transport layer, but also supposes actions at the logistical layer in terms of coordination and orchestration.

3. Good coordination of the transport chain.

4. Sustainable from an environmental point of view. The sustainability condition applies to the infrastructural layer, transport layer and logistical layer.

5. Attractive services (price and quality) of the service providers in the transport chain (terminal operators, carriers, ...), i.e. the transport layer.

11.1.3 Traffic Congestion in and Around Ports

Road traffic congestion costs money for both transporters and freight owners. Nowadays, the cost of congestion going to or from ports is extremely high, so it becomes unreasonable to improve logistic costs without doing something on the landside. The OECD study reported by Merk and Notteboom (2015, p. 29) indicates that:

> the price difference per FEU-km[9] between inland transport and long-haul liner shipping ranges from a factor 5 to a factor 30, further supporting the notion that inland logistics is one of the most vital areas for the competitiveness of seaports.

Port congestion is worse in developing countries where port queuing systems have not been set according to the demand for vehicle entry, and many operations are done manually. Rajamanickam and Ramadurai (2015) studied the Port of Chennai, India and found that "congestion or

---

9   FEU is forty-foot equivalent unit, as opposed to TEU twenty-foot equivalent unit.

queuing of trucks is due to the longer document processing and security check times that has a negative impact on the number of trucks serviced per hour" (p. 1914). The complication arises when the commodities sent or received are in the form of bulk commodities.

As opposed to the container terminal, where examination of the content and the size of the container are standardised, the bulk commodities often create difficulties, even for a modern port such as Singapore. It was observed that:

> complexity is further exacerbated due to uncertain vessel arrivals, weather-dependent loading and unloading to/from vessels, and heterogeneous types of equipment and vehicles required to handle the movements of goods in and out of the port. (Li et al. 2016, p. 2382)

The simulation work by Lima et al. (2015) has provided a better understanding on how traffic management and fleet/vessel scheduling can be coordinated to reduce queuing at port gates. The latter measure, also known as Truck Arrival Management (TAM), is the procedure to arrange the arrival of the vessel so that it will reduce the waiting time. A more advance version of TAM is using vessel dependent time window (VDTM) to ensure that the information on vessel arrival is conveyed to the land transport operators (Chen et al. 2013). Many methods can be applied and one of them is applying the optimisation model for truck appointments. With this method, the terminal can manage the maximum number of trucks that can be handled in a specific time segment.

There are several policy measures available to encourage off-peak inbound and outbound traffic. Merk and Notteboom (2015) have identified several of them: for example, PierPASS in Los Angeles and Long Beach; the use of distribution centres for small ports like Gothenburg to increase the use of rail; introducing extended gates developed successfully by the Port of Antwerp; or the dedicated road freight lane in the Alameda Corridor and rail freight lane of the Betuwe Line. The importance of gate management is critical and has been discussed in various academic and practical papers.

Another example mentioned by Acciaro and McKinnon (2013) and Maguire et al. (2009) is an appointment system (or TAS, Terminal Appointment System), which generates pros and cons. The gate appointment is often complimented with the extended gate hour's system. The supporters of TAS argue that the system brings down congestion and reduces emissions, by controlling the random arrival of trucks, modifying the peak hour demand, minimising congestion of idling trucks and improving the utilisation of terminal capacity.

The critics of the system state that the appointment system benefits the regulators but not the industry. Acciaro and McKinnon (2013, p. 9) also claim:

> effectiveness of an appointment system depends on the opening hours
> of distribution facilities and warehouses, and to some extent on labour
> and road regulation.

Chen et al. (2013) further indicates that the appointment system, using a vessel-dependent time window, will not be effective if the terminal does not operate 24-hours. Another innovative solution offered is the concession agreement in the Rotterdam Port which is designed to force terminal operators to meet the modal split target by giving bonuses or imposing penalties, thus providing more push for congestion-free modes of transport.

IT technologies, including automation systems, are an important advancement in improving the movement of fleets, and perhaps will be even more important in the future, together with the advancement of autonomous vehicles. This would range from the vehicle position and recognisance system, virtual yard system, to the automatic gate web-based system that allows only a particular assigned vehicle to enter the port area (Maguire et al. 2009).

At the other end of the spectrum, the reduction of traffic going in and out of the port area can be achieved through better container arrangements or improved trans-loading activities: port-centric logistics; consolidation of container loads; and repositioning of empty containers. In the case of Miami Port, the increase in traffic volume was addressed by the construction of Port Miami Tunnel that opened on 3 August 2014. O'Rourke (2016) measured the improvement in travel speed after the tunnel was opened. He found that the travel speed improved despite an increase in traffic. Obviously, on the other hand, the costs of constructing the tunnel should be taken into account, and a proper benefit cost analysis needed to be undertaken before it was implemented.

11.2 Case Studies of Indonesian Ports

11.2.1 Case I: The Need to Manage Land Use and the Local-Through-Access Traffic Separation for Tanjung Priok Port in Jakarta

As an archipelago state, Indonesian ports are the entrance and exit gates of goods and people. Tanjung Priok Port is the main port located in North Jakarta having the highest level of activity handling more than 50% of cargo flow in Indonesia. Currently, Tanjung Priok Port has a water area of 424 hectare, including the port area and breakwater, and has 604 hectare land area. The flow of containers at Tanjung Priok Port has tended to fluctuate since 2010. Whilst it experienced a decrease between 2012 and 2015, the flow increased in 2016 where domestic and international flows reached 165,387,000 and 82,239,500 TEU respectively. However, the flow of these containers decreased in 2017 (PT Pelabuhan Tanjung Priok 2017).

The movements of goods from their origin to destination to and from Tanjung Priok Port involves containers, as stated by Decree of Directorate General of Land Transportation no. SK.538/AJ.306/DJPD/2005 (amendment of Decree no. AJ.306/1/5 of 1992), that pass through the roads of: (i) Tanjung Priok — Cilegon, (ii) Tanjung Priok — Bogor, (iii) Tanjung Priok — Cirebon, and (iv) Tanjung Priok — Pulo Gadung (Fig. 11.4). The majority of heavy vehicles traveling from outside Jakarta towards Tanjung Priok Port originate from Bekasi, Karawang, and Cikampek.

Currently, the majority of export industries are located towards the east of Tanjung Priok Port, i.e. Cikarang and West Karawang, handling mostly export containers (and also imported raw materials). The existing Cikampek toll road is the main route on which trucks travel. The distance between Cikarang industrial area and Tanjung Priok is around 60 km. Due to the existing congestion on the toll roads, some exporters consider taking a longer route (nearly 800 km) with less congested toll and public roads to use another international port in Surabaya (Tanjung Perak).

Considering the land area of 604 hectare covered by Tanjung Priok Port and the huge number of stakeholders involved at the Port, land

Fig. 11.4 Hinterland areas and movement corridors of containers carrying goods towards Tanjung Priok Port. Source: adapted from Tanjung Priok Port, 11 September 2019.

management is essential. In the 2017 Master Plan of Tanjung Priok Port, the projection for containers shows that between 2020 and 2035, the volumes of containers at Tanjung Priok Port are predicted to reach 8,642,700 and 15,480,600 TEU respectively. The projection illustrates that in 2035, Tanjung Priok Terminal will reach its capacity to meet domestic and international demands. The high volumes of incoming and outgoing goods at Tanjung Priok Port require the management to improve the site to enhance its effectiveness.

The port area is the busiest area filled with heavy vehicles that impact on the performance and transport. Figure 11.5 shows the movements of heavy vehicles from the industrial areas in the hinterland that then impact heavily on the corridors leading into Tanjung Priok Port.

Figure 11.5 shows that the accumulation of heavy vehicles in industrial hinterland areas leads to a significant rise in vehicle volumes. This also leads to slower vehicle movements due to increased congestion on the roads. The combination of high volumes of traffic using toll roads, mixed use of land around the port, and local traffic has created a congested road network entering the port gate. Whilst the toll road is aimed at easing traffic from the industrial area, the traffic problem occurs when a container truck leaves the toll road and uses the public road to access the port gates. The elevated toll road known as "Access Tanjung Priok (ATP toll)", recently built using a loan from the Japanese Government, has not been able to relieve the congestion at the port gate.

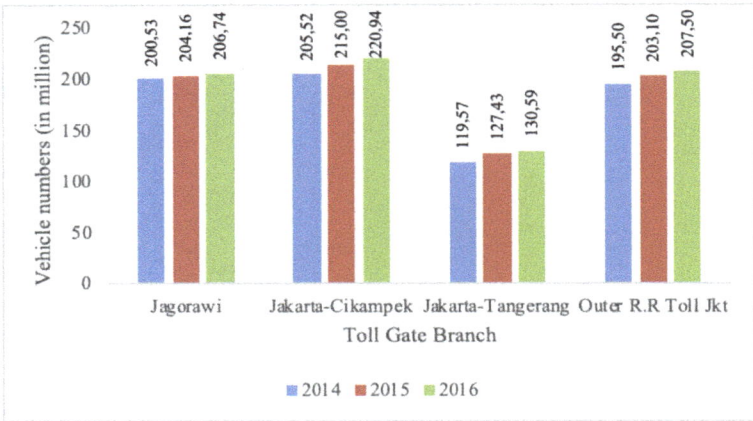

Fig. 11.5 Number of Vehicles through Toll Road by Toll Gate Branch, 2014–2016.
Source: adapted from PT Jasa Marga/Indonesia Highway Corp 2018.

Of the five existing toll roads — Jagorawi; Jakarta-Cikampek; Jakarta-Tangerang; Camareng, City Toll of Jakarta, Tol Sedyatmo; Outer Toll of Jakarta — the Jakarta-Cikampek Toll Road carried the highest number of heavy vehicles among other classifications of vehicles in 2014 (Indonesia, Highway Corp, 2018). This data remained consistent in 2015 and 2016 with the average growth of 3.25% (Fig. 11.6).

11.2.1.1 Congestion around the Port of Tanjung Priok and the Failure to Comply with Land-Use Regulations

Land-use problems arise in some cities in Indonesia related to the lack of land-use controls, and the dominance of property developers to dictate the development plan and real estate. Tanjung Priok Port has the same problem where the port development area and entrance and exit access are in conflict with the surrounding non-commercial or residential areas that border the port.

From the traffic map in Figure 11.6, it can be seen that the area where the speed of vehicles around Tanjung Priok Port slows is Tanjung Priok Toll Road, where the interactions with local residents and commuters occurs in the morning peak hours. This shows the negative impact on the port region caused by the activities of the local population where there is the urgent need to access a way to and from the port. The

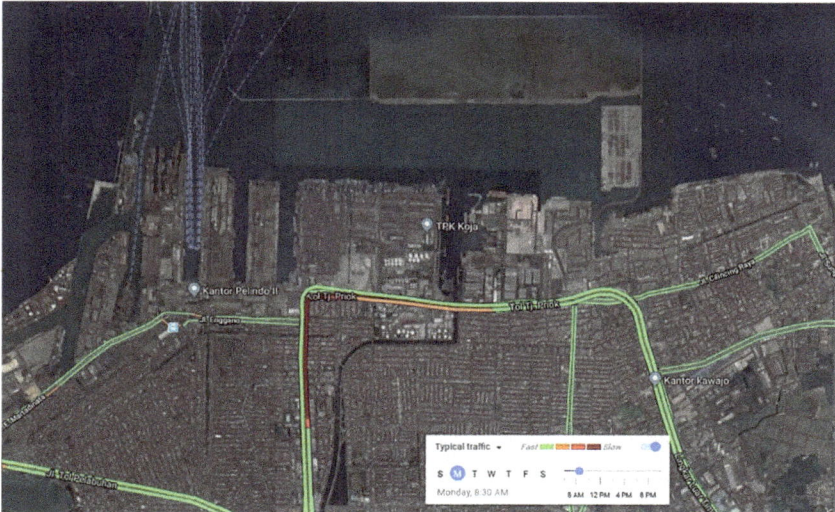

Fig. 11.6 Traffic Conditions around the Tanjung Priok Port (morning peak hour).
Source: adapted from Google Maps. 11 September 2019.

establishment of the DLKr or *Daerah Lingkungan Kerja Pelabuhan* (*Work Area of Port*) directly adjacent to legal residential areas has created a mobility problem for container vehicles leading to and from the Tanjung Priok Port (Fig. 11.7).

Fig. 11.7 Mix of through traffic and the movement of local traffic.
Source: adapted from Google Maps, 11 September 2019.

11.2.1.2 Reactivation of Railway Access to Port Terminal

A way to improve the flow of container vehicle traffic leading from and to the port, as well as the traffic caused by the local travel, is to develop a special access road to the Port. In general, constructing toll roads is expected to provide optimal output if those toll roads are developed on an elevated basis. Separate to the construction of toll roads with access to the port, the development of railways is also important.

Tanjung Priok Port has limited access to railway services and has not made railways the main mode for freight transport. Interviews with the authority reveal that door-to-door delivery with rail is more expensive than trucks. An example is the at-grade rail intersection that disrupts the rail arrival/departure schedule, and the port loading and unloading system required by railway containers. Furthermore, the expectation of producers or exporters that the custom clearance be completed prior to entering port gates cannot be fulfilled.

11.2.1.3 The Development of Dedicated Toll Access

Figure 11.8 shows the toll road network that supports the access to Tanjung Priok Port, which is Jakarta Outer Ring Road, Tanjung Priok Access, and the Plan of Cibitung Cilincing Toll Road.

The Tanjung Priok Access Toll Road currently consists of five sections: E-1 Section for Rorotan-Cilincing along 3.4 km, E-2 Section for Cilincing-Jampea along 2.74 km, E-2A Section for Cilincing-Simpang Jampea along 1.92 km, NS Link for Yos Sudarso-Simpang Jampea along 2.24 km, and NS Direct Ramp along the 1.1 km.

The important toll road segment that will greatly assist continuous freight movement to and from Tanjung Priok Port are the two toll roads (Fig. 11.8) namely Cibitung-Cilincing (no. 11) and Tanjung Priok Access (no. 10). These two toll segments will completely separate through traffic to the Port of Tanjung Priok from the local traffic.

Inland Waterways. To develop the connection between Tanjung Priok Port and its hinterland, an alternative transport mode is needed. Current connections are limited to toll roads and railways and therefore, a more modern and less costly transport mode has been suggested in the form of inland waterways. The Cikarang-Bekasi Laut (CBL) Inland Waterways will connect Tanjung Priok Port to Industrial Areas

Fig. 11.8 Toll Roads Network (include Access Toll Road to Tanjung Priok Port).
Source: adapted from Toll Road Management Agency, 2018.

in Cibitung, Cikarang, and Karawang by utilising the CBL Canal (Fig. 11.9). The development of the water line of CBL with a total length of 25 km, consists of widening its width, dredging, and developing the Inland Terminal around Cikarang Industrial Area. This is expected to reduce congestion on the toll roads around Cibitung, Cikarang, and Karawang. In addition, it is also expected to provide a less costly but more efficient logistic solution. CBL Inland Waterway is projected to increase the volume of container flow to Tanjung Priok Port from Cibitung, Cikarang, and Karawang with a total capacity of its operational stage at 3 million TEUs annually.

In Stage 1, the canal transportation system will utilise the existing canal built by the Ministry of Public Work and People Housing located in Cikarang Bekasi Sea passing through Marunda, North Jakarta. In addition, for Stage 2, PT Pelindo II (the State Owned Enterprise that owns the Port of Tanjung Priok) plans to add more routes from Tanjung Priok to Cikampek where the canal will link the logistics from Tanjung Priok and the Industrial Areas of Cibitung-Cikarang in Bekasi, Cikampek, and Karawang.

The plan to operate New Priok is an effort to optimise the capacity of Tanjung Priok from 7.1 million TEU to 10 million TEU (PT Pelabuhan

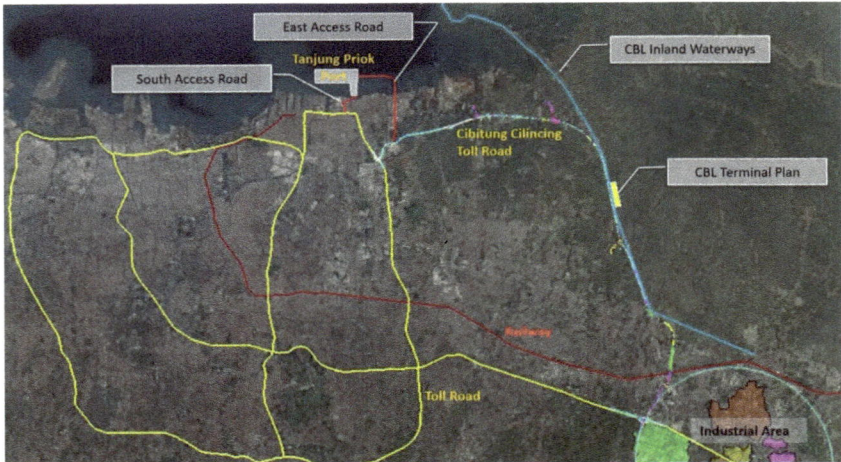

Fig. 11.9 Proposed Cikarang Bekasi Laut (CBL) Inland Waterway for container access to Tanjung Priok Port. Source: adapted from PT Pelindo II, 11 September 2019.

Indonesia II, 2016), where the role of CBL inland waterways becomes so important. New Priok is a project implemented by PT Pelindo II undertaken through private concession to invest in the port reclaimed land and port infrastructure. CBL Inland waterways will reduce the flows of containers heading into Tanjung Priok Port since vehicles will pass through the canals and dock at the port. To optimise the use of CBL terminal, the development of Cibitung Cilincing Toll Road (Fig. 11.8) should be accelerated to relocate the container loads from land transport to the canal.

11.2.1.4 Ensuring Control of Inbound and Outbound Traffic: Pelindo II Corporate Actions

At Tanjung Priok Port, eight entrance and exit gates are operated to serve the conventional, container, and car terminals as shown in Figure 11.10.

The conventional terminal of Tanjung Priok Port has four entrance and exit gates, which are Gates 1, 3, 8, and 9:

- Gate 1 is provided for vehicles from and to the east part of the port. This Gate connects Nusantara II Street with Martadinata Street and is the main gate for vehicles leading to the conventional terminals of Nusantara I and II.

- Gate 3 links Martadinata Street and Padamarang Selatan Street and is an alternative gate for vehicles leading from the west toward Birai 1 and Birai 2. According to the short-term plan, this gate will be closed following the development of Pasoso flyover.

- Gate 8 connects Bangka Street with Enggano Street. This gate is an alternative exit gate for vehicles from the port as well as the special entrance for motorcycles.

- Gate 9 joins Port Main Street with Jampea Street where it is the main entrance and exit gate for vehicles from and to the east part mainly those that lead to the Industrial Area of KBN-Marunda, KBN-Cilincing, Cikarang, Bekasi, Cikampek, and Bekasi as well as vehicles from North Jawa Road network.

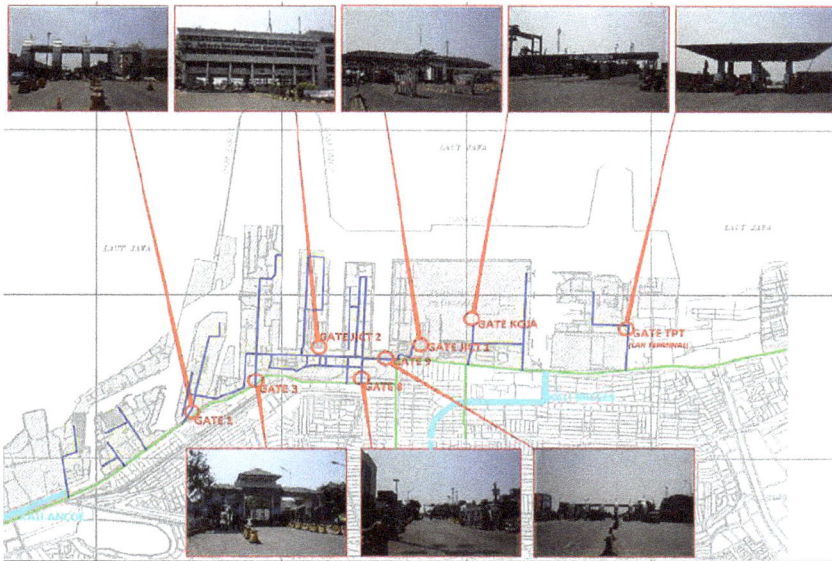

Fig. 11.10 Gates available at Tanjung Priok Port. Source: adapted from Masterplan of Tanjung Priok Port (2017).

The application of ICT can be used to control the port's incoming and outgoing traffic, making the operational system for cargo handling more efficient. Nowadays, both sides of service — shipping and land transport — have been optimised. These two sides have been strengthened by IT where the registered trucks are allowed to enter the port with contracts to deliver or carry goods. At the same time, the docked, loading, and unloading ships can control their positions and determine the trucks that will carry their loads. This IT application under Truck Arrival Management (TAM) gives effectiveness to administration, schedules, and coordination amongst trucks and with the ship arrivals. PT Pelabuhan Tanjung Priok (PT JICT) is managing productivity and efficiency by having developed the JICT Auto Gate (Automatic Gate System) and JICT Weighing in Motion (WIM) systems, which weigh vehicles with sensors without asking the trucks to stop.

Empty Trips. If congestion at corridors leading towards the port and around the port occurs due to high volumes of trucks, this inefficient movement needs a solution. In a freight transport system, one problem is vehicles without loads. Trucks entering and leaving the port can be engaged in three different activities: pick up/export, delivery/import, and Simultaneous pick-up and Delivery (SPD). Figure 11.11 illustrates three situations related to the movements of trucks and container loads when entering and leaving the port gates. The studies previously conducted at Tanjung Priok Port (Herdian, et al. 2017) showed that empty trucks moving towards TPK (Container Terminal) Koja reached 51% (6% combo and 45% single) in 2015 and empty trucks leaving the terminal reached 44% in the same period.

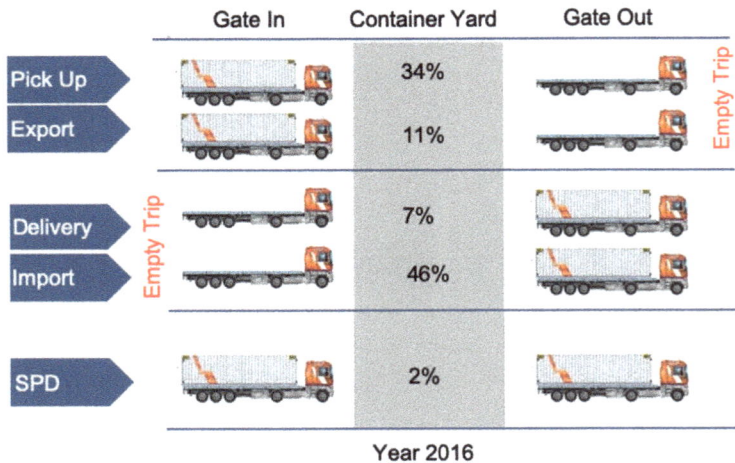

Fig. 11.11 The movement pattern of incoming and outgoing trucks at the port of Tanjung Priok. Source: adapted from Herdian et al. 2017.

In 2016, empty trucks moving towards TPK Koja reached 53% (7% combo and 46% single) and empty trucks leaving the terminal reached 45%. Here, combo means container trucks carrying two containers at the same time. The ideal condition of vehicle movements is the SPD (Simultaneous Pickup and Delivery) pattern, where the trucks entering and leaving the port are carrying loads. Greater efficiency can be achieved by equipping trucks with double loads (combo).

The above-mentioned 'ideal' situation can be achieved through using IT solutions where the trucks must have two related and simultaneous tasks, which are pick up (export activity) and delivery (import activities). To reduce the number of trucks and movements at the port, it is important to optimise the existing IT by utilising it more effectively.

11.2.2 Case II: Importance of Rail Traffic to Support Efficient Operation of Belawan Port, North Sumatera

Belawan International Port is the main focus of the strategic development of the port area in Medan to support the function of Medan city[10] as part of the National Centre of Activities of Mebidangro Metropolitan Region. The importance of this port is largely due to its strategic position in the north part of Sumatera, and on the busiest Malacca straight (Fig. 11.12). Currently, PT Pelindo I, a port company wholly owned by the Indonesian Government, operates Belawan Port. This port serves passenger, containers, bulk and general cargo. Pelindo I is currently developing a multi-purpose container port in another area (Kuala Tanjung) in response to the high demand for container traffic shown in Figure 11.13.

By referring to Figure 11.13, we can see the increased trends in both export and import volumes over the years, while in 2016 volume decreased. The projections for freight loads and unloads at Belawan Port (Masterplan of Port Belawan) can be seen in Table 11.2 below.

---

10   As part of the National Centre of Activities of Mebidangro City Area (Decree of Medan City no. 13 Year 2011; article 12 verses 2 point d).

Infrastructure Investment in Indonesia

Fig. 11.12 Belawan Port and Its Hinterland. Source: adapted from Masterplan of Belawan Port, 11 September 2019.

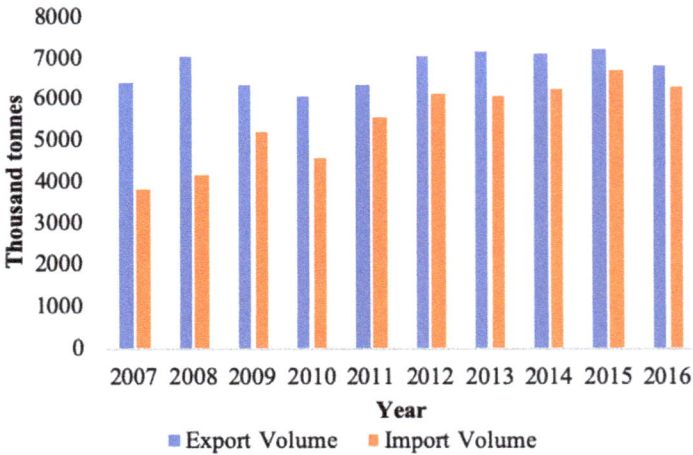

Fig. 11.13 Export and Import Volumes from Belawan Port. Source: adapted from Central Bureau Statistics of Sumatera Utara Province, 2017.

Table 11.2 Projections of cargo loads and unloads at Belawan Port

Description	Year	
	2025	2030
Exports	8,266,070.54	10,008,680.94
Imports	3,444,689.14	4,170,880.76
Inter-island Loading	1,749,915.45	2,118,823.60
Inter-island Unloading	10,301,202.88	12,472,849.39
Total	23,761,878.01	28,771,234.69

Source: adapted from Masterplan of Belawan Port, 29 March 2018.

Based on data presented in Table 11.2, Belawan Port has characteristics marked by domestic incoming freight and international outgoing freight (exports) as the dominant activities. Forecast data of cargo flows can be seen in Table 11.3.

Table 11.3 Forecast data of cargo flows at Belawan International Container Terminal (BICT)

Year	International	Inter-island	Total
2020	963,009	764,157	1,141,915
2028	1,422,802	1,522,630	2,945,432
2030	1,568,640	1,809,037	3,377,676

Source: adapted Masterplan of Belawan Port, 29 March 2018.

The capacity increase of the BICT Terminal is due to the extension of its length at 700 m built in the short-term development period (2011–2015) and 1,250 m that will have been built in the middle term (2016–2025) to handle 2,900,000 TEU. Based on forecast projections, BICT will reach its maximum capacity in 2028 when the containers at BICT will be relocated to Kuala Tanjung Port. The increase of traffic in Belawan Port has resulted in demand for land transport services (Fig. 11.14). Congestion in the port area and in the existing transport corridors in the Northern part of Sumatra has increased significantly. The existing road network has not been able to cope with this demand. As a response, the government through its toll road authority is currently planning and constructing a new road network using PPP schemes and government assignments to state-owned companies.

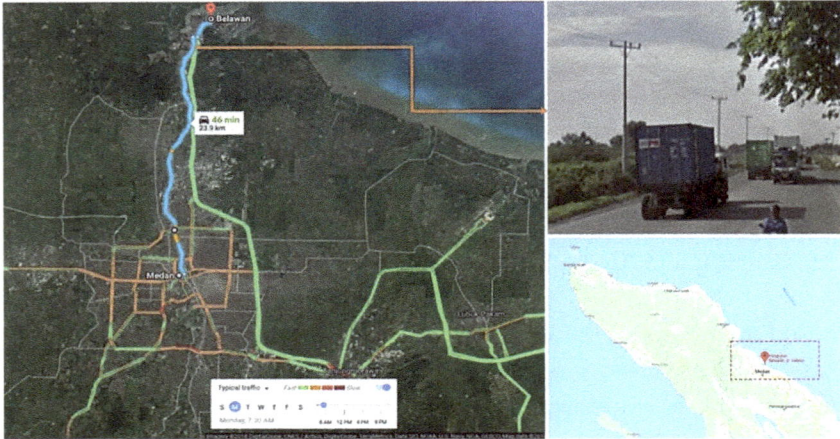

Fig. 11.14 Main Road Networks Going from and To Belawan Port. Source: adapted from Google Map, 11 September 2019.

Those important routes are Port road, Flyover/CBD Toll Road of Polonia-Belmera Toll Road, and Medan-Belawan Toll Road. The Balawan Port Action Plan projects that the average daily traffic will reach 2,340, 2,860 and 3,370 trucks in 2020, 2025 and 2030, respectively. The negative impact caused by this traffic is the congestion of 2 km of road at the main entrance gate to the port.

11.2.2.1 Sei Mangkei Special Economic Zone (SEZ) and Connectivity to Belawan Port: Railway Experience

The slow progress of toll road development is responded to by a proposal for a railway service to carry containers from Sei Mangkei Special Economic Zone (SEZ) to Belawan Port. The expectation is that, with a dedicated line, freight trains are more competitive than trucks in terms of travel time. The Industrial Area of Sei Mangkei is located at Simalungun Regency with crude palm oil (CPO) as the main source of raw material for further processing. This industrial area occupies an area of around 2,000 hectare pioneered by a state-owned company (PTPN III). The industrial area of Sei Mangkei is supported by the development of a railways system and a dry port.

Data obtained from the national railway company PT KAI Regional I of North Sumatera, for the period of January to June 2017, showed daily trips between Sei Mangkei and Belawan Port were 36 TEU (1,080 TEU on a monthly basis). Figure 11.15 contains photographs of container loading at the Sei Mangkei container yard at their inaugural railway trip to Belawan Port.

Fig. 11.15 Loading and Unloading Activities at the Industrial Area of Sei Mangkei. Photo courtesy: Danang Parikesit, 2017.

Through the development of Kuala Tanjung Port,[11] the Industrial Area of Sei Mangkei has become part of the Kuala Tanjung Port hinterland. This development will accelerate the connectivity from the hinterland through to the port. Rail will be the preferred option for the transport of goods from the Industrial Area of Sei Mangke through to Kuala Tanjung Port as it has the capacity of delivery in a single trip and it will not be affected by congestion.

Existing Railway Lines. Development of the rail mode, primarily the freight trains to support Belawan Port, would benefit the freight requirements of the wide hinterland, which needs a more efficient transport mode. The railway line connecting Medan-Binjai-Besitang in North Sumatera Province is now operational. To extend the rail-based transport service, a railway connecting Aceh and North Sumatera is currently planned through the railways of Sigli-Bireun and Lhokseumawe-Langsa-Besitang servicing 417,541 km. These railways

---

11   The Ministry of Transportation and the state-owned company PT Pelindo I are currently constructing a multi purpose port in Kuala Tanjung, a new port adjacent to the SEZ Sei Mangkei. The container port terminal is planned to be financed using PPP scheme.

will later pass through eight regencies/cities in Aceh and one city in North Sumatra (see Fig. 11.16).

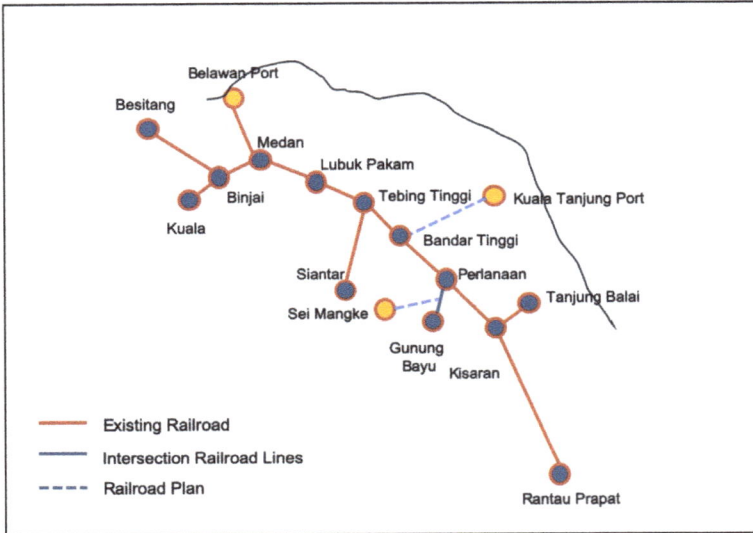

Fig. 11.16 Existing and planned railway lines in North Sumatra. Source: adapted from Masterplan of Kuala Tanjung Port, 11 September 2019.

11.2.2.2 *Belawan-Kuala Tanjung Port System and the Design of Access Traffic*

Pelindo I developed Kuala Tanjung Port as part of the development plan of a port system. The plan is to comprehensively develop Kuala Tanjung Port in four stages.

1. Stage I: Development of Multipurpose Terminal of Kuala Tanjung (2015–2017)

2. Stage II: Development of Industrial Area of 3,000 hectares (2016–2018)

3. Stage III: Development of Dedicated/Hub Port (2017–2019)

4. Stage IV: Development of Integrated Industrial Area

Belawan-Kuala Tanjung Proposed Toll Road. Congestion is an important consideration in an urban area and its surrounds. The development of

Belawan-Kuala Tanjung Toll Road, as well as the access road from and to production centres, is important to support the connectivity and effective movements of goods. The road connection between Belawan and Kuala Tanjung Ports, as stated in the draft document of the Revised Masterplan of Belawan Port, is around 140 km in length. Considering the two existing transport modes, which are road and railway, and by combining the advantages of these concepts, the government considers a scenario of intermodal system implementation (Fig. 11.17), which can facilitate the delivery of goods through greater capacity without causing congestion.

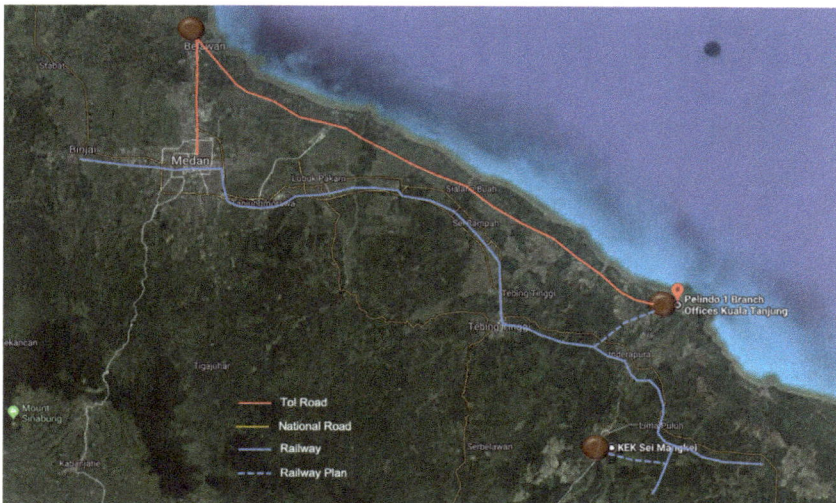

Fig. 11.17 The transportation networks of roads and railways, as well as the corridors of Belawan and Kuala Ports. Source: adapted from Google Maps, 11 September 2019.

11.2.3 Case III: Pelindo III Green Port Terminal of Teluk Lamong, Surabaya

Teluk Lamong Port Terminal, located in the Tanjung Perak Port area of Surabaya, is the first semi-automatic terminal in Indonesia using environmental-friendly technology with the green port concept. The goal in the establishment of Teluk Lamong Port Terminal is to develop Tanjung Perak Port with the aim of reducing the waiting time of ships at

Tanjung Perak Port, which is the economic gate of East Java and Eastern Indonesia. The Teluk Lamong Port Terminal facilities built in Stage 1 include: a container dock (500 m x 80 m); a dry bulk dock (250 m x 30 m); a dry bulk field (7.6 ha); and a container field (24.2 ha). This terminal was built via a reclamation method with an entirely new terminal on reclaimed land. It lies around 3.5 km from the shoreline and is connected by a 2 km bridge from Tambak Osowilangun beach. The Teluk Lamong Port Terminal is part of the Port Action Plan, and integrated into Tanjung Perak Port as well as Gresik Port and Magyar Terminal in the Gresik Regency, and Socah Terminal and Tanjung Bulupandan Terminal at the Bangkalan Regency (Fig. 11.18).

Fig. 11.18 Teluk Lamong Port Terminal (no. 2) as one of the terminals in the Operational Area of Tanjung Perak Port. Source: adapted from Pelindo III, 11 September 2019.

The increasing productivity of Teluk Lamong Port Terminal can be seen in Figure 11.19 where the recorded container flows were 1,442 and 120,688 TEU in 2014 and 2015 respectively (Pelindo III, 2016). This showed an eight-fold increase even though container flows were lower compared to those from the other ports or terminals presented in Figure 11.19.

This increase of productivity will affect the high volume of vehicles carrying goods entering and leaving the terminal area that need traffic management and good infrastructure. The projections of ship visits to

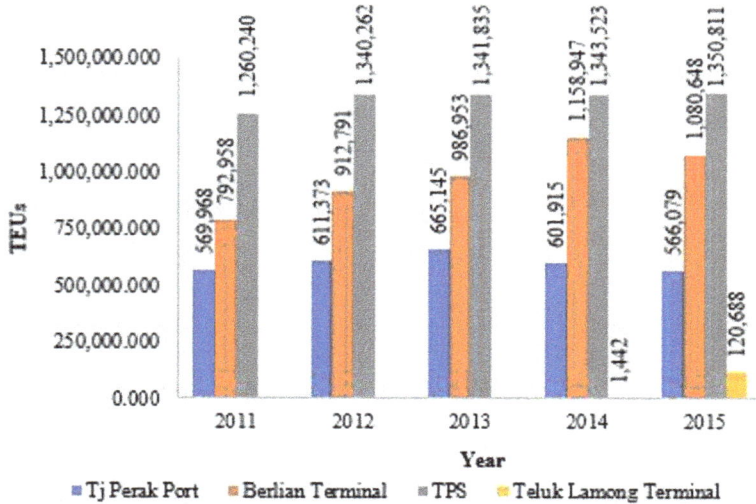

Fig. 11.19 Container Flows at Tanjung Perak Port and Teluk Lamong Port Terminal, in TEU (2011–2015). Source: adapted from Pelindo III, 29 March 2018.

Teluk Lamong Port Terminal in the Master Plan of Tanjung Perak Port and terminals surrounding it can be seen in Table 11.4.

Table 11.4 Projection of Ship Visit Flows to Teluk Lamong Port Terminal

Type of Ship	Data Projection Output		
	2020	2025	2035
International Containers	365	775	1,072
Domestic Containers	1,395	2,618	7,828
Dry Bulk	101	106	166
Liquid Bulk of LPG	33	39	46
Liquid Bulk of LNG	33	39	51
Total	1927	3577	9163

Source: Masterplan of Tanjung Perak Port and its surrounds, 2017.

With the projected increase in ship visits, Teluk Lamong Port Terminal will need to have a good strategy to provide optimum services to all parties utilising the port services, not only going in and out of the port area but also container movements inside the port area. The existing port has limited area for container yards: as a consequence, the port operators have several areas dedicated for container yards (empty and loaded), for the collective use by various terminals in Tanjung Perak Port. Figure 11.20 below shows the existing container movement in the port area.

Fig. 11.20 Current Movement of Container System in Tanjung Perak Port. Source: PT Pelindo III, 11 September 2019.

11.2.3.1 *The Design and Private Sector Initiative for Inter Terminal Freight Transport within Tanjung Perak Port*

The high demand on freight movements, namely containers, needs infrastructure that can guarantee efficient freight movement. Congestion occurring at some points in Surabaya is caused by high flow volume of transport of goods, mainly containers, occupying some roads which have low capacities. The utilisation of the container train for efficient transportation of goods, can be a solution to overcome the movement of container boxes to Teluk Lamong.

As seen in Figure 11.21, it is recognised that connecting depots, which are the supporting facilities for the movement of goods by freight trains, will reduce the level of congestion on the roads. The development and operation of depots around Teluk Lamong, managed by private parties, are essential leading to the smooth relocation of activities from

Fig. 11.21 The Application of Rail-based Container Trains as a form of transportation of goods at Teluk Lamong Port Terminal. Source: adapted from PT Terminal Teluk Lamong, 11 September 2019.

Tanjung Perak Port to Teluk Lamong Port Terminal. This is necessary if a good solution to the container movements is not available. The private sectors have relocated their activities to Teluk Lamong Port Terminal by building some depots around that terminal so that congestion occurring around Tanjung Perak Port will move to Teluk Lamong Port Terminal.

To accommodate the movements of these containers, besides utilising the elevated toll roads, Pelindo III plans to provide an Automatic Container Transporter (ACT). This plan will be developed as a monorail project for container movements from Tanjung Perak Port in Surabaya to Terminal Multipurpose Teluk Lamong (TMTL). This monorail will have a route length of 5.6 km and use the ACT system.

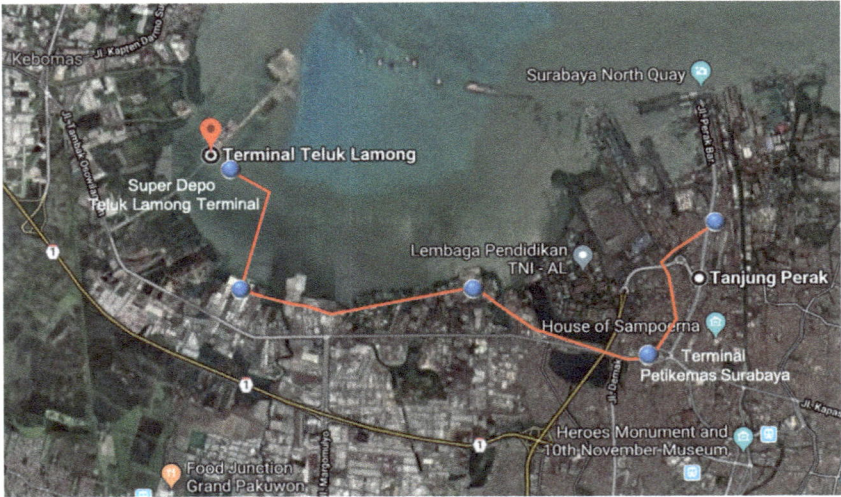

Fig. 11.22 Automatic Container Transporter Development Plan. Source: adapted from PT Teluk Lamong, 11 September 2019.

From the design shown on Figure 11.22, the container movement method between terminals will minimise the use of the road transport, by constructing most of the monorail over the bay.

Traffic Movements in and out of Tanjung Perak Port. As part of the development of Tanjung Perak Port, the Teluk Lamong Port Terminal shares the same hinterland areas, mainly all areas in East Java Province and some parts of Central Java and the Special Region of Yogyakarta Province.[12] The road network around the terminal area consists of an arterial road and a toll road with a physical separator. The existing road to Teluk Lamong Port Terminal is an arterial road (Tambak Osowilangun) that connects Surabaya City and Gresik City. This is a four-lane road with two lanes in each direction. The problems related to road capacity are caused by the constriction at two points — the Osowilangun and Branjangan bridges — with their narrow width of only 8.2 m. These points restrict traffic movement around the terminal.

---

12   Executive Summary Review of Tanjung Perak Master Plan, July 2017.

Improved access to the port can also be created by the construction of new road segments. The new access development is a step towards separating the heavy vehicle flows leading to the terminal from the local traffic. Considering the problem of providing enough space for roads (where there is constriction at some points along the existing road), it is difficult to create a separation by building new lanes. In the case of Teluk Lamong Port Terminal, where the toll roads exist near the terminal access, a solution is to develop a flyover and tapper[13] leading to Teluk Lamong Port Terminal by integrating the existing toll roads (Fig. 11.23).

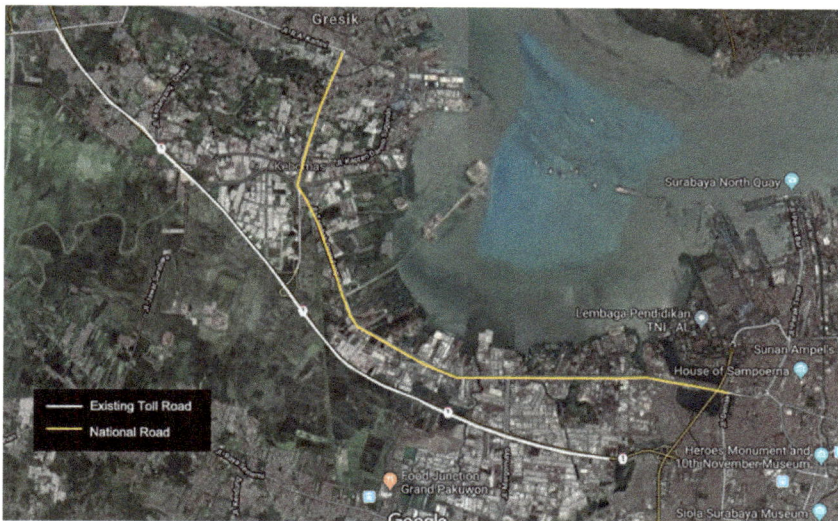

Fig. 11.23 The proposed Integrated Toll Roads to Teluk Lamong Port Terminal. Source: adapted from PT. Teluk Lamong, 11 September 2019.

This infrastructure consists of a flyover 2.4 km in length with the flyover contour of 1.8 km length, the land road at the Benowo side 363 m in length, and on the Lamong Bay side at 350 m length. The flyover width is 40 m. By building this flyover, the management of traffic movement entering and leaving Teluk Lamong Port Terminal can be improved. The current mixed traffic from and to Teluk Lamong Port Terminal with local access that is still using Artery Osowinangun Street can be avoided making the vehicle movements more efficient.

---

13 https://kppip.go.id/proyek-strategis-nasional/a-sektor-jalan/pembangunan-fly-over-dan-menuju-terminal-teluk-lamong/

*11.2.3.2 Competing Port Terminals and the Opportunity to Manage
Container Traffic among Terminals*

The high and stable growth of East Java Province has led to the increasing demand for port services. Many industrial areas in the region have invested heavily in constructing ports for their own use, mostly managed by Pelindo III. The expansion of ports managed by Pelindo III stretches from Gresik, Socah to Bulupandan Port Terminal. As a result, the flows of goods at Teluk Lamong Port Terminal are currently relatively low. The low operational performance of Teluk Lamong Port Terminal, as reported by the Tanjung Perak Port Authority (2016), can be shown by its Berth Occupancy Ratio (BOR) and Yard Occupancy Ratio (YOR) at 18.28% and 13.40% respectively. This is an opportunity for the Port operators and terminal operators to work collaboratively in dealing with future demand, using a combination of infrastructure and IT solutions.

11.3 Lessons Learned from the Literature and Case Studies

11.3.1 Importance of Land Connectivity in Ensuring Lower Logistics' Costs

The international literature reviewed in this chapter has identified that, although land connectivity is considered as the most important issue in port productivity, policy intervention is often neglected, or is not the focus of the authority. In the case of Tanjung Priok Port, the government realised that land connectivity is an important element of logistics costs because 70% of the container movements, mostly for export purpose, are transported from Cikarang Industrial area to the port. Traffic performance on the existing toll road has been unsatisfactory in terms of punctuality and cost of travel. The existing dry port, which is running below its capacity, has not been successful in attracting cargo owners to use their rail facility. Another on-going initiative is using river/drainage channel transport from the industrial zones directly to the port terminal. The latter scheme is designed as a PPP to attract private investors for the project. Some of the project risk, especially demand risk, will be absorbed by the government.

Land connectivity is also important, not only because it determines the biggest cost of commodities, but also because it is a factor expressing the competitiveness of a commodity in the global market. For an island country, Indonesia will largely depend on the combination of sea and land transport in moving goods for both domestic and international market. The number of mode changes, cost of travel, time required to reach port gate, number of companies involved in moving containers or bulk products, are all factors important to consider in creating a competitive pricing. In the case of Tanjung Perak Surabaya, because of the geographical separations of different port terminals, the operator (i.e. Pelindo III and its subsidiaries) needs to find an innovative solution to deal with inter-terminal movements.

In all ports researched in these case studies, the transport authorities focused on the infrastructure solutions, ranging from rail access and elevated toll access for Tanjung Priok Jakarta port, and rail access from the special economic zone for Belawan Medan port. For Tanjung Priok port the Indonesian government has an ongoing PPP project in preparation to implement inland water transport connecting the Cikarang Industrial area directly to the port terminals. An inter-terminal container rail connection system for Tanjung Perak Surabaya has been studied for implementation.

To fulfil the needs of information technology-based transactions, Tanjung Priok Port has collaborated with PT Telkom, a state-owned telecommunication company. This partnership is manifested in a project with the Indonesia Logistic Community Service (ILCS), based on information and communication technology to create an integrated online platform. This platform covers operational, financial, technological, and human resource aspects. In addition, this helps the strategic partnership develop the National e-Trade Logistic that mainly supports the implementation of the Indonesian National Single Window.

There has not been a comprehensive study/*ex-post* analysis of the commercial and economic viability of the abovementioned infrastructure projects. The rail operation from the special economic zone to Belawan Medan was discontinued after several trials. The traffic volumes for the elevated toll road access are less than predicted, resulting in lower revenue to the government.

Local authorities and port operators in the three case studies presented in this chapter have not worked together on traffic management solutions despite various experiences documented in international studies.

11.3.2 Road versus Rail Connectivity to Ports, and the Role of Government Support for Commercial Rail Operations

Rail service provides technical advantages compared with road transport in delivering both bulk commodities and containers. It can provide an uninterrupted service, without exposing its services to traffic congestion, even when a grade separation is not provided. The Indonesian Railway Act has mandated authority to give top priority to rail service in land transport operations. Using the existing configuration of 12–30 carriageways of 40 TEU, the use of rail will obviously relieve the pressure of traffic congestion, reduce traffic congestion, and improve the air quality along the corridor and in the port area. However, in the two ports where rail services were introduced, both have shown unsatisfactory results. For Belawan port, the service from the special economic zone stopped after several service trials; for Tanjung Priok port, the rail service from Bandung Gedebage dry port was unsuccessful and currently services have been reduced to one train operation per day.

There are several reasons for this situation. The first reason is the imbalance of traffic from both the special economic zone and Bandung Gedebage dry port. The container traffic is dominated by one-way service from the production centres carrying outbound export products, with almost no return traffic. As a result, the cost of freight charged by the rail operator to the cargo owners is extremely high compared with the trucking service. The second reason is rail requires LO-LO (Lift On — Lift Off) service at both ends, and therefore requires a higher cost of transport imposed on cargo owners. For example, from Bandung to Jakarta using rail it takes two hours and costs USD 250 per container, whereas LO–LO service at both ends requires USD 50 per container. This means that the rail service is uncompetitive compared with direct tracking services. Thirdly, the rail infrastructure at the port area is financed by either rail operators or port operators, resulting in the need for investment recovery cost charged to the cargo owners. In various international cases, the cost of infrastructure is born by the government in order to keep rail services competitive with road transport services.

If the Indonesian government wants to keep the balance of traffic between road and rail, there are several policies that should be considered. Infrastructure investment for rail services should be separated from rail operation using a vertical separation/unbundling framework. Therefore, investment projects should be procured by government either using the government/national budget or by attracting private sector investment using PPP schemes. The second policy that should be undertaken, in cooperation with the Ministry of Industry and the Ministry of Trade, is to have a regulation on the mandatory use of rail transport for raw materials to industrial areas, especially for the import of raw materials used in export-oriented products. This regulation allows for the higher return of cargo from ports to the special economic zones, industrial areas and dry ports. This regulation will dramatically reduce the freight cost using rail to and from the ports.

There are several other policies that can be introduced. The first policy is to reduce the fuel tax for diesel use in rail operations. At the moment, the Indonesian government is applying zero fuel tax for the trucking industry and imposing industry fuel tax for rail operations. Although in recent years the government has eased the fuel tax by introducing a quota system for fuel consumed in rail operations, an excess of fuel above the quota is still charged with a fuel tax. Encouraging the transport industry to consolidate road and rail operations would create the most effective solution for cargo owners. This latter solution has already been tested by dry port operators in Cikarang. In recent years it has resulted in an increasing demand for rail services. If the government can promote the above solution across the industry, dry port with rail operations will have an opportunity to be the breakthrough needed to reduce logistics costs in Indonesia.

11.3.3 Managing Land Uses around Ports

Many ports in Indonesia were built during the Dutch colonial period and at that time, ports were situated at a distance from the city centre. The rapid growth of cities and port areas after Independence in 1945, was due to job creation in large metropolitan areas. However, the lack of land-use controls by the Indonesian Government has resulted in highly dense urban areas around ports with no separation between local and through traffic. The Spatial Plan Act was introduced in 2007 and imposed stringent controls over land use in urban areas. All local governments have to submit a spatial plan for approval by local parliaments, which comply with the National Spatial Plan of the Indonesian Government. This is an ongoing process and until today not all local governments have submitted nor received approvals from local parliament/national governments for their local spatial plans. In the case of the three ports reviewed in this study, they all suffered from this particular issue.

The recommendation to the Indonesian Government is to separate local and regional traffic as well as access traffic to the port areas. Whilst the current traffic management scheme introduced by the government of Jakarta is the "odd-and-even" number scheme for different days in a working day, the use of traffic management measures, such as lane separation, rerouting of through traffic; introducing a time windows scheme and truck appointment schemes for entering the port, can be introduced to alleviate traffic congestion around the port area. A specific traffic problem in Tanjung Priok Port in Jakarta is the fact that export activities are concentrated during the Friday-Sunday period, which is affected by international mother vessel schedules in Singapore port.

Local governments can start improving land use by relocating freight forwarding company offices to dedicated inland container depots to allow stuffing and un-stuffing activities around ports. Inland Container Depot (ICD) Lat Krabang in Thailand has provided international evidence on how relocation of container stuffing and un-stuffing activities can make transport moving to and from ports more effective. Indonesian ports could test such a solution to immediately release the pressure of congestion around ports caused by inefficient land-use configurations.

References

Acciaro, M, and McKinnon, A 2013. *Efficient hinterland transport infrastructure and services for large container ports*, paper presented at The International Transport Forum OECD, Paris, France.

Álvarez-SanJaime, Ó, Cantos-Sánchez, P, Moner-Colonques, R, and José J. Sempere-Monerris, JJ 2015. 'The impact on port competition of the integration of port and inland transport services', *Transportation Research Part B: Methodological*, 80, pp. 291–302, https://doi.org/10.1016/j.trb.2015.07.011

Bomba, M, Mazumder D, Hutson, N and Harrison, R 2006. *Landside access needs for deepwater ports*, technical report for The Center for Transportation Research, Texas, United States:The University of Texas at Austin.

de Borger, B, Proost, S and Van Dender, K 2008. 'Private port pricing and public investment in port and hinterland capacity', *Journal of Transport Economics and Policy*, 42:3, pp. 527–61, core.ac.uk/download/pdf/6978989.pdf

de Borger, B and De Bruyne, D 2011. 'Port activities, hinterland congestion, and optimal government policies: The role of vertical integration in logistic operations', *Journal of Transport Economics and Policy*, 45:2, pp. 247–75, www.jstor.org/stable/23072177

Chen, G, Govindan, K and Yang, Z 2013. 'Managing truck arrivals with time windows to alleviate gate congestion at container terminals', *International Journal of Production Economics*, 141:1 pp 179–88.

Cullinane, K and Khanna, M 2000. 'Economies of scale in large containerships: optimal size and geographical implications', *Journal of Transport Geography*, 8, pp. 181–95.

Fan, L, Wilson, WW and Dahl, B 2012. 'Congestion, Port Expansion and Spatial Competition for US Container Imports', *Transportation Research Part E: Logistics and Transportation Review*, 48, pp. 1121–36, https://doi.org/10.1016/j.tre.2012.04.006

Freightera, 2017. Shipping by road or rail: pros and cons', www.freightera.com/blog/shipping-road-vs-rail/

Herdian, T, Kusumastanto, T, Sartono, B, Fahmiasari, H 2017. 'Operational analysis of container truck on congestion at Tanjung Priok port', *Advances in Engineering Research (AER)*, 147, pp. 70–85.

de Langen, PW and Sharypova, K 2013. 'Intermodal connectivity as a port performance indicator', *Journal of Research in Transportation Business and Management*, 8, pp. 97–102, https://doi.org/10.1016/j.rtbm.2013.06.003

Li, B, Tan, KW, Tran, TK 2016. 'Traffic simulation model for port planning and congestion prevention', in *Proceedings of the 2016 Winter Simulation Conference* (T M K Roeder, P I Frazier, R Szechtman, E Zhou, T Huschka, and S E Chick, eds.), New York, USA: IEEE, pp. 2382–93.

Lima, ADP, de Mascarenhas, FW and Frazzon, EM 2015. 'Simulation-based planning and control of transport flows in port logistic systems', *Mathematical Problems in Engineering Journal*, 2015, https://doi.org/10.1155/2015/862635

Maguire, A, Ivey, S, Golias, MM, Lipinski, ME 2009. *Relieving congestion at intermodal marine container terminals: Review of tactical/operational strategies',* report for the Center for Intermodal Freight Transportation Studies, Tennessee, USA: University of Memphis, pdfs.semanticscholar.org/b38f/1c df94f612b8d1410bb7d09ce940e7bb29ee.pdf

Merk, O andNotteboom, T 2015. *Port hinterland connectivity*, discussion paper no. 2015–2013 presented at The International Transport Forum OECD, Paris, France.

Monios, Jand Wilmsmeier, G 2012. 'Giving a direction to port regionalisation', *Transportation Research Part A Policy and Practice*, 46, pp. 1551–561.

Monios, J and Wilmsmeier, G 2013. 'The Role of intermodal transport in port regionalisation', *Transport Policy*, 30, pp. 161–72, https://doi.org/10.1016/j.tranpol.2013.09.010

Ng, AKY, Ducruet, C, Jacobs, W, Monios, J, Notteboom, T, Rodrigue, J-P, Slack, B, Tam, K, Wilmsmeier, G 2014. 'Port geography at the crossroads with human geography: Between flows and spaces', *Journal of Transport Geography*, 41, pp. 84–96, https://doi.org/10.1016/j.jtrangeo.2014.08.012

Notteboom, TE, and Rodrigue, J-P 2005. 'Port Regionalization: towards a new phase in port development', *Journal of Maritime Policy and Management*, July–September, 32:3, pp. 297–313, https://doi.org/10.1080/03088830500139885

Notteboom, T 2008. *The relationship between Seaports and the intermodal hinterland in light of global supply chains: European challenges*, presented at the Research Round Table, 'Seaport Competition and Hinterland Connections', April 10–11, Paris, France.

O'Rourke, P 2016. 'Examining the Impacts of the Port Miami Tunnel: A before and after study of truck counts and travel speed in the vicinity of PortMiami', *ITE Journal*, 86:11, pp. 28–33.

Pelindo III, 2016. Company website of Pelindo III, www.pelindo.co.id

PT Jasa Marga/Indonesian Highway Corporation, 2018. Company website of PT Jasa Marga, www.jasamarga.com/public/id/home.aspx

PT Pelabuhan Tanjung Priok, 2017. Company website of IPC, priokport.co.id/

Rajamanickam, GD and Gitakrishnan, R 2015. 'Simulation of truck congestion in Chennai port', in *Proceedings of the 2016 Winter Simulation Conference* (TMK Roeder, PI Frazier, R Szechtman, E Zhou, T Huschka, and SE Chick, eds.), IEEE, pp. 1904–15.

Robinson R, 2002. Integrated and intermodal Freight Systems: A conceptual Framework, *Proceedings of the IAME Conference*, Panama.

Roso, V 2007. 'Evaluation of the dry port concept from an environmental perspective: A note', *Transportation Research Part D Transport and Environment*, 12:7, pp. 523–27, https://doi.org/10.1016/j.trd.2007.07.001

Wilmsmeier, G, Monios, J and Lambert, B 2011. 'The directional development of intermodal freight corridors in relation to inland terminals', *Journal of Transport Geography*, 19:6, pp. 1379–86, https://doi.org/10.1016/j.jtrangeo.2011.07.010

Wilmsmeier, G, Monios, J and Pérez-Salas, G 2014. 'Port system evolution — the case of Latin America and the Caribbean', *Journal of Transport Geography*, 39, pp. 208–21, https://doi.org/10.1016/j.jtrangeo.2014.07.007

Zhang, X Zeng, Q and Chen, W 2013. 'Optimization model for truck appointment in container terminal', *Procedia — Social and Behavioral Sciences*, 96, pp. 1938–47, https://doi.org/10.1155/2018/5165124

12. Potential Infrastructure Enhancements for Ports and Cities
Conclusions, Future Research and Policy Concepts

C. F. Duffield,[1] S. Wahyuni,[2] D. Parikesit,[3]
F. K. P. Hui,[4] and S. Wilson[5]

12.0 Overview and Conclusions

This monograph maps the research journey undertaken by the policy and finance team within the infrastructure cluster of the Australia-Indonesia Research Centre. An outline of the research approach and collaboration is provided in the paper titled 'Collaborative international industry-university research training in infrastructure projects: an Australian-Indonesian case study' by Hui et al. 2018.[6]

---

1   Professor of Engineering Project Management, Deputy Head of Department (Academic), Dept of Infrastructure Engineering, The University of Melbourne.
2   Associate Professor, Dept. of Management, Faculty of Economics and Business, Universitas Indonesia.
3   Professor of Transporation Engineering, Dept. of Civil and Environmental Engineering, Universitas Gadjah Mada.
4   Senior Lecturer and Academic Specialist, Dept. of Infrastructure Engineering, The University of Melbourne.
5   Research Fellow, Dept. of Infrastructure Engineering, The University of Melbourne.
6   Hui, F, Duffield, C, Wahyuni, S, Parikesit, D, and Wilson, S 2018, 'Collaborative international industry-university research training in infrastructure projects: an Australian-Indonesian case study', 42nd *Australasian Universities Building Education Association (AUBEA) Conference 2018: Educating Building Professionals for the Future in the Globalised World*, September 26 – 28, pp. 48 –57.

                    https://doi.org/10.11647/OBP.0189.12

The chapters presented have captured the essence of this research project and outline a scope that started with the contextualisation of the economic situations that confront both Australia and Indonesia and then investigated the issues surrounding major investment in infrastructure, focusing attention on the ways by which both countries seek to enhance the services offered in and around their sea ports. Having explored many of the constraints to port investment (like availability of land, planning integration, finance, project implementation approaches) the research progressed to clarifying areas where improvements can best be made, including financing initiatives, improved focus on the integration of hinterland logistics with port operations, areas where efficiency gains may be possible and benchmarking with international best practice. In each of these areas some key findings were:

Synergies between Australia and Indonesia (Chapter 1): Both countries face the need for urgent infrastructure investments to assist in improving their productivity. Australia and Indonesia are rich in natural resources including coal, minerals, gold, copper, nickel, oil, gas and fertile land (giving rise to agricultural products). Unfortunately, however, both countries face more than their share of natural disasters. For Indonesia the impact of being in the ring of fire brings frequent volcanic eruptions, tsunamis and earthquakes as well as frequent floods. Flooding in Australia is also an ongoing concern along with cyclones, bushfires and extreme heat. The vast expanse of both countries places ongoing pressure on fiscal budgets and results in competing demands for investment on worthwhile infrastructure projects.

The positioning of both countries in the Southern hemisphere results in the countries being adjuncts to major trade routes between Europe, the Americas and the emerging powerhouse economies of China and India. The location of major trading partners has both countries looking north for opportunities. The economies of both countries are robust and growing consistently and this growth places further urgency on the need for infrastructure development if their global competitiveness is to be maintained and enhanced.

Infrastructure planning (Chapter 2): It is evident that many worthwhile infrastructure projects have been identified. The Government of Indonesia has recognised this, incorporating targets and strategies into a number of national plans which aim to address the issues. In Australia, the establishment of Infrastructure Australia in 2008 acknowledged that independent advice would assist to prioritise and progress nationally significant infrastructure. This approach has resulted in a detailed audit of Australian infrastructure needs followed by a plan and ratification of priority projects based on their merit. There remain significant challenges, risks and issues associated with delivering the required infrastructure. Priority areas identified for Indonesia include better integration of transport into and out of the country and the linking of a nation of islands. For Australia, infrastructure is lagging the population growth being experienced in the major centres of Sydney, Melbourne, Perth and Brisbane along with the tyranny of distance and the need for equitable access to services by the population. These priority areas of infrastructure investment led to the focus of the research aligning to major ports and their interface to cities.

To understand the priority barriers to achieving the necessary development in ports a survey of port executives, government officials, financiers and consultants supporting this sector was undertaken in both Indonesia and Australia. The survey considered twenty-nine variables, including the World Bank's ten topics used to measure the ease of doing business and the World Economic Forum's Executive Opinion Survey's most problematic factors for doing business enhanced with the specific infrastructure related topics of affordable energy availability, land acquisition and regulatory uncertainty. Major issues identified in this survey for Indonesia were corruption, inefficient government bureaucracy, policy instability, inadequate supply of infrastructure, regulatory uncertainty and land acquisition. In Australia, inadequate supply of infrastructure, policy instability, affordable energy availability, restrictive labour regulations, and land acquisition were identified as key barriers.

Funding and financing infrastructure (Chapter 3): The ability to afford the extent of required infrastructure investment identified emerged as a major hurdle for delivering the assets in the expected timeframe for both countries. Australia's banking system, and the underpinning financial strength of the country, make Australia attractive as an investment location. This, along with AAA credit ratings for most Australian states and the federal government, has assisted in the development of active international investing in Australian infrastructure assets. At the same time Australian governments are very sensitive to borrowing limits and maintenance of their good credit rating.

A range of alternate investment approaches were explored that included direct funding and or borrowing by government, private corporations, or international sponsors, the use of Public Private Partnerships, the development of special economic zones to asset recycling and even privatization. Whist there are examples where each of these financing alternatives have been successfully used there were also numerous examples where the approaches either did not work well or were simply not acceptable to the government of the day. Privatisation was clearly considered unacceptable politically in both Australia and Indonesia.

To further understand what financing approach is preferable for port development, the aforementioned survey included questions regarding financing preferences. Conclusions drawn from the survey findings were:

- Current government policies are perceived to be supporting and facilitating direct government investment in Indonesia, more so than in Australia, where investment is dominated by the private sector.

- Australia seems to have access to finance whereas Indonesia would like more.

- Ports appear to get more attention in Indonesia than in Australia. This is not surprising as the Indonesian President has made port enhancements a priority for the country.

- Some think Australia has excessive administration/control mechanisms.

The focus for future attention was to understand how to generalise the good outcomes Australia has achieved from asset recycling strategies, to direct investment towards improving hinterland transport assets surrounding ports, to continue the refinement of Public Private Partnerships such that they deliver value in Australia and that improved mechanisms to facilitate such projects in Indonesia are developed. There was also the need to continue strengthening the banking sector in Indonesia to increase their capacity for involvement in infrastructure investment.

Efficient facilitation of infrastructure assets (Chapter 4): Appropriate structuring and planning for major infrastructure is essential if the investment in correct assets are to be made for an affordable cost and appropriate management of risk. Poor project initiation frequently leads to expensive rework, truncated projects, poor quality or even the building of assets well in advance of the need for the facility. The Indonesian Government have been working to improve project initiation through more attention to the development of business cases, through the undertaking of institutional reform, the identification of funding arrangements, land management and general upskilling of project resources. In Australia, the emphasis for improvement comes by way of independent analysis and recommendation of projects via the conduct of independent project reviews (Gateway Reviews or project assurance mechanisms) in advance of major decisions and an ongoing discipline to undertake business cases that rigorously investigate the need for a project and its alignment with policy, economic benefits, clear investigation of viable options and consideration of how value with be achieved by the recommended procurement approach. In short, for increased project surety focus is required on early risk identification, improved planning and robust decision-making processes.

In addition to the above best practice concepts, the Jokowi government is actively encouraging foreign investment by improving its attractiveness, stability and functionality for other trades, making Public Private Partnerships (PPP) a viable option for procurement of infrastructure projects. It has established a web of supporting government organisations to support the various stages of procurement.

A number of detailed case study projects have been considered in this chapter, these present sobering examples of why further improvements are required.

Integration of port and hinterland facilities (Chapter 5): As domestic and international trade increased in volume and ship technology improved, so did the need for more efficient intermodal transfers and space landside for port functions. Unfortunately, there are few international examples where the landside of seaports function effectively, particularly where city expansion and congestion impact on port operations. Pressures of globalisation, the widespread use of container ships and the need for associated storage, stuffing and un-stuffing of containers, and port access by road and rail have governments and port operators seeking alternative solutions like dry ports, or intermodal logistics terminals. International ports like the reclaimed land options at Hanshin and Tokyo Bay in Japan along with intermodal concepts such as at Botany Bay in Sydney have been explored.

Port expansion *in situ* can only occur if port activities encroach upon surrounding residential, commercial and industrial areas, or if land is reclaimed from the sea. Both options bring into play the regulatory powers of national, state and local governments. In the case of Port Botany, it has been shown how local government has imposed land-use zoning policies to facilitate port (and airport) related activities. Solutions to the general logistics or supply-chain management problem invariably involve political decisions of government and other stakeholders in the planning of seaports and dry ports in any urban system. The means of regulating urban system growth, mechanisms of resolving environmental conflicts and the relative power of political parties and different stakeholders and the community requires further investigation, but such a solution needs to be found if efficiencies between ports and hinterland areas is to be found.

Queueing of trucks on streets surrounding ports remains an issue in Indonesia. Stevedore vehicle booking systems (VBS) provide potential for a solution involving the use of information technology to reduce congestion around ports. Integration of sea, road and rail systems also appear to offer scope for improvement.

International efficiency of Australian and Indonesian ports (Chapter 6): Benchmarking port facilities internationally provides guidance on areas for improvement. A comparative analysis of efficiency between international ports and port terminals in Indonesia and Australia was undertaken for these close neighbours and major trading partners. The efficiency was examined using Data Envelopment Analysis (DEA) where various logistical inputs that affect overall port performance are determined, and corresponding outputs compared. Ports included in the benchmarking included major Australian, Indonesian and Chinese international ports. It was found that Australian ports are slightly more efficient than Indonesian ports and terminals, with China as a leader in the overall efficiency ranking in the analysis. Constant and variable returns to scale models were both considered. Comparisons with Singapore or Hamburg (the most efficient international ports) can be misleading due to the high volume of inter-vessel cargo handled in these ports, whereas Indonesia and Australia tend to be destination locations.

It was found that Indonesian ports can improve turn-around times in sea-side operations, while Melbourne was found to have a relatively lower efficiency in crane operations in the sea-side operations. Both areas require transport and logistic improvements along with institutional reform that includes the customs interface with ports and terminals.

Innovation in port development — a quad helix model (Chapter 7): Improving productivity requires ongoing management and detailed planning which is frequently top-down driven by government. Early engagement with wider stakeholders in the port-city interface provides an innovative concept for improvement. This chapter reviewed a comprehensive case study on how Academic-Business-Community-Government plus bank partnerships can be nurtured to create innovation. It was observed from Japan, Shenzen, Hong Kong and other ports in China that there is a need for a systematic cluster strategy that includes: the cultivation of key persons for local industrial vitalisation; analysis for new industries; input into planning through industrial vitalisation; integration of other areas (e.g. city development and SMART technology); and overseas marketing.

It was shown that to develop a successful cluster of supporting activities, there is a need for the development of a systematic cluster strategy and that such a strategy is enhanced with assistance from Academics, Business (particularly banks), Community and Government. This strategy should include cultivation of key resources for local industrial vitalisation and the development of new industries.

Specific competitiveness of Indonesian ports (Chapter 8): Specific factors and problems impacting Indonesian port competitiveness and related financing decisions for seaport projects in Indonesia were explored using a series of focus group discussions with key industry leaders. The focus group meetings were complemented by a detailed questionnaire and in-depth interviews with port experts, financial bodies, port corporations, and government officials.

The results indicate that there is still a gap between policy expectation and the realisation of port development facilitation. Causes for this gap include inefficient workings of government's bureaucracy, customs clearance, and strategic decision making.

Specific efficiency of Australian ports (Chapter 9): In recent years, efficiency improvements in Australian ports have been sought using asset recycling. This approach facilitates the furtherance of private sector management and development processes along with the release of financial capital from such long-term held assets. In preparation for this transaction there have been a series of Australian Ports reform strategies, development of private investment markets, and consideration of where the released capital can be best re-invested to improve amenity and overall port productivity.

To encourage state governments to participate in the recycling of assets using long-term leases to the private sector, the Australian government provided a 15% cash bonus of the sale price for infrastructure investment for those jurisdictions who participated. Other strategic changes included freeing up investment decisions with landlord decisions being controlled by the private operators rather than by government. Government retained regulator responsibilities with regulation being most important as ports tend to be monopolistic businesses. The development of the private sector port investment market has seen strong commitment from Australian and international superannuation and investment funds. Issues to be overcome as part of the asset recycling processes include: development of techniques to value the assets, management of diverse political positions, and development of processes for future development.

Outcomes from focus group discussions with port industry stakeholders showed that to improve the governance and policy in ports in Australia the government needs to remain as a key player and provide regulations that coordinate the work of the relevant port stakeholders. Further, port stakeholders need to work together to create a clear vision and plan for the port's future and strategies.

Alternative techniques for financing Indonesian seaports (Chapter 10): Current financing arrangements in Indonesia fall short of requirements for port infrastructure investment. Building on an online survey and focus group discussions, a detailed case study was conducted on the New Priok Container Terminal One (NPCT-1). This port development forms part of the Indonesian Governments National

Development Planning Agenda 2015–2019 for sea transportation infrastructure development. Some twenty-four selected seaports were part of the plan (five main seaports and nineteen feeder seaports). This plan includes major developments of Kalibaru (The New Priok) Port, Cilamaya Port, Makassar New Port, Port of Kuala Tanjung, and Port of Bitung (Bappenas, 2014). Investment in these facilities has a major impact on financing schemes and how project risks are allocated.

It was found that Indonesian domestic bank syndication and Public Private Partnership (PPP) schemes with government fiscal support are the two most awaited financing vehicles. In reality, however, the domestic banks have limited capacity and the PPP schemes remain ineffective. The cash flow simulation showed that, if the decision to distribute project dividends is based on a project's internal rate of return, the project sponsors could benefit from adjusting the project's capital structure. The current market continues to rely on government guarantees.

The critical importance of transport when considering port developments (Chapter 11): The importance of integration of the hinterland with port development has been previously discussed. This chapter expands on this concept and considers so called "self-generating ports", which includes the integration between a port and an industrial area, often developed as a single or joint investment. The idea of the self-generating port emerged because the business risk associated with the traffic coming from and going to its hinterland is too complicated to be mitigated by the port operator. Ports can no longer rely on the traffic generated by their hinterland but need to produce their own traffic by having manufacturing industries inside the port area supplying cargos and bulk commodities, as well as receiving them.

Issues surrounding the use of multimodal ports are explored through a review of the international literature followed by consideration of three ports in Indonesia namely: Belawan Port in Medan, North Sumatera; Tanjung Priok Port in Jakarta; and Tanjung Perak/Teluk Lamong Port Terminal in Surabaya.

It was found that whilst the idea of regional or international hub ports and self-generating ports are appealing for both policy makers and investors, most ports still rely on their hinterland. Not only because these new types of ports are costly, but they require delicate coordination efforts between national and sub-national governments, and between governments and the private sector, especially the main industry players. Small ports in a country like Indonesia are likely to serve as hinterland ports, facilitating economic development of the region, far more than ensuring financial sustainability of those ports. The national and sub-national governments provide large subsidies to fill in the financing gap between the revenue and income from port operations. For instance, many of the ports in Eastern Indonesia are fully financed by the national government and treated as Public Service Agencies.

12.1 Future Research

Each of the chapters articulates how current research has led to an improved understanding of the ways in which Australia and Indonesia can improve infrastructure investment, and, more particularly, investment that enhances port functionality. Ongoing research is considered a vital for continuous improvement in ports. The concept of enhanced outcomes being derived from Academic-Business-Community- Government co-operation was amplified by Sari Wahyuni's study into the Quad Helix model detailed in Chapter 7.

The early chapters elude to the potential for neighbouring countries, having similar commodities, to block trade and thus increase scale and enhance their global returns through enhanced leverage Further research is required as to how to make this ideal a reality. The issue of attracting ongoing international investment and having the strength of economy to repay such debt is also an ongoing problem. Mechanisms to leverage Public Private Partnerships requires development. Improved planning warrants further research, in particular, to overcome the major issues identified: inefficient government bureaucracy; inadequate supply of infrastructure; ongoing issues of corruption; energy affordability; regulatory uncertainty; policy stability; restrictive labour regulations; and poor work ethic in the national labour workforce and tax regulations as they apply to infrastructure finance. It seems that development and refinement of Australia's success with asset recycling is urgently needed so that the positive aspects from this financing mechanism can be applied more effectively for both countries.

Aligned with better infrastructure planning is the need for efficient project management processes to select and procure those projects of highest priority.

For ports a continuing theme was that of hinterland/port integration. It is worth speculating on the value of research into ports and their hinterlands both for Australia and Indonesia. Difficulties in achieving this is the lack of appetite to fund evidence-based policy analysis in the Australian transport sector. As one anonymous, senior government transport bureaucrat put it: "there are no votes in conducting such studies: Ministers love to cut the ribbon on an infrastructure project and not to worry about on-going maintenance nor potential problems." Nevertheless, given the Federal Government's policy of making gateway ports (seaports and airports) the "engines of economic productivity" it seems that port-hinterland research funding is needed to learn from the outcomes of past policies and to determine those transport policy options that will not burden future generations with economic, social and environment costs. Independent analyses are needed in the era of Public Private Partnerships for inter-modal terminals as demonstrated by the controversy surrounding Moorebank Intermodal Terminal.

Throughout the stages of acquiring data and performing DEA analysis, it was recognised that there are limitations in our current research approach and future research into Australian and Indonesian port efficiency can benefit from detailed investigation into global benchmarks. The current DEA approach used in this study did not consider the time temporal scale efficiency. It would be beneficial in future research to include datasets of various time periods to investigate temporal changes which can further strengthen the DEA results. Conceptually, a complete port operational review study, including landside data from ports and terminals could be included in the analysis.

For Indonesian ports there remains the need to identify how to improve the government's consistency and commitment to further encourage investor interest. Furthermore, transportation and energy infrastructure need to be made more accessible. Road connectivity, intermodal transportation, and energy need to be enhanced to increase operational performance.

12.2 Lessons Learnt and Policy Implications

This study has identified the "low hanging fruit" for financing infrastructure. Policy makers would benefit from focusing attention on these achievable mechanisms for financing future infrastructure projects. At a macro scale a trading alliance between Indonesia and Australia may provide break throughs for future trade.

Collaborative international research as kindled by this research creates a model for capacity building and knowledge transfer.

Specific to infrastructure and ports, the importance of land connectivity in ensuring lower logistics' costs cannot be underestimated. To further develop this area, it has been identified that although land connectivity is considered as the most important issue in port productivity, policy intervention is often neglected, or is not the focus of the authority. In the case of Tanjung Priok Port, the government realised that land connectivity is an important element of logistics costs because 70% of the container movements, mostly for export purpose, are transported from Cikarang Industrial area to the port. Traffic performance on the existing toll road has been unsatisfactory in terms of punctuality and cost of travel. The existing dry port, which is running below its capacity, has not been successful in attracting cargo owners to use their rail facility. Another on-going initiative is using river/drainage channel transport from the industrial zones directly to the port terminal. The latter scheme is designed as a PPP to attract private investors for the project. Some of the project risk, especially demand risk, will be absorbed by the government.

Land connectivity is also important not only because it determines the biggest cost of commodities, but because it is a factor expressing the competitiveness of a commodity in the global market. For an island country, Indonesia will largely depend on the combination of sea and land transport in moving goods for both the domestic and international market. The number of mode changes, cost of travel, time required to reach port gate, number of companies involved in moving containers or bulk products, are all factors important to consider in creating competitive pricing. In the case of Tanjung Perak Surabaya, because of the geographical separations of different port terminals, the operator (i.e. Pelindo III and its subsidiaries), needs to find an innovative solution to deal with inter-terminal movements.

In all ports researched in the case studies presented in this research monograph, the transport authorities focused on infrastructure solutions, ranging from rail access and elevated toll access for Tanjung Priok Jakarta port, and rail access from the special economic zone for Belawan Medan port. In the case of Tanjung Priok port the Indonesian government has an ongoing PPP project in preparation to implement inland water transport connecting the Cikarang Industrial area directly to the port terminals. An inter-terminal container rail connection system for Tanjung Perak Surabaya has been studied for implementation.

To fulfil the needs of information technology-based transactions, Tanjung Priok Port has collaborated with PT Telkom, a state-owned telecommunication company. This partnership is manifested in a project with the Indonesia Logistic Community Service (ILCS) based on information and communication technology to create an integrated online platform. This platform covers operational, financial, technological, and human resource aspects. In addition, this helps the strategic partnership develop the National e-Trade Logistic system that mainly supports the implementation of the Indonesian National Single Window.

There has not been a comprehensive study/ex-post analysis of the commercial and economic viability of the abovementioned infrastructure projects. The rail operation from the special economic zone to Belawan Medan was discontinued after several trials. The traffic volumes for the elevated toll road access are less than predicted, resulting in lower revenue to the government.

It appears that there is scope for local authorities and port operators to work more closely on traffic management solutions.

Even within the transport portfolio there is scope for refined use of integrated road/rail connectivity to ports, and the role of government support for commercial rail operations. This could provide an uninterrupted service, without exposing its services to traffic congestion, even when a grade separation is not provided. The Indonesian Railway Act has mandated authority to give a top priority to rail service in land transport operations. Using the existing configuration of 12–30 carriageways of 40 TEU, the use of rail will obviously relieve the pressure of traffic congestion, reduce traffic congestion, and improve the air quality along the corridor and in the port area. However, in the two ports where rail services were introduced both have shown unsatisfactory results. For Belawan port, the service from the special economic zone stopped after several service trials; for Tanjung Priok port, the rail service from Bandung Gedebage dry port was unsuccessful and currently services have been reduced to one train operation per day.

If the Indonesian government wants to keep the balance of traffic between road and rail, there are several policies that should be considered. Infrastructure investment for rail services should be separated from rail operation using a vertical separation/unbundling framework. Therefore, investment projects should be procured by government either using the government/national budget or by attracting private sector investment using PPP schemes. The second policy that should be undertaken, in cooperation with the Ministry of Industry and the Ministry of Trade, is to have a regulation on the mandatory use of rail transport for raw materials to industrial areas, especially for the import of raw materials used in export-oriented products. This regulation allows for the higher return of cargo from ports to the special economic zones, industrial areas and dry ports. This regulation will dramatically reduce the freight cost using rail to and from the ports.

There are several other policies that can be introduced. The first policy is to reduce the fuel tax for diesel use in rail operations. At the moment, the Indonesian government is applying zero fuel tax for the trucking industry and imposing industry fuel tax for rail operations. Although in recent years the government has eased the fuel tax by introducing a quota system for fuel consumed in rail operations, an excess of fuel above the quota is still charged with a fuel tax. Encouraging the transport industry to consolidate road and rail operations would create the most effective solution for cargo owners. This latter solution has already been tested by dry port operators in Cikarang. In recent years it has resulted in an increasing demand for rail services. If the government can promote the above solution across the industry, dry port with rail operations will have an opportunity to be the breakthrough needed to reduce logistics costs in Indonesia.

Managing land uses around ports remains unresolved. The Spatial Plan Act was introduced in 2007 and imposed stringent controls over land use in urban areas. All local governments must submit a spatial plan for approval by local parliaments, which comply with the National

Spatial Plan of the Indonesian Government. This is an ongoing process and currently not all local governments have submitted nor received approvals from local parliament/national governments for their local spatial plans. This continues to create difficulties.

The recommendation to the Indonesian Government is to separate local and regional traffic as well as access traffic to the port areas. Whilst the current traffic management scheme introduced by the government of Jakarta is the "odd-and-even" plate number scheme for different days in a working week, the use of traffic management measures, such as lane separation, rerouting of through traffic; introducing a time windows scheme and truck appointment schemes for entering the port, can be introduced to alleviate traffic congestion around the port area. A specific traffic problem in Tanjung Priok Port in Jakarta is the fact that export activities are concentrated during the Friday-Sunday period, which is affected by international mother vessel schedules in Singapore port.

Local governments can start improving land use by relocating freight forwarding company offices to dedicated inland container depots to allow stuffing and un-stuffing activities around ports. Inland Container Depot (ICD) Lat Krabang in Thailand has provided international evidence on how relocation of container stuffing and un-stuffing activities can make transport moving to and from ports more effective. Indonesian ports could test such a solution to immediately release the pressure of congestion around ports caused by inefficient land-use configurations.

Ongoing development of hub ports and "self-generating ports" provides the possibility for quantum change in port efficiency. Such changes will require policy enhancement.

Questions as to how and when subsidies, guarantees or gap funding warrant support requires further investigation for both small ports acting as hinterland ports and the national and sub-national governments support of larger facilities.

Appendix

Research Methodology:
Efficient Facilitation of Major Infrastructure Projects

A1.0 Introduction and Methodology

The research (**Efficient Facilitation of Major Infrastructure Projects**) is based on several different methodologies to investigate the perceptions of the various stakeholders associated with ports. It utilised: forums; online surveys; focus group discussions (FGD); in-depth interviews; and workshops.

Ethics approval for the *Efficient Facilitation of Major Infrastructure Projects* was obtained from the Human Research Ethics Committee of The University of Melbourne on 9 August 2017 (Ethics ID number 1749875). The Indonesian University partners also followed the requirements of their individual Universities.

This section describes the research process — the development and refinement of the research questions, the development of the methodology, the development of the survey tools and the conduct of the research itself.

A background literature review and evaluation of case study projects was undertaken to better understand the underlying issues relating to port infrastructure finance and project initiation. This literature review and evaluation of case study projects served to inform the methodology used in the research.

Key port-related personnel, industries and organisations were approached by the researchers, (both in Australia and Indonesia), to take part in the FGDs, to complete the online survey or to take part in the in-depth interviews. Participation was voluntary, and participants could withdraw at any time from the study.

A1.1 Research Forum

The vast amount of literature reviewed in the early stages of the research project led to a need for an exploratory tool to further refine the research objectives. A research forum involving Australians and Indonesians was held in Melbourne, Australia in July 2017 to exchange ideas and discuss how best to explore the research topic and progress the study. The forum participants included researchers/government advisors, university research staff and private sector advisors: the study chief investigator from The University of Melbourne, the co-lead researcher from the Universitas Gadjah Mada, Indonesia; academics/researchers in project management, finance, international business and supply chain; professors of Transport and Law; a finance lawyer; University research staff; a PhD student and four Masters by research students.

The forum provided an opportunity to clarify thoughts, to update all the attendees on the work that had been done so far, to discuss the content of the online surveys that were being developed, and to refine the key questions that needed to be asked during the study. One of the outputs of the forum was to agree on the final output of the research as being a research monograph on *Infrastructure Investment in Indonesia* with a focus on ports. This was agreed as a project deliverable.

The discussion identified the work being done by the World Bank and World Economic Forum related to ease of and barriers to doing business in countries around the world. It further highlighted recent reforms made by the Indonesian Government to reduce high logistics/freight costs in that country. Aspects of these business barriers were subsequently incorporated in the online surveys and among other important themes to be investigated. The research forum also identified a number of key qualitative questions that can only be effectively explored using focus group discussions and face-to-face interviews.

A1.2 Online Surveys

A1.2.1 Development of the Online Surveys

A survey tool was developed to investigate various themes related to Efficient Facilitation of Major Infrastructure Projects port planning and development — namely: investment decisions; port/city performance; barriers to doing business; funding and financing decisions; port sustainability; procurement; and capacity building.

The questions in the survey tool were reviewed by the Australian (The University of Melbourne (UoM)) and Indonesian University partners (Universitas Indonesia (UI) and Universitas Gadjah Mada (UGM)) via email and then via video conferences. An Australian and Indonesian language version of the survey was prepared. The surveys contained both quantitative and qualitative questions. Most questions were the same in both questionnaires except for a few that related to specific funding models only available in Australia or in Indonesia. They also differed slightly on the demographic information being sought where descriptions of Government agencies in the two countries were different.

The Indonesian version of the survey was translated into Indonesian by an Indonesian post-graduate Engineering student enrolled at the UoM who was also engaged as a research assistant (RA) on the project. Questions were offered in both Indonesian and English on the Indonesian online survey. The surveys were hosted by SurveyMonkey™.

The questionnaires consisted of several sections. They included questions related to demographics of the survey participants and their organisations; gender and age; country of main professional/work experience; area of specialisation; experience; years of work with/in/ related to ports; association with ports; which port(s) they are currently working in/with; if they were responding at a port level or terminal level; and if their port undertakes international benchmarking.

There were also questions related to investment decisions and how important it is to make investment decisions in various areas to improve ports; competitive strengths of ports were explored; and areas where investments should be directed to improve port operations.

The online port survey included a question asking participants to indicate from a list of twenty-nine factors provided, how problematic these factors are to doing business in Indonesia (in the Indonesian Survey) and in Australia (for the Australian survey). Respondents were required to indicate how problematic the factors are on a scale of 1 to 5 where 1 is most problematic to 5 being least problematic. The list was made up from the sixteen factors that the World Economic Forum (WEF) uses in their Executive Opinion Survey, the ten indicators used by the World Bank for their 'Doing Business' rankings (WB) and three additional factors included in the questionnaires: affordable energy availability, land acquisition, and regulatory uncertainty that were identified as issues in Indonesia.

Funding and financing decisions were explored in the questionnaires by asking survey participants to indicate the relative effectiveness of twenty-nine listed financing methods. The usefulness of the Indonesian Governments reform package to reduce high logistics/freight costs in Indonesia to improve the supply chain was examined. Obtaining finance with consideration to port sustainability was considered. Lastly, procurement of port development projects and capacity building was explored.

A1.2.2 Conduct of the Online Survey

The Indonesian survey was launched 7 September 2017 and the Australian version of the survey on 1 November 2017. Both surveys closed on 14 May 2018.

The surveys targeted senior port personnel, including senior executives, port/terminal operators, project managers, engineers, government representatives and senior bureaucrats, finance organisations, and industry organisations that work with or in ports. Participants approached to take part in the surveys included individuals associated with ports — for instance, transport providers/companies, logistics companies/logistics managers, representatives from financial institutions including banks and infrastructure financing companies, legal practitioners, shipping organisations, consultants, maritime unions, transport planners and university researchers.

A plain language statement (PLS) and consent form were prepared in both English and Indonesian. Both documents contained a link to the online survey in their respective countries.

Participants from Indonesia were invited to take part in the online survey by the research partners in Indonesia. Participants to the survey from Australia were invited either by phone or email. Interested parties received an email invitation with a link to the PLS, consent form and online survey. The peak professional bodies representing ports in Australia and supply chain/transport and logistics organisations in Australia were contacted to advise them about the online port survey and to ask them to either alert or advertise the survey to their membership.

At the completion of the survey, the responses to qualitative questions from the Indonesian survey were translated into English by the Indonesian Research Assistant in Australia whereas the Indonesian partners were provided with the excel databases directly downloaded from SurveyMonkey™.

Survey data was downloaded from SurveyMonkey into an SPSS (IBM SPSS Statistics 24) and Excel database for analysis. All data was deidentified. The a-priori statistical value was set at $p \leq 0.05$.

Qualitative data analysis was undertaken for text responses from the surveys, FGDs and in-depth interviews and included the use of NVivo 11 software (QSR International Pty Ltd) to assist with this analysis.

A1.3 Focus Group Discussions

The focus group discussions that were held in Jakarta, Indonesia in September 2017 and in Australia in February 2018 were organised by the respective University research partners in each country.

In Indonesia, the University research partners from that country invited port stakeholders and senior port executives known to them and contacted port, government and industry stakeholders to invite them to take part in the FGD.

The research team from the UoM joined the team from UI and UGM and attended the FGD in Jakarta in 2017. Whilst in Jakarta for the FGD, the research team together with their Indonesian University research partners met with senior Government representatives to discuss major infrastructure and port development and met with senior port executives at the major port in Jakarta.

Questions explored at the FGDs aligned with the online survey. The key questions are shown in Table A1. The FGD sessions were divided into two parts: the first session focused on questions related to Port Development. The second session focused on questions related to Funding and Financing.

Table A1 Focus Group Discussion Questions

First FGD session — Port Development	Second FGD session — Funding and Financing
a. What is needed to improve governance/policy in ports?	g. What are the benefits to port efficiency if in a Special Economic Zone (in Indonesia)/Special Tax Zone (in Australia) compared to a port in a high activity region, e.g. industry linked?
b. What is needed to improve management structures in ports?	
c. What decisions and IT could be improved to enhance efficiency at ports?	h. What strategies could best increase port competitiveness? E.g. supply chain connectivity.
d. Which landside infrastructure developments would be most effective? E.g. improved customs, container movements, port services, dry ports, intermodal terminals, hinterland connection.	i. What strategy do you recommend to attract port investments? E.g. Commercial Structure, Financial leverage/ mechanism.
e. Would improved IT, crane rates, customs clearance and rail/road infrastructure into terminals improve handling rate of containers-container throughput and reduce ship dwelling times and ease congestion at your port?	j. How could investment risks be reduced?
	k. Do cost-benefit analyses adequately support your investment decisions?
f. What infrastructure is required to best interface landside operations with the port?	

Transcripts made from the FGDs in both countries were analysed.

A1.4 In-Depth Interviews

In-depth interviews of senior port executives were conducted in Surabaya, Indonesia in April 2018. In-depth interview participants were drawn from relevant industries and government agencies around Surabaya. Thanks to Ibu Hera from ITS for arranging the contacts and generous time provided by the contacts.

Australian research team members were also present at the interviews. Questions discussed were the same as for the FGDs (Table A1). The questions asked of attendees at the FGDs and in-depth interviews are consistent and relate to port development and funding and financing.

Transcripts were made of the interviews and analysed.

A1.5 Response Rates

A1.5.1 Australia — Online Survey

Email invitations were sent to key port stakeholders around Australia to invite them to take part in the online port survey, for example: senior port executives, peak Australian port association and logistics and transport professional associations, terminal operators/management, port related organisations, government personnel, consultancies, transport personnel, logistics personnel, finance personnel, fund managers, technical experts, stevedores, legal personnel, maritime safety personnel, academics and shipping personnel. Some approaches were initially made by phone and followed up by email. The majority of contact was via email invitation. All email invitations were accompanied by a link to the PLS and consent form.

There were sixty-four full and in-part and partial responses to the online Australian Port Planning and Development survey of which not all responded to each question. The specific number of responses to individual questions are referred to by the individual researchers in their chapters.

The survey targeted senior individuals in their organisations, so it is felt that the responses obtained should be representative of the industry as a whole.

A1.5.2 FGD — Australia

Eleven senior port stakeholders took part in the Australian FGD in February 2018. Stakeholders were senior executives from port operations, senior logistics operations, consultants, finance and government.

A1.5.3 Indonesia — Online Survey

The survey was emailed to governmental agencies, major port operators, banks, terminal operators and other institutions involved in port operations in Jakarta and Surabaya. There were eighty-one full and in-part responses and partial responses to specific questions in the online Indonesian port survey. The number of responses received for specific questions have been referred to by the specific investigators.

A1.5.4 FGD — Indonesia

The FGD session held in Jakarta, Indonesia in September 2017 was attended by more than three dozen high-ranking officials and representatives of the government, major corporations in logistics and development, banks, associations, universities, and other experts. Twenty-six participants took part in the first session of the FGD: Indonesian Ports Planning and Development. Twenty-four participants took part in the second session, which focused on Indonesian Ports Financing.

Attendees came from Government Ministries, State Owned Enterprises, senior port and terminal executives, finance, banking, transport, construction, fund managers, private associations, technical experts, logistics/procurement.

A1.5.5 In-Depth Interviews — Indonesia

In total, six in-depth interviews were conducted with key personnel from three different ports in Surabaya.

List of Illustrations and Tables

Chapter 1

Chapter 2

Chapter 3

Chapter 4

Chapter 5

Chapter 6

Chapter 7

Chapter 8

Chapter 9

Chapter 10

Chapter 11

Appendix

This book need not end here...

At Open Book Publishers, we are changing the nature of the traditional academic book. The title you have just read will not be left on a library shelf, but will be accessed online by hundreds of readers each month across the globe. OBP publishes only the best academic work: each title passes through a rigorous peer-review process. We make all our books free to read online so that students, researchers and members of the public who can't afford a printed edition will have access to the same ideas.

This book and additional content is available at:
https://doi.org/10.11647/OBP.0189

Customise

Personalise your copy of this book or design new books using OBP and third-party material. Take chapters or whole books from our published list and make a special edition, a new anthology or an illuminating coursepack. Each customised edition will be produced as a paperback and a downloadable PDF. Find out more at:

https://www.openbookpublishers.com/section/59/1

Donate

If you enjoyed this book, and believe that research like this should be available to all readers, regardless of their income, please become a member of OBP and support our work with a monthly pledge — it only takes a couple of clicks! We do not operate for profit so your donation will contribute directly to the creation of new Open Access publications like this one.

https://www.openbookpublishers.com/supportus

Like Open Book Publishers [f]

Follow @OpenBookPublish [twitter]

Read more at the Open Book Publishers **BLOG**

You may also be interested in:

The Infrastructure Finance Challenge

Edited by Ingo Walter

https://doi.org/10.11647/OBP.0106

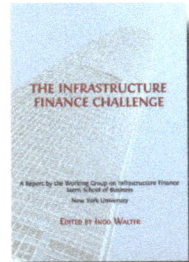

Complexity, Security and Civil Society in East Asia. Foreign Policies and the Korean Peninsula

Edited by Peter Hayes and Kiho Yi

https://doi.org/10.11647/OBP.0059

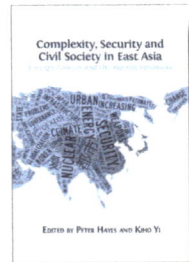

www.ingramcontent.com/pod-product-compliance
Lightning Source LLC
Chambersburg PA
CBHW042312210326
41598CB00042B/7371